THE CAMBRIDGE COMPANION TO

ARCHAIC GREECE

The Cambridge Companion to Archaic Greece provides a wide-ranging synthesis of history, society, and culture during the formative period of Ancient Greece, from the Age of Homer in the late eighth century to the Persian Wars of 490–480 BCE. In ten clearly written and succinct chapters, leading scholars from around the English-speaking world treat all aspects of the civilization of Archaic Greece, from social, political, and military history to early achievements in poetry, philosophy, and the visual arts. Archaic Greece was an age of experimentation and intellectual ferment that laid the foundations for much of Western thought and culture. Under the rule of strongmen known as "tyrants," individual city-states in Greece rose to great power and wealth, and after a long period of isolation, many cities sent out colonies that spread Hellenism to all corners of the Mediterranean world. The Greeks came together in great sanctuaries like Delphi and Olympia to compete in athletic contests and celebrate their gods with the earliest examples of monumental architecture and sculpture. The book offers a vivid and fully documented account of this critical stage in the history of the West.

H. A. Shapiro is the W. H. Collins Vickers Professor of Archaeology and Professor of Classics at The Johns Hopkins University. A Fellow of the Guggenheim Foundation, the Alexander von Humboldt Foundation, and the American School of Classical Studies at Athens, he is the author of *Art and Cult under the Tyrants in Athens* (1989), *Personifications in Greek Art* (1993), and *Myth into Art: Poet and Painter in Classical Greece* (1994) and coauthor of *Women in the Classical World* (1994). He has been a Visiting Professor at Munich University, Princeton University, and the University of Cape Town.

THE CAMBRIDGE COMPANION TO

ARCHAIC GREECE

Edited by

H. A. SHAPIRO

The Johns Hopkins University

CAMBRIDGE UNIVERSITY PRESS
Cambridge, New York, Melbourne, Madrid, Cape Town, Singapore, São Paulo

Cambridge University Press
32 Avenue of the Americas, New York, NY 10013-2473, USA

www.cambridge.org
Information on this title: www.cambridge.org/9780521822008

First published 2007

Printed in the United States of America

A catalog record for this publication is available from the British Library.

Library of Congress Cataloging in Publication Data

Cambridge companion to archaic Greece / edited by H. Alan Shapiro.
p. cm.
Includes bibliographical references and index.
ISBN-13: 978-0-521-82200-8 (hardback)
ISBN-10: 0-521-82200-9 (hardback)
ISBN-13: 978-0-521-52929-7 (pbk.)
ISBN-10: 0-521-52929-8 (pbk.)
1. Greece – Civilization – To 146 B.C. I. Shapiro, H. A. (Harvey Alan),
1949– II. Title.
DF77.C317 2007
938 – dc22 2006026059

ISBN 978-0-521-82200-8 hardback
ISBN 978-0-521-52929-7 paperback

CONTENTS

Part 3: History and Material Culture

List of Illustrations, Maps, and Tables

Illustrations

Illustrations follow page 158.

Maps

Tables

Contributors

CARLA M. ANTONACCIO is Professor of Classical Studies at Duke University and former Dean of Arts and Humanities at Wesleyan University. She is the author of *An Archaeology of Ancestors* (1995). She is currently co-director of the Morgantina Project in Sicily and is working on the publication of the archaic settlement, as well as a book on the archaeology of colonization.

JONATHAN M. HALL is the Phyllis Fay Horton Professor in the Humanities, Professor and Chair of Classics, and Professor of History at the University of Chicago. He is the author of *Ethnic Identity in Greek Antiquity* (1997), *Hellenicity: Between Ethnicity and Culture* (2002), and *A History of the Archaic Greek World* (2007).

JEFFREY M. HURWIT is Professor of Art History and Classics at the University of Oregon. He is the author of *The Acropolis in the Age of Pericles* (2004) and co-editor of *Periklean Athens and Its Legacy: Problems and Perspectives* (2005). A former Guggenheim Foundation Fellow, he served in 2000–2001 as the Martha S. Joukowsky Lecturer for the Archaeological Institute of America.

DEBORAH KAMEN is a Humanities Fellow at Stanford University and an Assistant Professor of Classics at the University of Washington. She is the author of a Bryn Mawr Commentary on Isaeus.

PETER KRENTZ is W. R. Grey Professor of Classics and History at Davidson College. He served as Elizabeth A. Whitehead Visiting Professor at the American School of Classical Studies in 2000–2001. He is the author of "Fighting by the Rules: The Invention of the Hoplite *Agon*," in *Hesperia* (2002).

LESLIE V. KURKE is Professor of Classics and Comparative Literature at the University of California, Berkeley. She is the author of *The Traffic in Praise: Pindar and the Poetics of Social Economy* (1991) and *Coins, Bodies, Games, and Gold: The Politics of Meaning in Archaic Greece* (1999). She is currently at work on two separate projects: one on the figure of Aesop and ancient Greek popular culture, the other on archaic Greek choral poetry in its local ritual contexts.

RICHARD T. NEER is Professor and Chair of the Department of Art History at the University of Chicago. He is the author of a fascicle of the *Corpus Vasorum Antiquorum* for the J. Paul Getty Museum and of *Style and Politics in Athenian Vase-Painting* (Cambridge 2002). His forthcoming book is on the origins of the Classical style in Greek sculpture.

ANDREA WILSON NIGHTINGALE is a Professor of Classics and Comparative Literature at Stanford University. She is the author of *Genres in Dialogue: Plato and the Construct of Philosophy* and *Spectacles of Truth in Classical Greek Philosophy:* Theoria *in Its Cultural Context*. She has received an ACLS and a Guggenheim Fellowship.

VICTOR PARKER, currently Senior Lecturer in the Department of Classics in the University of Canterbury in Christchurch, New Zealand, studied at Harvard and Heidelberg. He has written some thirty specialized studies on Greek history and historiography ranging from the Mycenaean period to the Maccabaean revolt, but concentrated on the archaic period. He has also published on Near Eastern, especially Hittite, as well as Roman history.

JONATHAN L. READY received his Ph.D. in Classics from the University of California, Berkeley, in 2004 and is now an assistant professor in the Department of Classical Studies at Indiana University. His current project examines similes spoken by characters in the *Iliad*.

H. A. SHAPIRO is the W. H. Collins Vickers Professor of Archaeology and Professor of Classics at The Johns Hopkins University. A Fellow of the Guggenheim Foundation and the Alexander von Humboldt-Stiftung, he is the author of *Art and Cult under the Tyrants in Athens* (1989) and *Myth into Art: Poet and Painter in Classical Greece* (1994) and co-author of *Women in the Classical World* (1994). In 2006 he was Langford Eminent Scholar at Florida State University.

PREFACE

The present volume joins a growing list of titles in the Cambridge Companion series in the fields of Classics and Ancient History. Its origins go back to the turn of the millennium, when Beatrice Rehl of Cambridge University Press invited me to organize a collection of chapters on the history and culture of Archaic Greece. She has gently but firmly guided the book through its long gestation period, and I owe her both my sincere thanks and an apology for taking so long.

This book is the work of ten scholars who represent the best of the Anglo-American tradition in Classical scholarship and have worked hard to produce substantial essays that would be both readable and accessible to university students and, at the same time, offer new approaches to traditional topics and questions in the study of Archaic Greece. I am grateful to all of them for their collegial willingness to re-think various points and to work in a spirit of cooperation and free exchange of ideas. I have learned a great deal from all of them, especially those outside my own field of art and archaeology. A particular debt of gratitude is owed to Deborah Kamen and Jonathan Ready, who joined the project at a late stage and, with great enthusiasm and efficiency, saved it from even further delays.

Each contributor was given considerable freedom in determining the best format for his or her chapter. Thus, some have chosen to document their discussions with full references to recent scholarship, while others have provided few or no footnotes but instead annotated their bibliographies to guide the reader toward more specialized sources. Similarly, the always-contentious issue of transliterating Greek names has not been addressed here with even an attempt at standardization (which inevitably fails). Rather, each chapter is internally consistent, and the attentive reader will observe a range of very different styles current among classical scholars, ranging from the hard-core hellenizers (e.g. Kretan, Boiotia, Drakon) to the old-fashioned latinizers.

On behalf of all the contributors, I wish to thank Greta Ham, who worked hard on the final preparation of the manuscript for publication, as well as on the securing of photos and permissions. The index was prepared by Jeffrey Rosenberg of the Johns Hopkins Classics Department.

My own work on this project was facilitated by the hospitality of several institutions where I spent a sabbatical in 2004, especially Corpus Christi College and the Sackler Library at Oxford University.

Baltimore
October 2006

Abbreviations

Diehl	E. Diehl, *Anthologia Lyrcia Graeca.*
DK	H. Diels and W. Kranz, eds., *Die Fragmente der Vorsokratiker.*
FGrHist	Jacoby, F., ed., *Die Fragmente der griechischen Historiker.*
Fornara	C. W. Fornara, ed. and trans., *Archaic Times to the End of the Peloponnesian War.*
GHI^2	P. J. Rhodes and R. Osborne, eds., *Greek Historical Inscriptions*: 404-323 BC.
LP	E. Lobel and D. L. Page, eds., *Poetarum Lesbiorum Fragmenta.*
ML	R. Meiggs and D. Lewis, eds. *A Selection of Greek Historical Inscriptions to the End of the Fifth Century BC.*
PMG	D. L. Page, ed., *Poetae Melici Graeci.*
W, W^2	M. L. West, ed., *Iambi et Elegi Graeci.* (W^2 = 2nd edition specifically.)

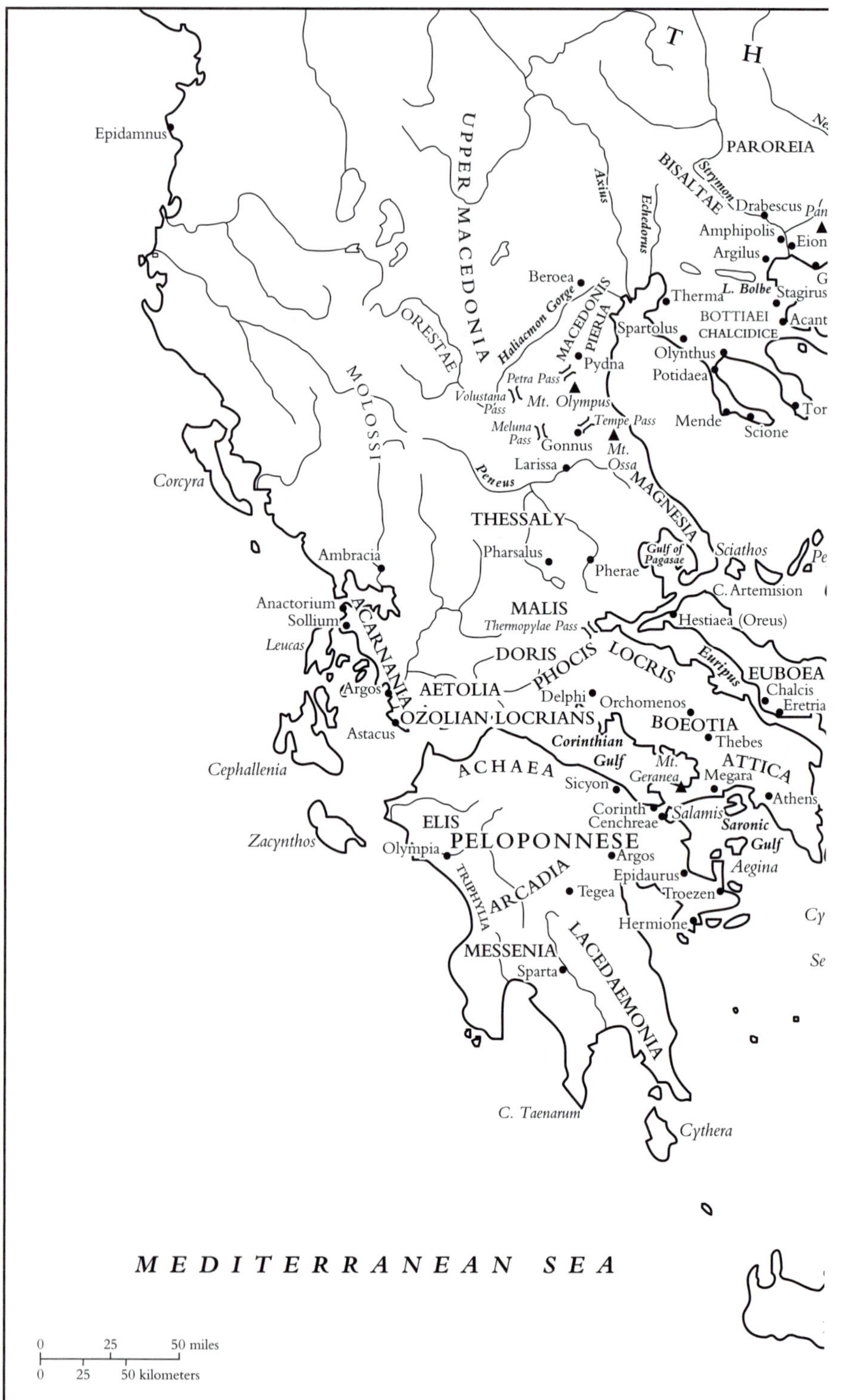

Map 1. Greece and Asia Minor.

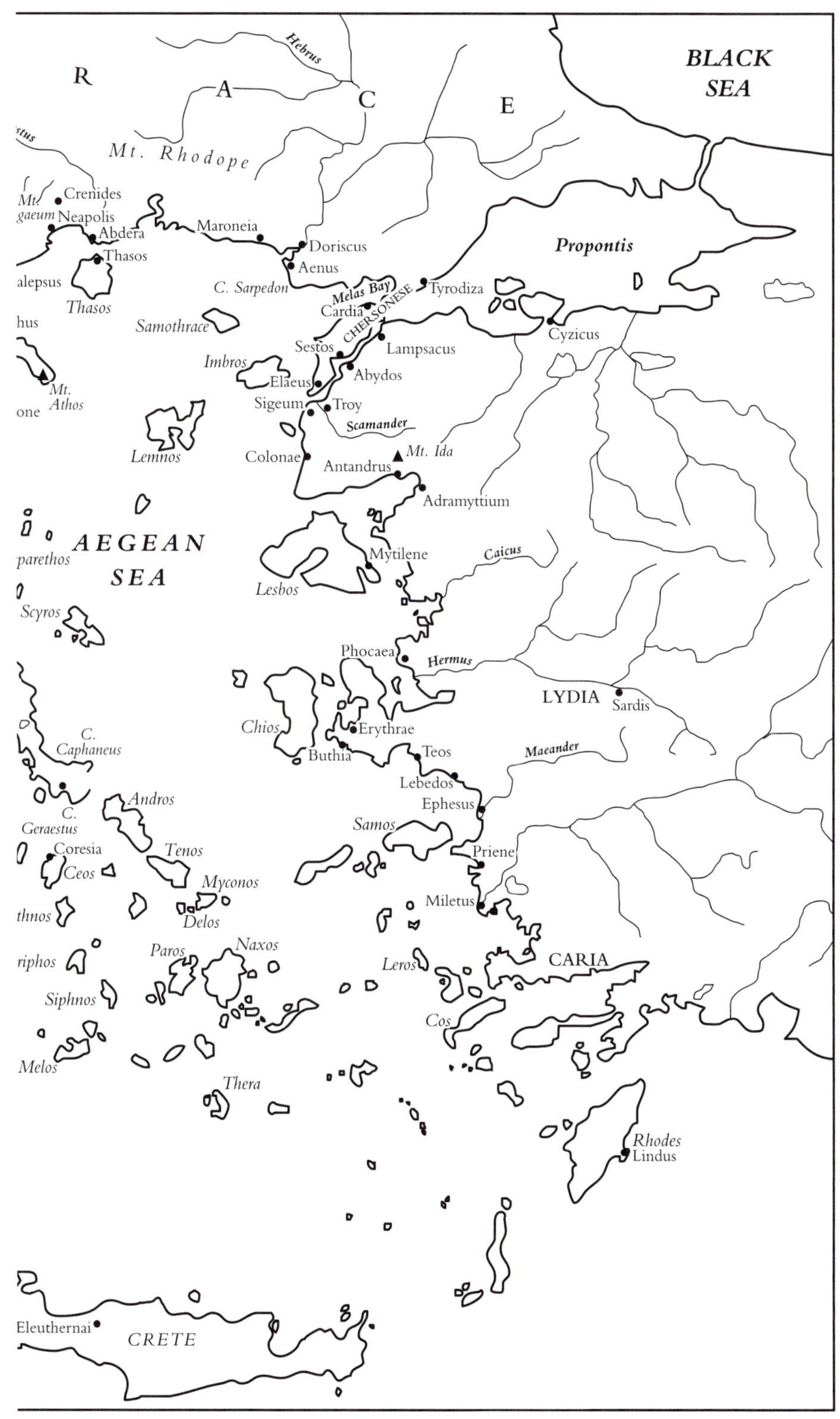

BLACK SEA
R
A
C
E
Hebrus
Mt. Rhodope
Crenides
Neapolis
Abdera
Thasos
Maroneia
Doriscus
Aenus
Proportis
C. Sarpedon
Melas Bay
Cardia
CHERSONESE
Tyrodiza
Samothrace
Sestos
Lampsacus
Cyzicus
Imbros
Elaeus
Abydos
Mt. Athos
Sigeum
Troy
Scamander
Lemnos
Colonae
Antandrus
Mt. Ida
Adramyttium
AEGEAN SEA
Mytilene
Caicus
Lesbos
Scyros
Phocaea
Hermus
Chios
Erythrae
LYDIA
Sardis
C. Caphaneus
Buthia
Teos
Maeander
Lebedos
Ephesus
Andros
C. Geraestus
Samos
Coresia
Ceos
Tenos
Priene
Myconos
Miletus
Delos
Naxos
Paros
Leros
CARIA
Siphnos
Cos
Melos
Thera
Rhodes
Lindus
Eleuthernai
CRETE

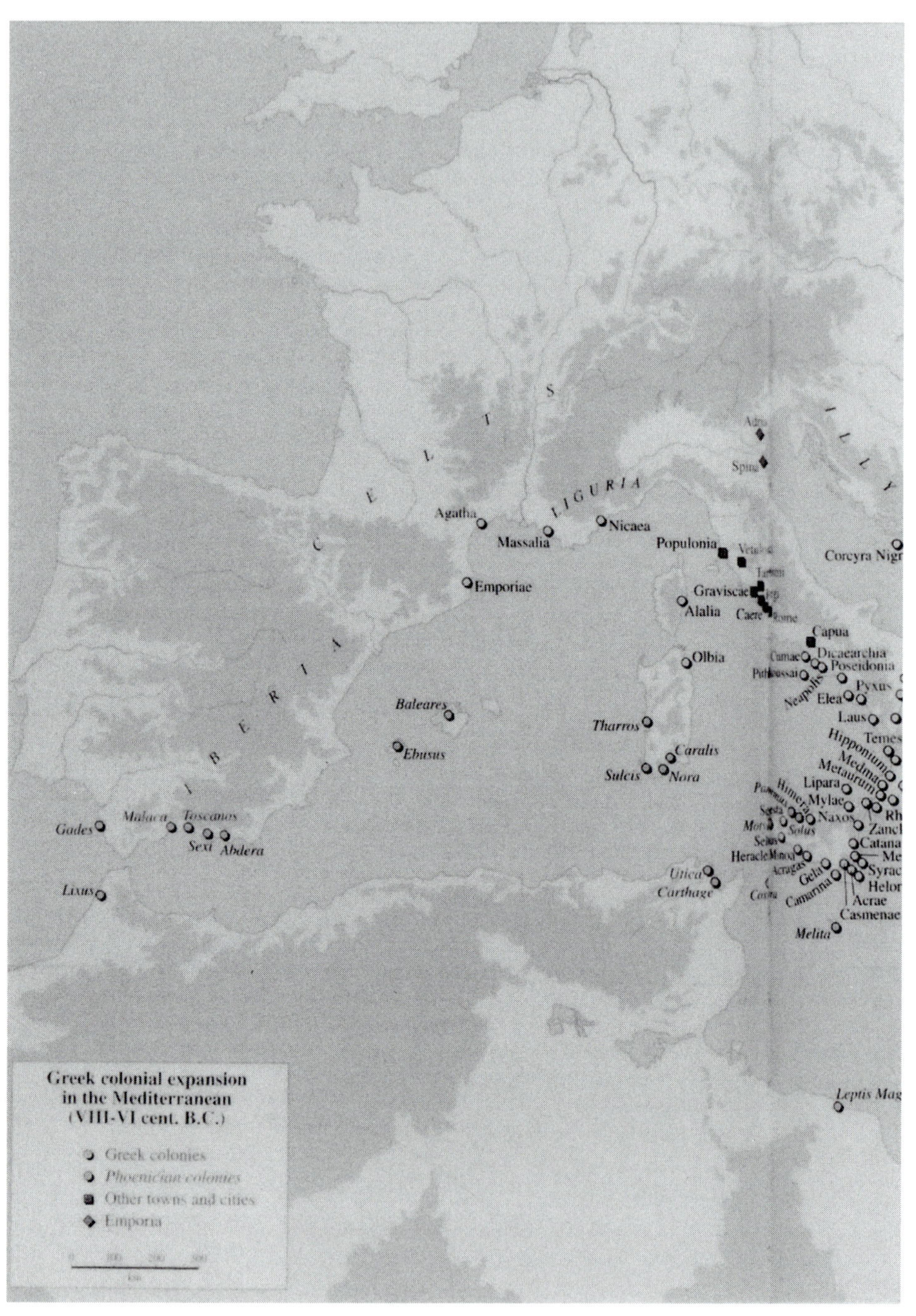

Map 2. Greek colonization.

Tanais
S C Y T H I A
Olbia
Phanagoria
Panticapaeum
Tyras
Theodosia
COLCHIS
Phasis
Istrus
Tomis
Cerasus
Trapezus
Sinope
Cotyora
Amisus
Odessus
Mesembria
Apollonia
Tieum
Heraclea Pontica
Byzantium
Chalcedon
THRACIA
Abdera
Cyzicus
Thasos
MYSIA
Epidamnus
Apollonia
Tarentum
Metapontum
Siris
Sybaris
Croton
Terina
Caulonia
Locri Epizeph.
Corcyra
Phocaea
Chios
Chalcis
Eretria
Samos
CARIA
PAMPHYLIA
CILICIA
Al-Mina
SYRIA
Megara
Corinth
Athens
Argus
Miletus
Phaselis
Celenderis
Nagidus
Cnidus
Rhodes
Sparta
Thera
CYPRUS
Sidon
Tyre
PHOENICIA
CRETE
Jerusalem
Apollonia
Cyrene
Taucheira
Barca
Euhesperides
LIBYA
Naucratis
AEGYPTUS
Memphis

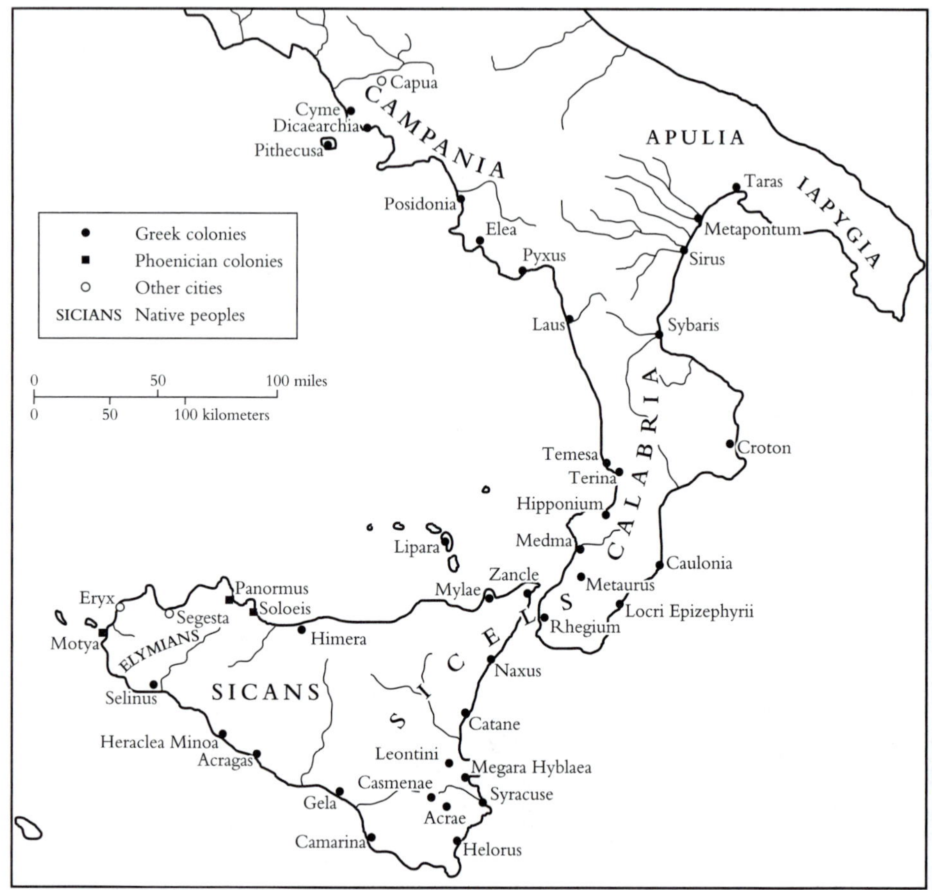

Map 3. Magna Graecia and Sicily.

Introduction

H. A. Shapiro

Terms and Definitions

The ten essays in this volume aim to provide an overview of the culture and society of ancient Greece during the formative years that we conventionally refer to as the Archaic period, from about 800 to 480 BCE. It was in these years that all the elements we think of as making up Greek civilization, from poetry and philosophy to architecture and city planning, were created and experienced their earliest stages of development. This was an exciting period of discovery and experimentation, without which we cannot understand or appreciate the achievements of Classical Greece that have shaped the civilization of the West ever since.

Our word "archaic" derives from the Greek *archaios*, meaning simply "old" or "ancient." It is, for example, the word that Modern Greek uses to describe what we call Ancient Greece or the Ancient Greek language. There is none of the negative connotation implied in our use of the word "archaic" to describe something that is hopelessly old-fashioned, primitive, or out of date. On the contrary, *archaios* was often a mark of respect, especially in the area of religion, where whatever is older – a temple, say, or a cult statue – is better, more sacred. The Greeks of the Classical period and later did not refer to what we call Archaic Greece by this name, for they did not divide their earlier history into periods as we do. But they did describe as *archaios* certain objects, especially works of art and architecture, that would fall into what we call the Archaic period, and in this sense the choice of the word Archaic is reasonably faithful to the Greeks themselves. Though some scholars have objected to the use of this term as "archaic" (i.e., outmoded), no one has come up with a better alternative.

It is much easier to define the end point of the Archaic period than its beginning. Ancient historians all agree that the Persian Wars (comprising two separate campaigns, in 490 and then in 480–79 BCE) mark the boundary between the Archaic period and the Classical. The Persians did not, of course, appear out of nowhere in 490. The Greeks who lived on the eastern shores of the Aegean (what is now the west coast of Turkey) and on the islands just off those shores had lived in the shadow, and in some cases under the domination of the Persian Empire for more than half a century. But it was the crossing of vast Persian armies into mainland Greece, and more specifically the ability of the outnumbered Greeks to fight them off, that proved the watershed event in the formation of a distinctive Greek identity. That so many Greek city-states, heretofore living as autonomous and culturally quite distinct political entities, were able to come together to defeat the invaders was both the culmination of their earliest phase and, ironically, the last great display of Greek unity. For with the birth of the Classical era in the aftermath of the Persian Wars came the start of rivalries among the Greek states that would tear apart this fragile alliance and result in intra-Greek warfare for the next century and a half.

There is no one great event, comparable to the Persian Wars, that can be said to mark the beginning of the Archaic period. There was, instead, a gradual emergence from the dormant and impoverished centuries we traditionally call the Dark Age – though this very notion has been challenged by recent archaeological discoveries. What we can say with certainty is that, in the century between 800 and 700, so many fundamental changes came about – alphabetic writing, monumental architecture, overseas trade, and colonization, to name just a few – that the Greek world of 700 would have been unrecognizable to a man living in 800. For convenience, then, we have set our starting point at 800, though in some areas (see, for example, Chapter 8 on colonization and Chapter 9 on Panhellenic sanctuaries), we must reach back at least to the ninth century to understand the origins of the Archaic period.

The many tales of gods and heroes that we refer to as Greek mythology were, for the Greeks themselves, part of their early history, continuous with and inseparable from what we understand as the "historical" age. This discrepancy between modern and ancient notions of history and myth is especially acute in the Archaic period, when the proximity of gods and heroes was keenly felt and the "rationalizing" tendency of the Classical Greeks was still far away. Thus Hesiod could organize all of human history into his "Five Races of Man," with his own era of toil and suffering, the Age of Iron, in a direct line from the earlier, happier ages enjoyed by gods and heroes. Aristocratic families in the Archaic period could plausibly claim descent from a particular hero and often, through that hero, from a god or goddess, without raising eyebrows. If we press too hard our modern distinction between what is myth and what is history, we will fail to understand a fundamental quality of Archaic Greek thought.

WHY A COMPANION TO ARCHAIC GREECE?

One of the main purposes of this book is to encourage more serious study of Archaic Greece by undergraduate students in the English-speaking world. Among scholars and advanced students of ancient history, archaeology, Greek literature, and philosophy, there is no shortage of interest in the Archaic period. Indeed, this period has experienced something of a boom in scholarship in recent decades, but the teaching of Archaic Greece has not kept pace with new developments in research. This may be due in part to the view, prevalent since the Enlightenment of the eighteenth century, that privileged the Classical period as the "Golden Age" of Greek civilization, the age that produced the greatest art and literature (especially Greek tragedy) and gave the world its first democracy, in Athens. The Archaic period was far less well known, and, though Homer was acknowledged as the starting point of Western literature, his epics were not seen as rooted in a particular time and place and culture, but as timeless works of poetic genius. This is still the way Homer is often read and studied today. The Archaic period also suffers from the lack of a towering figure around whom to build an introductory course. The "Age of Pericles" and the "Age of Alexander" have an immediate appeal. The "Age of Periander" or the "Age of Peisistratos" would be just as fascinating, but they lack name recognition.

At the other end of the chronological spectrum, the study of the Hellenistic period (ca. 323 BCE–31 BCE) has also suffered from the effects of the Enlightenment model, which dismissed everything after the Classical period as a steady decline until the rise of a new Golden Age under the first emperors of Rome. After Alexander the Great (356–323 BCE), we must move all the way down to Cleopatra or Augustus Caesar, three centuries later, to find a figure who is a household name. Yet, like the Archaic period, the Hellenistic has experienced a resurgence of scholarly interest, perhaps because the tremendous wealth of primary sources, especially inscriptions and papyri, allows us to ask and answer questions that are not possible in earlier periods. We may hope that the recently published *Cambridge Companion to the Hellenistic World* will contribute to a renewed interest in the teaching of Hellenistic history and culture.

The complete overhaul of the study of Archaic Greece in recent years is owed to several factors. First, the accelerating pace of archaeological fieldwork throughout the Greek world tends to impact our understanding of the Archaic period, with its relative dearth of written sources, even more than it does later periods. There is simply more new evidence for Archaic Greece than for Classical Greece, and this makes the study of the earlier age especially appealing. Second, the recognition that the older cultures of the Ancient Near East had a profound impact on the formative period of Greek civilization has opened up new approaches that were barely acknowledged a generation ago. The notion that some kind of "Greek miracle" gave birth to all of Western art, literature, and philosophy in splendid isolation can no longer be sustained, and the idea of an "Orientalizing Revolution" has made the study of Archaic Greece much richer and more sophisticated. Third, after many generations in which the study of Archaic Greece was defined by a set of conventional topics – the "rise of the *polis*," "hoplite warfare," "mother city and colony," "the Greek tyrants," among them – the scholarship of recent years has brought to the fore long-neglected aspects of life and art. Thus, for example, the traditional study of Archaic poetry by genres (epic, lyric, epinician, etc.) has been enlivened by what one of the contributors to this book, Leslie Kurke, has called "cultural poetics," setting the poetry into a context of performance and of political and social realities. In the sphere of social and private life, the intensive study of the institution of the symposium, or all-male drinking party, pioneered by the Oxford classicist Oswyn Murray, has added a whole dimension to our understanding of Archaic Greek society that was missing from traditional political and military history.

Sources and Evidence

Despite the seamless continuity, in many respects, from the Archaic period into the Classical, there are some fundamental differences between the two eras and especially in the ways in which we study them today. Herodotus, who was born at about the time the Persian Wars were being fought, is known to us as the Father of History, because in the Archaic period the writing of history as we know it did not yet exist. Indeed, it seems likely that it was the epoch-making Persian invasions that first inspired the Greeks to want to record their own history systematically. Although many later historians – starting with Herodotus – wrote about the period we call Archaic, there are no eyewitness historians. This is very different from, say, the period of the Peloponnesian War, for which we have two eyewitness accounts (covering different stages of the war) by Thucydides and Xenophon. This does not mean we have no record of events by contemporary writers in the Archaic period. Solon, the Athenian statesman, tells us quite a lot about the reforms he implemented in Athens (see Chapter 1), and Tyrtaeus gives us a vivid picture of warfare in seventh-century Sparta (see Chapter 3). But we must always remember that these men were writing poetry, not history, and interpret their evidence accordingly. There is plenty of historical information contained in the Homeric epics (see Chapter 5), but how do we use it, so long as the debate is unresolved on what period Homer is describing: that of the Late Bronze Age (ca. 1200 BCE), that of his own time (late eight/early seventh century), or some period in between? Hesiod is also more poet than historian, yet his *Works and Days* is an invaluable source on life in Greece in the years around 700.

Although the invention and spread of writing is one of the key criteria by which we define the Archaic period, this does not mean that writing was prolific or in common use at any time. What writing does survive invariably gives us precious information that would be unavailable from other sources: dedications carved on marble votive statues, names of potters and painters scratched or painted on vases, short epigrams carved on funerary monuments, even a few excerpts from early law codes (see Chapter 1). But, valuable as they are, these are tiny snippets compared with the steady stream of documents that were produced in Athens and other cities starting in the mid-fifth century – decrees, magistrates' reports, building accounts, sacrificial calendars, and much more – and turns into a flood once we reach Late Classical and Hellenistic times.

If literary and epigraphical documents for the Archaic period are scanty, what do we have to go on? The archaeological record for the Archaic period is extremely rich – in some respects, surprisingly, even richer than for later periods. For example, the intense building activity in the Panhellenic sanctuaries of Delphi and Olympia during Archaic times (described in Chapter 9) was never matched again. The monumental funeral vases of the later eighth century (see Chapter 10) dwarf any pottery made later in Greece, and the marble *kouroi* and *korai* that populate Archaic sanctuaries and cemeteries (see Chapter 10) essentially died out after the early fifth century. Of course Classical Greek art is very rich too, but there is no form of art or architecture that does not have well-preserved examples in the Archaic period, except perhaps the art of large-scale fresco painting, which is virtually all lost (except in Macedonia) anyway. The study of Archaic Greek art has one more big advantage: whereas the great masters of Classical sculpture are known to us almost entirely through Roman copies of lost originals, in Archaic sculpture everything is an original.

For the student of ancient Greece, the geographical definition of what we call the Greek World is continually expanding and contracting as we move through time. Like an hourglass, it is narrowest at the midpoint. That is, for the High Classical period of the fifth century, we tend to focus almost exclusively on the city of Athens, simply because the surviving material – from buildings, inscriptions, and vases to drama and philosophy and historiography – is so overwhelmingly rich. There was no "Athens" of the Archaic period, that is, no one *polis* that was both a dominant military/political power in the Aegean and a cultural capital. There is, of course, an Archaic Athens, but it is only one of many prosperous centers, and in fact the literary output of Archaic Athens is astonishingly slight. To find the cutting edge of Archaic Greek culture we must look to Miletus for philosophy, to other Ionian cities and the islands for poetry, to Euboea for trade and colonization, to Corinth for vase-painting (until eclipsed by Athens ca. 550), and to south Italy and Sicily for architecture and architectural sculpture. In other words, the history and culture of Archaic Greece is a regional history, with flashes of brilliance all over the Aegean and beyond. It is also a period of great mobility, and, without a single great center to serve as a magnet, as Athens did later on, the movement was in all directions. A poet from Asia Minor could settle in Sparta (Alcman), another in Athens (Anacreon), whereas a philosopher from the island of Samos could end up in south Italy (Pythagoras) and a trader from Corinth in Rome (Demaratus). It is not until the conquests of Alexander the Great that the Greek world again opens up into a series of regional histories through the Hellenistic period, this time dwarfing the geographical limits of preceding ages.

The Elements of Archaic Greece

Each chapter in this book synthesizes the results of the latest research on an aspect of the Archaic period and offers a fresh approach to long-studied questions. In many instances, the author of the chapter has made significant contributions in the specialized literature to shaping the way the subject is approached today. What all chapters have in common is that they demonstrate the need for combining different kinds of evidence, primary source material, and theoretical models in trying to understand the complex and ever-changing world of Archaic Greece.

The study of Classical Antiquity has traditionally drawn on four fairly distinct disciplines: language and literature (philology); history; philosophy; and archaeology and art. The authors of this volume would each probably identify themselves with one of these four subdisciplines, yet each is keenly aware of the need to break down disciplinary boundaries in order to achieve a fuller understanding of the remote past. The chapters are here grouped into three sections of unequal size, on history, literature/philosophy, and art and material culture, but different groupings would have been possible and they may be read in any order. Fully half of the ten chapters would most likely fall under the broad heading of "history," but together they demonstrate how that term has come to embrace much more than the conventions of Greek political and military history. Even those subjects are now benefiting from new approaches. Thus Peter Krentz's chapter on warfare in the Archaic period draws on both poetry and artistic sources to explore the social values that were expressed in the pervasive institution of war. Political history used to mean the history of the *polis*, or city-state, but Jonathan Hall shows that the *polis* is but one definition of Greek identity – albeit a crucial one – that must be set alongside the issue of ethnicity and examined on a regional basis to avoid generalization and oversimplification.

The Greeks saw their own culture as being first and foremost about individuals rather than institutions. In Archaic Greece the individuals we hear most about fall into two overlapping categories, tyrants and lawgivers. In his chapter, Victor Parker shows how these two make an "odd couple" and yet can illuminate the whole period by being studied in tandem. For many historians, Archaic Greece is the "Age of Colonization," for this phenomenon was so widespread and the duration of the colonization movement is almost exactly coextensive with the conventional dating of the Archaic period on other grounds. With the rise of twentieth century archaeology, the study of Greek colonization has gone from a game of historical speculation based on a modicum of information in Herodotus and Thucydides combined with a welter of quasi-legendary heroes, founders, and stories to a fully rounded picture, in which history is written largely out of material culture. Carla Antonaccio, herself an archaeologist as well as a historian, shows how the next step is to explore the different models of interaction between Greek colonists and native populations that emerge from the material evidence.

Deborah Kamen presents the kind of social and family history that was largely absent from the study of Ancient Greece until recent years. Though the study of women and gender is no longer as new or radical a subfield of Classics as it once was, the focus in Greece still tends to be on the Classical period, when we have such rich source material as tragedy and comedy or the imagery of Athenian vases. But Kamen here demonstrates that all the institutions and beliefs pertaining to the life-cycle, for both women and men, have their origins in the Archaic period.

The remaining five chapters of this book take in areas that are equally diverse, from philosophy and religion to poetry and art. No study of Archaic Greece, indeed of Greece at all, can get around the figure of Homer. In Jonathan Ready's chapter, Homer is considered alongside the second great early epic poet, Hesiod. Together they shaped more than a literary genre, indeed the whole belief system of all later Greeks. No topic in Greek literature is more hotly debated at the present time than the origins of the poetry we call Homer's and how it was transmitted to us, and Ready presents a balanced account of the state of the question. If Homer remains an elusive individual, and Hesiod only slightly less so, the lyric poets of the seventh and sixth centuries are just the opposite: the first vivid, idiosyncratic characters in the history of poetry. Leslie Kurke considers how these personalities emerge even more clearly when we can reconstruct the settings in which their verse was performed. This is especially crucial for the first distinctively female voice preserved to us, that of Sappho of Lesbos.

Andrea Nightingale, in her chapter on early Greek philosophy, demystifies the debate about rational versus nonrational thought, or mythic thought versus philosophy in early Greece, by showing that the figures we call the pre-Socratic philosophers, as much as their contemporaries the poets, were citizens of various cities around the Greek world, exposed to the cultural cross-currents of the age, and integral to the lives of those cities. They were not solitary thinkers, nor the head-in-the-clouds philosopher type that was already caricatured in Classical Athens. Their concerns were as much religion and theology as the moral and ethical issues we think of as the province of philosophy. That they usually wrote in the same forms of verse as the poets is further evidence that the two groups cannot be artificially separated.

The visual arts are too often marginalized in general studies of Greek history and culture, or treated as mere illustration. In his chapter,

Jeffrey Hurwit analyzes the representation of the human figure in sculpture and painting as part of a broader theme that cuts across much of this book, the self-fashioning of the individual in Archaic Greece.

Last, themes of religion, identity, and material culture come together in Richard Neer's chapter on the Panhellenic sanctuaries during the Archaic period. For all the tremendous diversity of the Greek *poleis*, they were acutely conscious of their shared Greekness, and nothing expressed this better than the great sanctuaries where they came together, whether to worship, to compete in athletic contests, or to glorify themselves and their cities through expensive dedications. In many ways, the great era of the Panhellenic sanctuaries was the Archaic, even though they continued to operate throughout Antiquity, and Neer shows how these sacred spaces were essential to the formation of a Greek identity.

This volume does not pretend to be an exhaustive or systematic survey of Archaic Greece. There are several topics that might easily have formed the basis of additional chapters but for various reasons have not been treated in this way. Religion, for example, is a fundamental aspect of Archaic Greek culture and society, so fundamental in fact that it permeates every subject discussed in this book, from law and warfare to poetry and architecture. Instead of in a separate chapter, religion is treated in each of its many contexts, and for a survey of Greek myth and religion the reader is referred to any of several handbooks in this field. Likewise, the economic life of Archaic Greece is not dealt with in a chapter, because the evidence is extremely sparse and can only be discerned in a few specific instances, such as the crisis in Athens at the time of Solon (see chapter 1). The one economic issue that deserves fuller treatment is the invention of coinage in Archaic Greece and its implications for social life, a subject brilliantly explored by Leslie Kurke in her recent book *Coins, Bodies, Games and Gold: The Politics of Meaning in Archaic Greece*. Yet another subject of current interest is the genesis of sports and athletic competition in the Archaic period. This is touched on in the discussions of the Panhellenic sanctuaries where the games took place (see Chapter 9) and of the victors for whom poems were written (see Chapter 6).

Part One

HISTORY OF ARCHAIC GREECE

1: Tyrants and Lawgivers

Victor Parker

Introduction and Attempts at Definition

Lawgivers and tyrants seem at first an odd couple: of the latter we have a negative view, whereas the former make a more positive impression. Certainly, so wise a sage as Solon, the sixth-century BCE lawgiver of Athens, has found many admirers throughout history, whereas few have confessed to liking his near contemporary, Periander the tyrant of Corinth – certainly not after reading this impassioned denunciation of him:

> Now while Periander was in the beginning milder than his father [Cypselus, also tyrant of Corinth], he later, owing to a correspondence with Thrasybulus, the tyrant of Miletus, became far more murderous than Cypselus . . . Periander . . . understood that Thrasybulus was advising him to murder those among the townsmen who were in any way pre-eminent. So Periander then unleashed every savagery upon the citizens, for he finished off whatever Cypselus had omitted to do in the way of killing people or sending them into exile.
>
> (Herodotus 5.92)

Now I have started off with this passage on Periander for several reasons: first, because it shows us what sort of a reputation the tyrants in the end had, but, second, because another fact about Periander helps make a link between tyrants and lawgivers. For both Solon and Periander belonged to a select "canon" of men traditionally renowned for their wisdom, the so-called Seven Sages.

These Seven Sages, according to the later tradition, had among other things coined the Delphic sayings "nothing in excess" and "know thyself." Although different versions of the canon remained in circulation, in a standard version it consisted of these seven men:[1]

Cleobulus of Lindos
Solon of Athens
Chilon of Sparta
Thales of Miletus
Pittacus of Mytilene
Bias of Priene
Periander of Corinth

Shockingly, two of the seven men on the list ruled their respective cities as tyrants. As we will see, we can consider a third, none other than Solon himself, a tyrant also – from a certain point of view. And of those three "tyrants," two were also lawgivers. This should justify a chapter treating the two types together: after all, both tyrants and at least some lawgivers held near-despotic power over their respective communities.

This finally leads us to formulating the question: What then are lawgivers and tyrants? We begin with the lawgiver, for his is the simpler case. First, the Greeks drew a sharp distinction between a "law" and a "decree": a "decree" is an enactment of an assembly and may be superseded or revoked at any time by an assembly, but a "law" is, in theory, a permanent rule made by a man or commission duly authorized to make "laws" unfettered by any restraints. Once this man, the lawgiver, has set his "laws," they count and no assembly may alter or revoke them – except by the same process by which they were made, that is, by the due authorization of a new lawgiver with the same unfettered competence. Let us take a look at one such lawgiver:

> The Cyreneans sought, and the Mantineans gave them a man, most distinguished amongst his fellow-townsmen, by the name of Demonax. Now when this man had come to Cyrene and had learnt about affairs there, he arranged them in three tribes, distributing them as follows: He formed one division of the Thereans and their neighbors, the other of the Peloponnesians and Cretans, and the third of all the Islanders. Moreover he set aside plots of land for the King, Battus, as well as sacral offices, but all the other prerogatives which the kings had previously held, he opened up to the people.
>
> (Herodotus 5.161.2–3)

The Cyreneans called in Demonax, whose decisions they bound themselves to accept in advance. Obviously, much weight fell on the choice of lawgiver: the choice of an outsider betrays a fear that a native Cyrenean would be biased, and at all events the lawgiver had to have an established reputation for wisdom and prudent evenhandedness. After all, a city was giving him unlimited power to rearrange its constitutional and juridical ordinances in binding fashion, theoretically forever. The (mostly) legendary Spartan lawgiver Lycurgus had arranged for his ordinances to be binding on the Spartans forever.[2] The great law code composed by the anonymous lawgiver of Gortyn in the fifth century BCE was still proudly displayed centuries later in Roman times.[3] Given how many areas of life the Gortynian Code affected, one man's apodictically proclaimed views on propriety and justice must have had a profound effect on life in Gortyn for many generations. This theoretically unlimited, even dictatorial power of the lawgiver makes another link with the figure of the tyrant. We shall see others as we proceed.

That brings us now to the more difficult question: What is a tyrant? The word in Greek is *tyrannos*, and its meaning changed from its first attested usage in the mid-seventh century BCE (as a mere synonym for *basileus* or "king") until it eventually acquired its standard meaning of a brutal despot, in particular one who seizes power.[4] We see the concrete result of this development in Thucydides, who wrote ca. 400 BCE. Thucydides uses the two words *tyrannos* and *basileus* in a mutually exclusive way: the *basileus* is a ruler (especially of a non-Greek people, but also of contemporary Greek states such as Sparta or Thessaly, as well as of Greeks in mythological times) who lawfully held his position, whereas the *tyrannos* is a ruler (always of a Greek city) who seized power. By and large we follow Thucydides' distinction today and class as "tyrants" a certain group of Greek rulers from the seventh and sixth centuries BCE.

Thus it can come as a shock to read a pre-Thucydidean author such as Herodotus who still uses the two words interchangeably: Herodotus (5.113.2) classes among the "tyrants" an hereditary ruler of the Greek city of Soloi on Cyprus, whom Thucydides would surely have called a *basileus*, whereas rulers who (presumably) seized power in several Greek cities in southern Italy are called "kings" (3.136.2; 5.44.1). Herodotus can speak of a *basileus* assuming a "tyranny" and of a *tyrannos* holding the "kingship" (3.52.3–4; 5.35.1). The upshot of this brief discussion is simply to indicate how blurred a line runs between "kings" and "tyrants" in pre-Thucydidean works. Herodotus does not distinguish in his mind between "tyrants" and "kings" in the way in which Thucydides and we, in his train, still do.

The difficulty increases when we turn from Herodotus and Thucydides to Aristotle, the first philosopher who tried systematically to investigate the phenomenon of tyranny. Aristotle (*Politics* 1295a) defined three types of "tyranny": (1) that exercised in accordance with law and tradition among non-Greek peoples (i.e., the non-Greek rulers for whom Thucydides used the word *basileus*); (2) that exercised in Greece by an absolute ruler appointed by the people (more on this in a moment); and (3) that characterized by sheer despotism and lawlessness (the names of rulers in this class show that Aristotle has in mind the same group of rulers whom Thucydides terms "tyrants"). All the same, Aristotle classes the first two kinds as "kingship" and states that some hereditary Greek "kings" actually became "tyrants" (of the third class) by overstepping their lawful authority. As we see, the line between "kings" and "tyrants" still remains exceedingly difficult to draw.

Now we too can collect the material that Aristotle attempted systematically to classify, and thus we can see his problem. For example, one hereditary king, Pheidon of Argos, counted in pre-Aristotelian literature as a tyrant – owing to, primarily, his wanton act in sacrilegiously deposing the lawful governors of the Olympic Games and organizing the Games himself (Herodotus 6.127.3; cf. Aristotle *Politics* 1310b). To take another example: the poet Alcaeus had so thoroughly branded his contemporary, the lawgiver Pittacus of Mytilene, as a tyrant, that neither Aristotle (*Politics* 1285a) nor anyone else could deny the fact. Yet, among other things, Alcaeus had this to say about Pittacus:

> [The Mytileneans] have made base-born Pittacus tyrant of the enervated, luckless city; all of them together have praised him greatly.
>
> (Alcaeus fr. 348 LP)

Even Alcaeus could not withhold that the Mytileneans themselves had gladly installed Pittacus as "tyrant." But such a tyrant was surely different from those tyrants who had seized power – hence Aristotle's second category of "tyrants." Again, if a "king" ruled lawfully, he was not a "tyrant," but if he overstepped his lawful bounds (as Pheidon had), he became a "tyrant" – of Aristotle's third category. The essential distinction for Aristotle, with regard to his third category, lay here: the "tyrant" rules without law; the "king" rules according to law. This of course conflicted with the definition for the "lawful" second category of tyranny – so Aristotle tended to treat that type as really being "kingship." Aristotle then knew of a certain group of rulers whom consensus classed as "tyrants," but whom he could not very well define so that they were truly distinct from "kings." As the inclusion of Pittacus amongst the tyrants shows, lawgivers too might be considered as "tyrants."

Let us now compare Pittacus with another lawgiver, Solon. Pittacus was installed as ruler of Mytilene, allegedly for a period of ten years (Diogenes Laertius 1.75), during which he held unlimited power. Solon was installed as ruler of Athens (probably as an annual "archon" – the later term for the highest executive official in Athens) with unlimited powers. Both Pittacus and Solon made new laws for their respective cities; both also stepped down from power when their set time expired. Both gained a great reputation for wisdom; hence their position amongst the traditional "Seven Sages." Why, then, is Pittacus a tyrant, but not Solon? No other answer emerges than that Solon himself emphatically denied that he was a tyrant or had ever sought the tyranny:

> I grasped not tyranny nor implacable violence.
>
> (Solon fr. 32 W; cf. fr. 33 W)

In the same way as Alcaeus in his poetry had irrevocably pinned the tag of "tyrant" on Pittacus, so Solon, by means of his poetry, had incontrovertibly rejected the label. We today, however, looking back on the two, can see very little difference between them. If Pittacus was a tyrant, then so was Solon. For the analytically minded, Solon belongs in Aristotle's second category of tyrants. We have now come full circle: from a certain point of view the "lawgiver," with his unlimited power to set binding and permanent rules for a state and his occasional actual rule for a set period of time, is a "tyrant" – a ruler with unlimited power. Furthermore, the distinction between lawfully ruling "kings" and lawlessly ruling "tyrants" often seems highly artificial. In discussing the "lawgivers" and "tyrants" of the Archaic period – in our context, ca. 650–500 BCE – we will then do well to remember that we are dealing with an amorphous and highly varied group that resists easy definition: both positively (solely on the basis of inherent characteristics) as well as negatively (in contrast against other rulers).

Individual Lawgivers and Tyrants

In this section I would like now to look at the circumstances of several individual tyrants and lawgivers, with a view towards collecting a body of evidence on the basis of which we may draw some, albeit tentative, conclusions in a third section.

The Cypselids of Corinth (ca. 630–550 BCE)[5]

A standard principle of historical argument dictates that sources closer in time to the events that they relate have more claim to accuracy than sources much farther away in time. Any treatment of any event or person in Greek history must begin with those sources, should they exist, that are contemporary with the event or person depicted. In the case of Cypselus, mercifully, two such pieces of evidence exist. We can assert their contemporaneity on the basis of a simple reflection: whereas later sources view the Cypselid tyranny in unrelentingly hostile fashion, these two alleged utterances of the Delphic Oracle present Cypselus in a positive light. In fact they look suspiciously like pro-Cypselid propaganda:

> Eëtion, no-one honors you who are worthy of much honor.
> Labda is pregnant, and will bear a millstone: but he [i.e., the stone] will fall upon
> The dictatorial men and bring justice to Corinth.
> (Herodotus 5.92b.2; Eëtion and Labda are Cypselus' parents)
>
> Happy is this man who enters my house,
> Cypselus, son of Eëtion, King of famous Corinth!
> (Herodotus 5.92e.2; a third line was added later and has here been omitted)

From these two pieces of evidence we may conclude the following: Cypselus presented himself (or delighted to have himself presented) as someone who would bring justice to Corinth, whereas the previous régime (that of the Bacchiads, an aristocratic clan) had allegedly been unjust. As little as we may wish to think of a tyrant as bringing justice to a city, the concept finds a place in the sixth-century poet Theognis of Megara:

> Cyrnus, this city is pregnant, and I fear that she'll give birth to a man
> Who'll be a straightener of our evil insolence.
> The townsmen are still sensible, but the rulers
> Have turned to fall into great baseness.
> Good men, Cyrnus, never wrecked a city,
> But whenever evil men decide to commit insolence

And ruin the people and favor the unjust in judgment
For the sake of personal profit and power,
Don't expect that that city will remain quiet for long,
Not even if she now has deep peace.
Whenever the following things become dear to evil men,
(Namely) profits that accompany the people's detriment;
For from these things (come) civil wars and internecine murders
And a monarch [i.e. . a "tyrant"]: may this never befall this city!
(Theognis ll. 39–52 W with emendation; Cyrnus is a young friend of Theognis' to whom Theognis addresses his poem)

Here, the tyrant is someone who will "straighten" a city, correct the "insolence" of its abusive, mercenary, and unjust governing cadre. This closely parallels the presentation of the pre-Cypselid régime in Corinth. Let us make one final point about the second of our two pro-Cypselid poems: in the second Cypselus bears the title "King of Corinth." We recall the difficulty involved in distinguishing "kings" from "tyrants" and now note that we know of not one tyrant who ever called himself "tyrant."

When we proceed from those two contemporary poems about Cypselus to later evidence we run up against a common fact of Greek historiography: as time passes, stories become embroidered and acquire more and more legendary elements. Already Herodotus (writing in the second half of the fifth century BCE) tells a story of how Cypselus as a baby narrowly escaped death at the hands of the authorities in Corinth (5.92). Such legends are told of leaders as diverse as Cyrus the Great and Moses – how a man who would become a great leader was almost killed in infancy and how Providence (in some shape or form) protected him. These legends are not historical evidence in the strictest sense. Almost no historically sound information survives in Herodotus about Cypselus. When we turn to even later historiography, we must exercise even greater skepticism. Nicolaus of Damascus, the court historian ("plagiarist" would be a better term) of Herod the Great, also tells us of Cypselus' rise to power. Nicolaus wrote about the time of the birth of Christ, but was probably copying (verbatim) from the mid-fourth century BCE historian Ephorus of Cumae, whom Diodorus of Sicily (another plagiarist, writing in the first century BCE) copied as well.[6] This presumably Ephoran account adds several interesting details, namely that the previous régime had annually appointed one of its number to bear the title *basileus* and that Cypselus, when he slew that annual title-holder, took over the title (Diodorus 7.9.6; Nicolaus of Damascus FGrHist 90 fr. 57.1 and 6). We have already seen a contemporary piece of verse refer to Cypselus as *basileus*. This might (but clearly need not) corroborate Ephorus' account.

One further thing we may say about Cypselus. During his rule, which Herodotus (5.92f.1) sets at thirty years (clearly a round figure to be taken with a grain of salt), the Corinthians founded several colonies. Cypselus arranged for his sons to be the *oikistai* ("founders") of these colonies. Because the citizens of a colony traditionally buried its *oikistes* with heroic honors (ever after maintained) in its marketplace, they always knew their *oikistes'* name.[7] When Nicolaus (i.e., probably Ephorus) tells us that Cypselus sent out Pylades and Echiades as *oikistai* of the colonies of Leucas and Anactorium, respectively, we can accept this information, because Ephorus could easily enough have found that out on the basis of still extant founder-cults (Nicolaus of Damascus FGrHist 90 fr. 57.7). The use of the tyrant's (king's?) sons as founders of colonies indicates that Cypselus was trying to tie these colonies very closely to Corinth and to Corinth's ruling house.

Cypselus' son Periander succeeded him. We note that this "tyranny" (like the old ancestral kingship) was hereditary. Periander had married Melissa, the daughter of Procles, the tyrant of neighboring Epidaurus (Herodotus 3.50.2). We have already looked at Periander's later reputation, and this later reputation makes judging the information recounted of him difficult. Too much simply emphasizes his brutality (e.g., his murder of his wife, or his attempt to have 300 Corcyraean boys castrated – Herodotus 3.50.1 and 3.48.2). Herodotus does, however, mention a conquest of Epidaurus and also of Corcyra (3.52.6–7). Now the Bacchiads had founded Corcyra, and given Cypselus' attempts to bind new colonies to Corinth, an attempt by Periander forcibly to bring an old colony back into the fold would at least make sense – as would his installation of his son Lycophron as Corcyra's ruler. Finally, Periander sent out another son, Evagoras, as the *oikistes* of yet another colony, Potidaea (Nicolaus of Damascus FGrHist 90 fr. 59.1).

Periander's reputation for wisdom must have preceded the growth of the stories about his brutality. How he earned this reputation as a sage lies mostly outside our knowledge – the later stories simply crowded the earlier ones out. Herodotus (5.95.2) mentions his role as an arbitrator in a war between the Athenians and the Mytileneans during the time of Peisistratus of Athens and Pittacus of Mytilene, and a fragment of the contemporary poet Alcaeus might (but clearly need not) have mentioned this.[8] Periander ruled for forty years (thus Aristotle's round number) and was succeeded by his nephew Psammetichus, whose name (that of a contemporary Egyptian pharaoh) attests to some contact between the tyrant dynasty and the Egyptians (Aristotle *Politics* 1315b). Psammetichus' power soon collapsed; with him the tyrant dynasty fell.

The Orthagorids of Sicyon (ca. 620/610–520/510)[9]

In Sicyon resided the longest-lived of all the tyrant dynasties, its 100 years' duration unmatched. Now 100 years is obviously a round figure (cf. the Hundred Years' War between England and France), and we should not take it as exact. We may reconstruct the family tree of this dynasty as follows:

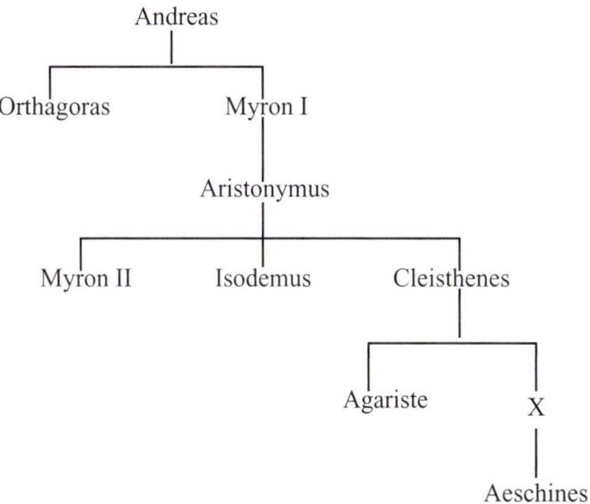

The founder of this dynasty remains a shadowy figure; for more information than his name (attested in Aristotle *Politics* 1315b), we rely on a papyrus fragment that possibly preserves part of Ephorus' history (Fornara 10). According to this fragment Orthagoras' father Andreas (whose name Herodotus attests, 6.126.1) received the high honor of accompanying a sacral embassy to Delphi in the capacity of a sacrificial butcher, whereas Orthagoras himself achieved fame as a military commander. None of this finds corroboration, although it does fly in the face of a common misunderstanding of this tyrant dynasty. Let us just say that the alleged factual details that we do receive attest this family's high social standing within Sicyon.

Myron I and Aristonymus, whose names Herodotus (6.126.1; cf. Pausanias 2.8.1) attests, are truly nothing more than names – they need not even have been tyrants. For Myron II and Isodemus we have some information from Nicolaus of Damascus, presumably again following

Ephorus. Isodemus allegedly had killed his brother, the tyrant Myron II, for adultery with Isodemus' wife. Isodemus, who thereafter became tyrant, was ritually impure and thus prevented from carrying out sacrifices on behalf of Sicyon. He was therefore persuaded to lay down the tyranny; thereupon Cleisthenes became tyrant. This story will be bear little weight; all the same it does posit that their position obligated the tyrants of Sicyon (one of whom, incidentally, it calls a *basileus*) to sacrifice on behalf of their city (Nicolaus of Damascus FGrHist 90 fr. 61).

When we come to Cleisthenes, the sources of information finally begin to flow more freely. This wealthy tyrant's renown spread far and wide, so that he could turn his daughter's (Agariste's) wedding into a Panhellenic spectacle (Herodotus 6.126; the date can be fixed somewhere in the 560s[10]). He invited all eligible bachelors who considered themselves worthy of becoming his son-in-law to present themselves in Sicyon. The extravaganza harked back to the mythological wooing of Helen, and Cleisthenes on this occasion took every opportunity to emphasize his wealth, status, and power. Curiously, Herodotus makes no mention of any son of Cleisthenes, though one must have existed, for when Cleisthenes married his daughter off, he never hinted that he was considering his new son-in-law as an heir. At any rate, descendants (at least sons of sons) of Cleisthenes are attested as ruling Sicyon much later (Scholiast to Aeschines 2.77).

Although the story of Cleisthenes' daughter's wedding attests Cleisthenes' wealth and renown, it tells us little of how he gained it. Aristotle (*Politics* 1315b) mentions Cleisthenes' warlike character, but ventures no details. A scholiast to Pindar (*Nemean* 9 Inscr.) speaks of Cleisthenes' participation in the First Sacred War (a war against the town of Crisa in Phocis that probably belongs to the 590s BCE and concerned the Delphic Oracle); Pausanias (10.7.3) speaks of Cleisthenes' victory in the newly introduced chariot races at the Pythian Games after the First Sacred War. Herodotus speaks of a similar victory in the Olympic Games (6.126), and Cleisthenes is also said to have founded local Pythian Games in Sicyon with the spoils from the First Sacred War (Scholiast to Pindar, *Nemean* 9 Inscr.). This interest in "games" is a recurring theme for the tyrants, as we shall see.[11]

Finally, Herodotus (5.68) tells us of a tribal reform that Cleisthenes carried out in Sicyon. Greek communities typically comprised several "tribes" that tended to have political, religious, and even military significance. Various circumstances occasioned large-scale tribal reforms by which the members of the community were redistributed either among the existing tribes or into entirely new ones. Now the Greeks themselves conventionally divided their "people" up into three large "tribes": Dorians, Ionians, and Aeolians. The Dorians conventionally subdivided themselves into three further "tribes": Hylleis, Dymanes, and Pamphyli. Sicyon, as a Dorian community, possessed these three tribes – plus one additional non-Dorian tribe, the Aegialeis. The family of the Orthagorids belonged to this tribe; if our information about the careers of Orthagoras and his father is correct, this non-Dorian tribe was not disadvantaged in comparison with the Dorian ones. According to Herodotus, however, Cleisthenes altered the names of all the tribes: the new names were (for the Dorian tribes) Hyatai, Oneatai, Choireatai and (for the non-Dorian tribe) Archelaoi. Herodotus interprets the first three names – which remained in use for sixty years after Cleisthenes' death – as purposefully mocking the Dorians: (roughly) "pig-ians," "ass-ians," and "piglet-ians." Now stories about tyrants routinely acquire embellishments, and we must always take stories of tyrants' doing mean things to people with several tons of salt. In my opinion it is more likely that Cleisthenes carried out a tribal reform (similar to that of, e.g., the lawgiver Demonax in Cyrene) and instituted completely new tribes. The new tribes were geographically based (similarly, e.g., to the Spartan Obes), and the names were derived from toponyms. "Hyatai" then means not "pig-ians," but rather "People of (the place) Hya." Simply going by the rules of word formation in Greek, the latter is actually rather more probable than the former. At some point, however, someone noticed that the name could be taken to mean "pig-ians" – and the other two names were then altered a bit to make them mean "ass-ians" and "piglet-ians." So another story of a mean, snide tyrant arose.[12]

We have finally to deal with the downfall of the tyranny in Sicyon. This seems to have come towards the end of the sixth century at the hands of the Spartans. Three sources attest to this; although none of them inspires much confidence by itself, a case can be made for accepting them together: Plutarch *De Herodoti malignitate* (*On the Malice of Herodotus*) 21 (p. 859); Rylands Papyrus 18; and the Scholiast to Aeschines 2.77. In each case we are dealing with a general tradition that the Spartans suppressed tyrannies in Greece. To summarize very briefly the argument: Herodotus says that Cleisthenes' arrangements for the Sicyonian tribes remained in force for sixty years after his death (probably not an exact figure; it may mean "about two generations"). Now Cleisthenes' rule seems to have ended in the 560s, so if we assume that the institutions of the tyranny lasted only as long as the tyranny itself and were overturned with the tyranny, then the final Orthagorid tyrant, Aeschines, lost power in the 510s BCE. This fits well with the implication of the scholiast to Aeschines (2.77) that at least two generations of Orthagorids ruled after Cleisthenes. Interestingly, the deposition of the last tyrant of Athens, Hippias, in 511 BCE by the Spartan king Cleomenes I, is well attested (Herodotus 5.64–5; for the date Thucydides 8.68.4), and this expedition would provide not just a good contemporary parallel for the Spartans' deposition of Aeschines, but perhaps even a convenient occasion for it.

Solon

The first lawgiver of Athens was said to be Draco. He remains for us a shadowy figure, difficult even to date. Proverbially, however, his laws counted as particularly harsh: a liberal use of the death penalty (allegedly) had characterized them (Plutarch *Solon* 17). With the exception of the law on homicide,[13] all were abolished by the next lawgiver, to whom we now turn.

In the early sixth century, traditionally in 594 but quite possibly as many as twenty years later, Solon was selected to resolve a severe social, economic, and political crisis in Athens. The choice clearly appealed to most people in Athens – Solon had enough respect from all parties and did not appear biased in anyone's favor. At any rate Solon received absolute power for (apparently) one year to execute whatever reforms he saw fit. Because Solon described and defended his reforms in his poetry, both the ancient commentators (such as the author of the pseudo-Aristotelian *Constitution of Athens* [the *Athenaion Politeia* or *Ath.Pol.*] or Plutarch, the author of a biographical essay on Solon), as well as modern scholars, are in a far better position than usual to discuss an early Greek ruler.

The measures that Solon instituted give the clearest insight into the problems that Athens was facing. Solon made illegal a practice common throughout Greece, that of using one's own person as security for a loan (Plutarch *Solon* 15.3; *Ath.Pol.* 6.1). In default of payment a creditor could legally seize the debtor's person and even sell him abroad as a slave in an attempt to recoup the loss. Furthermore, Solon freed those debt-slaves still within Athens and bought back many whom their creditors had sold abroad (Solon fr. 36 W). Debt-slavery had clearly gone beyond being an occasional phenomenon affecting individuals and had grown to become a crisis affecting society as a whole. A curious law of Solon's sheds further light on the crisis: he forbad the export of any natural produce other than olive oil (Plutarch *Solon* 25.1 = T 5, fr. 56 Ruschenbusch). In another law Solon supposedly encouraged fathers to teach their sons a trade

(Plutarch Solon 22.1 = fr. 56 Ruschenbusch). These laws' relevance will become clear in a moment.

The origin of this crisis we can sketch only theoretically. Several things contributed: First, during the seventh century the population in Athens had grown dramatically[14] – severe stress on Athens' ability to produce enough food for its population may well have resulted from this. Second, the Greeks did not practice primogeniture: a man's sons all inherited equally. If a landholder had more than one son, then they subdivided his plot equally when he died. A given holding of land might from generation to generation suffer subdivision until the resultant plots became too small to support a family. If such a smallholder could not gain additional land (by whatever means), then he had to borrow – mostly grain, because this was still a premonetary economy – against next year's harvest or against his land or against his person (or his children's). Third, while many smallholders were falling into desperate straits, large landholders were aggrandizing their own estates: for example, by lending to smallholders against the latter's land. In brief, many people were losing land and thereby their means of feeding themselves. Fourth, large landholders might then trade grain abroad to obtain goods unavailable in Athens, thus further reducing the supply of grain in Attica and making it even more difficult for those with inadequate land to acquire sufficient food – hence Solon's law allowing only the export of olive oil, as the production of olive oil has little impact on the production of grain (olive groves tend to lie in marginal land unsuited for grain). The other law of Solon's, mentioned above, perhaps also belongs in this context: the "industrial" produce of people whose fathers had taught them a trade provided them with the means to acquire natural produce from those who owned land.

If the crisis originated in this way, then we can also see that Solon treated only the symptoms, but not the causes. A treatment of the causes would presumably have mandated a large-scale redistribution of land so that the existing productive capacity better served the needs of the population as a whole. Such a redistribution, however, is difficult to achieve even under the best of circumstances and will always meet with determined resistance (see, e.g., Plutarch's biographies of Agis IV and Cleomenes III, two third-century Spartan kings who sought to carry out a redistribution of land in Sparta). Solon never attempted it (cf. Plutarch *Solon* 16.1). He merely treated the effects of debt-slavery and abolished the practice itself; ironically, this also made it more difficult for smallholders to borrow in time of need. Furthermore, he attempted to retain within Athens what grain was being produced. Although Solon may have provided welcome relief, he deferred resolution.

We now come to Solon's political reforms. He instituted a second council (from which we may conclude that a first already existed) and reformed the census of classes. The second, new council consisted of 400 members, 100 from each inner Athenian "tribe" (*Ath.Pol.* 9.4). The mode of members' selection is unknown. Furthermore, we can only guess at the duties of this new council: as the predecessor of the well-known Council of 500 (instituted by Cleisthenes at the end of the sixth century), it may well have had that council's probouleutic function, that is, the preparation of the agenda for the Assembly. The functions of the council that already existed in Solon's day, the Council of the Areopagus, also remain obscure. In the early fifth century it allegedly functioned as "guardian of the constitution" (*Ath.Pol.* 25.2; cf. 9.4 and Plutarch *Cimon* 15.3). Modern scholars have frequently interpreted this as meaning that it had some sort of "veto power" over decrees of the Assembly. We will come to the composition of this council in a moment.

For now let us turn to Solon's reforms of the class census. In the fifth century, Athenian society was divided up into four classes, defined in terms of wealth:

Pentacosiomedimnoi = men whose property produced more than 500 bushels of grain
Hippeis = more than 300 bushels of grain
Zeugitai = more than 200 bushels of grain
Thetes = everyone else[15]

This system was attributed to Solon, and although Solon himself does not mention it in his own poetry (i.e., we have no contemporary evidence), we can show by argument that this attribution is correct. This system assesses wealth in bushels of agricultural produce, not in coin. Now coinage was introduced into west Aegean Greece starting from the mid-sixth century[16]; the clearly clumsy premonetary definitions of the Athenian classes antedate this. This brings us into Solon's time.

Now the made-up word *Pentacosiomedimnoi* literally means "500-bushel-men" and owes its coinage to this new definition of a class. That the names of the other three classes did not have to be coined on the basis of their new definitions shows that these names already existed, whatever political or social significance they may have had. At any rate these names imply slightly different definitions of the people so denoted:

Hippeis = "horsemen," that is, men who could afford to maintain a horse; *Zeugitai* = "yoke-men," that is, men who could afford to maintain a brace of oxen. In these cases the name was old; the definition in terms of natural produce was attached to the old name.

Political rights in Athens depended on class. In 453 BCE, it became possible for members of the third class, the *Zeugitai*, to hold the highest offices (*Ath.Pol.* 26.2). This implies that hitherto the highest offices had been reserved for the two highest classes. This feature of the constitution is usually assumed to be Solonian in origin (*Ath.Pol.* 7.3). If, as Plutarch *Theseus* 25.2, states, the "aristocrats" in Athens (called Eupatridai, i.e., "sons of noble fathers") had once possessed the sole right to hold office, then Solon did away with this in the course of his class reforms. However that may be, the most important officials in Athens (even if their roles grew more and more ceremonial during the fifth century) were the nine archons. An additional advantage of holding this office in the fifth and fourth centuries (*Ath.Pol.* 3.6) was that the Council of the Areopagus consisted of all former archons. If the same rules held in Solon's day, then the chief magistracies in Athens were strictly limited to the two wealthiest classes, and membership of the Council of the Areopagus (which may have had a veto right over decrees passed by the Assembly) was limited to the former archons (cf. Plutarch *Solon* 29). That all of this extrapolation is fraught with danger is clear. If, however, Solon did institute all of these reforms (introduction of a new council, restructuring of both councils' competence, introduction of a new class census) strictly on his own say-so, surely we begin to see why it is useful to look upon him as an absolute ruler comparable to the tyrants, and in this context we should perhaps recall Cleisthenes' tribal reforms in Sicyon.

In addition to all of these reforms, Solon reformed the Athenian legal code (Herodotus 1.29). Although this reform, too, had far-reaching importance, the later Athenians' habit of attributing any law to Solon renders its discussion, in my view, almost impossible.[17] Worse, far too many laws, even those that are cited to us according to the so-called *axones* (the rotating prisms on which these laws were publicly displayed), contain references to coinage that Solon (as his use of bushels of grain to measure wealth shows) did not as yet know. An example will make this clear:

> Of natural produce [Solon] allowed the sale abroad of olive oil alone, but forbad the export of everything else: and he ordained that the Archon should curse those who did export,

> or he himself was to pay one hundred drachmas into the public treasury. It is the first "axon" which contains this law.
> (T 5, fr. 65 Ruschenbusch = Plutarch *Solon* 24.1)

We can probably assume in this case that the monetary fine was later added to the original punishment, namely a curse from the Archon, and guess further that the law itself does go back to Solon, whereas the later "editing" was limited to the introduction of the monetary fine. But we have such a guide all too rarely. At any rate the present author has not much faith in his ability to guess which laws attributed to Solon are genuinely Solonian.

To conclude, then: In a severe crisis the Athenians turned to a trusted man, Solon, and gave him absolute power to institute political and legal reforms in dealing with the crisis however he saw fit. We have also seen that his reforms, although far-reaching, dealt only with the immediate crisis and not with its long-term causes. Yet even such relief as he provided was clearly welcome.

The Peisistratids of Athens

A few years after Solon's one-year "tyranny," a new tyrant arose in Athens. This was Peisistratus, and unlike Solon he seized power. What follows derives entirely from Herodotus 1.59–64. Peisistratus built up a local support base in northern Attica, on the other side of the hills from Athens – hence Peisistratus' "faction's" nickname, the Hyperacrii, "the people beyond the hills." (Both this name and its variant, Diakrii [Plutarch *Solon* 29.1], emphatically do not mean "people of the hills.") Peisistratus managed to get the Athenians to provide him with a personal bodyguard with whom he proceeded to seize the Acropolis. Possession of the Acropolis was tantamount to possession of Athens, and unlike the case of a would-be tyrant many years earlier, Cylon, when the Athenians had blockaded the Acropolis (Herodotus 5.71; Thucydides 1.126), the people of Athens this time seem to have acquiesced in Peisistratus' tyranny. I would like to propose, with all due tentativeness, a simple reason: the recourse to the rule of one man – after Solon's example – seemed logical, indeed compelling: after all, it had helped the last time. We have already seen that Solon probably treated only the symptoms of the economic crisis in Athens, not its causes. It may well be that the problems that Solon had sought to relieve had flared up again. Be that as it may, two powerful aristocratic families – normally at loggerheads – joined forces to drive Peisistratus from the city. No sooner was Peisistratus gone than the leaders of their two families (the Alcmeonids and the Philaids) fell out again, and the leader of the Alcmeonids (Megacles) conspired to bring Peisistratus back. A marriage alliance was arranged, and a cheering populace welcomed Peisistratus back into Athens. But Peisistratus and Megacles shortly fell out, and Peisistratus went into exile a second time. After ten years he returned. He set out from Eretria (a town in Euboea that seems to have maintained friendly relations with Peisistratus) and received financial support from Thebes and military support from some Argives, as well as from a Naxian blade-for-hire called Lygdamis. Peisistratus easily defeated the army brought against him by the authorities in Athens – in fact, the opposing army mostly melted away without a fight, as few truly wanted to fight to keep Peisistratus out. Only the aristocratic Alcmeonids and their supporters actually fought. After their defeat, they fled. Peisistratus now consolidated his position as tyrant. He died in the tyranny and passed it on to his son Hippias, who ruled until 511 BCE – thirty-six years after his father's third seizure of power, according to Herodotus (5.65.3).

Before we go on to the tyrants' achievements in Athens, let us spare a word on the chronology of this house. The third seizure of the tyranny we can securely date to 547 – not just by adding 36 to 511, but by corroborating argument as well: the third seizure must antedate the Persian taking of Sardis (Herodotus 1.64 and 84), fixed by the Babylonian Nabonidus Chronicle to 546.[18] At any rate, the second exile lasted ten years, so the second seizure belongs to 557. Thereafter – and this we must say as firmly as possible – our chronological data end. The pseudo-Aristotelian *Constitution of Athens* pretends to give further information, which, however, was long ago shown to be faked.[19] It is illustrative to show up the fraud. Remember that Herodotus fixed the length of the third tyranny at thirty-six years, a figure we can substantiate. According to the *Ath.Pol.* (14.3; 15.1; 17.1; 19.6) the three "tyrannies" had the following lengths (in years):

First:	6
Second:	7
Third:	6 (Peisistratus)
	17 (Hippias)

I confess that I enjoy putting this up on the blackboard in lectures – and then watching as individual students begin to laugh as they figure out the fraud. It only requires simple addition: 6, 7, 6, and 17 add up to 36! The author of the *Ath.Pol.* misunderstood the figure of thirty-six years in

Herodotus and arbitrarily divided it up over all three "tyrannies." (The same error underlies the figure of thirty-five years in Aristotle's *Politics* 1315b.) I trust it is becoming clear how carefully we must scrutinize our sources before we blindly accept what they say. The end result is this: we have no idea when Peisistratus seized power for the first and second time, save that it was before 557.

We come finally to the acts of the Peisistratids. From Herodotus we know that the Alcmeonids fled from Athens in 547. They, of course, possessed large estates – the formation of which had presumably played its part in the economic crisis we discussed above in the section on Solon. It is inconceivable that these estates lay fallow during the Alcmeonids' exile. Unfortunately, no source tells us what became of them, so we must guess. Usually, scholars have assumed that Peisistratus confiscated these properties and redistributed them. In other words, the Alcmeonids' flight cleared the way to a long overdue land reform. At any rate, the economic crisis that had earlier seemed so severe simply disappeared during the tyranny. The author of the *Ath.Pol.*, following on his discussion of Peisistratus' agrarian policy, remarks that people remembered the tyranny of Peisistratus as a "golden age" (*Ath.Pol.* 16.7), and here we can believe him, as no one would have thought to invent such a statement after the tyranny's fall.

Peisistratus, like most tyrants, was interested in games and festivals. He founded the Greater Panathenaean Games (Aristotle fr. 637); if the traditional date of the games in Eusebius (566) be accepted, then we should probably think of Peisistratus' first tyranny. Like most other tyrants Peisistratus (and his son) carried out large building projects: a temple of Olympian Zeus (Aristotle *Politics* 13134b) and the archaeologically attested sixth-century temple to Athena on the Acropolis, as well as a sixth-century temple to Dionysus on the slope of the Acropolis, can probably be attributed either to Peisistratus or his son Hippias. We also know of the *Enneakrouros*, a fountain house that helped secure the water supply in Athens (Thucydides 2.15.5).

After his father's death Hippias became tyrant. He married his daughter Archedice to Aeantides, the son of Hippocles, the tyrant of Lampsacus. We are best informed of the end of Hippias' reign, when the tyranny turned brutal. Three years before the tyranny's end Harmodius and Aristogeiton – motivated by a purely private grudge – assassinated Hippias' brother, Hipparchus. Hippias, thoroughly alarmed, turned to increasingly repressive measures to retain control. Thucydides tells us how Hippias took hostages from various prominent families and had them kept on Delos against their families' good behavior (Thucydides

6.59). But it was not the Athenians themselves who deposed Hippias. The Alcmeonids had over the years attempted to cajole the Spartans into invading Athens to topple the tyranny (Herodotus 5.64–65), and King Cleomenes obliged in 511. The Peisistratids fled to Sigeium, an extraterritorial possession (whether technically Athenian or personal) in Asia Minor, over which Peisistratus had once appointed another son, Hegesistratus, as governor (Herodotus 5.94.1).

Pittacus of Mytilene and His Predecessors

Thanks to the poems of Alcaeus we have contemporary evidence for the tyranny in Mytilene, the largest city on the island of Lesbos. Alcaeus' own politics, however, made him implacably hostile to all who gained power in his city. (Alcaeus himself seems routinely to have stood on the losers' side.) Unfortunately, many of his poems are preserved only on papyrus scraps, which, however, do sometimes contain commentary summarizing additional poems' contents. On the assumption that various ancient authors who still had the poems in their entirety before them have (more or less) accurately described parts now lost, we can make out the following succession of régimes in Mytilene:

First, an aristocratic clan, the Penthilidae, held sway over Mytilene. Alcaeus briefly mentions them in a fragmentary context (Alcaeus fr. 75 LP); according to Aristotle (who we can only hope was relying on parts of Alcaeus that we no longer possess), the Penthilidae were cruel rulers against whom the Mytileneans revolted when the former went through the marketplace striking people with clubs (*Politics* 1311b).

Then, two tyrants ruled: Melanchrus and Myrsilus. Until the discovery of the relevant fragments of Alcaeus, we knew these tyrants only from late sources. According to Diogenes Laertius (1.74), writing in the third century CE, Alcaeus' brothers assisted Pittacus in deposing the tyrant Melanchrus, whom the tenth century CE Byzantine lexicon, the "Suda" (Suidas, s.v. Pittacus) also says Pittacus deposed. We do know that Alcaeus at least mentioned Melanchrus (fr. 331 LP), and we can surmise that Diogenes and the compilers of the "Suda" gathered their additional information about Melanchrus from other poems of Alcaeus' no longer available to us.

Several poems of Alcaeus' mention the next tyrant, Myrsilus. Alcaeus apparently participated in a plot against him (Commentary to fr. 113 LP) and went into exile when it failed. One of the conspirators, Pittacus, later double-crossed the others and colluded with Myrsilus (Alcaeus fr. 70 LP), whose death Alcaeus celebrates (fr. 332 LP).

Thereafter Pittacus became tyrant (fr. 348 LP), allegedly for a term of ten years. After the violent overthrow of the Penthilidae and later that of Melanchrus, after all the civic strife surrounding the tyranny of Myrsilus, Pittacus established peace: "He liberated his native land from the three greatest evils: tyranny, civic strife, and war" (Diodorus 9.11.1).

Although Alcaeus heaped invective on Pittacus, calling him "base-born," "fox," and even "potbelly," Pittacus (like Solon) gained a reputation as a wise lawgiver even if we learn of few specific laws (see Aristotle *Politics* 1274b and Diogenes Laertius 1.76). Herodotus attests to his reputation for wisdom (1.27.2), as does his inclusion among the Seven Sages. Even if we know little securely about his deeds while tyrant, we do know that his reputation stood high among the later Mytileneans. A later song implicitly makes much of his simplicity; Plutarch (*Septem sapientium convivium* [*Dinner of the Seven Sages*] 14, p. 157) recounts a Mytilenean work-song of a woman grinding grain with a mill:

> Grind, mill, grind!
> For even Pittacus ground
> When he was King of great Mytilene!

We also note that this particular Mytilenean song also calls Pittacus a "king."

Conclusions

We have now looked at three tyrant dynasties (the Cypselids of Corinth, the Orthagorids of Sicyon, the Peisistratids of Athens) and two lawgivers (one of whom was considered a tyrant and the other of whom we may usefully consider as a tyrant). We must remember, however, that this was only a selection mandated by strict limitations of length. It would be fascinating to cover the Aeacids of Samos, Thrasybulus of Miletus, Pheidon of Argos, Theagenes of Megara, and many others as well. The same applies to the lawgivers. As it is, we will have opportunity to refer to some of them in this section.

First, we note that "tyranny" was not an isolated phenomenon. Even if a traditional term such as "the Age of Tyranny" goes perhaps too far, tyrants were extremely common (if by no means universal) in the period from about 650 to 500 BCE If we include lawgivers such as Pittacus and Solon as absolute rulers, then we get even more tyrants. What caused so many cities to have recourse to tyranny? In the terms of evolutionary biology, which general circumstances favored the development of tyranny in the time period in question?

We have several hints. In the case of Solon we see a severe economic crisis, a crisis that he apparently did not solve, but rather another tyrant, Peisistratus, who (probably) carried out a large-scale redistribution of land when his opponents, the wealthy aristocratic clan of the Alcmeonids, fled into exile. Extrapolation is terribly dangerous, but Cypselus, for example, *may* have done something similar in Corinth when the members of the aristocratic clan, the Bacchiads, that had hitherto governed Corinth fled into exile (Herodotus 5.92e.2 – presumably the Bacchiads belonged to those whom Cypselus drove into exile). A sense of economic crisis also emerges from Aristotle's comment that Theagenes of Megara, a sixth-century tyrant, slaughtered the livestock of the wealthy who were letting their herds graze on others' land (*Politics* 1305a), that is, were in some way appropriating it from the poor, depriving them of the means to feed themselves.

Together with the economic crisis, we get some sense of a political crisis as well. Solon also tried to deal with political problems, stemming perhaps from the prerogative of the aristocrats, the Eupatridai, to hold office (if we can take Plutarch's word for this). This prerogative of the Eupatridai should remind us of the régime of the Bacchiads in Corinth (whose alleged injustice and unpopularity Cypselus attempted to turn to his own advantage). We may also refer to the allegedly brutal Penthilidae in Mytilene. When we contemplate the régimes that preceded the tyrannies, we perhaps begin to understand why Theognis viewed a tyrant as someone who would "straighten" a city. Moreover, Theognis put the blame for the tyrant whom he feared as inevitable squarely on the shoulders of the evil men who governed his city.

This, however, raises the next question: Why did cities turn to an absolute ruler? Why give a lawgiver unlimited power to reform the city's institutions as he saw fit? Why receive a despot into one's city with cheers (as in the case of Peisistratus' first return from exile)? Why tolerate despotic rule? My own tentative (and partial) answer to this (and it is hardly consensus opinion) is that many tyrants presented themselves as legitimate kings and their rule as the return to an ancestral mode of government.[20] Their subjects seem to have viewed them as kings as well. This is even true for a "lawgiver" such as Pittacus. Certainly, as we have seen, distinguishing "tyrants" from "kings" by some clear definition is difficult. In the famous story of Polycrates' ring, when the fisherman brings the ring back to Polycrates, he addresses the tyrant as "King" (Herodotus 3.42.2). The tyrants thus laid (tenuous) claim to a legacy of legitimate one-man rule that (with the exception of Athens) probably still lay within living memory and may often have seemed preferable to the current régime, which the would-be tyrant might convincingly promise to "straighten." All the same, each case on some level is unique, and individual tyrants' paths to power probably varied greatly. Some may have parleyed a military command into the tyranny, others some civic office, and so on (Aristotle *Politics* 1310b).

Second, having made some tentative suggestions as to the origin of tyranny, let us proceed to ask, what were the characteristics of a tyrant's rule? In some cases, the period of rule was limited (Solon or Pittacus). In others, the tyrants themselves clearly viewed their position as hereditary: whether successful or not, they all seem to have sought to hand over the rule to a son or, barring a son, some other male relative such as a nephew (e.g., Periander passed on the tyranny to his nephew Psammetichus). To take another example, three generations of Aeacids ruled on Samos (Aeaces I, his sons Polycrates and Syloson, and Syloson's son Aeaces II).[21] More often than not, however, tyrants were toppled before it came to an orderly succession.

Some tyrants seem to have held an office. Pittacus was made "tyrant" by the Mytileneans: clearly he held an office of some sort, even if we assume that the title of which Aristotle (*Politics* 1285a) speaks, *Aisymnetes*, is generic rather than specific. Thucydides (6.54.6) tells us that the Peisistratids took good care to hold the chief offices themselves (or, perhaps, at least to make sure that allies filled all major offices). Aeaces II refers in an inscription either to his (or to his grandfather's, another tyrant's) holding the position of *epistates* (a general title for any supervisor, but also for a ruler).[22] We have seen that there is a chance that the Cypselids and the Orthagorids held the position of a *basileus*.

It is difficult to characterize tyrants' (and lawgivers') policies in any but the most sweeping terms, because each was responding to a large degree to a local (and thus unique) situation. All the same, certain trends emerge. We have already looked briefly at how various rulers responded to an economic and social crisis. We can say a little more about these responses now. Many tyrants channeled public wealth into building projects. In addition to the Peisistratids' temples, we may here note the architectural achievements of Polycrates of Samos: the temple of Hera, the mole in the harbor, and the mile-long tunnel of Eupalinus driven through solid rock to a spring to secure the city's water supply (Herodotus 3.60; Aristotle *Politics* 1313b). This last reminds one not only of the *Enneakrouros*, but also of the fountain house built in Megara by its tyrant Theagenes (Pausanias 1.40.1). Greece is a hot, thirsty land, and if tyrants secured their cities' water supplies, they rendered their subjects a valuable service.

Yet such buildings did more than serve the public benefit. By such works the tyrants emphasized their power and status, their role as public benefactors. The building of temples underscored their piety: many tyrants also erected structures in Panhellenic sanctuaries such as Delphi, where the tyrant Cypselus had one of the so-called treasuries built (Herodotus 1.14.2). Finally, the erection of such large buildings had an economic impact within the communities that the tyrants ruled: they provided mass employment. We have seen the ways in which various lawgivers and tyrants attempted to deal with an economic crisis in which not enough people had access to land from which to support themselves directly. Building projects were another such way.

As a rule the tyrants also enjoyed the great athletic festivals, which were (difficult as it may be for us to accept) religious festivals foremost. Many tyrants are somehow associated with the Olympic Games (in honor of Zeus Olympios), from Pheidon of Argos who, with an army to back him, celebrated the games in his own name all the way to Cleisthenes of Sicyon, who announced his daughter's impending marriage at Olympia after winning the chariot race there (Herodotus 6.127.3 and 126.2). Many tyrants founded games at home: Peisistratus established the Panathenaean Games (a torch-relay race in honor of the goddess Athena); Cleisthenes founded Pythian Games in Sicyon (in honor of Apollo Pythius and in imitation of the Pythian Games at Delphi, in which he once won the chariot race); Polycrates of Samos was about to found games in honor of either Apollo Pythius or Apollo Delius when death intervened (Suidas, s.v. *tauta soi kai Pythia kai Delia*). Because these games were first of all religious festivals, the tyrants' participation in (indeed foundation of) them emphasized, once again, their own piety. Of course, the games also provided entertainment for the masses, entertainment in which the tyrants could play an important role. For the tyrants (who enjoyed competing in the chariot races, especially as the victor in this contest was not the driver, but the financier, i.e., the tyrant) benefited greatly from the public status gained by having won at, for example, Olympia.

In addition to their patronage of games, the tyrants also sought to foster the arts. Their building projects, of course, gave free scope to architecture and architectural sculpture. But the tyrants also supported the literary arts: under Peisistratid patronage the Homeric epics were edited in Athens;[23] Cleisthenes specifically banned the recital of Homeric epics from Sicyon, but may have encouraged the performance of the

Argonauts' saga;[24] Periander patronized the poet Arion at his court (Herodotus 1.23–4); Ibycus of Rhegium worked at tyrants' courts both in Sicyon and on Samos (Ibycus fr. 27 and 1 Page).

Finally, the tyrants tended to build up a network of mutually supportive ties with one another. If a Naxian adventurer called Lygdamis helped Peisistratus become tyrant of Athens, then Peisistratus later helped Lygdamis become tyrant of Naxos (Herodotus 1.64.2). According to a late source (Polyaenus 1.23), Lygdamis later helped the Aeacid Polycrates regain control of Samos for his dynasty. Marriage alliances between tyrants' houses did their part as well: Cypselus saw his son and successor Periander married to Melissa, the daughter of the tyrant of neighboring Epidaurus, Procles. Hippias' daughter married the son of the tyrant of Lampsacus. Theagenes of Megara provided troops for his son-in-law's (Cylon's) failed attempt to make himself tyrant of Athens (Thucydides 1.126.3; Pausanias 1.40.1). Even beyond marriage alliances and mutual support, friendship between tyrants existed: that between Periander of Corinth and Thrasybulus of Miletus was, if not proverbial, at least anecdotal. In addition, when the tyrants expanded abroad, some at least preferred to keep it in the family: Cypselus, Periander, and Peisistratus placed their sons in charge of colonies/possessions abroad (see also *Tyrants and Patronage* in Chapter 8). In general (though exceptions exist), this finely meshed "network" of contacts and alliances seems to have served the keeping of the peace.

Let us now try to pass judgment on the "tyrants" and "lawgivers," these two variations on the theme of "absolute rule" in Archaic Greece, and their role in Greek development. Many of them played a role in the long-term political organization of their communities: one thinks of Solon's class census in Athens, Cleisthenes' tribal reform in Sicyon, or Demonax' tribal reform in Cyrene. Economically, they sought to find solutions for communities whose land's (practical) productive capacity seems often to have fallen short of actual need. They ruled during a time when trade as well as trades were becoming increasingly important, so we find such considerations playing a part in their economic policies insofar as we can discern them. And, certainly, many a community benefited from the fountain houses, harbors, and temples that the tyrants built.

But the so-called age of tyrants did pass, and here at the end of this essay we may speculate as to why: First, if we take them as "kings" (or would-be kings), then the tyrants stand at the very end of a long political development that was making one-man rule obsolete anyway. They were hopelessly exposed to these same long-term trends, and the tyrants, owing to the youth of their régimes, could not, ultimately, lean on tradition as a support for their rule convincingly. Second, even if the tyrants did "straighten" their communities, once the necessary "straightening" had taken place, there was little need, necessarily, to keep the tyrants on. Third, the tyrants seem to have grown increasingly repressive towards the end of their reign in order to stay in power (Hippias' is the best-attested case) – with the result that they undermined their own popularity and thus dug their own graves more effectively than any freedom fighters could have. Moreover, the final period of tyranny seems to have remained best in communities' collective memory; hence the savage reputation of someone such as Periander, with whom we began. The "lawgivers," with their fixed appointments, obviously fared much better. They did not become involved in a vicious struggle to maintain power once they had outlived their usefulness, even if they owed their appointment to their "monarchies" to the same factors that had once made tyrants seem like "straighteners."

NOTES

1 Demetrius of Phalerum 10.3 DK; cf. Stobaeus 43.131 Meineke = 4.1.134 Hense; cf. Diogenes Laertius 1.13.

2 Plutarch *Lycurgus* 29. If Lycurgus was a real person, he stands beyond the reach of historians: the later Spartans routinely attributed all their laws and customs to Lycurgus, so we cannot judge which laws (if any) are genuinely his. Unlike Solon (on whom see below), Lycurgus left behind no writings.

3 Willetts 1967.

4 On this and what follows see Parker 1998, 145–72; cf. Fornara 8.

5 The chronology has been much disputed; I follow that advanced in Parker 1993, 385–417.

6 On the attribution of this material to Ephorus see FGrHist, II C 248 (commentary to 90 fr. 57–61).

7 For an extended discussion of Archaic Greek colonization and colonies, see ch. 8.

8 Alcaeus fr. 10.7 LP; Page 1955, 159 with n. 1.

9 The chronology has been much disputed; I follow that advanced in Parker 1992, 165–75.

10 For this see Parker 1992, 165.

11 See also ch. 9, *The Sycionian Tyrants at Delphi and Olympia.*

12 See further Parker 1994, 404–11; see also ch. 2 on the tribes as a subdivision of the *polis* and, in particular, the Sicyonian reforms.

13 Stroud 1968.

14 See, e.g., Snodgrass 1980, 22–3.

15 Most scholars have generally assumed that, after the advent of coinage in the mid-sixth century, monetary definitions replaced these clumsy ones in bushels of grain, so that "1 bushel" equaled "1 drachma." The conversion stems from Plutarch *Solon* 23.3.

16 See Kraay 1988, 435–7.
17 See on this Hignett 1950, 18–19.
18 Grayson 1975, 107.
19 Heidbüchel 1957, 70–89. No attempt at "rescuing" the chronological data in the *Ath.Pol.* convinces.
20 Parker 1996, 165–86.
21 For the Aeacid dynasty, see White 1954, 36–43.
22 GHI² no. 16 = Sylloge³ no. 10. On this see Parker 1996, 181–2.
23 For this see Davison 1955, 1–21.
24 For the arguments involved see Parker 1994, 418–21.

BIBLIOGRAPHY AND SUGGESTED READINGS

General Works

Anderson, G. 2005. "Before *Turannoi* were Tyrants: Rethinking a Chapter of Early Greek History." *Classical Antiquity*. 24: 173–222.

Andrewes, A. 1956. *The Greek Tyrants*. (A very dated general guide in English.)

Berve, H. 1967. *Die Tyrannis bei den Griechen*. (This remains the standard reference work for the Greek tyrants.)

Cawkwell, G. L. 1995. "Early Greek Tyranny and the People." *Classical Quarterly* 89: 73–86.

Grayson, A. K. 1975. *Assyrian and Babylonian Chronicles*.

Kelly, T. 1976. *A History of Argos*. (It contains a chapter on tyranny.)

Kraay, C. M. 1988. "Coinage." *Cambridge Ancient History*, IV². 431–45.

McGlew, J. F. 1993. *Tyranny and Political Culture in Ancient Greece*.

Page, D. 1955. *Sappho and Alcaeus*. (A gold mine of information for the tyranny in Mytilene.)

Parker, V. 1996. "Vom König zum Tyrannen: Eine Betrachtung zur Entstehung der älteren griechischen Tyrannis." *Tyche* 11: 165–86.

______. 1998. "Τύραννος. The Semantics of a Political Concept from Archilochus to Aristotle." *Hermes* 126: 145–72.

Snodgrass, A. M. 1980. *Archaic Greece*.

Willetts, R. F. 1967. *The Lawcode of Gortyn*.

The Tyranny in Athens (Solon and the Peisistratids)

Davison, J. A. 1955. "Peisistratus and Homer." *Transactions of the American Philological Association* 86: 1–21.

Frost, F. J. 1985. "Toward a History of Peisistratid Athens." In *The Craft of the Ancient Historian. Essays in Honor of C. G. Starr*. Eds. J. W. Eadie, and J. Ober, 57–78.

Heidbüchel, F. 1957. "Die Chronologie der Peisistratiden in der Atthis." *Philologus* 101: 70–89.

Hignett, C. 1950. *History of the Athenian Constitution*.

Lavelle, B. M. 1991. "The Compleat Angler: Observations on the Rise of Peisistratos in Herodotos (1.59–64)." *Classical Quarterly* 85: 317–24.

______. 1993. *The Sorrow and the Pity. A Prolegomenon to a History of Athens under the Peisistratids, ca. 560–510 B.C.*

Rhodes, P. J. 1976. "Pisistratid Chronology Again." *Phoenix* 30: 219–33.

Ruschenbusch, E. 1966. *Solonos Nomoi. Die Fragmente des Solonischen Gesetzwernes mit einer Text und Überlieferungsgeschichte.*
Stanton, G. R. 1990. *Athenian Politics, ca. 800–500 B.C.: A Sourcebook.* (In my opinion, the best introduction is this collection of source material with commentary.)
Stroud, R. S. 1968. *Drakon's Law on Homicide.*
Waters, K. H. 1971. *Herodotos on Tyrants and Despots. A Study in Objectivity.*

The Tyranny at Corinth

Oost, S. I. 1972. "Cypselus the Bacchiad." *Classical Philology* 67: 10–30.
Parker, V. 1993. "Zur griechischen und vorderasiatischen Chronologie des sechsten Jahrhunderts v. Chr. unter besonderer Berücksichtigung der Kypselidenchronologie." *Historia* 42: 385–417.
Salmon, J. B. 1984. *Wealthy Corinth.*

The Tyranny at Megara

Legon, R. P. 1981. *Megara.*
Oost, S. I. 1973. "The Meagara of Theagenes and Theognis." *Classical Philology* 68: 186–96.

The Tyranny in Samos

Barron, J. P. 1964. "The Sixth-Century Tyranny of Samos." *Classical Quarterly* 68: 210–29.
Shipley, G. 1987. *A History of Samos.*
White, M. 1954. "The Duration of the Samian Tyranny." *Journal of Hellenic Studies* 74: 36–43.
Woodbury, L. 1985. "Ibycus and Polycrates." *Phoenix* 39: 193–220.

The Tyranny at Sicyon

Bicknell, P. J. 1982. "Herodotos 5.68 and the Racial Policy of Kleisthenes of Sicyon." *Greek, Roman, and Byzantine Studies* 23: 193–201.
Griffin, A. 1982. *Sikyon.*
Leahy, D. M. 1968. "The Dating of the Orthagorid Dynasty." *Historia* 17: 1–23.
Ogden, D. 1993. "Cleisthenes of Sicyon, Λευστήρ." *Classical Quarterly* 87: 353–63.
Oost, S. I. 1974. "Two Notes on the Orthagorids of Sicyon." *Classical Philology* 69: 118–20.
Parker, V. 1992. "The Dates of the Orthagorids of Sicyon." *Tyche* 7: 165–75.
______. 1994. "Some Aspects of the Foreign and Domestic Policy of Cleisthenes of Sicyon." *Hermes* 122: 404–24.

2: Polis, Community, and Ethnic Identity

Jonathan M. Hall

Defining the *Polis*

Traditionally, treatments of the Archaic Greek world have been dominated by discussion of the *polis* – a term that is often loosely (but not entirely erroneously) translated as "city-state." Victor Ehrenberg, who in many ways pioneered modern research into the origins of the *polis*, described it as the very "foundation and support of Greek culture"[1]; more recently, Oswyn Murray has characterized it as "the dominant form of government in the Greek-speaking world for roughly a thousand years, enabling city dwellers to control directly all or much of their own government, and to feel a local loyalty to an extent which no modern society has achieved."[2] In reality, this emphasis on the *polis* has tended to obscure the fact that in numerous regions of Greece, especially in the north and west, it was not the exclusive or even dominant form of sociopolitical organization until fairly late in the Classical period. On the other hand, there is no denying that much of the literature that survives from the Archaic period betrays the perspective of poets for whom the *polis* constituted an important point of reference, and this should at least serve to justify continued interest in how and when this characteristically Greek institution arose. To answer these questions, however, we first need to define what the *polis* was. Although it would be a mistake to assume that every *polis* developed in the same way or as a result of the same factors, there are nevertheless certain shared defining characteristics that can be identified.

Modern definitions of the *polis* typically emphasize its smallness of scale – limited to a single urban center and its immediate hinterland – and its independent and autonomous status. Yet the latter criterion, although undoubtedly a cherished ideal, seems to have played a less significant role in ancient conceptions. The Perioikic ("surrounding") settlements of Lakonia, whose foreign policies were determined by Sparta, and the allied communities of the Delian League, which were compelled to pay tribute to Athens in the fifth century, are all described in ancient sources as *poleis*. For the ancients, instead, the term *polis* – at least by the Classical period – signified three things simultaneously. As Aristotle (*Politics* 1.1.1) famously pointed out, it meant a political community of citizens, but it could also be used synonymously with the word *asty* to indicate an urban settlement and with the word *ge* or *chora* to denote a territory that included both the urban center and its hinterland.

There is good reason to suppose that these three meanings were not all inherent in the term from the outset. Cognate with Old Indian *púr*, Lithuanian *pilìs*, and Latvian *pils*, *polis* probably originally designated a stronghold – in fact, the term is occasionally employed interchangeably with "acropolis" and may have carried this meaning in the Bronze Age. It seems reasonable to suppose, then, that the signification of the term was extended to signify first an urban settlement around the acropolis and then a broader territorial state before coming to designate also the political participants of that state. Such an inference finds some support in the *Iliad*, where in the majority of cases *polis* is used synonymously with *asty* to denote a physical place and is often juxtaposed with the word *demos*, which seems to denote both a people and the land it occupies. The elegiac poet Kallinos of Ephesos (fr. 1 W) urges his fellow citizens to fight on behalf of their *ge* rather than their *polis*. Similarly, the Spartan poet Tyrtaios (fr. 10 W) declares that it is a fine thing for a man to fall in the front ranks while fighting for his *patris* (homeland) and discusses the misery that ensues when one is forced to leave "one's *polis* and rich fields." Elsewhere (fr. 2 W), Tyrtaios's reference to the *polis* of Sparta, given "to the descendants of Herakles with whom we left windy Erineos and arrived in the wide island of Pelops," also appears to connote a place rather than a community. Whether this implies that the term *polis* continued to retain its more restrictive sense of urban center into the middle of the seventh century – the traditional date for both Kallinos and Tyrtaios – or whether the two poets were consciously employing the term in its Homeric sense is harder to determine. By the time of Solon in the early sixth century, *polis* could certainly be used to describe a political community: the Athenian statesman argues that it is not the gods but foolish, slavish citizens, guided by unjust leaders, who run the risk of destroying the *polis* (fr. 4 W).

The Urban Center and Its Territory

Let us consider first the urban aspect of the *polis*. The term "city" – even with the definitions of the preindustrial city offered by the German sociologist Max Weber and the Australian archaeologist Gordon Childe – is not entirely appropriate for the settled communities of the Archaic age, which lacked the sort of complexity and monumental grandeur that we normally associate with cities. Nor is it easy to establish a settlement hierarchy (i.e., city–town–village) on the basis of population thresholds – first, because we can make only very rough estimates for the populations of Archaic settlements, and second, because certain regions of Greece were more densely inhabited than others, making any universal benchmark meaningless. In the tenth and ninth centuries, the settlement of Nichoria in Messenia probably numbered around forty households, whereas in the eighth century, the population of Zagora on the island of Andros has been estimated at between 225 and 375 inhabitants. By today's standards, both settlements would barely qualify as villages, but in the less populated landscape of early Greece, modern categories may be misleading. One interesting feature that occurs at Zagora from the middle of the eighth century is a marked distinction between larger residences on the upper plateau of the site and smaller dwellings on the southeastern slopes. This might suggest a rudimentary process of social stratification, which would certainly be a feature of the developed *polis*.

Zagora was abandoned ca. 700 BCE, although a sanctuary situated in the center of the settlement continued to attract worshippers into the fifth century. It is likely that its inhabitants – like those of nearby Hypsele, which was abandoned at about the same time – decided that their needs would be better met by relocating to the principal settlement of the island at Palaiopolis. This is a process that is generally known as synoecism, though the term embraces a variety of patterns. In speaking of the synoecism of Attika, Thucydides (2.15) imagines a scenario in which the inhabitants of the entire region agreed to yield deliberative powers and authority to Athens while maintaining residency in their own towns and villages. This is clearly a different situation from the one that occurred on Andros, where small settlements were physically abandoned in favor of a single, larger urban center. But when Thucydides (1.10) describes Sparta as an "unsynoecized *polis*," it is clear that he is operating with an entirely different notion again. Settlement at Sparta extended over an area of some 300 hectares – more than forty times the size of Zagora – but we know from literary sources that within this area the population lived within the four nucleated villages (*komai*) of Pitane, Mesoa, Limnai, and Kynosoura, which remained detached from one another even as late as the fifth century. The eighth-century settlements at Athens, Argos, and Eretria also extended over large areas, and here too distribution maps of burials and settlement traces suggest originally detached nuclei of activity, although at all three sites the adoption, toward the end of the eighth century, of large extramural cemeteries and the simultaneous decline in the numbers of burials made within the confines of the later settlement probably indicates a physical coalescence of villages to form a single, more integrated community. In some cases, the new physical unity of the settlement was marked by the construction of defensive walls: Old Smyrna was walled by at least the middle of the eighth century, whereas fortification circuits are attested at Abdera and perhaps Korinth, Miletos, and Eretria by the mid-seventh century. As at Zagora, indications of social stratification become visible in the latter part of the eighth century – most notably in terms of the different types of burial rites adopted and the varying amounts of wealth deposited in graves.

It is probably no accident that, in the course of the eighth century, the number of retrieved burials in many regions of Greece increases sharply (by as much as seven times in the case of Attika). Although it would be unwise to postulate a direct correlation between numbers of burials and population size – meaning that, in certain periods, part of the population may have been disposed of in less formal ways that have left little or no archaeological trace – most historians and archaeologists agree that the population of Greece increased significantly in the eighth century. There are also some indications that more settled conditions favored the practice of sedentary agriculture. Residence in an urban center obviously offered better protection but, by making possible a basic division of labor, it also allowed residents to satisfy their economic needs more efficiently. At the same time, as Anthony Snodgrass has pointed out, the emergence of urban centers necessitates new forms of organization: "[a] loose organization under a dominant family, with *ad hoc* decisions taken by a local ruler and only occasional assemblies of any larger group, becomes unworkable when the community more than doubles in size within a single generation."[3]

Whether the emergence of urban communities finds its reflection in cultic behavior is a more complicated issue. The eighth century certainly witnesses a significant increase in votive offerings at a large number of sanctuaries, some of which had been abandoned or frequented only very spasmodically during the previous centuries. This is also the period when the first monumental cult buildings are constructed – for example, the 100-foot-long temples (*hekatompeda*) at the Samian Heraion and in the sanctuary of Apollo Daphnephoros at Eretria. The construction of such buildings evidently testifies to a fairly advanced organization of resources and labor and it may well be that it also reflects a communal effort to give religious expression to a nascent *polis*-centered ideology. Yet whereas finds of relatively cheap offerings such as terracotta figurines probably indicate the presence of fairly low-status worshippers, there are also more spectacular offerings of expensive items of military equipment, bronze tripods, and cauldrons (and we have to remember that these are only the items that escaped the clutches of cash-starved Hellenistic generals and postclassical looters). One gets the distinct impression that such conspicuous displays of consumption on the part of elites were designed to impress not only social inferiors within the urban settlement but also peer groups beyond it, and this in turn might suggest that the construction of the first monumental temples was not exactly a voluntary, communal effort.

The complexities are highlighted by what have been called "extraurban" sanctuaries. Starting from the observation that the earliest and most important religious sanctuaries were often located not within the heart of the *polis* but in the countryside at some distance from the urban center, François de Polignac has argued that the function of these sanctuaries was to mark out the territory that belonged to the urban center – that is, the second of the three criteria that, for the ancients, defined the *polis*. Yet doubts have been raised as to whether such extraurban sanctuaries were, in fact, so closely associated with the *polis* (at least originally). I have argued elsewhere that the sanctuary of Hera, 8 km to the northeast of Argos, was almost certainly a common sanctuary for the various political communities of the Argive plain rather than the exclusive extraurban sanctuary of Argos down until the 460s BCE, when Argos destroyed Mykenai, Tiryns, and Midea. At Poseidon's sanctuary on the Korinthian isthmus, cult activity is attested from around the middle of the eleventh century, almost three centuries before any urban settlement springs up at Korinth (though the emergence of Korinth does appear to coincide with an increase of activity at Isthmia). The sanctuary of Hera Akraia at Perachora displays all the characteristics of an "international" sanctuary rather than a shrine belonging to the Korinthian *polis*, and the same is true of the Samian Heraion. In short, although the continued references in the Homeric epics to terms such as *demos*, *gaia* ("land"), and *patris* indicate that notions of territoriality were roughly contemporary with the emergence of urban centers, it is not yet entirely clear what role – if any – sanctuaries played in establishing either territorial boundaries or a sense of political community.

The Emergence of Political Communities

There are some reasons to suppose that the emergence of a political community – for Aristotle, the most important attribute of the *polis* – was a far more gradual development that had its roots in the Dark Age but had still not come to fruition by the seventh and perhaps even sixth century. One pitfall that we need to avoid is that of thinking backward from the developed Athenian democracy of the fifth century and assuming that equality had anything to do with political participation. Ian Morris, for example, has argued that the eighth-century increase in burials is a consequence of the fact that a broader cross-section of the political community was now granted access to formal (and hence archaeologically visible) burial and that this marks the first manifestation of what he terms a "middling ideology." This middling ideology, he explains, which is given literary expression by Hesiod and the elegiac poets, excluded women, slaves, and outsiders to construct a community of equal male citizens. As a reaction, epic and lyric poets formulated an "elitist ideology" that sought to elide distinctions between Greeks and non-Greeks, males and females, and mortals and divinities in order to highlight a basic division between elites and nonelites (see Chapter 6). When, however, the elitist ideology collapsed in the final quarter of the sixth century, the middling ideology provided firm foundations for a "strong principle of equality" that would eventually make democracy "thinkable."

Ideology is, of course, by definition not the same as reality. Morris does not attempt to deny that power in Archaic Greek *poleis* was invariably in the hands of the few. Literary accounts tell how *poleis* were governed by groups of endogamous elite families such as the Bakchiadai at Korinth, the Eupatridai at Athens, or the Basilidai at Ephesos (see Chapter 1). The rise of tyrants in several Greek states can only really be satisfactorily explained against the background of internal friction among elites, and the earliest law codes appear to be concerned primarily with regulating potential conflict among aristocratic officeholders by setting fixed procedures and terms of office (see Chapter 1 on lawgivers and tyrants). Yet it is far from clear that the elegiac poets – whose verses were, as Morris concedes, probably composed for performance at aristocratic *symposia* – really professed a middling ideology that reflected a latent egalitarianism. An attentive reading of the fragments attributed to Tyrtaios, for example, reveals that his exhortations are directed almost exclusively to the more noble Spartans who claimed descent from Herakles and fought in the front rank of the phalanx. Admonitions to practice moderation in all things and a disdain for excess are recurrent *topoi* in the elegiac poets but this is primarily a matter of comportment that has little to do with social egalitarianism. Solon (fr. 34 W) explicitly says that he was not minded "to divide equally the rich land of the country between the nobles and the base," and his confession that "I desire to have money but I do not want to acquire it unjustly" (fr. 13 W) is just one of a series of comments that demonstrates that supposedly "middling" poets had no objections to wealth *per se*, provided that it was not ill-gotten. Along similar lines, it is corruption and injustice rather than the principle of aristocratic rule that lie behind Hesiod's criticism (*Works and Days* 36–41) of the "bribe-devouring *basileis*" (a word that is best translated "chiefs"), and the fable of the hawk and the nightingale (202–12) appears to be an utterly unapologetic assertion that the vise-like rule of the community's leaders conforms to the rule of nature. In light of this, the emergence, in the late sixth and early fifth centuries, of more democratic governments in *poleis* such as Athens, Naxos, Kos, and Syracuse is better viewed not so much as the fulfillment of a latent egalitarianism but as a veritable revolution whereby the *demos* (a word that now signified "masses" or "nonelites") wrested control of the state away from the aristocracy. It is hardly accidental that the word that would be chosen to define this new political order was not *isonomia* ("equality before the law") but *demokratia* ("the rule of the masses").

Rather than egalitarianism, then, the key concept is the sense of belonging to a political community by participating in it and recognizing the authority of those entrusted with overseeing it. This was largely achieved through the convening of an assembly, originally termed an *agora* (from the verb *ageirein* ["to gather together"]). In the Homeric epics, the assembly is generally presided over by a council of elders. Most of the discussion takes place among the councilors, but it is clear that the larger assembly was expected to ratify by verbal assent the proposals put before it. Though we lack any written sources, it is probably the case that the Homeric-style assembly was simply an enlarged and more formalized version of earlier communal councils in which the heads of Dark Age villages sought broader acquiescence for their decisions. Some *poleis* were eventually to acquire more representative councils: a law from Chios, dated to 575–50 BCE, refers to a "people's council"

(ML 8 = Fornara 19). In other *poleis* such as Sparta, the assembly seems to have been little different from its Homeric counterpart (Aristotle *Politics* 2.8.3).

We know neither the regularity nor the frequency of these early assemblies. When Telemachos summons a meeting of the assembly (*Odyssey* 2.25–34), an elder notes that this is the first meeting since Odysseus left for Troy twenty years earlier, though this is probably intended deliberately to illustrate the fact that all is far from well on Ithaka. At a certain point, the signification of the word *agora* was extended to designate not only an assembly of individuals but also the place where that assembly met, and it might be supposed that the designation and laying-out of a specific area for meetings of the assembly would offer some guide to its importance within the day-to-day governance of the community. Unfortunately, it is seldom clear in our literary sources when *agora* is being used to define a specific place and when it merely denotes a meeting of the assembly. A permanent meeting place appears to be mentioned in connection with Troy (*Iliad* 18.274) and Scheria (*Odyssey* 6.266–7), but when Hesiod advises Perses to avoid listening to "the quarrels of the *agora*" (*Works and Days* 30) or when Alkaios tells how he yearns "to hear the *agora* being summoned" (fr. 130B LP), we cannot be certain that either poet has in mind a single, specific space.

In fact, early *agorai* are relatively difficult to identify in the archaeological record. It is often claimed that the *agora* in the Sicilian colony of Megara Hyblaia was laid out from the inception of the settlement in the last third of the eighth century (see Figure 18), but in reality there is little compelling evidence that it served this function much before its monumentalization a century later. Open spaces within the eighth-century settlements at Zagora, Dreros on Krete, and Emborio on Chios could have housed assemblies, but their proximity to cult buildings makes it virtually certain that their primary function was to host ritual observances; the oft-cited *agora* in the Kretan city of Lato may not pre-date the Hellenistic period and was similarly the seat of predominantly cultic activity. At Argos, a formal *agora* seems not to have been laid out before the drainage of the marshy area at the foot of the Larissa acropolis toward the end of the sixth century. The Athenian *agora*, on the northwest slopes of the acropolis, probably also dates to this period, though later authors were to refer to a quarter on the eastern side of the acropolis as the "old (*archaia*) *agora*."[4] It is likely that a permanent location became highly desirable once the *agora* also developed a commercial function, but our first explicit testimony for an economic role appears in the fifth-century law code from the Kretan city of Gortyn.

Participation in the governance (and, of course, the defense) of the *polis* would certainly have engendered an awareness of belonging to a political community, but the political community can only take collective cognizance of itself when its own contours or boundaries are explicitly defined. Archaic poets seem to have been fairly clear about the distinction between the aristocracy – denoted by terms such as *esthloi* ("noble") and *agathoi* ("good") – and the masses (*demos*), even if they disagreed as to whether birth or wealth should qualify an individual for membership of the elite class. Needless to say, they are less interested in defining the lower limit of the *demos*. Presumably those who fought in the hoplite phalanx were included in the *demos*, though the same may not have been true of lighter-armed troops. And because it is generally assumed that hoplites were responsible for providing their own equipment, there was probably a minimum wealth qualification, meaning that landless agricultural laborers (*thetes*) are unlikely to have been included in the political community. In fact, there are hints that, in Attika at least, these issues had still not been resolved at the beginning of the sixth century. Solon (fr. 36 W) tells how he repatriated Athenians who had been sold abroad and liberated those who had been enslaved on their own land (see Chapter 1). The author of the Aristotelian *Constitution of the Athenians* (6) adds that he prohibited the practice of offering one's own person as security for loans, thus eliminating debt slavery. It was this reform that – perhaps for the first time at Athens – established a "glass floor" between poorer citizens and slaves, thereby formalizing the boundaries of the political community.

Above the *demos* were those it entrusted with political counsel, military command, and the administration of justice. In the Homeric epics it is clear that the authority of the *basileis* is "achieved" rather than "ascribed." That is, authority derives not from the office one holds but from one's own charisma and ability to persuade, manifested through the demonstration of military prowess and conspicuous generosity. Typically, achieved statuses are highly unstable and the hereditary transmission of such authority is seldom guaranteed. In the *Iliad*, Agamemnon is generally recognized as the supreme commander of the Achaian expedition, though he is not always able to compel his peers – or sometimes even the army – to accept his wishes. In the *Odyssey*, Odysseus assumed authority on Ithaka even though his father, Laertes, was still alive, but it is sympathy and respect for Odysseus rather than recognition of a "kingly" office that impels anybody to pay regard to Telemachos in his father's absence. The situation is less clear in the Hesiodic poems, though the description of the *basileis* in the *Theogony* (80–93) emphasizes the sort of persuasive qualities normally associated with achieved statuses and also implies that such status might be inherited at birth (though presumably it had to be defended in adulthood).

At a certain point, however, ascribed status became important – meaning that emphasis was given to the office itself, rather than the person who held it. And once offices are fixed and regularly filled by a succession of candidates, one can talk of a basic administrative machinery that distinguishes states from chiefdoms or stateless societies. One indication for this shift from achieved to ascribed status may be found in references to the establishment of annually rotating, named magistracies in place of the more generic term *basileis*. By the later fifth century, the Athenians believed that the annual archonship had been introduced in 683/2, with a ten-year archonship existing for seven decades before that, but the evidence is of dubious value, as is Diodoros' assertion (7.9) that the Bakchiadai of Korinth annually elected one of their own to the office of *prytanis* from ca. 745 BCE. More plausible is the reference to fifty-one *ephetai* in the late fifth-century republication of Drakon's homicide law of 621/0 BCE (ML 86 = Fornara 15B), but the most reliable evidence comes from a law, displayed in the temple of Apollo Delphinios at Dreros and dated to the second half of the seventh century, that specifies that the office of *kosmos* could be held only once in any ten-year period (ML 2 = Fornara 11). This would suggest, then, that the shift from achieved to ascribed statuses was under way by around the middle of the seventh century. Naturally, such offices continued to be restricted to the elites.

POLIS AND *ETHNOS*

The *polis* was by no means the universal or exclusive form of state organization in Archaic Greece. Conventionally, a distinction has been drawn between the *polis* and the *ethnos* – a looser type of political organization associated above all with regions such as Achaia, Elis, Aitolia, Akarnania, Thessaly, and Makedonia. One of the best known portrayals of an *ethnos* is Thucydides' description of the Aitolians as "a large, bellicose *ethnos*, settled in dispersed, unwalled villages (*komai*) and lightly armed"; he also adds that the Eurytanes, "who constitute the greater part of the Aitolians, are incomprehensible with regard to their speech and eaters of raw meat, or so it is said" (3.94.4–5). The fact that the historian notes elsewhere (Thucydides 1.5–6) that the practice of carrying arms in public – once widespread throughout Greece – was, in his own day, confined to "barbarians" and those regions "settled according to the old fashion" such as West Lokris, Aitolia, and Akarnania has suggested to modern scholars that the *ethnos* represents a more "primitive" form of organization out of which, in some areas, the *polis* later evolved.

This distinction between *polis* and *ethnos* was not, however, one that was recognized by ancient writers. The supposition that it was rests on a passage in the *Politics* (2.1.5) where Aristotle, in discussing the differences between a *polis* and an alliance (*symmachia*), says: "In the same way, a *polis* differs from an *ethnos* whenever the people are not scattered among villages but like the Arkadians." But, as Mogens Hansen has pointed out, the real distinction that is being drawn here is between a *polis*, whose constituent elements are different, and an alliance or an *ethnos* "like the Arkadians," whose constituent elements are the same. From another passage in the *Politics* (3.5.11), we know that the elements that constitute the latter are *poleis*. In other words, Aristotle is differentiating between *ethne* settled in villages *(komai)* and *ethne*, like the Arkadians, settled in *poleis*. This notion is not limited to Aristotelian thought. Thucydides (3.92.2) observes that the Malians, classified as an *ethnos* by Aischines (*On the False Embassy* 115–6), were divided into three parts (*mere*) – the Paralioi, the Iries, and the Trachinians – and Herodotos (7.199.1) explicitly describes Trachis as a *polis*. Elsewhere, Herodotos (8.73) explains that the Peloponnese was inhabited by seven *ethne*: the Arkadians, the Kynourians, the Achaians, the Dorians, the Aitolians, the Dryopes, and the Lemnians. The *poleis* of the Dorians, Herodotos continues, are "numerous and well-known," whereas Elis is the only *polis* of the Aitolians, and to the Dryopes belong the *poleis* of Hermione and Asine. It is for this reason that Zosia Archibald has argued that "ethnos and polis should not be juxtaposed, since they do not represent *alternative* modes but rather *different levels* of social organization."[5]

The problem with this conclusion is that, in an inscription (ML 15 = Fornara 42) set up on the Acropolis shortly after 506 BCE and cited by Herodotos (5.77.4), the Athenians commemorate their victory over the *ethne* of the Boiotians and the Chalkidians, and although the Boiotians were indeed an *ethnos*, the Euboian city of Chalkis was undoubtedly a *polis*. One could perhaps suppose that it is the Boiotians' status as an *ethnos* that has determined the precise terminology employed on the dedication – they are, after all, named first – but Herodotos (7.161.3) also has an Athenian envoy refer to the Athenians as the "oldest *ethnos*," and nobody would dispute Athens' status as a *polis*.

In fact, it is not so much that *polis* and *ethnos* occupy different organizational levels as that they belong to entirely different categories. In Archaic literature, the term *ethnos* can denote flocks of birds, swarms of bees and flies, and even the ranks of the dead. Ultimately, it designates a class of beings that share a common identification and is therefore frequently employed in connection with populations that entertain a collective self-consciousness. The term *polis*, on the other hand, carries more spatial connotations – a legacy, as we have seen, of the original meaning of the word. Indeed the difference between the two terms is illustrated by the nomenclature that the Greeks employed to define population groups. It is well known that *poleis* were more commonly designated by "ethnics" – that is, by the names of their citizens (*hoi Athenaioi*; *hoi Korinthioi*; *hoi Milesioi*) – than by toponyms (*hai Athenai*; *he Korinthos*; *he Miletos*). Yet the adjectival -*i*- suffix in the ethnics reveals that they are secondary formations from the toponyms. By contrast, in *ethne* it is the population that gives its name to the territory it occupies: *Thessalia* is formed from *hoi Thessaloi*, *Boiotia* from *hoi Boiotoi*, and *Achaia* from *hoi Achaioi*.

If *ethnos* simply designates a population, then it is not inherently "primitive" in nature. In fact, it would be difficult to maintain that *ethne* were invariably less developed than regions in which *poleis* emerged at an early date. Achaia, for example, is credited with an early and prominent role in the colonization of South Italy and boasts one of the first peripteral (colonnaded) temples on the Greek mainland at Ano Mazaraki-Rakita. It may not be coincidental that another early peripteral temple is known from Thermon in Aitolia. We are, however, entitled to question whether the *ethnos* was necessarily anterior to the *polis*, and here it may be helpful to distinguish between consolidated *ethne* and dispersed *ethne*.

Consolidated *ethne* are represented by those groups such as the Aitolians, Achaians, or Thessalians that inhabited a contiguous tract of territory in the historical period. Whereas *poleis* were typically focused on a single urban center with a relatively small hinterland – the territory of Argos, for example, is unlikely to have exceeded 100 sq km prior to the middle of the fifth century – consolidated *ethne* normally occupied vastly greater expanses of land in which several settlements might coexist. Some of these settlements were fairly large (e.g., Pherai in Thessaly; Aigai and Aigeira in Achaia; Thessalonike-Therme and Kastanas in Makedonia) and most would eventually emerge as *poleis*. This is a development that seems to have already occurred in parts of eastern Arkadia by the sixth century but not until the fifth or even fourth century in Aitolia. Furthermore, settlements did not invariably serve as administrative units within *ethne* – a function fulfilled more regularly by regional sanctuaries such as those at Thermon in Aitolia, Olympia in Elis, or Dodona in Epeiros. It is interesting to note that several consolidated *ethne* are listed in the Homeric *Catalog of Ships* (*Iliad* 2.494–749) – a section that was almost certainly originally independent from the rest of the *Iliad* and may, according to some scholars, draw on a tradition dating back to the Late Bronze Age. At this early date, however, they seem to lack a concrete sense of territoriality: regional names derived from *ethne*, such as Thessalia or Boiotia (see above), are unattested in the poems of Hesiod and Homer.

Dispersed *ethne*, instead, are diaspora-type collectivities, whose members were in the historical period scattered throughout different communities – normally *poleis* – but who conceived of their unity in terms of an original homeland in which their ancestors had cohabited. Of the twelve *ethne* that constituted the Delphic Amphictyony (the League that administered the sanctuary of Pythian Apollo), two – the Ionians and the Dorians – were dispersed *ethne*.[6] Tradition told how the Ionians had originally inhabited mainland Greece and especially the Peloponnese (though there are, as we shall see, several variants) but had fled to Athens, from whence an expedition was dispatched to settle the island of Euboia, the Cyclades, and the central seaboard of Asia Minor. The cause of the Ionians' flight to Athens was reputedly the dislodgement of the Achaians from their former homes in Lakonia and the Argolid – regions that, along with Messenia, were captured by marauders from central Greece known as the Dorians, led by descendants of Herakles. Thucydides (1.12.3) dates the arrival of the Dorians to eighty years after the fall of Troy. Once established in the Peloponnese, tradition told how the Dorians set out to found secondary settlements on the islands of the southern Aegean, the Dodecanese, and the southwest coast of Asia Minor.

It is often claimed that vestiges of the original unity of dispersed *ethne* such as the Dorians and the Ionians can be seen in the similarities of dialect and common institutional features such as festivals and calendars that are shared by Dorian and Ionian cities respectively. Furthermore, in several Dorian cities the citizen body was divided into three tribes (*phylai*) that had the same names – representing, it is argued, the fossilized relic of an original tripartite tribal structure that had pertained in the premigratory period (a similar claim is sometimes made for the tribal institutions in Ionian cities). But even more importantly, although it was normally the *polis* that had first claim on a citizen's loyalty, the memory of a primordial integrity is supposed to have endowed the members of dispersed *ethne* with an ethnic consciousness that could be invoked in circumstances that extended beyond the confines of the *polis*. Thus, in the course of the Peloponnesian War (431–04 BCE), Sparta appealed to a Dorian heritage shared by many of its allies – especially Syracuse – whereas Athens sought to justify its hegemony over the member states of the Delian League by emphasizing a common Ionian patrimony.

Ethnic Consciousness in Archaic Greece

Recent research into ethnicity in antiquity, drawing on comparative studies from social anthropology and social psychology, would suggest that there is nothing inevitable or primordial about ethnicity, despite protestations to the contrary by members of ethnic groups. Biological features, language, religious professions, or cultural traits, far from defining ethnic groups, are variously harnessed to serve as visible markers for identities that are constructed discursively through appeal to common founding fathers, primordial homelands, and a shared history (all of which may be invented as much as remembered). Furthermore, ethnic self-identification responds to – and fluctuates with – specific historical circumstances. This means not only that the identity of any given ethnic group is seldom endowed with the same degree of salience over time, but also that entire ethnic groups may appear or disappear as a result of processes of social differentiation and assimilation. Even when individuals inherit an ethnic ascription at birth, they often have the choice whether to regard that specific component of their social identity as meaningful or not. In light of these observations, the notion that the Archaic *polis* faithfully preserved the inherited structures, habits, customs, and ethnic sentiment of *ethne* that had existed more than 350 years earlier is, to say the least, questionable.

If we examine a little more closely the cultural and institutional features that are thought to argue for premigratory integrity on the part of *ethne* such as the Dorians or Ionians, the evidence appears less compelling. Table 1 tabulates the calendars that have been reconstructed for the Ionian cities of Athens and Miletos and the Dorian cities of Rhodes and Epidauros. As can be seen, there are certainly correspondences between cities proclaiming an Ionian ethnicity: the second, third, fourth, sixth, eighth, and eleventh months of the year (which began in midsummer) bear the same names in both Ionian cities. What is harder to establish is whether these correspondences are due to a common

TABLE 1. *List of Months at Athens, Miletos, Rhodes, and Epidauros*

	Athens	Miletos	Rhodes	Epidauros
1	Hekatombaion	Panemos	Panamos	Azosios
2	Metageitnion	Metageitnion	Karneios	Karneios
3	Boedromion	Boedromion	Dalios	Proratios
4	Pyanepsion	Pyanopsion	Thesmophorios	Hermaios
5	Maimakterion	Apatourion	Diosthyos	Gamos
6	Poseideon	Poseideon	Theudaisios	Teleos
7	Gamelion	Lenaion	Pedageitnios	Posidauos
8	Anthesterion	Anthesterion	Badromios	Artamitios
9	Elaphebolion	Artemision	Sminthios	Agrianios
10	Mounykhion	Taureon	Artamitios	Panamos
11	Thargelion	Thargelion	Agrianios	Kuklios
12	Skirophorion	Kalamaion	Hyakinthios	Apellaios

inheritance or whether, say, the names of the Athenian months have been borrowed from those in use at Miletos (the upsilon in the name of the Athenian festival of the Apatouria, for example, indicates that it was derived from the East Ionic-speaking zone of Asia Minor). In the two Dorian cities, on the other hand, only the second month (Karneios) is the same: the names of three other months (Panamos, Artamitios, Agrianios) are common to both cities, but fall at different times within the year. More revealingly, however, there are clear correspondences with some of the names of the Ionian months (Panamos is the Doric for Panemos, Pedageitnios for Metageitnion, Badromios for Boedromion, Artamitios for Artemision, Posidauos for Posideion).

Table 2 lists the names of known tribes in twenty-one Dorian *poleis*, together with the dates at which they are first attested. According to Tyrtaios (fr. 19 W), the citizens of Sparta were brigaded in three tribal regiments known as the Hylleis, the Dymanes, and the Pamphyloi. The same three names occur at Megara, Kos, and Kalymnos and – alongside other tribal names – at Sikyon, Argos, probably Issa, and perhaps Troizen, Thera, and the Kretan *poleis* of Hierapytna and Olous. Yet there are many Dorian cities (including Korinth) where these tribal names are not attested, and, as is clear from the table, the earliest evidence for the existence of these names is often very late. In other words, we cannot exclude the possibility that the common names were borrowed rather than inherited.

TABLE 2. *Dorian Tribes*

City	Hylleis	Dymanes	Pamphyloi	Date (century)	Other Tribes
Sparta	X	X	X	7	
Sikyon	X	X	X	6	Archelaoi
Megara	X	X	X	5	
Argos	X	X	X	5	Hyrnathioi
Kerkyra				5	Aoreis; Makchidai; ?Antheia; ?Philoxenoi
Korinth				4/3	Aoreis
Epidauros	X	X		4/3	Azantioi; Hysminatai
Troizen	X	X		4/3	Scheliadai
Thera	X	?		4/3	
Kos	X	X	X	4/3	
West Lokris		X		3	
Issa	?	X	X	3	
Akragas	X			3	
Gortyn		X		3	Aithaleis; Ap[-] yma[-]; Archeia; Dek[-]
Lyttos		X		3/2	Diphyloi
Kalymnos	X	X	X	3/2	
Hierapytna		X	X	2	Kamiris
Olous		X	X	2	[-]on
Knossos			X	2	Aithaleis; Archeia; E[-]
Lato	X			2	Aischeis; Echanoreis; Synameis
Oleros			X	2/1	

Sikyon may be an interesting case in this respect. According to Herodotos (5.68), the Sikyonian tyrant, Kleisthenes, renamed the three Dorian tribes Hyatai ("pig-men"), Oneatai ("ass-men"), and Choireatai ("swine-men"), while naming his own tribe Archelaoi ("rulers of the people"); the Sikyonians endured this insult for a full sixty years after Kleisthenes' death but then changed the names back to Hylleis, Pamphyloi, Dymanes, and Aigialeis. Naturally enough, little credence has been given to the account: the abusive names are sometimes explained as humorous approximations to otherwise obscure tribal names in use at early Sikyon. If correct, this might suggest that there was a tribal reform at Sikyon around sixty years after the death of Kleisthenes – in other words, at about the exact same time that his grandson and namesake was reforming the tribal system at Athens – that resulted in the adoption, perhaps for the first time, of Dorian tribal names for three of the four tribes. The choice may have been justified on the – by this time unverifiable – grounds that the names had been in use prior to Kleisthenes' tyranny.[7] Be that as it may, the fact that tribes served as the fundamental basis for civic and military units presumes that they were approximately equal in size and this surely implies that the tribe was a subdivision of – and consequently, subsequent to – the *polis* rather than that the *polis* was an aggregate of preexisting tribes that belonged to an era prior to the migrations.

At first sight, the evidence of dialect looks more promising. By and large, the dialects of *poleis* that claimed a Dorian or Ionian identity share certain common characteristics (though Dorian Halikarnassos employed both the Ionic script and dialect). Yet the assumption that such correspondences are due to their shared descent from a protodialect perpetuates a nineteenth-century model of linguistic change that had already been called into question within a decade of its formulation (in 1863, by August Schleicher, who was heavily influenced by Darwinian evolutionism). In fact, a detailed study of the dialects spoken in the Argolid has concluded that, far from being the descendants of a proto-Doric dialect once spoken in a contiguous area of central or northern Greece, they evolved through close contact with both Doric and non-Doric dialects.

Archaeology has been unable to provide much in the way of concrete confirmation for the notion of mass migrations at the end of the Bronze Age. Newcomers or "refugees" do seem to have made their homes in Achaia during the twelfth century BCE, but their material culture owes very little to that of the Argolid, where tradition placed one of the original homelands of the Achaians. Attempts to trace the appearance in the Peloponnese of new artifacts or cultural forms with northern provenances have generally proved unsuccessful: such items as do appear to derive from the north either are attested first in regions such as Attika and Euboia that professed an Ionian affiliation (e.g., cremation or inhumation in cist graves) or were already present in the Mycenaean world prior to the period in which the migrations are supposed to have occurred (e.g., the "violin-bow" fibula or the Naue II slashing sword). Tenth-century pottery from Miletos and Ephesos shows some affinities with Attic styles, though much of the earliest pottery in the Ionian settlements of Asia Minor is locally made, deriving its influences as much from Euboia and Thessaly as from Attika. The absence of clear material indications is not decisive – there are documented cases of migrations that have left little trace in the archaeological record – though it hardly offers encouragement to those who place implicit trust in the literary traditions for the migrations.

Ultimately, however, it is the literary traditions themselves that betray their fictive nature. The tradition that the Ionians were the former residents of Achaia who fled to Attika before setting out to colonize the Anatolian coast is a fifth-century rationalization to account for the fact that both Attika and Achaia are independently named in earlier sources as the original Ionian homeland. But to confuse matters further, the seventh-century poet Mimnermos (fr. 9 W) says that Ionian Kolophon had been founded by Pylos in Messenia whereas, according to the fifth-century historian Hellanikos of Mytilene (4 FGrHist 101), the Ionian city of Priene considered itself a foundation of Boiotian Thebes. Despite various attempts to harmonize them, it is undoubtedly these conflicting accounts concerning Ionian origins that prompted Herodotos (1.146.1) to ridicule the Ionians' professions to pure, blue-blooded descent from Athenian progenitors. In the case of the ancestors of the Dorians, at least two originally independent traditions can be identified: one locates them in Doris, the hilly district on the north face of Mount Parnassos, under the rule of the eponymous Doros; the other names their founding father as Aigimios and their primordial homeland as the Thessalian region of Hestiaiotis. Herodotos (1.56.3) attempted to resolve the contradiction by proposing that the Dorians had wandered circuitously for many years before their arrival in the Peloponnese, whereas Strabo (9.5.17) suggested that Hestiaiotis had, at an earlier date, been called Doris. Neither explanation succeeds in dispelling the suspicion that the developed traditions on the migrations are a cumulative synthesis of originally independent accounts and a rationalized simplification of realities that were far more complex. The function of these traditions was not to preserve the genuine memory of prehistoric migrations but to charter the profession of ethnic identities in the protohistorical and historical periods.

It is less easy to trace the developmental stages of this process. The citizens of Sparta, probably founded in the second half of the tenth century, clearly regarded themselves as Dorians by Tyrtaios' day (fr. 2 W). It is far from clear, however, that the neighboring Messenians were considered – or considered themselves – Dorians at so early a date. Tyrtaios' repeated emphasis (frs. 2, 19 W) on the Spartans' Dorian ancestry in the context of what is generally agreed to be the seventh-century conflict between Sparta and Messenia possesses little rhetorical effect, unless it was regarded as a distinctive quality to which the Messenians had no equal claim. There is no unambiguous evidence for the Dorian identity of the Messenians prior to the fifth century. Similarly, the earliest evidence for Argos' subscription to a Dorian identity comes in a fragment of a poem entitled the *Catalog of Women* (fr. 10b Merkelbach-West), probably composed in the early or mid-sixth century, in which the daughter of Doros is given in marriage to the Argive culture-hero Phoroneus.

The Origins of the *Polis*?

It is likely, though not provable, that the consolidated *ethne* of the Archaic period traced their origins back into the Dark Age, if not further. That does not, however, appear to be the case with dispersed *ethne*, whose formation seems to have developed in tandem with the emergent *polis* – especially if, as suggested here, that was a more gradual and drawn-out process than is sometimes believed to be the case. If the idea of the *polis* was one that would eventually prove attractive to most *ethne*, consolidated *ethne* offered, in turn, a model of wider affiliation and networking that could not be satisfied so easily within the relatively narrow confines of the *polis*. It is also possible that ethnic classification served as a useful criterion in establishing who should be included in, or excluded from, the political community. But the consequence of these observations is that the standard evolutionist model that views the *polis* as emerging from the *ethnos* stands in need of correction. The real distinction that should be drawn is not between areas where the *polis* flourished and those where the *ethnos* was dominant but between regions where the *polis* emerged early and those where its existence is only attested later. What could account for this differential development?

It has often been noted that the earliest *poleis* appear in those regions of Greece that were most strongly influenced by Mycenaean administrative structures in the Late Bronze Age. We know from Linear B tablets found at Pylos that Mycenaean states were divided up into provinces, districts, towns, and villages to better organize the collection of taxes for the palatial center. And it can hardly be accidental that the term *basileis*, employed to denote the leaders of the nascent *polis*, had in the Mycenaean period defined local officials at the town or village level. The fact that physical place constituted such an important criterion within early conceptions of the *polis* suggests, then, that this form of political and social organization could have been a lingering legacy of the administrative and territorial subdivisions of Late Bronze Age Greece.

At first sight, Boiotia appears to represent an exception to the rule: taking its name from the *ethnos* of the Boiotoi, Late Bronze Age Boiotia was administered through palatial centers such as Thebes, Orchomenos, and perhaps Gla. In reality, however, the *polis* developed earlier and more prolifically in Boiotia than in almost any other consolidated *ethnos*, whereas the sort of organizational structures normally associated with *ethne* were not really exploited prior to the last quarter of the sixth century, when they served as the foundation for the Boiotian League. Sandwiched between consolidated *ethne* such as the Thessalians to the north and the Phokians to the west and the *poleis* of Athens, Megara, and Korinth to the south, it is hardly surprising that Boiotia represents a hybrid case.

I am certainly not suggesting, as some scholars have, that the *polis* was a creation of the Late Bronze Age: the notion of a political community, which is so essential to Classical definitions of the *polis*, was barely developed as late as the seventh century. Yet, although the recent archaeological illumination of the Dark Age has hardly served to dispel the general picture of insecurity, introspection, and isolation, it is also evident that the social and political forces that would eventually give shape to the *polis* were already at work in the eleventh, tenth, and ninth centuries and that notions of central places and territorial subdivisions almost certainly represent a legacy from the Mycenaean period. The observation provides yet one more salutary reminder that little is gained by maintaining the traditional date of ca. 700 BCE for the start of the Archaic period.

Notes

1 Ehrenberg 1937, 147.
2 Murray 1993, 62.
3 Snodgrass 1980, 24.
4 Papadopoulos 1996 even suggests that the Classical *agora* was not laid out until after the Persian War of 480–79 BCE.
5 Archibald 2000, 214.
6 See Chapter 9 for further discussion of this sanctuary and its activities.
7 See Chapter 1, *The Orthagorids of Sicyon*, for further discussion of the tribal reform.

Bibliography and Suggested Readings

Archibald, Z. 2000. "Space, Hierarchy and Community in Archaic and Classical Macedonia, Thessaly, and Thrace." In Brock and Hodkinson, eds. 2000, 212–33.

Brock, R. and S. Hodkinson, eds. 2000. *Alternatives to Athens: Varieties of Political Organization and Community in Ancient Greece.*

Childe, V. G. 1950. "The Urban Revolution." *Town Planning Review* 21: 9–16.

Ehrenberg, V. 1937. "When Did the Polis Rise?" *Journal of Hellenic Studies* 57: 147–59.

Fisher, N. and H. van Wees, eds. 1988. *Archaic Greece: New Approaches and New Evidence.*

Hall, J. M. 1995. "How Argive was the 'Argive' Heraion? The Political and Cultic Geography of the Argive Plain, 900–400 BC." *American Journal of Archaeology* 99: 577–613.

______. 1997. *Ethnic Identity in Greek Antiquity.*

______. 2002. *Hellenicity: Between Ethnicity and Culture.*

______. 2003. "The Dorianization of the Messenians." In *Helots and Their Masters in Laconia and Messenia: Histories, Ideologies, Structures.* Eds. N. Luraghi and S. E. Alcock, 134–60.

______. 2007. *A History of the Archaic Greek World ca. 1200–479 BCE.*

Hansen, M. H. 1999. "Aristotle's Reference to the Arkadian Federation at *Pol.* 1261a29." In *Defining Ancient Arkadia.* Acts of the Copenhagen Polis Centre 6. Eds. T. H. Nielsen and J. Roy, 80–88.

Hansen, M. H., ed. 1997. The Polis as an Urban Centre and as a Political Community. Acts of the Copenhagen Polis Centre 4.

Mitchell, L. G. and P. J. Rhodes, eds. 1997. *The Development of the Polis in Archaic Greece.*

Morgan, C. 2003. *Early Greek States: Beyond the Polis.*

Morris, I. 2000. *Archaeology as Cultural History: Words and Things in Iron Age Greece.*

Murray, O. 1993. *Early Greece.* Second ed.

Papadopoulos, J. K. 1996. "The Original Kerameikos of Athens and the Siting of the Classical Agora." *Greek, Roman and Byzantine Studies* 27: 107–28.

Polignac, F. de 1995. *Cults, Territory, and the Origins of the Greek City-State.* Transl. J. Lloyd.

Schleicher, A. 1863. *Die darwinische Theorie und die Sprachwissenschaft.*

Snodgrass, A. M. 1980. *Archaic Greece: The Age of Experiment.*

Weber, M. 1922. *Wirtschaft und Gesellschaft.*

3: Warfare and Hoplites

Peter Krentz

For most of the twentieth century, scholars believed that the Archaic period saw dramatic changes in Greek military practices, significant enough to merit the name "hoplite revolution" or at least "hoplite reform."[1] This revolution was thought to have had major social and political consequences, especially for the development of Greek democracy. In brief, the story went as follows. In Early Iron Age fighting, as described by Homer, aristocrats dominated the battlefield, fighting heroic duels in front of a large, but largely uninvolved, mass of supporters. The invention of new equipment, especially the double-handled hoplite shield, led to the adoption of a close-ordered formation, the hoplite phalanx, that relied not on individual exploits but on group solidarity. Aristocrats had to welcome anyone who could afford the new equipment into the phalanx, in order to make it as large as possible. Hoplites adopted new unwritten military protocols that made warfare more ritualistic and confined it largely to competitions for status rather than survival. In individual communities, hoplites gained a sense of group identity and demanded a greater voice in politics. In many early *poleis* they supported tyrants who broke the aristocrats' stranglehold on power and paved the way for democracy.

In the last thirty years, scholars have challenged every part of this story, despite its undeniable explanatory power. In what follows, I will first explain the traditional view in more detail, and then look at the challenges.

The Hoplite Revolution

The hypothesis of a hoplite revolution received its classic statements in English sixty years ago, though it appeared earlier in German.[2] In

1947, H. L. Lorimer argued that the invention of the double-handled shield caused a "momentous change" from the eighth-century BCE style of fighting, in which warriors constantly scattered and regrouped. The round shield previously in use had a central hand grip, and could be suspended by a strap from the shoulders, especially to cover the back during a retreat. The new shield, the round *hoplon* from which the hoplite took his name (Diodorus 15.44.3), had instead a bronze armband (*porpax*) through which the user inserted his arm up to the elbow; he then grabbed a leather handgrip (*antilabe*) attached just inside the rim (see the third figure from the left top row, in Figure 1). The shield varied in diameter from 0.80 to 1.00 m. Concave, with a sharply offset rim, it could rest on the left shoulder, which would relieve some of the weight.

Because of its weight and distinctive handles, a *hoplon* protected its user's left side better than his right. Thucydides describes the result (5.71.1):

> All armies, as they come together, push out toward the right wing, and each side overlaps the enemy's left with its own right, because in their fear each man brings his uncovered side as close as possible to the shield of the man stationed to his right, thinking that the best protection is the tightness of the closing-up (*synkleisis*).

A soldier who turned and ran usually ditched his bulky shield – hence the Spartan mother's admonition to her son as she handed him his shield, "With it or on it," that is, bring your shield back or die with it (Plutarch *Moralia* 241F). In Athens, "throwing away one's shield" was an actionable offense punished by disenfranchisement.

When asked why the Spartans disgraced those who threw away their shields but not those who abandoned their breastplates or helmets, the Spartan king Demaratus replied that soldiers wore breastplates and helmets for their own sakes, but carried shields for the sake of the whole line (Plutarch *Moralia* 220A). A hoplite wore a set of bronze armor, including a helmet, a breastplate, and shin-guards (see Figure 2). The most common helmet was the Corinthian, hammered (including cheek-pieces and a nose-guard) out of a single sheet of bronze. The breastplate consisted of front and back plates hinged together on the side and fastened on top of the shoulders. The finest shin guards, each made out of a single piece of bronze, fit the individual wearer's leg as a soccer shin guard does.

With his right hand a hoplite carried a single spear, which he thrust rather than threw. He had a sword as a secondary weapon. He fought hand to hand at close quarters, but he was no Homeric hero, no soloist fighting duels in front of his followers. Weighed down by perhaps 30 kg of defensive equipment, with limited vision and limited hearing due to his helmet, he relied on his fellow soldiers for protection from the sides. The preeminent hoplite virtue was standing one's ground. Tyrtaios, the hoplite poet *par excellence* who wrote ca. 640–600 BCE, encouraged the Spartans as follows (fr. 11.11–34):

> Those who dare to remain in place at one another's side
> and advance together toward hand-to-hand combat and
> the frontline fighters,
> they die in lesser numbers, and they save the army behind
> them;
> but when men flee in terror, all soldierly excellence is lost.
> No one could ever come to an end in recounting all
> the evils that befall a man if he learns to do shameful things:
> grievous it is to be struck from behind in the small of the back
> as a man is fleeing in the deadliness of war;
> and shameful is a body lying stretched in the dust,
> driven through the back from behind with the point of a
> spear.
> So let each man hold to his place with legs well apart,
> feet planted on the ground, biting his lip with his teeth,
> thighs and shins below and, above, chest and shoulders
> covered by the belly of his broad shield.
> In his right hand let him brandish his mighty spear,
> let him shake the fearsome crest upon his head.
> By performing mighty deeds let him learn the skills of warfare,
> and not stand with his shield beyond throwing range,
> but moving in close let each man engage hand to hand
> and, wounding with long spear or sword, let him kill an
> enemy.
> Setting foot beside foot, leaning shield against shield,
> crest ranged against crest, helmet against helmet,
> chest against chest drawn near, let him fight his man,
> with sword hilt or long lance gripped in his hand.

After the invention of hoplite equipment, many more warriors mattered on the battlefield. The formation, the hoplite phalanx, was what counted. Each side tried to push through the other in a shoving match known as the *othismos* (from the verb *othein*, meaning "to push"). Once one side broke, the battle ended, and the winners erected a trophy at the place where the losers turned to run.

Lorimer dated all the new items of equipment to the first half of the seventh century. By about the middle of the century, a famous pot, the Chigi olpe of ca. 640 BCE, shows two opposing phalanxes (see Figure 3). The piper used by the Spartans to keep the men in step, the tight formation, and all the items of defensive equipment mentioned above are present.

In 1953, A. Andrewes elegantly restated the case that these military changes quickly created a new class of warriors who wanted a larger political voice. When they did not get what they wanted, they backed tyrants such as Kypselos, who seized power in Corinth ca. 655 BCE. In support of the hypothesis that military revolution led to political revolution, Andrewes cited Aristotle,[3] who claimed in his *Politics* (1297b12; compare 1289b27) that

> the earliest form of constitution among the Greeks after the kingships consisted of those who were actually soldiers, the original form consisting of the cavalry (for war had its strength and its pre-eminence in cavalry, since without orderly formation a hoplite force is useless, and the sciences and systems dealing with tactics did not exist among the men of old times, so that their strength lay in their cavalry); but as the states grew and the armed men had become stronger, more persons came to have a part in the government.

After making a detailed study of early Greek armor and weapons, A. M. Snodgrass challenged this theory in the 1960s.[4] Bronze shin guards, bronze breastplates, bronze helmets, and even the hoplite shield – if one accepts the argument that an upright shield emblem proves a *porpax* shield that would not be held upside down – all appeared before 700 BCE, though they do not appear together on a vase painting until about 675 BCE. Snodgrass therefore preferred to speak of a "hoplite reform," and held that hoplites appeared first as individuals. Even by mid-century, when there were enough hoplites to create a phalanx, they were unlikely to have become at once a political force.

The painter of the Chigi vase, however, seems to have made earlier attempts to show a phalanx: on the Berlin aryballos of ca. 650 BCE, close-ordered hoplites oppose each other in three small groups,[5] and on the Macmillan aryballos of ca. 655 BCE the hoplites advancing from the right defeat their opponents in a series of duels (see Figure 4). J. Salmon suggested that the pipe player on an aryballos from Perachora, ca. 675 BCE, indicates a phalanx, because even though the fighting is disorganized, a pipe player would only have been needed for a disciplined advance in formation (see Figure 5, leftmost man). Salmon concluded that the hoplite phalanx could have existed in time for hoplites to have played a role in seventh-century political struggles.

Recent studies suggest that military change was neither so significant nor so rapid as even Snodgrass thought. In what follows, I will discuss reinterpretations of Archaic poetry, of military equipment, and of the nature of hoplite battle in particular and of hoplite warfare more broadly.

REINTERPRETATIONS OF ARCHAIC POETRY

The gulf between Homeric warfare and hoplite warfare no longer appears as wide as it once did. Following a path-breaking study by J. Latacz in 1977, most scholars have accepted that Homer focuses on heroic duels not because they were all that mattered in Early Iron Age battles, but because, like a modern movie director, he can most effectively tell his story by shifting his gaze from the mass melée to the individual fighters.[6] Homer's warriors engage in mass but not massed battles. A large number of men fight, but they do so in a loose, fluid formation rather than in a massed phalanx. At times soldiers bunch together, as when nine named champions

> formed apart and stood against the Trojans and brilliant Hektor
> locking spear by spear, shield against shield at the base, so buckler
> leaned on buckler, helmet on helmet, man against man,
> and the horsehair crests along the horns of their shining helmets
> touched as they bent their heads, so dense were they formed on
> each other,
> and the spears shaken from their daring hands made a jagged
> battle line.
>
> (Homer *Iliad* 13.129–34)

At other times, however, wide gaps enable chariots to move among the men on the battlefield, and individuals move now forward, now back. Men fight at close range with thrusting spears and swords, but also at a distance by throwing rocks and spears. Archers step out from the cover of neighbors' shields to shoot arrows. Leaders encourage their brave men to fight in the front line. Everyone knows that

> if one is to win honor in battle, he must by all means
> stand his ground strongly, whether he be struck or strike down
> another.
>
> (Homer *Iliad* 11.409–10)

Nestor puts his best men in the front and the back, so that the cowards in the middle have to fight even if they do not want to (Homer *Iliad* 4.297–300). Standing one's ground is easier if men stay together; two men together can frighten off even a great warrior such as Aeneas (Homer *Iliad* 5.571–2).

Tyrtaios stresses many of the same themes. Brave men should close to fight hand to hand; they should stay together and support each other; they should not shame themselves by running away. Tyrtaios wrote for soldiers who fought in a loose formation; otherwise they would not have to be told to fight among the frontline fighters rather than stand with their shields beyond throwing range. Tyrtaios' battlefield contained light-armed troops too, mixed right in with the best-armed men. Fragment 11, quoted above, continues (fr. 11.35–8):

> And as for you light-armed soldiers, crouching here and there
> behind the shields, keep hurling great rocks,
> and fling your smooth javelins against them,
> standing hard by the soldiers in full armor.

Tyrtaios differs from Homer in some respects. He does not mention chariots, and his hoplites do not throw spears. Otherwise there really seems to be no gap at all between the two poets, and these omissions might be a function of the audience Tyrtaios was addressing rather than a reflection of battlefield reality. Another seventh-century poet, Kallinos, says to his fellow Ephesians, "let every man, as he dies, hurl his javelin one last time" (fr. 1.5), and many seventh-century vases show hoplites with two spears (for examples see Figures 3 and 4). One advantage of the *porpax* shield, in fact, was that a man could carry an extra spear. As for chariots, they may have continued in use as transport for warriors who fought on foot. In the Classical period, Sparta and Thebes had elite infantry units known as "horsemen" and "charioteers," names that probably reflect their origin as mounted infantry. Some sixth-century Athenian vases portray chariots, and there are a great many examples of squires holding horses for their dismounted riders.[7] An Archaic parade in Eretria featured 60 chariots, 600 horsemen, and 3,000 hoplites, perhaps an indication of the proportion of mounted infantry (Strabo 10.1.10).

ARMOR

In an interesting study published in 1995, E. Jarva reexamined Archaic Greek body armor. He counted the dedications found at Olympia, with the following results:

- about 350 helmets, more than two-thirds of them Corinthian;
- about 280 shields, starting late seventh century (so quite comparable to helmets, if the earlier helmet examples are excluded);
- about 225 greaves (shin guards);
- about 33 breastplates, slightly more ankle guards, and lower numbers of belly guards, arm guards, thigh guards, and foot guards.

Jarva suggests that this quantitative evidence implies that the use of bronze armor was relatively limited: If the numbers are taken as significant, it appears that fewer than half of the soldiers who wore a helmet and carried a shield also wore shin guards, and only about one in eight wore a bronze breastplate.

Because Greek soldiers brought their own armor and weapons – only for Sparta can a case be made that the state supplied military equipment – variety is not surprising. Linen corselets appear not only in Homer, but also in a poem by Alkaios of Mytilene (born ca. 620 BCE) listing defensive equipment:

> The great house glitters
> With bronze. The entire ceiling is decorated
> with shining helmets, down
> from which white plumes of horsehair
> nod, the adornments of
> men's heads. Greaves of bronze
> conceal the pegs they hang on,
> shining bright, a protection against strong arrows,
> while corselets of new linen
> and hollow shields lie thrown about.
>
> (fr. 140.1–10)

The traveler Pausanias denigrated the quality of linen corselets, but he also noted that one could see many of them dedicated in sanctuaries (Pausanias 1.21.7). An amusing anonymous poem (ca. 700–550 BCE) even suggests that Argives wearing linen corselets were once recognized as the best fighters:

> Of all soils Pelasgian Argos is the best,
> and best are the horses of Thessaly, the women of
> Lakedaimon,
> and the men who drink the waters of lovely Arethusa;
> but better even than these are they who dwell
> between Tiryns and Arkadia, rich in sheep,
> the linen-corseleted Argives, goads of war.
> But you, Megarians, are neither third, nor fourth,
> nor twelfth, nor in any reckoning or account.
> (*Palatine Anthology* 14.73)

Armor made of organic materials, of course, would not survive to be found by archaeologists, but it was cheaper than bronze and, up to a thickness of about 1 mm, provided better protection for its weight.[8] A leather corselet cut out of oxhide would cost perhaps half as much as a bronze breastplate, and weigh only half as much as well. Though the literary record attests linen corselets earlier than leather, leather would have been cheaper. Jarva argues that it was probably in common use throughout the Archaic period; it certainly appears in Attic black-figure vase painting by about 560 BCE.[9]

Helmets also varied. The Corinthian helmet restricted both vision and hearing, and several kinds of open-faced helmets were used in the seventh and sixth centuries: Insular on the islands, Illyrian on the mainland. The sixth century also saw the introduction of the Attic type with hinged cheek-pieces and the Chalkidian with cutouts for the ears. At Marathon in 490 BCE the Plataians wore a Boiotian leather cap (literally, a "dog's skin"), later recommended by Xenophon for horsemen because of its good visibility.[10] A hoplite could also wear a leather cap.[11] Poorer men may even have made do with a felt cap known as a *pilos*. The Spartans wore this *pilos* at Sphakteria in 425 BCE, and J. K. Anderson has suggested that it was part of a general lightening of equipment in the Classical period. But it appears in Athenian black-figure, so evidently some Archaic warriors were already wearing it.[12] The relative proportions of these different kinds of headgear in Archaic armies are difficult to gauge. Corinthian helmets dominate in vase paintings – especially

Corinthian vase paintings – as they do among extant examples. If we relied on vases, however, we would think horses were far more common in ancient Greece than donkeys and mules. Artists may similarly have preferred to portray the more valuable helmets.

All this equipment the Greeks called *hopla*, a generic word. A hoplite (*hoplites*) was an armed warrior who took his name from his equipment, not simply from his shield. J. F. Lazenby and D. Whitehead have pointed out that our sources call the *porpax* shield an *aspis*, not a *hoplon*.[13] A hoplite did not necessarily have a *porpax* shield: Greek writers applied the term "hoplite" to Egyptians carrying shields that reached to their feet, and to Macedonians who used a much smaller shield (Xenophon *Anabasis* 1.8.9 and Arrian *Anabasis* 1.6.2, respectively).

The most common Greek shield, at least later, consisted of a wooden core faced with bronze, sometimes with a leather lining on the inside. Though both ancient and modern writers refer to it as a bronze shield, the wood did the real work, because the bronze veneer was too thin to improve the resistance of the shield significantly. Men paid for the bronze to impress their friends and dazzle their enemies. Xenophon, who credits the legendary Lykourgos with introducing the bronze shield to the Spartan army, comments that it could be polished quickly and tarnished slowly (Xenophon *Constitution of Sparta* 11.3). More often the bronze was limited to the rim, or the blazon, and the *porpax*.

Two *porpax* shield cores are preserved well enough for the wood to be analyzed. One, dated to the mid-sixth century BCE, probably came from a grave in eastern Sicily and is now in Basel. It was made of willow strips, 0.14 m wide, laminated and pegged together. The other, dated to the early fifth century BCE, probably came from an Etruscan tomb at Bomarzo and is now in the Vatican. It was made of poplar boards 0.20–0.30 m wide, glued together with no trace of lamination.[14] The Chigi olpe seems to show the first type, strips of wood laminated across each other in layers to prevent splitting (see Figure 3).[15] It continued in use a long time: A fourth-century BCE *porpax* shield found at Olynthos in northern Greece consisted of crossing pieces of wood 0.06 m wide.[16] Poplar and willow are both on the list of woods recommended for shields by the Roman naturalist Pliny; they are flexible, rather soft woods that tend to dent rather than split (Pliny *Natural History* 16.209). A cheaper version might be made out of wicker, which remained in use throughout the Classical period, at least when nothing better was available. Demosthenes armed his sailors at Pylos in 424 BCE with wicker shields (*aspides*; Thucydides 4.9.1), and in 403 BCE the Athenian democrats made themselves wicker shields before their battle against the oligarchs' forces (Xenophon *Hellenica* 2.4.25). Aineias Taktikos, writing in the fourth century BCE, describes an incident in which conspirators inside a city imported osiers and wove baskets during the day and shields at night. Elsewhere he says that wickerwork can stop missiles coming over city walls (Aineias Taktikos 29.11–12, 32.2).

There is good iconographic evidence for another kind of shield, the round or oblong Boiotian shield, found in Archaic vase painting and on coins, in addition to the Dodona figurine (Figure 2). No examples have been found, and scholars have often dismissed the Boiotian shield as an unrealistic heroic marker, adapted from Mycenaean figure-of-eight shields and out of place in a hoplite phalanx. But these objections can be overcome.[17] The shields appear to have two cutouts, one on each side, probably because they were constructed originally of animal hides stretched over a wooden frame. Shields made of these organic materials would have vanished without a trace. This kind of shield can have a single central grip (see the fourth figure from the left in Figure 1) or be supplied with a *porpax* and *antilabe*. If it is a *porpax* shield, it is held with the arm straight rather than bent.

To judge by vase paintings, this shield remained an attractive option for a minority of fighters throughout the Archaic period. A leather shield could be a source of pride, as in the drinking song of Hybrias the Cretan, usually dated to the late Archaic period:

> My wealth is great; it is a spear and a sword,
> And the grand hairy shield to guard my body.
> With these I plow, with these I harvest,
> with these I tread the sweet wine from the grapevine,
> with these I am called master of the rabble.
> And they who dare not carry the spear and sword
> and the grand hairy shield to guard their bodies,
> all these fall down before me, kiss my knee, hail me
> their high king and master.
>
> (Athenaios *Deipnosophistai* 695f–696a)

In equipment too, then, the best-equipped Archaic soldiers were not so different from Homer's heroes, who wore helmets, breastplates, and shin-guards, and carried shields, spears, and swords. Variety ruled in Archaic armies just as it does in Homer. We should not imagine all Archaic fighters lumbering under 30 kg or more of defensive equipment. The two most recent studies of hoplite equipment conclude that even the heavily armed hoplite carried less than 30 kg – no more than a

TABLE 3. *Weight in Kilograms of a Greek Hoplite's Equipment Compared to a Roman Legionnaire's*

Equipment	Archaic Hoplite (Jarva 1995)	6th Cent. Hoplite (Franz 2002)	Augustan Legionnaire (Junkelmann 1986)
Shield	6.2–7.2	6.5–8	9.65
Helmet	1.2–1.5	1.5–2.6	2.1
Breastplate/coat of mail	4–8	4.6–5.5	8.3
(Leather corselet)	(3.5–5.5)		
(Linen corselet)	(6–7)		
Greaves (pair)	1	1.2–2.2	
Other	0–1.8	0–3.6	
Spear/pilum	1.5	1.6–4	1.9
Sword	1.5–2	2.2	2.2
Dagger			1.1
Clothing (including sandals)	2	1	4.15
Total	**17.4–25**	**18.6–29.1**	**29.4**

Roman legionnaire during the age of Augustus (see Table 3). Many well-equipped men fighting in the front rank might have had a panoply of less than 20 kg, while the minimum Homer's Odysseus said he needed to fight – helmet, shield, spears – would have weighed no more than about 12 kg, and would have protected all vital organs (Homer *Odyssey* 18.376–80). If he wore only a felt *pilos* on his head, a hoplite could have carried less than 10 kg.

The cost of this equipment is difficult to ascertain, but should not be exaggerated. A shield and spear probably cost no more than a month's wages for a skilled worker, and a full panoply perhaps three months' pay. The equipment could be handed down from father to son, borrowed from a friend, or acquired from an enemy.[18] The modern idea that the criterion for hoplite service at Athens was economic capacity – that is, that the *zeugitai*, the third of Solon's four census classes, were the hoplites "yoked" together in the phalanx – is a mirage. No ancient source equates the *zeugitai* with the hoplites, and if all hoplites were required to be *zeugitai*, Attica could not have fielded armies of the attested strength, for it lacked sufficient land.[19] Athenian hoplites were "those who provide *hopla*" (Thucydides 8.97.1). The philosopher Sokrates – whose total property, including his house, was worth no more than 500 drachmas, or about a year and a half's wages if he had a regular job, which he did not – nevertheless served at least twice, in the siege of Potidaia in 432–29 BCE and in the invasion of Boiotia in 424 BCE (Xenophon *Oikonomikos* 2.3; Plato *Apology* 28d, *Symposion* 219e–221c; Plutarch *Alkibiades* 7.2–3).

The "Storm of the Spear"

The traditional understanding of Archaic battle, exemplified by V. D. Hanson's *Western Way of War*, has both phalanxes deploy with about a meter per man, or even less, each forming an unbroken wall of shields.[20] The two sides then close to fight hand to hand and ultimately to push, leaning into their shields. Widespread though it is, this view rests on an excessively literal interpretation of the sources both for the formation and the manner of fighting.

Formation first. The double-handled shield, like any shield carried on one arm, would have protected one side of the body better than the other. But it did not make a hoplite so vulnerable that he must have put his right side behind his neighbor's shield. Hoplites carried the *porpax* shield while climbing scaling ladders placed against city walls (see Figure 6) and while serving as marines on board triremes. As H. van Wees has pointed out, a hoplite could have covered himself nicely by turning sideways to the enemy.[21] This stance, with right foot planted behind left, would also have enabled a more powerful spear thrust.

W. K. Pritchett collected the literary evidence for the width of file in battle formation, concluding that each man occupied about three feet.[22] Most of his passages, however, apply to the Macedonian phalanx. For the earlier Greek phalanx, the case rests on Thucydides' comment in 5.71.1, quoted above, to the effect that each hoplite tried to get as close as possible to the man on his right and relied on the tightness of the *synkleisis* ("closing-up"). Even if we assume that Thucydides did not exaggerate and should be taken literally, this passage does not prove that Greek hoplites each occupied about three feet. We do not know how close Thucydides thought was "as close as possible" for warriors fighting with spears and swords. The next paragraph, in which Thucydides uses the verb *synkleio* twice, shows that a lack of *synkleisis* can mean a gap large enough for at least a fifth of the Spartan army, so a compact *synkleisis* does not have to be three feet per man (Thucydides 5.72.1, 3). According to Polybios, the Roman infantry fought at six feet per man, because each man needed room to use his shield and sword.[23] If we allow the Greek hoplite up to six feet, the evidence that the Macedonians tightened the formation makes better sense.

Vase paintings suggest that the Greeks began their advance in a closer formation than they fought in. On the Chigi vase (Figure 3), for example, where the opponents appear to be in a close-order formation, they have not yet engaged. On the Berlin aryballos, the hoplites in a close-order formation have not engaged, while those who fight are no longer in line. On the Macmillan aryballos (Figure 4), which shows general fighting, no more than two fighters are in close formation at any one place. Another Protocorinthian vase, the oinochoe from Erythrai first published in 1992, also shows a formation breaking up as it engages.[24] Of course these scenes are all small, and one would like to have the large-scale paintings of historical battles seen by Pausanias in the Stoa Poikile at Athens (Pausanias 1.15). The painting of the battle of Oinoë showed the two sides on the point of engaging, while the painting of the battle of Marathon actually showed several different stages, including the beginning of the hand to hand fighting and the rout.

Most Greeks rushed into battle "violently and furiously" (Thucydides 5.70). As troops advanced over an irregular Greek plain, broken up by trees, huts, stones, field walls, ditches, and undulating ground, they spread out.[25] Homer provides an appropriate simile. The Myrmidons deploy in a tight formation (*Iliad* 16.212–17):

> And as a man builds solid a wall with stones set close together
> for the rampart of a high house keeping out the force of the
> winds, so
> close together were the helms and shields massive in the middle.
> For shield leaned on shield, helmet on helmet, man against man,
> and the horse-hair crests along the horns of the shining helmets
> touched as they bent their heads, so dense were they formed on
> each other.

When they charge, Homer compares them to wasps coming out of a nest (*Iliad* 16.259–267):

> The Myrmidons came streaming out like wasps at the wayside
> when little boys have got into the habit of making them angry
> by always teasing them as they live in their house by the roadside;
> silly boys, they do something that hurts many people;
> and if some man who travels on the road happens to pass them
> and stirs them unintentionally, they in heart of fury

come swarming out each one from his place to fight for their
children.
In heart and in fury like these the Myrmidons streaming
came out from their ships, with a tireless clamor arising.

However neat the phalanx was when it began to move, by the time it reached the enemy it tended to dissolve into small clusters and individuals, the braver men striking out on their own, the less confident men bunching together. Archaic hoplites were amateurs, mostly farmers, who lacked the training necessary to advance in an evenly spaced formation.

The nature of the fighting once the opponents came "to hands" has also been debated. Despite its frequent appearance in modern writers, the noun *othismos* occurs rarely in battle contexts in the classical historians: twice in Herodotos, once in Thucydides, and never in Xenophon. On the other hand, the verb *othein* and its compounds occur frequently. This use of *othein* goes back to Homer, in passages exemplified by the following lines describing what happened when Hektor and the Trojans attacked the nine Greek champions who resisted them (*Iliad* 13.136–48):

The Trojans came down on them in a pack, and Hektor led
them raging
straight forward, like a great rolling stone from a rock face
that a river swollen with winter rain has wrenched from its socket
and with immense washing broken the hold of the unwilling
rock face;
the springing boulder flies on, and the forest thunders beneath it;
and the stone runs unwavering on a strong course, till it reaches
the flat land, then rolls no longer for all its onrush;
so Hektor for a while threatened lightly to break through
the shelters and ships of the Achaians and reach the water
cutting his way. But when he collided with the dense battalions
he was stopped, hard, beaten in on himself. The sons of the
Achaians
against him stabbing at him with swords and leaf-headed spears
thrust (*othein*) him away from them so that he gave ground
backward, staggering.

Here Greeks, drawn tightly together, push Hektor back. But this passage is very poor evidence for a mass shove in general battle. First of all, the Greeks are fighting inside their camp wall, with their backs to their ships.

Second, not all Greeks, but only a small group of nine named champions who rallied together, "push" by stabbing with their weapons. Homer means that the Greeks used their weapons to force Hektor to back up, slowly – pushed back as opposed to routed.

Archaic warriors fought hand to hand with spears and swords. They also threw javelins and rocks, slung lead bullets, and shot arrows. We should not imagine too great a distinction between hoplites and light-armed in the Archaic period. The Chigi vase (Figure 3) shows fully armed hoplites – bronze breastplates, greaves, helmets, and double-handled shields – with two spears each, one a javelin. Elsewhere we see archers wearing some pieces of hoplite equipment.[26]

Eventually Greek armies had separate contingents of hoplites, archers, and horsemen, but such sophistication probably did not appear until *after* the Persian invasions. Earlier armies probably looked quite Homeric: the rich men, the ones who called themselves the beautiful and the good, rode their horses to battle, dismounted, and fought in the front.[27] Others too might make their way to the front, depending on their personal temperaments as well as on their equipment. The frontline fighters might back off, rest, and fight again. Only in the fifth century do we have literary and visual evidence for the custom of erecting trophies, victory markers put up at the *trope*, the place where the enemy turned and ran. These simple trophies of armor hung on a tree or post also mark a real change in warfare. Instead of the fluid, back-and-forth fighting that occurred earlier, classical battles usually meant a general engagement until one side fled once and for all.

This understanding of Archaic fighting solves an old puzzle. If hoplite phalanxes dominated Archaic warfare, why did Greek artists concentrate so heavily on one-on-one combats? For the entire Archaic period, A. Stewart recently counted eight extant depictions of massed formations (seven vases plus the Siphnian Treasury frieze; see Figure 7).[28] His list could be extended if three closely packed hoplites are always taken as a phalanx, but representations of warriors in ranks are indeed rare compared to duels. The usual explanations of this conundrum suggest that Greek artists portrayed mythological scenes, or that the emphasis on a warrior's loneliness reflected the psychological reality of battle.[29] The latter is closer to the truth. Although hoplites deployed in a massed formation, they fought as individuals against other individuals, or in small groups. In looking for depictions of hoplites fighting in large massed formations, we were looking for the wrong thing. For the best representations of Archaic fighting, we should look not at the Chigi vase, but at other battle paintings from the Chigi group, such as the aryballos in Paris (Figure 8) and the aryballos in Syracuse (Figure 9). The Paris aryballos shows two one-on-one duels and one two-on-one fight, with an archer supporting the single fighter. The Syracuse aryballos shows only hoplite duels, with considerable variety among the shields in size, shape, and style.

Agonal Warfare?

Archaic Greek warfare has often been characterized as "agonal," from the Greek work *agon*, meaning "contest."[30] According to this view, Archaic Greeks fought more for status than survival. The family farmers who formed the backbone of the hoplite army ritualized warfare in order to restrain its destructive force. Hoplites fought according to unwritten customs or protocols: They formally declared war before invading an enemy; they confined warfare to set battles in open plains, seldom employing deception; they did not attack noncombatants; they did not pursue a defeated enemy very hard or long; they claimed victory by erecting a trophy and conceded defeat by asking for permission to bury their dead; they offered prisoners of war for ransom rather than killing them or forcing them into slavery; they accepted the outcome of a battle as decisive. In the words of V. D. Hanson, "for at least the two centuries between 700 and 500 BCE, and perhaps for much of the early fifth century BCE as well, hoplite infantry battle determined the very nature of Greek warfare, and became the means to settle disputes – instantaneously, economically, and ethically."[31]

This interpretive model rests on evidence no earlier than the second half of the fifth century.[32] Euripides, Thucydides, and Xenophon refer to various Greek *nomoi* or *nomima* (unwritten rules). Most famously, Herodotos has the Persian general Mardonius tell King Xerxes that "When the Greeks declare war on one another, they find the fairest and most level piece of ground, go down into it and fight, so that the winners come off with great losses; I say nothing of the losers, for they are utterly destroyed" (7.9b.1). But when we look at the Archaic evidence, patchy though it is, the case for new military protocols evaporates: Some customs – especially those involving the gods – go back to Homer, some turn out to be matters of practical military tactics rather than conventions designed to ameliorate warfare, and some do not appear until the mid-fifth century.

Nor does the evidence support the claim that single battles ended wars quickly and economically. The Messenians and the

Lakedaimonians fought twice in the seventh century, each time for about twenty years. The Lelantine war, fought between Chalkis and Eretria and their allies, included fighting at the time of Hesiod (ca. 700) and Archilochos (at least twenty years later). The first Sacred War is said to have lasted ten years in the early sixth century. The Athenians and Mytileneans fought for "a long time" over Sigeion. The war of Athenian settlers in the Chersonesos against Lampsakos began during the reign of Peisistratos, when Miltiades came to the Chersonesos, and continued until the time of Stesagoras, Miltiades' nephew, who was killed about 516, so it lasted at least a dozen years. Fighting between Athens and Aigina began about 505, broke out again about 490, and was at its height in 483, when the Athenians built the fleet they actually used against Persia.

Archaic wars sometimes resulted in significant territorial gains.[33] To say nothing of what happened on Crete or in various colonies, the Spartans, Sikyonians, Argives, and Thessalians turned defeated opponents into serfs, and the Lokrians, Megarians, Epidaurians, and Eleians may have too. If the Athenians did not create serfs, they began to send out their own citizens to settle on defeated land already in the late sixth century, when 4,000 Athenians moved to Chalkis.

Another Model

The most detailed extant description of Archaic warfare comes from the second-century CE travel writer Pausanias, who narrates the Lakedaimonians' conquest (and reconquest) of Messenia in Book 4 of his *Periegesis*. S. E. Alcock has recently provided a corrective to the usual view that this narrative is only "pseudo-history": Messenian social memory might have been kept alive in villages – the conquered Messenians continued to live in villages, rather than being dispersed among Lakedaimonian farms, at least in the region around Pylos – or in gatherings at sacred sites and tombs.[34] Emigrants might also have kept traditions alive until their descendants returned to Messenia in the fourth century. Pausanias tells a story that he found not incompatible with – and perhaps even based on – Tyrtaios, whom he cites four times.

The First Messenian war broke out after a quarrel over cattle escalated into murder. Attempts at resolving the matter failed, and some months later, without declaring war, the Lakedaimonians captured the Messenian town of Ampheia by a surprise attack at night. Then the Lakedaimonians plundered Messenian territory – though they did not demolish buildings or cut down trees, because they hoped to conquer the land for themselves – and unsuccessfully assaulted other fortified towns. Meanwhile, the Messenians raided the Lakonian coast and the cultivated land round Mt. Taÿÿgetos.

Three years after the capture of Ampheia, both sides marched out for battle. The Messenians, however, deployed behind a ravine that prevented the forces from fighting hand to hand. Skirmishing over the ravine was indecisive, and because the Messenians had fortified their position with a wooden palisade, the Lakedaimonians returned home.

One year later, the Lakedaimonians invaded again, and this time a battle took place. Mounted men were few, and the light-armed on both sides were stationed behind the hoplites. The Messenians charged recklessly, while the Lakedaimonians maintained their formation. Before engaging they threatened each other, brandishing their weapons, and then fought using the *othismos* and man against man. (By *othismos* Pausanias does not mean a mass shove, because he goes on to describe some Messenians leaping forward, out of formation, and javelins killing men who tried to strip corpses.) Though the Lakedaimonians had a numerical advantage and a deeper formation, the Messenians finally pushed back King Theopompos and routed the Lakedaimonian right wing, while King Polydoros and his men routed the Messenian right wing. Darkness ended the fighting with no clear winner.

The Messenians then abandoned their inland towns and settled together on Mt. Ithome. Five years passed before the Lakedaimonians invaded again. The resulting battle ended again in darkness with no clear decision, but this time it seems to have been a less general engagement. Instead the best men stepped forward and fought in the space between the two sides, so that neither side broke. Following four years of small-scale raiding on both sides, the Messenians won the next battle by setting an ambush of light-armed troops. Nevertheless, the Lakedaimonians were able to besiege Ithome, and after a series of depressing omens the Messenians lost all their generals and their best men in a final battle. After holding out for five months, they evacuated Ithome. The Lakedaimonians razed the town to the ground, and then assaulted and captured the remaining cities. They annexed all of Messenia, turning the survivors into serfs known as helots.

Some years later, the Messenians revolted. In the first year after the revolt, they fought an indecisive battle; in the next year, joined by allies, the Messenians won a victory. The Messenian hero Aristomenes then led several raids: on Pharae in Laconia, Sparta itself (from which he was deterred by the appearance of Helen and the Dioskouroi), Karyai, and Aigila. In the third year, the Lakedaimonians bribed the Arkadian general Aristocrates, who deserted with his men in the middle of a battle at the "Great Trench."

The Messenian survivors abandoned most of their towns and collected on Mt. Eira, where they held out for eleven years. They plundered and raided Messenia (because it was now held by the Lakedaimonians) and Lakonia, coming as close to Sparta as Amyklai. Once they engaged more than half the Lakedaimonian infantry. Aristomenes was captured, escaped, resumed his raids (including a night attack on a sleeping contingent of Corinthians on their way to help the Lakedaimonians at Eira), was captured again, and escaped again. Eira finally fell on a moonless, stormy night. When rain drove the guards away from their posts, the Lakedaimonians assaulted and took the acropolis. After three days of vicious street fighting, Aristomenes led the Messenians away.

This story represents the antithesis of agonal warfare. Set battles do not begin and end wars. Each long war saw at least three battles, none of which was decisive. The fighting otherwise takes place on a smaller scale, each side raiding the other. Deceptions – surprise attacks and ambushes – seem common. Noncombatants are sometimes captured. Sieges can go on for years. And in the end, the struggle *is* about the survival of a community as an independent community, not simply about status. Thucydides could dismiss the Messenian Wars as border fights that involved no great alliances and no great acquisition of power (1.15.2). But these long, intermittent wars determined the Messenians' fate for the next several hundred years.

Though Classical Greeks romanticized the way their ancestors fought, saying that they had an unwritten code that limited the costs of war, Archaic Greeks knew better. "War is sweet to the inexperienced," Pindar wrote near the end of the Archaic period, "but anyone who has experienced it fears its approach in his gut" (fr. 110).

CONCLUSION

Archaic Greece did not experience a military revolution, much less one that led to political revolutions as well. Mass fighting took place already in the Early Iron Age, as described by Homer. Equipment evolved, including the Corinthian helmet and the *porpax* shield, but it developed in order to help a man do better what he was already doing. It did not compel a change in the manner of fighting. Because hoplites provided their own equipment, they could choose what to bring, and many humble farmers fought in lighter gear than their wealthier comrades carried. Aristotle's belief that hoplites replaced cavalry as the dominant military arm rests on a misconception of how Archaic horsemen fought. They were mounted infantry. They may have been the flashiest foot-soldiers, but they fought in the same conglomeration that everyone else did, including archers, javelin-throwers, and slingers.[35]

This mass was necessarily loose. It may have tightened somewhat when light-armed troops ceased to fight within the phalanx, perhaps as a result of contact with more sophisticated eastern military forces at the end of the Archaic period. Greeks believed that Kyaxares, king of Media 625–585, first separated the spearmen, archers, and horsemen (Herodotos 1.103.1). For the Athenians, the battle of Marathon may have been the turning point. Herodotos says that at Marathon the Athenians were "the first Greeks, as far as I know" to charge the enemy at a run, and they did so with no horsemen or archers (6.112.2–3). Scholars have dismissed these claims on the grounds that running into battle was nothing new, and that the Athenians brought even their slaves to fight. But Herodotos should not be dismissed so lightly. What was remarkable about the Athenian charge was that all ran together, rather than each man advancing at his own pace, and what was remarkable about the Athenian formation was that it excluded horsemen and archers – which is not to say that every man had identical equipment.

Though the Athenian gamble at Marathon succeeded, the Persian invasions taught the Greeks the value of specialist forces. In the fifth century, separate contingents of cavalry, archers, and even mounted archers (normally associated with Persia) appeared in Greece. Light-armed fighters no longer fought mingled with hoplites. Not until the fourth century, however, when Philip II of Macedon copied the Athenian Iphikrates' abortive experiment and trained his light-armed infantry to fight in a close formation with long, thrusting spears, did the phalanx become the tight formation Aristotle knew.[36]

Hoplites, then, did not *qua* hoplites drive political changes in Archaic Greece. As K. A. Raaflaub has put it, "the men who owned the land fought in the army to defend the territory of the *polis* and sat in the assembly to participate in its decisions."[37] Their role became more formalized by the end of the Archaic period, but they did not begin to play a new part.

NOTES

1 For the following authors, I have taken and adapted translations from the following: Alkaios, Kallinos, and Tyrtaios from A. M. Miller; Aristotle's *Politics* from H.

Rackham; Athenaios and Homer from R. Lattimore; and *The Palatine Anthology* from W. R. Paton.

2 Nilsson 1928.

3 Aristotle still has his champions: see Cartledge 2001, 153–66.

4 Snodgrass 1965. On archaic armor, Snodgrass 1964 remains fundamental; the appendix in Snodgrass 1999 provides an update.

5 For a drawing of the Berlin aryballos, see Salmon 1977, 86.

6 Latacz 1977; Pritchett 1985a, 7–44; and van Wees 2004b, 151–65.

7 Greenhalgh 1973.

8 Blyth 1977.

9 Jarva 1995, 33–46 and 152–4.

10 Demosthenes 59.94; Xenophon *On Horsemanship* 12.3. Snodgrass 1999, 94–5 believes a metallic hat can take the same form.

11 Lissarrague 1990. For an example, see the interior of an Athenian black-figure cup, ca. 560, which shows a warrior with a cap, greaves, two spears, and a round shield with a shield device (Moore and Philippides 1986, pl. 109 no. 1678).

12 Thucydides 4.34.3, with Anderson 1970, 29–34. See *CVA* Greece 3, pl. 14–17.

13 Lazenby and Whitehead 1996, who note that even Diodoros 15.44.3 calls the shield an *aspis*.

14 For the shield in Basel, see Seiterle 1982 and Cahn 1989, 15–17. For the shield in the Vatican, see Blyth 1982. Aristophanes (fr. 65) and Euripides (*Cyclops* 7, *Herakleidai* 376, *Suppliants* 695, *Trojan Women* 1193) mention shields made of willow.

15 A contemporary ovoid krater from Aigina also shows shield interiors with concentric hatched triangles (Morris 1984, 79). Morris notes a different pattern on Protoattic cups found in the Kerameikos cemetery at Athens.

16 Robinson 1941, 443–4. Unfortunately the remains of the wood were not analyzed.

17 Boardman 1983, 27–33; Franz 2002, 183–4; and van Wees 2004b, 50–52 defend the Boiotian shield's authenticity.

18 On the cost of hoplite equipment, see recently Hanson 1995, 294–301 and Jarva 1995, 148–54. Franz 2002, 351–3 stresses that for the Archaic period, we really do not know. Snodgrass 1985 publishes a Corinthian helmet found in the Persian siege ramp at Paphos, which he believes was used for more than thirty years before it was lost during the building of the ramp in 498 BCE.

19 Rosivach 2002 makes the first point, van Wees 2004b, 55–7 the second. Van Wees suggests that the *zeugitai* were obligated to fight, while the poorer men could volunteer. See also van Wees 2006.

20 Hanson 2000, Lazenby 1991, and Cartledge 2001, 152–66 also defend the traditional view.

21 van Wees 2004b, 168–9.

22 Pritchett 1971, 144–54.

23 Polybios 18.30.6–8. Goldsworthy 1996, 179 finds the three feet given by Vegetius 3.14–15 "more plausible" than Polybios, comparing space allotments in eighteenth- and nineteenth-century armies using firearms. But Polybios is the earlier source and is quite explicit.

24 Akurgal 1992, Fig. 2.

25 Goldsworthy 1997.

26 Lissarrague 1990.

27 Greenhalgh 1973.
28 Stewart 1997, 89 with a list on 247.
29 Hannestad 2001, 112; Stewart 1997, 91.
30 Vernant 1968 was especially influential. In English, see particularly Connor 1988, Hanson 1995, and Ober 1996. Important, but very different, recent studies on competition within and between Greek armies include Lendon 2005 and Dayton 2006.
31 Hanson 2000, xxvi.
32 Krentz 2002.
33 van Wees 2004a.
34 Alcock 2002, 132–75. Pritchett 1985b, 1–68 defends Pausanias' topography. Figueira 1999 argues that the stories we have about the Messenian past have been refracted through the lens of later history, especially the Peloponnesian War. The same could be said of all later sources on Archaic warfare, including those used to construct the agonal model. My point is not that we should believe everything Pausanias says, but that he provides an alternative model of Archaic warfare.
35 van Wees 2004b, 78–9.
36 van Wees 2004b, 197.
37 Raaflaub 1997, 55. See also Hanson 1995, 181–219 on "agricultural egalitarianism" throughout Archaic and Classical Greece.

Bibliography and Suggested Readings

Akurgal, E. 1992. "Eine protokorinthische Oinochoe aus Erythrai." *Istanbuler Mitteilungen* 42: 83–96.

Alcock, S. E. 2002. *Archaeologies of the Greek Past.*

Anderson, J. K. 1970. *Military Theory and Practice in the Age of Xenophon.*

Andrewes, A. 1956. *The Greek Tyrants.*

Blyth, P. H. 1977. "The Effectiveness of Greek Armour against Arrows in the Persian War." Dissertation, University of Reading.

Blyth, P. H. 1982. "The Structure of a Hoplite Shield in the Museo Gregoriano Etrusco." *Bolletino dei Musei e Gallerie Pontifice* 3: 5–21.

Boardman, J. 1983. "Symbol and Story in Geometric Art." In *Ancient Greek Art and Iconography.* Ed. W. G. Moon. 15–36.

Cahn, David. 1989. *Waffen und Zaumzeug.*

Cartledge, P. 2001. *Spartan Reflections.*

Connelly, P. 1981. *Greece and Rome at War.*

Connor, W. R. 1988. "Early Greek Land Warfare as Symbolic Expression." *Past & Present* 119: 3–28.

Dayton, J. C. 2006. *The Athletes of War: An Evaluation of the Agonistic Elements in Greek Warfare.*

Figueira, T. J. 1999. "The Evolution of the Messenian Identity." In *Sparta: New Perspectives.* Eds. S. Hodkinson and A. Powell. 211–244.

Franz, J. P. 2002. *Krieger, Bauern, Bürger.*

Goldsworthy, A. K. 1996. *The Roman Army at War, 100 BC–AD 200.*

______. 1997. "The *Othismos*, Myths and Heresies: The Nature of Hoplite Battle." *War in History* 4: 1–26.

Greenhalgh, P. A. L. 1973. *Early Greek Warfare: Horsemen and Chariots in the Homeric and Archaic Ages.*

Hannestad, L. 2001. "War and Greek Art." In *War as a Cultural and Social Force: Essays on Warfare in Antiquity*. Eds. T. Bekker-Nielsen and L. Hannestad. 110–119.

Hanson, V. D. 1991. *Hoplites: The Classical Greek Battle Experience.*

______. 1995. *The Other Greeks.*

______. 2000. *The Western Way of War: Infantry Battle in Classical Greece*. Second ed.

Jarva, E. 1995. *Archaiologia on Archaic Greek Body Armour.*

Junkelmann, M. 1986. *Die Legionen des Augustus.*

Krentz, P. 2002. "Fighting by the Rules: The Invention of the Hoplite *Agôn*." *Hesperia* 71: 23–39.

Latacz, J. 1977. *Kampfparänese, Kampfdarstellung und Kampfwirklichkeit in der Ilias, bei Kallinos und Tyrtaios.*

Lazenby, J. F. 1991. "The Killing Zone." In *Hoplites*. Ed. V. D. Hanson. 87–109.

Lazenby, J. F. and D. Whitehead. 1996. "The Myth of the Hoplite's Hoplon." *Classical Quarterly* ns 46: 27–33.

Lendon, J. E. 2005. *Soldiers & Ghosts: A History of Battle in Classical Antiquity.*

Lissarrague, F. 1990. *L'autre guerrier: Archers, peltastes, cavaliers: Sur l'iconographie du guerrier.*

Lorimer, H. L. 1947. "The Hoplite Phalanx." *Annual of the British School at Athens* 42: 76–138.

Moore, M. B. and M. Z. P. Philippides. 1986. Agora XXIII: *Attic Black-Figured Pottery.*

Morris, S. P. 1984. *The Black and White Style: Athens and Aigina in the Orientalizing Period.*

Nilsson, M. P. 1928. "Die Hoplitentaktik und das Staatswesen." *Klio* 22: 240–249.

Ober, Josiah. 1996. "The Rules of War in Classical Greece." In idem, *The Athenian Revolution*. 53–71.

Pritchett, W. K. 1971. *The Greek State at War*, Vol. 1.

______. 1985a. *The Greek State at War*, Vol. 4.

______. 1985b. *Studies in Ancient Greek Topography*, Vol. 5.

Raaflaub, Kurt A. 1997. "Citizens, Soldiers, and the Evolution of the Early Greek Polis." In *The Development of the Polis in Archaic Greece*. Eds. L. Mitchell and P. J. Rhodes. London. 49–59.

Robinson, D. M. 1941. *Excavations at Olynthus, X: Metal and Minor Miscellaneous Finds.*

Rosivach, V. J. 2002. "*Zeugitai* and Hoplites." *Ancient History Bulletin* 16: 33–43.

Salmon, J. 1977. "Political Hoplites." *Journal of Hellenic Studies* 97: 84–101.

Seiterle, G. 1982. "Techniken zur Herstellung der Einzelteile (Exkurs zum Schild Nr. 217)." In *Antike Kunstwerke aus der Sammlung Ludwig, II. Terrakotten und Bronzen*. Ed. E. Berger. 250–263.

Snodgrass, A. M. 1964. *Early Greek Armour and Weapons.*

______. 1965. "The Hoplite Reform and History." *Journal of Hellenic Studies* 84: 110–22.

______. 1985. "A Corinthian Helmet from the Persian Siege Ramp at Palaepaphos." In *Alt-Paphos auf Cypern*. Ed. F. G. Maier. 45–49.

______. 1999. *Arms and Armor of the Greeks*. Second ed.

Stewart, A. 1997. *Art, Desire, and the Body in Ancient Greece.*

van Wees, H. 2004a. "Conquerors and Serfs." In *Helots and Their Masters*. Ed. S. Alcock and N. Luraghi. 29–76.

______. 2004b. *Greek Warfare: Myths and Realities*.

______. 2006. "Mass and Elite in Solon's Athens: The Property Classes Revisited." In *Solon of Athens*. Ed. J. H. Blok and A. P. M. H. Lardinois. 351–389.

Vernant, J.-P., ed. 1968. *Problèmes de la guerre en Grèce ancienne*.

4: The Life Cycle in Archaic Greece

Deborah Kamen

Arnold van Gennep's *The Rites of Passage* (1909; English trans. 1960) has had a profound impact on how we understand the nature of the "life cycle" and its *rites de passage* – each of which consists (to varying extents) of stages of separation, transition, and (re)incorporation. The life cycle, particularly in a community-oriented culture such as Archaic Greece, cannot be examined merely at the level of the individual; it must also be considered from the perspective of the individual vis-à-vis both household and society. In this chapter, I will examine the Archaic Greek rites of birth, initiation, marriage, and death in light of van Gennep's schema and attempt to ascertain the ways in which the Greeks negotiated these potentially anxiety-producing passages. Rites of passage are considerably better attested in the Classical period than in the Archaic, but the fragments available to us – literary, archaeological, and iconographic – allow us to see that many of the "Classical" life-cycle rituals are in fact rooted in Archaic practice.[1]

Stages of Life

Before we address the specifics of the Archaic Greek rites of passage, we should examine the ways in which the life cycle was divided. Not surprisingly, there were a number of ways to classify the stages of life. A common Archaic conception was that life was divided into periods of seven years called hebdomads. Solon, the early sixth-century BCE Athenian lawgiver and poet, describes the age classes (of men) thus:

> A prepubescent child (*pais anebos*), while still immature (*nepios*), in seven years grows a fence of teeth and loses them

> for the first time. When the god completes another seven years, he shows the signs of coming puberty (*hebe*). In the third [hebdomad] his body is still growing, his chin becomes downy, and the skin changes its hue. In the fourth everyone is far the best in strength, whereby men (*andres*) show their signs of physical excellence. In the fifth it is time for a man to be mindful of marriage and to look for a line of sons to come after him. In the sixth a man's mind is being trained for everything and he is no longer willing to commit acts of foolishness. In the seventh and eighth, a total of fourteen years, he is far the best in thought and speech. In the ninth he still has ability, but his speech and wisdom give weaker proof of a high level of excellence. If one were to complete stage after stage and reach the tenth, he would not have death's allotment prematurely (*aoros*).
>
> (Solon fr. 27 W)

This notion of life being divided into hebdomads was not restricted to the Archaic period; it continued into the Classical era and later. Hippocrates, the famous fifth-century BCE physician, is said to have developed the following schema of age classes (again, for males):

> The first [stage is from] from birth to 6; the second from 6 to 13; the third from 13 to 20; the fourth from 20 to 27; the fifth from 27 to 34; the sixth from 34 to 41; the seventh from 41 to 48. The first [is called] *paidion*; the second, *pais*; the third, *meirakion*; the fourth, *neaniskos*; the fifth, *aner*; the sixth, *geron*; the seventh, *presbytes*.
>
> (Pollux 2.4)

At least after *paideia* (childhood), the life stages for females were defined somewhat differently than for males; that is to say, the terms used were concerned less with chronological age than with marital or maternal status. When a girl reached puberty, she became a *parthenos*, a term referring to a marriageable but still unmarried young woman. The term *nymphe* designates both bride and new wife; but after her first child's birth, a woman was henceforth called a *gyne*, a word meaning both woman and wife.

Finally, one could also divide the stages of life – for both males and females – quite simply as young, middle-aged, and old. The eighth-century BCE poet Hesiod, for instance, refers to "the deeds of the *neoi* [young], the counsels of the *mesoi* [middle-aged], the prayers of the *gerontes* [old]" (fr. 321 M-W). Moreover, this tripartite division – like the division by hebdomads – is one we find in the Classical period as well, as for example in Greek tragedy (we might think of the riddle of the Sphinx).

BIRTH

Let us now examine the very first stage of the life cycle: birth. Unfortunately, our evidence for birth rites in the Archaic period is particularly scant, in some cases negligible: vase paintings, for instance, almost never depict childbirth and its associated rituals. Much of what we do know about birth practice in Archaic Greece derives from Plutarch's first-century CE account of Archaic and Classical Sparta – where, it so happens, the rituals surrounding birth were quite aberrant. Nonetheless, if we read Plutarch's account alongside Archaic literary and archaeological evidence, we can try to reconstruct an Archaic Greek "norm" for birth rites.

The baby's separation from its mother – including its passage through the birth canal and the cutting of the umbilical cord – was an anxiety-producing event for the entire household (*oikos*). Due to subpar standards of hygiene and an absence of sophisticated medical knowledge, both the mother's and the child's lives were truly in peril. As a result, goddesses of childbirth were called upon to aid in the delivery, the most prominent of whom was Eileithyia, the daughter of Zeus and Hera (Hesiod *Theogony* 922). "The goddess of birth labor" is in fact a common Homeric epithet for her (e.g., *Hymn to Apollo* 97, 115), and her very appearance prompts Leto to deliver Apollo on Delos (*Hymn to Apollo* 115–16). Moreover, we sometimes find Eileithyia associated with the Fates (Moirai) in childbirth (e.g., Pindar *Olympian* 6.42–4, *Nemean* 7.1–3). Finally, Archaic votive offerings to Eileithyia have been found in a number of places, such as sixth-century BCE terracotta representations of childbirth (figurines of pregnant and birthing mothers, replicas of the uterus, etc.) from Cyprus. In addition, from the sanctuary of Artemis Orthia in Sparta, archaeologists have uncovered (among other things) seventh-century BCE figurines of goddesses assisting a new mother and her baby, a bronze die with Eileithyia's name inscribed in Archaic script, and a pair of ivory figures sitting on a double throne, possibly representing Artemis Orthia and Eileithyia.

Against this background, let us look at part of Plutarch's account of Spartan birth rites, which I mentioned above:

> The women used to bathe their newborn babies not with water, but with wine, thus making a sort of test of their constitutions. For it is said that epileptic and sickly infants are thrown into convulsions by the strong wine and lose their senses, while the healthy ones are rather tempered by it, like steel, and given a firm habit of body. Their nurses, too, exercised great care and skill; they reared infants without swaddling bands (*spargana*), and thus left their limbs and figures free to develop. . . .
>
> (Plutarch *Lycurgus* 16.2–3)

There are a couple of things worth noting in this passage. First of all, Plutarch points out as strange the fact the Spartans bathed their newborns with wine. Ritual bathing with water was presumably the norm in most Archaic *poleis* (city-states), as we see, for instance, in the mythical account of Apollo's birth in the *Homeric Hymn to Apollo*: Leto's divine helpers "washed you, great Phoebus [Apollo], purely and cleanly with sweet water" (120–1). (We will see throughout this chapter that the ritual bath marked several other of the life cycle's major passages as well.) Second, the fact that babies at Sparta were not swaddled is also marked as unusual. In addition to copious Classical evidence for the practice of swaddling newborns, we can look again at the "Homeric" account of Apollo's birth, in which the goddesses "wrapped (*sparxan*) you [Apollo] in a white garment of fine texture, new-woven, and fastened a golden band about you" (121–2).

These practices of separation (delivery and umbilical cord-cutting) and transition (bathing and swaddling) were then followed by a number of rites of incorporation. In Sparta – again, a somewhat aberrant case – the baby had to be "approved" by the community before incorporation into the family and the state:

> Offspring was not reared at the will of the father, but was taken and carried by him to a place called Lesche, where the elders of the tribes officially examined the infant, and if it was well-built and sturdy, they ordered the father to rear it, and assigned it one of the nine thousand lots of land; but if it was ill-born and deformed, they sent it to the so-called Apothetae, a chasm-like place at the foot of Mount Taÿgetus,

> in the conviction that the life of that which nature had not well equipped at the very beginning for health and strength, was of no advantage either to itself or the state.
>
> (Plutarch *Lycurgus* 16.1–2)

Sparta was not the only place where infanticide was practiced – indeed, all over the Greek world, "flawed" newborns were exposed, whether because they were sickly, crippled, the "wrong" gender (female), or illegitimate – but only in Sparta (as far as we know) was exposure legally prescribed.

In Athens, and perhaps elsewhere, the first incorporation of the newborn infant into the family was effected through a ritual called the Amphidromia (literally, the "running-around"). According to later lexicographers, this rite involved someone – most often the father – carrying the baby around the domestic hearth. Although there are no mentions of the Amphidromia in Archaic Greek literature, it is possible that Demeter's placement of the baby Demophoön in the hearth (*Homeric Hymn to Demeter* 239–40) is an aetiological explanation for this rite, in which case, the rite was likely known in the Archaic period. In any event, after the baby's integration into the *oikos* (including his naming at the "tenth-day rites," the *dekate*, at least in the Classical period), he then had to be incorporated into the broader community. According to Herodotus (1.147.2), nearly all of the Ionians, including the Athenians, celebrated a yearly festival called the Apatouria in the month of Pyanepsion. Our only evidence for the details of this practice, however, comes from literary material from the Classical period. From these sources, we learn that on the third day of the festival, called the Koureotis, male offspring who had been born within the preceding year were registered in their fathers' phratries (pseudo-kinship groups; literally, "brotherhoods"), and a sacrifice called the *meion* was performed. It was at this same festival that boys were reintroduced at the age of sixteen, at which point they cut their hair as a symbolic marker of their separation from boyhood. Through this second presentation to the *phrateres* (phratry members), coupled with a second sacrifice (*koureion*) and the *phrateres*' acceptance, boys progressed toward incorporation into the *polis* as citizens; the next step involved admission to the *deme* (local unit of political subdivision) of residence. We can only guess whether all of these rituals existed already in the Archaic period, but given the festival's apparently early Ionian origins, it seems plausible that the Apatouria was itself quite old.

Initiation

The next major *rite de passage* in the Archaic Greek world, as in many societies, was the initiation of young people at puberty, a process sometimes referred to as *agoge* (literally, the "leading of a horse by one's hand"). Puberty was thought a dangerous time of life (Hippocrates, for example, believed that *parthenoi* were particularly susceptible to a number of illnesses), eased by the rituals performed either by all or more often some of the young people in a given community. These rites were quite sex-specific, as one might expect given their purpose: namely, to prepare boys and girls for their particular – and quite different – domestic and societal roles. The rites were also generally class-specific, open often only to the elite classes. This fact is significant, as it says something about the way Archaic *poleis* defined their boundaries: whereas every child obviously underwent physical puberty, many *poleis* chose to mark the *social* puberty – the incorporation into an adult community – only of their aristocratic youth.

Initiation of Boys

I will begin with an examination of initiation rites for boys, which are particularly well attested in Archaic Crete and Sparta. In both places, boys were removed from their families at a young age and grouped with their age-mates in companies called *agelai* (literally, "herds"). In Crete, we learn that when boys were still "rather young," they were brought to *syssitia* (mess-halls), where they were compelled to "sit on the ground and eat together wearing shabby clothes, the same in winter as in summer, and wait on one another as well as on the men." Their education consisted of learning their letters, the songs prescribed by law, and "certain types of music" (Ephorus FGrHist 70 F 149, quoted by Strabo 10.4.20). For Sparta, Plutarch again provides us with quite a bit of information: Boys were taken from their households by the state at age seven and provided with an education that was mostly "calculated to make them obey commands well, endure hardships, and conquer in battle"; they learned only as much reading and writing as was needed to get by. We also hear that Spartan boys kept their hair very short, generally went barefoot, were provided with minimal clothing, bathed infrequently, and slept on rough bedding (Plutarch *Lycurgus* 16.4–7).

When boys reached a prescribed age in both Crete and Sparta, rituals were held to mark their passage into puberty. One component of initiation, as in other parts of the Greek world, was a homoerotic relationship between the boy (*eromenos*; literally, "beloved") and an older male lover (*erastes*), a practice called pederasty. Archaic Greek poetry testifies to the prevalence of pederastic relationships. A fragment of Solon, for instance, reads, "until [a man] falls in love with a *pais* in the lovely flower of *hebe*, desiring thighs and a sweet mouth . . . " (fr. 25 W). Likewise, in the poetic corpus of Theognis, we find a number of erotic addresses to and encomia of boys. Thus, for example,

> there is some pleasure in loving a boy (*paidophilein*), since once in fact even the son of Cronus [Zeus], king of the immortals, fell in love with Ganymede, seized him, carried him off to Olympus, and made him divine, keeping the lovely bloom (*anthos*) of boyhood (*paideia*). So, don't be astonished, Simonides, that I too have been revealed as captivated by love for a handsome boy.
>
> (1345–50)

These poetic fragments are complemented by hundreds of representations of pederastic relationships on Archaic black-figure vases, some of which depict the *erastes* offering gifts to the boy, others overt sexual acts (see Figure 10 and, e.g., Dover's appendix of vases).

Let us turn now to Crete, where a particularly elaborate homoerotic initiation rite is attested, wherein older males ritually carried off (*harpage*) beloved boys: first,

> the *erastes* informs the friends of the *pais* three or four days beforehand that he intends to abduct him. It is most disgraceful for his friends to conceal the *pais* or to prevent him from journeying upon his appointed road, this course of action being regarded as a confession, so to speak, that the *pais* does not deserve the favors of such an *erastes*. When the encounter takes place, if the *erastes* is the boy's equal in social status (*time*) as well as in other respects, the friends pursue the *pais* and gently lay hold of him, thereby satisfying the claims of custom. But in other respects they cheerfully consent to lead him away. If he is unworthy, however, they remove him. The abduction ends when the *pais* has been brought to the men's quarters (*andreion*) of his abductor. The Cretans think a *pais* worthy of love not for his looks, but for his manliness and propriety of behavior.

> After giving the boy gifts, his abductor leads the boy off to any place in the countryside that he wishes. Those who were present when the abduction took place follow behind, and when they have feasted and hunted together for a period of two months (this being the maximum permissible period to detain the *pais*) they return to the *polis*. The boy is set free after receiving a military uniform, an ox, and a goblet, which are the gifts required by law, as well as many other costly presents, to which his friends make a contribution because of the expense involved. He then sacrifices the ox to Zeus and gives portions to those who returned with him. Afterwards he discloses details about his affair with his *erastes*, whether he derived any satisfaction from it or not, the law granting him this privilege, so that if any force was applied to him at the time of the abduction, he would be able to avenge himself on his lover on the spot and so be rid of him.
>
> It is considered a mark of disgrace for those who are handsome and have illustrious forebears not to obtain a lover, the failure to do so being judged a mark of character. But the *parastathentes*, which is the name given to those who are abducted, receive honors. In both the dances (*choroi*) and the races (*dromoi*) they have the most honored positions, and they are allowed to dress differently from all the rest, that is, in the clothes they have been given by their lovers. And not only now [i.e., when they are still young] but even when they are *teleioi* [i.e., fully adult] they wear a distinctive dress which indicates that each is regarded as "celebrated" (*kleinos*). They call the loved one "*kleinos*" or celebrated and the lover "*philetor*" or paramour.
>
> (Ephorus FGrHist 70 F 149, quoted by Strabo 10.4.21)

Thus in Crete, initiation into sexual maturity involved a two-month ritual separation of boys – specifically, boys from elite classes – from their age-mates. These boys then underwent a liminal stage in which they were geographically removed (i.e., brought to the countryside) and sexually initiated. Finally, after learning to hunt (see Figure 11) – a "wild" activity characteristic of initiation rites – and acquiring a number of gifts from their lovers, these *paides* were reincorporated into society with a new, celebrated status.

In Sparta, too, we find pederastic initiatory rites for boys approaching adolescence. Plutarch tells us that at the age of twelve, Spartan boys "were favored with the society of lovers (*erastai*) from among the reputable young men" (*Lycurgus* 17.1). A more egalitarian society than that found on Crete, Sparta apparently had all of its boys participate in pederastic relationships. Moreover,

> the boys' *erastai* also shared with them in their honor or disgrace; and it is said that one of them was once fined by the magistrates because his favorite boy had let an ungenerous cry escape him while he was fighting. Moreover, though this sort of love was so approved among them that even the *parthenoi* found lovers in good and noble women (*gynaikes*), still, there was no jealous rivalry in it, but those who fixed their affections on the same boys made this rather a foundation for friendship with one another, and persevered in common efforts to make their *eromenos* as noble as possible.
>
> (Plutarch *Lycurgus* 18.4)

Spartan boys' separation from the community – a lengthier one than we find in the Cretan ritual – came later, with their service in the *krypteia*, a sort of "secret police" force. Apparently not all young men took part in this service: according to Plutarch, only the "most astute" Spartans were chosen (*Lycurgus* 28.2). During their period of *krypteia* service, young men were isolated from society from age 17 to 19, relegated to the edges of the Spartan territory where, living hand to mouth, they policed the Helots (the enslaved population inhabiting Messenia). After these two years of "wildness," they were then ritually reincorporated into society – perhaps at a festival called the Hyakinthia – as proper hoplite-citizens. We might compare the *ephebeia*, an Athenian institution not formally instituted until the Classical period.

Initiation of Girls

And what about initiation rites for girls? In his work *Choruses of Young Women in Ancient Greece*, Claude Calame demonstrates that girls' initiation rites in Archaic and Classical Greece generally involved performances by choruses of age-mates. Scholars debate the precise function of these choral performances, but at the very least we might agree that the choruses served both to educate the girls and to integrate them into society as *nymphai*. As with the initiation of boys, it appears that the rites were not open to *all* girls, but were generally restricted to girls from elite families.

From the Archaic period, we find both iconographic representations of girls' choral performances (see Figure 12) and maiden-songs (*partheneia*), particularly from Sparta and possibly from Lesbos. Thus, for example, in a *partheneion* composed by the seventh-century BCE Spartan poet Alcman, a chorus of ten girls sings:

> And so I sing of the brightness of Agido: I see her like the sun, which Agido summons to shine on us as our witness; but our illustrious chorus-leader (*choragos*) [Hagesichora] by no means allows me either to praise or to fault her [Agido]; for she herself seems preeminent, just as if one were to put a horse among grazing herds, a sturdy, thunderous-hoofed prize winner, one of those seen in rock-sheltered dreams. . . .
>
> (fr. 1.39–48)

The chorus-leader Hagesichora is thus compared to a horse, the most beautiful and the fastest; next in beauty and speed is a girl named Agido, called a "race horse"; and Agido is in turn followed by other girls in the chorus (fr. 1.50–59). Such imagery of horses is found often in Archaic lyric poetry to refer metaphorically to the yoking and taming of young people. Allusion is also made in these lines to racing contests, which apparently formed a part of many choral ritual performances (see below on the Brauronia). Finally, we might note the degree to which the girls praise their leader's beauty: for instance,

> nor will you go to Aenesimbrota's and say, "If only Astaphis were mine, if only Philylla were to look my way and Damareta and lovely Ianthemis"; no, Hagesichora guards me [or wears me out (with love)]. For is not fair-ankled Hagesichora present here?
>
> (fr. 1.73–9)

Moreover, this praise, as well as the hypothetical desire to "possess" the other girls in the chorus (e.g., Astaphis, Philylla, Damareta, Ianthemis), is noticeably sexually charged; I will return to the homoerotic elements of female initiation rites in a moment.

As for girls' initiatory rites on Lesbos, scholars have interpreted some of the fragments of Sappho (late seventh/early sixth century BCE) as being performed by or with the help of choruses (see Chapter 6). An example of a possible choral song is Sappho's fr. 94 LP:

> . . . and honestly I wish I were dead. She was leaving me with many tears and said this: "Oh what luck has been ours,

> Sappho; truly I leave you against my will." I replied to her thus: "Go and fare well and remember me, for you know how we cared for you. If not, why then I want to remind you . . . and the good times we had. You put on many wreaths of violets and roses and (crocuses?) together by my side, and round your tender neck you put many woven garlands made from flowers and . . . with much flowery perfume, fit for a queen, you anointed yourself . . . and on soft beds . . . you would satisfy your longing (for?) tender. . . . There was neither . . . nor shrine . . . from which we were absent, no grove . . . nor dance . . . sound.
>
> (fr. 94 LP)

This may or may not be a *partheneion*, but one scholar points out that the particular activities mentioned – weaving garlands, going to holy places, dancing, and so forth – represent choral activities. Moreover, the use of the first-person plural (especially "*we* cared for you") indicates a group, not merely the poet and her addressee. (If so, the addressee is presumably a girl who has departed the choral group in order to marry.) And what about the elements of female homoeroticism underlying both Sappho's poems and Alcman's *partheneia*? This has long been a subject of debate: Some scholars believe that the desire expressed in these songs was indeed physically consummated (on "soft beds"?; see also Plutach's *Lycurgus* 18.4, above) – although perhaps only some of the girls had a sexual relationship with the chorus-leader (cf. the Cretan male initiatory practice). Other scholars, by contrast, deny that the poems tell us anything about the performance of female homoerotic acts. For our purposes, it is less important to determine whether acts actually took place than to note that elements of same-sex desire were incorporated into female initiatory rites.

For comparable rites in Archaic Attica, we have the most evidence for a festival called the Brauronia. In Aristophanes' *Lysistrata*, a chorus of women boasts of having been bears (*arktoi*) at the festival of Artemis Brauronia (line 645). But what does it mean to have been a "bear"? The "Suda" (Suidas), a tenth-century CE Byzantine encyclopedia, explains the festival practices thus:

> Women doing the bear ritual (*arkteuomenai*) used to perform a festival for Artemis, dressed in the *krokotos* (saffron robe), neither older than 10 nor younger than 5, placating the goddess. For there was a wild bear roaming the *deme* Philaidai,

> and it was tamed and lived with men. But a *parthenos* poked fun at it, and because of her insolence the bear was provoked and scratched her. Her brothers, angered by this, shot the bear, and as a result of this a plague befell the Athenians. The Athenians consulted an oracle and it said that there would be a release from their woes if, as penalty for killing the bear, they compelled their *parthenoi* to do the bear ritual. And the Athenians voted that no *parthenos* should be married to a man without first performing the bear ritual to the goddess.

The Suda entry notwithstanding, most scholars believe that not all but only a selective sample of Athenian girls became "bears," in which case, these *parthenoi*, likely culled from the elite classes, enacted a puberty ritual on behalf of all girls of the city. As such, they underwent a transitional period of "wildness" (cf. the boys' initiation rites in Crete and Sparta), after which they could be reintroduced to society as tame *nymphai*.

Our mostly Classical (and later) literary evidence for this rite is complemented by archaeological evidence dating to the Archaic period. For instance, excavation at Brauron has yielded a temple of Artemis (dated to ca. 500 BCE) near the "tomb of Iphigeneia"; in addition, an inscription naming a *parthenon* ("room of the maiden[s]") has been uncovered at the site, perhaps indicating a dormitory for the girl-bears (where they stayed during their period of separation). Moreover, spinning and weaving implements have been found in situ, as well as *krateriskoi* (miniature mixing bowls) dating from the late sixth and the first half of the fifth century BCE. Many of these *krateriskoi* depict girls variously dancing to *aulos*-players (seemingly in choral performance), progressing toward altars, holding garlands, sacrificing goats, and sometimes running races (cf. Alcman fr. 1). The girls are shown wearing either the *chiton* (a short undergarment) or nothing at all – the latter perhaps representing their state when the *krokotos* had been shed upon reincorporation into the community, to be put back on at marriage.

MARRIAGE

This brings us to the next major rite of passage, marriage, which was particularly fraught on all of the levels we have already discussed: those of the individual, the family, and the society. Thus the bride experienced a significant change in status, particularly upon the birth of her first child; each household lost or was forced to incorporate a new member; and the community as a whole shifted its notions of the connectedness of particular *oikoi*. The multiple rites of incorporation – detailed below – as well as the invocation of particular gods (e.g., Hymen) helped to ease this passage.

Let us begin with the question of age at marriage, which varied throughout the Archaic Greek world. Thus Hesiod gives the following advice:

> Bring home a wife to your house when you are of the right age (*horaios*), while you are not far short of thirty years nor much above; this is the right age (*horios*) for marriage. Let your wife be four years past puberty (*heboöi*), and marry her in the fifth. Marry a *parthenike* so that you can teach her careful ways, and especially marry one who lives near you, but look well about you and see that your marriage will not be a joke to your neighbors.
>
> (*Works and Days* 695–9)

According to Solon, "in the fifth [hebdomad; i.e., ages 27–34] it is time for a man to be mindful of marriage and to look for a line of sons to come after him" (27.9–10). Solon does not, however, specify an age for the bride. In Crete, all boys of a particular *agele* apparently married at the same time, at an age unspecified in our sources (Ephorus FGrHist 70 F 149, quoted by Strabo 10.4.20). The Gortyn law code (also from Crete), inscribed in the fifth century BCE but dating back at least in part to the seventh century, specifies only that an heiress (*patroïokos*) should marry "when twelve years of age or older" (*Inscriptiones Creticae* 4.72 xii 17–19). Finally, in Sparta, we hear that the legendary lawgiver Lycurgus "withdrew from men the right to take a wife whenever they chose, and insisted on their marrying in the prime (*en akmais*) of their bodies, believing that this too promoted the production of fine children"; but if a man did not wish to marry, he could select a *gyne* to bear his children, provided that he obtain her husband's consent (Xenophon *Constitution of the Lacedaemonians* 1.6, 8). Spartan women were to marry "not when they were small and underage (*aoroi*) for wedlock, but when they were in full bloom (*akmazousai*) and wholly ripe (*pepeiroi*)" (Plutarch *Lycurgus* 15.3).

For the nature of marriage rites in the Archaic period, we might start by looking at Homeric practice. In both the *Iliad* and *Odyssey*, we find solely aristocratic families forming alliances through the marriage of their children, with *nymphai* "exchanged" for *hedna* (bride-wealth). So, for example, in the *Odyssey*, a certain Amphinomus, one of Penelope's many suitors, says, "Let each man from his own palace woo her with *hedna* and seek to win her; and she then would wed him who offers most, and who comes as her fated bridegroom" (*Odyssey* 390–2). This institution most certainly continued among aristocrats in the Archaic period; but it was accompanied, at least from the sixth century on (and probably earlier), by the form of marriage we recognize from our Classical sources: namely, betrothal (*engue*) and the handing over (*ekdosis*) of the bride with dowry (*proix*). As early as Homer, we find instances of fathers promising their daughters to prospective grooms (if not with formal *engue*). Thus, in the *Odyssey*, Menelaus sends his daughter to marry Neoptolemus, in fulfillment of a promise he had made at Troy (4.5–7). Formal betrothal in the Archaic and Classical periods, on the other hand, was – at least among the elite – a public event at which an arrangement was made between the father and future son-in-law. Often this took place at a banquet, as for example in this ode of Pindar:

> a man takes from his rich hand a bowl foaming inside with dew of the vine and presents it to his young son-in-law (*gambros*) with a toast from one home to another – an all-golden bowl, crown of possessions – as he honors the joy of the symposium and his own alliance, and thereby with his friends present makes him envied for his harmonious (*homophronos*) marriage. . . .
>
> (Pindar *Olympian* 7.1–6)

We find another example of *engue* as early as ca. 575 BCE, when Cleisthenes of Sicyon betroths (*enguo*) his daughter to a man "in accordance with Athenian law" (Herodotus 6.130). Perhaps it was Solon who established this law on betrothal in Athens – we can only speculate – but in any case, the *engue* represented the beginning of the girl's separation from her natal *oikos*, after which she remained in a state of transition until marriage.

In Athens, the institution of the dowry may also have arisen through, or around the same time as, the legislation of Solon. All we hear, however, is that Solon limited the extravagance of the trousseau (*pherne*) the bride brought with her in marriage:

> the bride was to bring with her three changes of clothing, household stuff of small value, and nothing else. For [Solon] did not wish that marriage (*gamos*) should be a matter of

> profit or price, but that man and wife should dwell together for the delights of love and the getting of children.
>
> (Plutarch *Solon* 20.4)

From what we can tell, the *gamos* itself was a multistep ritual. In a preliminary rite (referred to as the *proteleia* or *progameia*), sacrifices were made and *nymphai* cut off their hair, dedicating it to Artemis and the Fates (cf. the boys' hair-cutting at the Koureotis). Our evidence for these preliminary rites is admittedly Classical or later (e.g., Greek tragedy and the lexicographer Pollux), but the practices may well date back to the Archaic period. The bride then took a bath in holy water (*loutra*) brought to her by her attendants, an event we find depicted particularly on *loutrophoroi* (*loutra*-carriers). (The *loutrophoros* was also used to carry the water for cleansing corpses. Cf. Figure 14 in *Death.*) Among the votive offerings presumably of new brides, found at a cave sacred to the Nymphs in East Attica, are a number of miniature *loutrophoroi*, some of which are of Archaic date.

After her ritual bath, the bride was then veiled and ritually transported to the groom's house in a torch-lit procession. This is in fact the part of the *gamos* most frequently depicted on black-figure vases (see Figure 13). Most likely, the procession was accompanied by the singing of marriage hymns (*epithalamia*) in honor of the god Hymen (e.g., Homer *Iliad* 18.493), for instance of the sort we find in Sappho: "On high the roof – Hymenaeus! – raise up, you carpenters – Hymenaeus! The bridegroom is coming, the equal of Ares, much larger than a large man" (Sappho fr. 111 LP). *Epithalamia* may also have been sung in or around the wedding chamber, as for example this fragment addressing a groom:

> Happy bridegroom, your marriage has been fulfilled as you prayed, you have the *parthenos* for whom you prayed. . . .
> Your form is graceful, your eyes . . . gentle, and love streams over your beautiful face. . . . Aphrodite has honored you outstandingly.
>
> (Sappho fr. 112 LP)

Hymns were sung for (or by?) the *nymphe* as well, as in this possible choral song: "'Virginity (*parthenia*), virginity, where have you gone, deserting me?' 'Never again shall I come to you, never again shall I come'" (Sappho fr. 114 LP).

Upon arrival at the groom's house – at least in the Classical period; evidence is scarce for the Archaic period – the bride was sprinkled with nuts and dried fruits (*katachysmata*) at the hearth (the same way a new slave was introduced to the *oikos*); and at some point thereafter she lifted her veil, a practice referred to as the *anakalypteria*. The groom then led the bride to the wedding chamber, outside of which a doorkeeper was placed (to ensure the consummation of the marriage?). One of Sappho's *epithalamia* refers to a particularly intimidating (or perhaps just oafish) guard, whose "feet are seven fathoms long, and his sandals are made from five ox-hides; ten cobblers worked hard to make them" (fr. 110 LP). The consummation was followed by a feast called the *epaulia*, depicted on vases especially at the end of the fifth and beginning of the fourth centuries BCE. At some point in the betrothal/marriage process – at least in Classical Athens, but perhaps earlier and elsewhere as well – the groom introduced his new bride to his phratry (at the Apatouria), at which point she was incorporated into the broader community.

The *gamos* practices I have outlined thus far represent the norm, from which variants were possible. In Sparta, for example, the *nymphe* was ritually carried off "by force" (*harpage*), although this abduction was presumably staged (cf. the Cretan male initiatory rite). Next,

> after the woman was thus carried off, the bridesmaid (*nympheuteria*), so called, took her in charge, cut her hair off close to the head, put a man's cloak and sandals on her, and laid her down on a pallet, on the floor, alone, in the dark. Then the bridegroom, not flown with wine nor enfeebled by excesses, but composed and sober, after dining at his public mess-table as usual, slipped stealthily into the room where the bride lay, loosed her girdle, and bore her in his arms to the marriage bed. Then, after spending a short time with his bride, he went away composedly to his usual quarters, there to sleep with the other young men. And so he continued to do from that time on, spending his days with his comrades, and sleeping with them at night, but visiting his bride by stealth and with every precaution, full of dread lest any of her household should be aware of his visits, his bride also contriving and conspiring that they might have secret rendezvous as occasion offered. And this they did not for a short time only, but long enough for some of them to become fathers before they had looked upon their own wives by daylight. Such rendezvous not only brought into exercise self-restraint and moderation, but united husbands and wives when their bodies were full of creative energy and

> their affections new and fresh, not when they were sated and dulled by unrestricted intercourse; and there was always left behind in their hearts some residual spark of mutual longing and delight.
>
> (Plutarch *Lycurgus* 15.3–5)

In Sparta, then, if we are to trust Plutarch's account, separation from the *oikos* was expressed as overt abduction; and during the bride's period of transition, she radically abandoned her *parthenia* by shedding the trappings of girlhood, even temporarily becoming a "man." Incorporation into her new status as *gyne* was then only gradually effected, by means of nocturnal "visits" from her new husband.

Death

Finally, death: quite obviously, it was the last rite of passage, removing the deceased from his family and community once and for all. Although death was, like all transitions in the life cycle, a source of some anxiety, most scholars agree that the Greeks of the Archaic and Classical periods considered death a necessary evil; in the words of the seventh-century BCE poet Callinus, "it is in no way fated that a man escape death" (fr. 1.12–13). Death was therefore "tame" – in the words of Philippe Ariès, a French medievalist and social historian – an accepted, rather than feared, part of the life cycle. We do, however, see a diachronic shift in how the "good death" was defined: Thus, in Homer, a good death was one that brought *kleos*, an aristocratic value entailing individual glory and survival in men's memory (see, e.g., Homer *Iliad* 22.71–3). With the rise of the *polis* in the Archaic period, a good death was defined rather in terms of civic service: it was now "a fine thing (*kalon*) for a brave man to die when he has fallen among the front ranks while fighting *for his homeland*" (Tyrtaeus fr. 10.1–2; my emphasis). And indeed, this is a notion that continued well into the Classical period (see, e.g., Herodotus 1.30–1 and Thucydides 2.42–6).

Let us turn now to the rituals performed on behalf of the deceased. In Archaic (and Classical) Greece, the "separation stage" of death consisted of three main steps: the *prothesis* (laying out of the corpse), the *ekphora* (carrying out of the corpse to the burial site), and the deposition. Much of our evidence for the first two practices comes from vase paintings; in fact, mourning for the dead is the only subject we find continuously represented in iconography from the Geometric period (ca. 900–700 BCE) to the Peloponnesian War. For deposition of the corpse, archaeological evidence is particularly useful.

After someone died, it was customary first to close his eyes and mouth (e.g., Homer *Iliad* 11.452–3, *Odyssey* 11.425–6 and 24.296). The women of the household then ritually bathed the corpse, clothed it, and laid it out on a bed (*kline*) with its feet facing the door (e.g., Homer *Iliad* 19.212). Perhaps an obol was placed in the corpse's mouth, understood to be the toll to cross the river Styx in Hades (but this is not attested literarily until Aristophanes, and there is no archaeological evidence until the Hellenistic period). Female family members – sometimes along with hired mourners – emitted wails (*gooi*) and sang dirges (*threnoi*) over the corpse; in a Homeric scene, those who

> had brought [Hector] to the glorious house set . . . by his side singers (*aoidoi*), leaders of the dirge (*threnoi*), who led the song of lamentation – they chanted the dirges and to it the woman added their laments (*stenachonto*). And among these white-armed Andromache led the wailing (*goos*), holding in her hands the head of man-slaying Hector.
>
> (*Iliad* 24.719–24)

A similar depiction of the "heroic" *prothesis*, complete with lavish displays of mourning, is found also in Geometric vase paintings.

In the early sixth century BCE, however, Solon passed legislation restricting the extravagance of funerals. Athens was not alone in implementing such laws: we find parallels in Archaic Gortyn, Mytilene, and Sparta. Among other things, this legislation attempted to curb ostentatious displays of wealth by aristocratic families, thereby easing competitive tensions within the community. Although Solon's laws ordained that "the deceased shall be laid out (*protithesthai*) in the house in any way one chooses" (pseudo-Demosthenes 43.62), the laws did in fact limit lamentation: "Laceration of the flesh by mourners, and the use of set lamentations, and the bewailing of anyone at the funeral ceremonies of another, [Solon] forbade" (Plutarch *Solon* 21.4). Despite this ordinance, scenes of *prothesis* in Archaic art – generally depicted on *pinakes* (plaques) and *loutrophoroi* – continue to show people (albeit fewer in number) tearing their hair and cheeks in mourning (Figure 14). We cannot tell whether these depictions reflect actual Archaic practice, or whether the representations simply hearken back to a Homeric model.

Next, on the day following the *prothesis*, the corpse was carried out for burial. An elaborate *ekphora* – that for Patroklos – is described in Homer thus:

> Achilles immediately ordered the war-loving Myrmidons to gird on their bronze, and yoke each man his horses to his chariot. And they rose and put on their armor and mounted their chariots, warriors and charioteers alike. In front were the men in chariots, and after them followed a cloud of foot soldiers, men past counting, and in their midst his comrades carried Patroklos. And as if with a garment they wholly covered the corpse with their hair that they cut off and cast on it; and behind them noble Achilles clasped the head, sorrowing.
>
> (*Iliad* 23.128–37)

Similar processions are depicted in Geometric art, but rarely appear in iconographic representations (at least from Athens) after the early sixth century. This may be due again to Solon's funerary legislation, which aimed in part to lessen the disorder and disruption caused by *ekphorai*: mourners, he ordained,

> shall carry out (*ekpherein*) the deceased on the day after that on which they lay him out, before the sun rises. And the men shall walk in front, when they carry him out, and the women behind. And no woman less than sixty years of age shall be permitted to enter the chamber of the deceased, or to follow the deceased when he is carried to the tomb, except those who are within the degree of children of cousins; nor shall any woman be permitted to enter the chamber of the deceased when the body is carried out, except those who are within the degree of children of cousins.
>
> (pseudo-Demosthenes 43.62)

Before this legislation, we should suppose that the *ekphora* was considerably more visible and public, presumably taking place during the daytime and attended by large numbers of people.

Finally, after the procession to the gravesite, the corpse was either inhumed or cremated. The beginning of the Archaic period saw a number of changes in burial procedure: Thus, for instance, around 750 BCE, the Greeks began to bury their adult dead extramurally, instead of within city walls as before, perhaps due to shifting notions of pollution (*miasma*);

the few exceptions included "special" burials (e.g., tombs of heroes and the public memorials of war dead) and burials at Sparta. Second, beginning in the eighth century BCE, the archaeological record demonstrates a huge increase in the number of graves. According to Ian Morris, this was due not to a huge population explosion but to a change in practice: it was no longer simply the elite classes who were being buried. This is a manifestation of a broader trend in the Archaic period, namely, an expansion of community boundaries to include nonaristocrats. Moreover, around 700 BCE, we see a sharp decline in the quality and extravagance of grave goods. These latter two changes were likely the product of a burgeoning egalitarian ideology, just like the funerary laws discussed above, as well as later legislation regulating tomb size, types of eulogies on behalf of the deceased, and number of visitors to the tomb (Cicero *Laws* 2.64–5). Finally, by the beginning of the Classical period (ca. 490–80 BCE), inscribed stone slabs (*stelai*) and funerary statues (*kouroi* and *korai*) – common markers of elite graves in the Archaic period – ceased being produced altogether (at least in Athens), probably for similar reasons.

In any event, burial of the corpse was considered extremely important (see, e.g., Homer and Greek tragedy) because it was thought to facilitate the passage of the deceased's soul into the next world. This was, however, a slow transition. For a certain period of time after deposition, the deceased was thought still to be present – at least in some sense – at his tomb. During the Classical period and perhaps earlier, family members held a funerary meal (*perideipnon*) soon after the deposition (e.g., *Iliad* 24.802), at which the deceased "presided." They also offered him rites on the third and ninth days (*trita* and *ennata*, respectively) after either death or burial. Exactly what these rites entailed is unclear, but we have archaeological evidence – from both the Archaic and Classical periods – of trenches for burnt offerings in the Ceramicus (the cemetery in Athens).

And what happened once the deceased's soul made its passage to the underworld? Our sources offer varying – and sometimes conflicting – views on this subject, reflecting the diversity of opinions about the afterlife in the Archaic Greek world. Thus, as one example, an early fifth-century BCE ode of Pindar, perhaps informed by Pythagorean or Orphic beliefs, states that

> the helpless spirits of those who have died on earth immediately pay the penalty [in Hades] – and upon sins committed here in

> Zeus' realm, a judge beneath the earth pronounces sentence with hateful necessity; but forever having sunshine in equal nights and in equal days, good men receive a life of less toil, for they do not vex the earth or the water of the sea with the strength of their hands to earn a paltry living. No, in company with the honored gods, those who joyfully kept their oaths spend a tearless existence, whereas the others endure pain too terrible to behold. . . .
>
> (Pindar *Olympian* 2.57–67)

The poem continues with a description of the triple reincarnation of the soul. For our purposes, I will focus here only on the above-cited lines, which indicate that the souls of "good men" were rewarded in Hades. (A similarly positive fate was thought to await the initiates into certain mystery cults; indeed, "happy is he among men who has seen [the Eleusinian Mysteries]; but he who is uninitiated and who has no part in them never has a similar lot of good things once he is dead, down in the darkness and gloom" [*Hymn to Demeter* 480–2].) Among those who "committed sins" on earth and were punished upon their deaths, perhaps the most famous are Tityus, Sisyphus, and Tantalus (e.g., Homer *Odyssey* 11. 576–600). We might contrast this Pindaric account with Homer's *Nekyia* (Book 11, *Odyssey*), in which the majority of the dead are neither punished nor rewarded, but instead face a relatively nondescript existence in the underworld.

After the soul was thought to reach its destination, the family members of the deceased, having undergone their own rites of separation and transition (e.g., mourning), were themselves reincorporated into "normal" society. And from that point on, the deceased was officially commemorated only once a year – at the Genesia. The lexicographer Hesychius refers to the Genesia as an "Athenian festival of mourning," although according to Herodotus it was known to all the Greeks (4.26). In any case, it was likely Solon's legislation that restricted this commemoration, at least in Athens, to a once-yearly event. Visits to the tomb nonetheless took place at unregulated times as well, just as in our day. The best evidence for this comes from the (primarily Classical) white-ground *lekythoi* (flasks) deposited at gravesites, which were used for making liquid offerings (wine, water, honey, milk, etc.) to the deceased, and which frequently depict mourners visiting the tomb. Through all of these assorted rituals, family members thus marked and facilitated the passage of a member of their *oikos* from life to death.

Conclusions

These, then, were the rites of passage in the Archaic Greek life cycle. We have noticed the division of these rites into ritualized stages of separation (e.g., having the umbilical cord cut, being physically removed from the natal *oikos*), transition (e.g., performing "wild" behavior, cutting one's hair, wearing special garments), and (re)incorporation (e.g., being celebrated at a household feast or public festival). Birth and death were probably the passages of greatest unease for the *oikos* and the broader community – possibly because, as Robert Parker has suggested, they represented events completely beyond human control. (So too was physical puberty, of course; but the rites I discuss above focus rather on the passage to social puberty.) By means of a defined set of cleansing rituals – bathing the newborn, washing the corpse, purifying the house, and so forth – the Greeks attempted to rein in the perceived *miasma* that these "uncontrollable" events generated. In the rest of the life cycle, too, it was ritual practices – accompanied, significantly, by the assistance of specialized deities (e.g., Eileithyia, Artemis, Hymen) – that helped to ease the difficult passage from one status to another.

Note

1 Translations of literary texts are adapted from the Loeb Classical Library (except of Ephorus, from Garland 1990); translations of the lexicographers are my own. I thank Leslie Kurke and Alan Shapiro for useful comments and assistance on this chapter.

Bibliography and Suggested Readings

General Works

Garland, R. 1990. *The Greek Way of Life.*

Patterson, C. 1998. *The Family in Greek History.*

van Gennep, A. 1960 [1909]. *The Rites of Passage.* Transls. M. B. Vizedom and G. L. Caffee.

Birth

Golden, M. 1990. *Children and Childhood in Classical Athens.*

Neils, J. and J. H. Oakley, eds. 2003. *Coming of Age in Ancient Greece: Images of Childhood from the Classical Past.*

Price, T. H. 1978. *Kourotrophos: Cults and Representations of the Greek Nursing Deities.*

Initiation

Calame, C. 1997 [1977]. *Choruses of Young Women in Ancient Greece: Their Morphology, Religious Role, and Social Function.* Trans. D. Collins and J. Orion.

Cole, S. G. 1984. "The Social Function of Rituals of Maturation: The Koureion and the Arkteia." *Zeitschrift für Papyrologie und Epigraphik* 55: 233–44.

Dover, K. J. 1978. *Greek Homosexuality.*

Dowden, K. 1989. *Death and the Maiden: Girls' Initiation Rites in Greek Mythology.*

Greene, E., ed. 1996. *Reading Sappho: Contemporary Approaches.*

King, H. 1993 [1983]. "Bound to Bleed: Artemis and Greek Women." In *Images of Women in Antiquity.* Eds. A. Cameron and A. Kuhrt. 109–27.

Sissa, G. 1990. *Greek Virginity.* Transl. A. Goldhammer.

Sourvinou-Inwood, C. 1988. *Studies in Girls' Transitions: Aspects of the Arkteia and Age Representation in Attic Iconography.*

Vidal-Naquet, P. 1981. "The Black Hunter and the Origin of the Athenian *ephebeia.*" In Myth, Religion and Society. Ed. R. L. Gordon. 147–62.

Marriage

Carson, A. 1990. "Putting Her in Her Place: Woman, Dirt, and Desire." In *Before Sexuality: The Construction of Erotic Experience in the Ancient Greek World.* Eds. D. M. Halperin, J. J. Winkler, and F. I. Zeitlin. 135–69.

Finley, M. I. 1981 [1954]. "Marriage, Sale and Gift in the Homeric World." In *Economy and Society in Ancient Greece.* Eds. B. D. Shaw and R. P. Saller. 233–45.

Morris, I. 1986. "The Use and Abuse of Homer." *Classical Antiquity* 5: 81–138.

Oakley, J. H. and R. H. Sinos. 1993. *The Wedding in Ancient Athens.*

Vérilhac, A.-M. and C. Vial. 1998. *Le mariage grec du VIe siècle avant J.-C. à l'époque d'Auguste. Bulletin de correspondance hellenique* Supplement 32.

Vernant, J.-P. 1990. Myth and Society in Ancient Greece. Transl. J. Lloyd. New York.

Death

Ariès, P. 1974. *Western Attitudes toward Death: From the Middle Ages to the Present.*

Garland, R. 1985. *The Greek Way of Death.*

Garland, R. 1989. "The Well-Ordered Corpse: An Investigation into the Motives Behind Greek Funerary Legislation." *Bulletin of the Institute of Classical Studies* 36: 1–15.

Kurtz, D. C. and J. Boardman. 1971. *Greek Burial Customs.*

Morris, I. 1989. "Attitudes toward Death in Archaic Greece." *Classical Antiquity* 8: 296–320.

Oakley, J. H. 2004. *Picturing Death in Classical Athens: The Evidence of the White Lekythoi.*

Parker, R. 1990 [1983]. *Miasma: Pollution and Purification in Early Greek Religion.*

Shapiro, H. A. 1991. "The Iconography of Mourning in Athenian Art." *American Journal of Archaeology* 95: 629–56.

Sourvinou-Inwood, C. 1996. *"Reading" Greek Death.*

Vermeule, E. 1979. *Aspects of Death in Early Greek Art and Poetry.*

Part Two

LITERATURE AND PHILOSOPHY

5: Homer, Hesiod, and the Epic Tradition

Jonathan L. Ready

A series of Greek vase paintings dating from 670 to 625 BCE depict up to five men blinding another figure with an elongated, pole-like object (see Figure 15). These vases have been thought to represent Odysseus' wounding of the drunken Cyclops, Polyphemus, as recounted by Odysseus himself in the *Odyssey* (9.105–566). Such an interpretation depends upon understanding the *Odyssey* to have been composed sometime before the first of these vase paintings and to have influenced artists soon after its appearance. Indeed, it is hard to overstate the importance of not only the Homeric but also the Hesiodic poems to the ancient world. Herodotus claimed the two taught the Greeks about their gods (2.53), and Homeric poetry became fundamental to Greek and Roman education. It was only natural that in order to examine the history of Rome and the domestic policies of the emperor Augustus, Virgil rewrote the stories of Achilles, Hector, and Odysseus. The popularity of the poems has hardly waned since then. In *Omeros* (1990), Derek Walcott explores the postcolonial Caribbean through the lens of Homeric epic. The narrators of Margaret Atwood's *Penelopiad* (2005) are Penelope and the maids whom Odysseus has killed after he dispatches the suitors (*Odyssey* 22.437–73). Yet despite all the attention lavished on the poems since antiquity they are far from known quantities. Let us return to Odysseus and the Cyclops.

In his version of the tale Odysseus emerges as a resourceful leader without whose specific brand of cunning his men would have perished. By contrast, only a few of the extant vases distinguish one of the blinders from the others. Is this an oblique comment on the nature of heroism? Perhaps the other painters did not think it necessary to distinguish Odysseus from his peers. His individual genius was less important than the fact that it took a group of men to blind the monstrous Polyphemus. Or perhaps the vases do not represent the scene from the *Odyssey* at all, but rather a traditional story about the blinding of an ogre.[1] Connecting the vase paintings with this folktale tradition instead of with a specific episode in the *Odyssey* reminds us that the Polyphemus episode in the *Odyssey* is itself indebted to other stories about the blinding of an ogre or other versions of a meeting between Odysseus and Polyphemus. If one favors, then, the identification of the vases with the Polyphemus episode in the *Odyssey*, questions arise about the relationship of the individual to the group. And if one prefers to challenge that identification, questions arise about the individual Homeric poems' relationships to the traditions that precede and inform them.

This essay will explore these sorts of questions about the relationships of the individual to the group in the poetry of Homer and Hesiod. Were these poets living and breathing individuals? How can Homeric and Hesiodic poetry's traditional components, passed down over countless generations, be seen to produce meaning in special ways? How do the trained oral poet's language and compositional techniques compare with those used by speakers in everyday situations? How estranged or distinct from their communities are Homer's Achilles and Odysseus? How does Hesiod's Zeus emerge as an all-powerful king by suppressing divine and cosmic forces that threaten him? How does Hesiod's *Works and Days* examine the communal value of justice by focusing on the personal matter of feeding oneself?[2]

Homeric Performance and Homeric Questions

Like other forms of poetry in ancient Greece, the Homeric epics were publicly performed.[3] A professional entertainer called a bard or a rhapsode would sing or recite these stories of gods and heroes. The *Odyssey* self-referentially presents two bards, Phemius on Ithaca and Demodocus on Scheria, who sing to the assembled members of an aristocratic household about the trials of the Trojans and Achaeans. The historical accuracy of such a portrait is less relevant than its insistence on a public performance context. In Plato's *Ion* the rhapsode Ion discusses the performance of his craft in the fifth and fourth centuries. He competes against other rhapsodes in reciting selections from the poems at festivals throughout Greece and the surrounding Mediterranean world. Other evidence concerns the competitive performance of the Homeric poems at the Great Panathenaic festival in Athens. The exact mechanisms of this poetic competition are unclear, with scholarly attention focusing on the "Panathenaic rule" whereby successive singers presented episodes from the *Iliad* or *Odyssey* in order.

In contrast to some lyric poetry (see Chapter 6), the epics were performed by men and depict epic performance as properly a male concern. Achilles sings to pass the time (*Iliad* 9.185–9), and the professional singers in the epics are male. The *Odyssey* casts female singers as threats to the hero: the sorceress Circe sings as she weaves (*Odyssey* 10.254–5); the Sirens enchant by singing about the adventures of the Trojans and Achaeans (*Odyssey* 12.182–92). In both epics the mortal female character consistently associated with song and authoritative speech is the troubling Helen. Furthermore, the poems not only deal with male heroes and with women only in relation to men but also align the narrator's voice with that of the male lead. Thus Odysseus acts as poet in narrating his adventures in books 9–12 of the *Odyssey*; his host Alcinous explicitly compares him to a bard (*Odyssey* 11.363–9). Richard Martin argues that the *Iliad* poet equates his own manipulations of Homeric speech with Achilles'. A bard can even be associated with a desire for *kleos* (glory), the goal of the epic hero himself.[4] Finally, I note Eva Stehle's examination of how a singer can authorize himself by claiming a "mobile" and/or "elevated," and so male, perspective in opposition to a "local" female perspective.[5] Given this backdrop, when Penelope comes downstairs to complain that Phemius' song about the Achaeans depresses her, Telemachus' response makes sense. He sends her away with a sharp retort: men will decide on the song to be sung (*Odyssey* 1.328–62). This characterization persists. Using epic phrasing, the chorus of Corinthian women in Euripides' *Medea* laments their exclusion from the performance of epic: "For Phoebus, the leader of songs, did not put in our mind the god-inspired song accompanied by the lyre. Since [if he had] I would have sung in opposition to the race of men" (424–9).[6]

Other generic features signaled a performance of Homeric epic. The poetry is in a meter called dactylic hexameter, most likely derived from joining or expanding the lyric meters that only appear to us in Greek poetry of the seventh and sixth centuries. Homeric poetry employs a *Kunstsprache*, or artificial epic dialect, made up primarily of Ionic and Aeolic forms and never spoken in daily conversation. The poems' monumental size reflects a brand of expansive composition distinct from the compositional practices of other epic traditions, such as the poems that have come down to us as the Epic Cycle or the songs of Hesiod. A related phenomenon is the poems' encompassing other genres of poetry, such as catalogs and laments. Finally, the epics are "Panhellenic," or at least "inter-communal."[7] Details related to local traditions or cults are absent. This practice distinguishes the epics from, say, local genealogical and *ktisis* (foundation) poetry (on which see Chapter 8) as well as epics oriented toward a particular audience, such as the *Thebaid*.

An ancient audience would have been attuned to these generic features and also comfortable with a facet of the poetry most challenging for today's readers – repetition. Individual epithets are repeated: Athena is gray-eyed and Achilles swift-footed; Hector often has a shining helmet. Whole lines or stretches of lines are repeated when, for instance, one character begins to speak to another ("he patted her with his hand and spoke a word and called her by name") or when a messenger repeats a message verbatim. Repeated epithets and lines are examples of the formulaic system evident in the Homeric poems. There is one way to state a given idea under given conditions. Larger schematic repetitions abound in the poetry as well. Scenes of arming, stabling a horse, or feasting, for instance, are constructed from a finite number of elements given in a particular sequence. We can compare Paris' arming in book 3 with Agamemnon's in book 11:

> First he [Paris] placed along his legs the fair greaves linked with
> silver fastenings to hold the greaves at the ankles.
> Afterwards he girt on about his chest the corselet
> of Lycaon his brother since this fitted him also.
> Across his shoulders he slung the sword with the nails of silver,
> a bronze sword, and above it the great shield, huge and heavy.
> Over his powerful head he set the well-fashioned helmet
> with the horsehair crest, and the plumes nodded terribly above it.
> He took up a strong-shafted spear that fitted his hand's grip.
> (*Iliad* 3.330–38)

> First he [Agamemnon] placed along his legs the beautiful greaves
> linked
> with silver fastenings to hold the greaves at the ankles.
> Afterwards he girt on about his chest the corselet
> that Cinyras had given him once, to be a guest present.
> ...
> Across his shoulders he slung the sword, and the nails upon it
> were golden and glittered, and closing about it the scabbard
> was silver, and gold was upon the swordstraps that held it.
> And he took up the man-enclosing elaborate stark shield

. . .
Upon his head he set the helmet, two-horned, four-sheeted,
with the horsehair crest, and the plumes nodded terribly above it.
Then he caught up two strong spears edged with sharp bronze
and the brazen heads flashed far from him deep into heaven.
(*Iliad* 11.15–20, 29–32, 41–4)

Formulaic and schematic repetitions distinguish the mechanisms of Homeric poetry from modern practices of valorizing an individual author's unique images or turns of phrase and ability to vary his or her pitch. This peculiar feature prompts "The Homeric Question": who or what produced the *Iliad* and *Odyssey*?

Before the research of Milman Parry and Albert Lord, scholars posited two models for the production of the poems. For the Unitarians, only the existence of a solitary genius poet could account for the masterful artistry of the epics. For the Analysts, the inconsistencies in the epics ruled out the possibility that one person authored the works. They tried to divide the texts into earlier and later layers contributed at different times. The Analysts also believed in a genius Homer. They thought that bards and redactors had added to an Ur-poem or put together a series of Ur-poems. Individual readers' subjective judgments about the quality of the Homeric texts prompted assertions that Homer single-handedly authored the poems or that they resulted from successive contributions by various poets and editors.

Parry and Lord reframed the debate. Parry's examinations of the formulaic mechanisms of Homeric poetry suggested that it was traditional, passed down over countless generations. He then found that contemporary twentieth-century traditional poetry was distinctly oral and postulated the same for Homeric poetry. The Unitarians and Analysts as they were currently defined had to step aside. No one man could have produced the rich and complex, yet strikingly thrifty, systems of formulae evident throughout the Homeric texts. Nor were questions of the temporal priority of one section over another relevant to the product of a traditional and oral poetic system. In place of one genius poet or a string of poets and redactors, Parry and Lord introduced a bard who composes as he performs. Like the singers in the then-Yugoslavia whom Parry and Lord recorded, the Homeric poets learned traditional systems of verse-making that allowed them to compose while singing. They practiced, but neither memorized hundreds of lines of verse nor labored over a small section.

Although most scholars accept Parry's analyses and Lord's subsequent expansion upon them and agree that the *Iliad* and *Odyssey* emerged out of traditions of oral poetry that stretch back centuries from the Archaic Period, new versions of the Homeric Question have emerged. When and how did the poems take the shape that we recognize as the *Iliad* and *Odyssey*? If an individual poet was responsible for one or both of the poems, what was his relationship to his peers and the poets who preceded him and to the oral tradition in which he worked? In short, how have we come to possess these poems? The entire history of the transmission of the poems is beyond the scope of this chapter.[8] Instead, I will outline the current differing positions of Anglophone scholars regarding the emergence of stable texts of the poems in antiquity.

The individual versus group metaphor remains pertinent. Some envision for each poem a moment of dictation (or even the use of writing) by an individual poet at some point between the eighth and the mid-sixth century. There is a two-part process in these arguments. First, scholars arrive at a *terminus post quem* and a *terminus ante quem* for the fixation of the poems. They point to allusions to or citations of the Homeric poems in other poems (or vice versa), the advent of vase paintings depicting recognizably Iliadic and Odyssean scenes, and even references in the epics to historical events. Others counter that such allusions and references (more often disputed than not) tell us little about the existence of complete and unified written works. The seeming intertexts with poems and vases signal rather a wide-spread knowledge of well-known episodes from the Trojan (or perhaps Iliadic and Odyssean) saga(s).[9] Another explanatory model used by those positing a dictated text, that of Richard Janko, attempts to distinguish the stage of linguistic development of the Homeric epics relative to that of other hexameter poems. In particular, the endings employed for various nouns mark the Homeric poems as the earliest of the extant hexameter corpus. Over Janko's objections, some have asserted that both earlier and later forms were current in the *Kunstsprache* in which the bards composed: one cannot determine a relative date for the poems based on the number of early forms.

After time frames for the fixation of the poems are determined, it is contended that the poems were set down in writing. There is no way the poems could have retained the linguistic, cultural, and historical features of the time frames to which they belong if they had not been written down at those times. Writing was not necessary for the composition of the poems, but for their fixation – thus the notion of the "orally dictated" text. One might question, first, the necessary condition for the dictation model, namely, the belief that one poet's version (usually at the instigation of an unknown patron) of the seminal events of the heroic past would be accepted as definitive by a wide range of audiences and performers and, second, the related necessary consequence of this model, namely, that the reperformance of the poems was now centered around this particular textual version.

The alternative model of Gregory Nagy posits the gradual concretization or "textualization" of the poems. As the Iliadic and Odyssean oral traditions "diffused" or "proliferated" over an ever wider area, they became more standardized. The same effect of "crystallization" was achieved by the poems passing through certain "bottlenecks," such as the competitive performance of the poems at the Panathenaic Festival in Athens, which validated some versions and rendered others moot. The Panathenaia was one all-important focal point from which relatively more fixed versions of the Iliadic and Odyssean sagas radiated out. Nagy argues that interactions of this sort among various communities of poets, politicians, and listeners and readers in various performance contexts resulted in "relatively most-fixed" versions of the *Iliad* and *Odyssey* sometime around 150 BCE. In this schema written texts play a part, as there is interplay between recorded texts and composition-in-performance, starting in the mid-sixth century.[10] Yet texts are not seen as a prerequisite for the fixation of the poem as they are in the dictation model. Critics of Nagy's model question the depiction of an oral tradition becoming ever more standardized as it becomes more widespread and the fixation (particularly in regard to linguistic features) of the Homeric poems without the use of writing at an earlier stage.

Both those who envision a moment of dictation and those who adhere to Nagy's model accept the notion of a stable text. But is "text" to be used literally or metaphorically? Is it the product of one poet's efforts or of more decentralized, yet ultimately just as formative, processes? Similarly, the word "stable" varies in meaning between the two schools of thought. Finally, all acknowledge that the epics come from an oral tradition. They disagree on just how "oral" the *Iliad* and *Odyssey* actually are.

Interpreting Traditional Oral Poetry

The Traditional Component

The emergence of the *Iliad* and *Odyssey* from an oral and traditional poetic system has interpretative consequences. I start with the importance of their being "traditional." Parry's findings on the formulaic and so traditional nature of Homeric diction led to a crisis of interpretation. Some judged his demonstrations to imply that repetitions between passages were the meaningless by-product of a poet's working with and within his traditional diction. Yet we might rather say that the traditional poet exploits schematic and formulaic elements to generate meaning.

Scholars tend to use the term "type-scenes" when speaking of recurring scenes of, for example, arming or feasting or sailing. The term "themes" is often applied to recurring scenes involving, for example, compensation or the mutilation of a corpse or the transgression of the boundary between god and man.[11] Because a traditional system is operative, some of the same words are repeatedly used in various instantiations of the same scenes, be they type-scenes or themes. The equation between a scene and its dictional cues becomes hard-wired in a traditional audience through the reperformance of the poetry.[12] The audience's familiarity with these building blocks of Homeric epic furnishes the poet with an interpretative ally. The audience appreciates his deployment and manipulation of such scenes and becomes attuned to making connections between the appearances of the same type-scene or theme in one performance and in different performances. Tracing the deployment of a particular scene throughout the poem accurately mimics an ancient audience member's reception of such passages.

John Miles Foley's work on "traditional referentiality" builds on research into such scenes. Words, phrases, and verses, as well as type-scenes, themes, and larger story patterns, acquire "inherent meaning" through their repeated use in the same contexts in reperformance. I provide three examples related to the first category (words, phrases, and verses). After killing Euphorbus, Menelaus is compared to a lion that provokes "green fear" among some shepherds and their dogs (*Iliad* 17.61–9). The phrase gives the audience a keen appreciation for the terror the lion and so Menelaus produce, because in its other appearances the formula "green fear" describes the sensation felt before a superhuman or divine entity.[13] The poet need not spell out the phrase's special resonance. It has become immanent in the phrase itself, as it is repeatedly deployed in the same contexts. Foley examines name-epithet combinations too. Even when the great warrior is sitting down, the phrase "swift-footed Achilles" sends important signals: "[It] is traditional epic code for the mythic entirety of the Achaean hero . . . It summons the larger traditional identity of the best of the Achaeans, using a telltale detail to project the complexity of a character with a resonant and singular history in the epic tradition."[14] Epithets abound, but we can also apply Foley's model (in an admittedly circular procedure) to extrapolating inherent meaning from a sample of two, that is, when we are dealing with specific cross-references between two passages. When Agamemnon decides that he can no longer continue the war, he weeps,

> like a spring dark-running
> that down the face of a rock impassable drips its dim water.
> (*Iliad* 9.14–15)

The same simile describes Patroclus' weeping in front of Achilles when Patroclus comes to chastise him for his intransigence and asks to be allowed to fight while wearing Achilles' armor (*Iliad* 16.3–4). The repetition shows us modern readers the simile's inherent meaning. Agamemnon and Patroclus are both desperate and ready to take drastic action. Who would have thought that Agamemnon would decide to leave Troy empty-handed? Or that Patroclus would request to don Achilles' armor and fight in his stead? A poet operating in the traditions of Homeric poetry could turn to the black water simile when describing a character who had little sense of what the future might hold, was in a state of near panic, and was willing to resort to measures that he never would have considered before. The black water image signals a character in desperate psychological straits. The poet, then, cross-refers to Agamemnon's and Patroclus' aporia by employing the black water simile.

Two questions arise in regard to the above discussion of type-scenes and themes and traditional referentiality. First, one may think that the genius audience member has replaced the genius poet, as is often the case with critical models that focus on reception. Yet, work on living oral traditions testifies to the interpretative sophistication of audience members raised within a culture that values traditional oral poetry. Plato represents Socrates in the *Ion* as having memorized obscure lines concerned with technical matters in the *Iliad*. Studying Homer was fundamental to Greek education, but Socrates was also exposed to countless public performances outside the classroom. In Xenophon's *Symposium*, a certain Niceratus characterizes himself as "listening to them [rhapsodes performing Homer] almost every day" (3.5–6). Poets honed their craft through constant reperformance, and audiences too learned the ins and outs of Homeric poetry. Second, some have urged seeking the referents of a word, theme, or larger story pattern not merely in similar manifestations in the records of traditional oral poetry but also in contemporary stories or myths on related topics regardless of genre and in the artifacts of the Near Eastern cultures with which archaic and classical Greece interacted.

Neoanalysis represents another approach to the traditional components of Homeric poetry. Unitarian scholars operating in this vein claim that the poet Homer adopted and adapted motifs or stories from other epic tales or traditions. They focus particular attention on the poems of the so-called Epic Cycle, especially the *Aethiopis* in which a hero named Memnon kills Nestor's son Antilochus and is then killed by Achilles . . . who is then killed by Paris and Apollo. A fight ensues over Achilles' body, and after Ajax recovers his corpse, the Achaeans hold a funeral complete with games in Achilles' honor. Replace Memnon with Hector and Antilochus with Patroclus and then replace the dead Achilles with the dead Patroclus, and the outline of books 16–23 of the *Iliad* appears. Neoanalysts contend that the *Iliad* poet reworked this or another actual poem or just a well-known story line in which Achilles dies. Thetis' lamenting Achilles upon hearing of Patroclus' death (*Iliad* 18.52–72) would be a remnant of this reworked poem or story line. Perhaps the *Iliad* poet is referring economically and movingly to Achilles' death by citing another traditional tale in which Thetis laments the dead Achilles. Achilles' own death, of course, emerges as a thematic concern of the *Iliad* starting in book 9. Ferreting out such influences, reworkings, or allusions is the project of Neoanalysis. This approach reminds us that a traditional poet works with but also reinterprets the plots and thematic components of those plots that make up the mythic background of his tales. In the agonistic performance context of Homeric poetry, poets will attempt this sort of capping and appropriating of previously told stories.

Focusing on the traditional aspects of the Homeric poems has made critics comfortable with the idea that the poetry can articulate sophisticated thematic concerns. The Western critic has often assumed that great art springs from individual genius, that when it comes to Homer, the unique moments show the poet at his best. But Homeric poetry values both the individual and the generic. Meaning is generated at all points along the spectrum bounded on either end by those two terms. A typical scene of feasting can have as much significance as a simile that appears only once.

The Oral Component

What of treating the *Iliad* and *Odyssey* as traditional *oral* poems? To get at the Homeric poet's concept of oral performance, Richard Martin examines the oral performers closest to hand: the *Iliad*'s characters and narrator. In general, characters compete publicly in three "heroic genres of speaking" – commanding, flyting (i.e., exchanging insults), and recollecting. In particular, Achilles possesses a unique ability to manipulate the formulaic patterns of Homeric speech through processes of expansion. Homeric poetry too sets itself up as a publicly performed feat of recollection, and Achilles' language mimics the techniques of Homeric poets competing to fashion the heroic past by simply outtalking their peers.

Whereas Martin is less interested in the epics' "sociolinguistic realism,"[15] other critics examine how the poems reflect speakers' actual linguistic and cognitive practices. Turning to the work of linguist Wallace Chafe, Egbert Bakker addresses why the hexameter line is often made up of short phrases arranged paratactically in a "strung-on style." Chafe proposes that a speaker usually speaks in three to five word chunks. Phrases or cognitive units of such length are all the human mind can grasp at one given moment. Analyzing transcripts from Chafe's experiments, Bakker sees the same degree of "appositional syntax and adding style attributed to Homer: one piece of information is heaped on another in small, relatively autonomous units."[16] For instance:

autar Alexandros	But Alexandros,
Helenes posis eukomoio,/	the husband of Helen of the fair hair,/
Tydeidei epi toxa titaineto,	to Tydeides his bow he aimed,
poimeni laon,/	the herdsman of the soldiers,/
stelei keklimenos	leaning on the gravestone,
androkmetoi epi tymboi/	on the man-made tomb,/
Ilou Dardanidao,	(that) of Ilus the son of Dardanus,
palaiou demogerontos.	the elder of the people.
(*Iliad* 11.369–2)	(Bakker 1990, 10)

Like speakers today, the Homeric poets presented their thoughts in discreet, discernable chunks understandable to listener and speaker. Bakker also addresses meter, one phenomenon marking epic as special speech. He argues that meter is a stylization and regularization of the rhythmical properties of ordinary cognitive units. Disjunctions between the metrical period of the hexameter line and the cognitive units of speech are also noteworthy. A cognitive unit may begin in one line and end in the next or run roughshod over a caesura. Bakker suggests that such "antimetry" tends to occur in clusters and would have engaged the audience's attention, thus becoming a rhetorical strategy on the part of the poet.

Elizabeth Minchin focuses on the workings of memory in the oral production of Homeric poetry, arguing for the relevance of cognitive scripts, for instance. A script is an expectation of the sequence of events related to a well-known cultural activity. One has a script related to cooking dinner or going to a movie. We use these scripts not only to go about our daily business but also to tell stories related to such topics, and in doing the latter we readily compress or expand the scripts as needed. Minchin suggests that "the episodic nature of the scripts which we are said to store in semantic memory appears to be mirrored in the recurrent narrative sequences of epic."[17] Type scenes are actually cognitive scripts related to particular topics, such as arming or lion hunts, and known by poet and audience. The variety in type scenes related to the same subject matter is a function of the poet's expanding or compressing his rendition of a given script or even merging one script with another. The variation within limits that characterizes such scenes does not reveal a poet wrestling with the tools of his trade but shows the mental workings of an oral performer.[18] Minchin also argues for the importance of visual memory to the poet. A mental picture of the scene prompts the script relevant to a simile, for instance. Here, too, the poet employs a cognitive device that all speakers use – the mind's eye. Like Bakker, then, Minchin explores the intersections between "normal" speech and the "special" speech of epic performance.

This presentation represents one take on a portion of the current scholarly activity surrounding the Homeric poems and on some of the interpretative tools applicable to the epics. The poems' thematic concerns may be further elucidated by examining Achilles' and Odysseus' relationships with the people with whom they interact: Just how individual are these two protagonists?

The *Iliad*

Nearly every activity in the heroic world is a site of competition. Speakers attempt to best one another in verbal duels (e.g., *Iliad* 20.176–258). Athletic events become heated contests (e.g., *Odyssey* 8.158–240). In the *Iliad* the most obvious site of competition is the battlefield, where warriors contend in exchange for the right to claim a *geras* (prize) when the spoils of war are distributed. The quarrel between Achilles and Agamemnon erupts over the allotment of these prizes.

When he is forced to give his *geras*, the captive girl Chryseis, back to her father Chryses, Agamemnon demands to be compensated for his loss. As king he is entitled to just as much as if not more than his followers: he will take Ajax's, Odysseus', or Achilles' prize if necessary (*Iliad* 1.118–20 and 133–9). Achilles objects to the idea that Agamemnon can take back spoils after they have been doled out (*Iliad* 1.124–6). When Agamemnon threatens to take Briseis, Achilles swears by the scepter, the staff that an Achaean chieftain holds while speaking in the assembly, that he will never return to the battlefield and tosses the scepter to the ground (*Iliad* 1.233–46). With this defiant gesture Achilles removes himself from the Achaean community. By the time the emissaries in book 9 beg him to return to battle Achilles has developed an almost existential awareness of and detachment from the folly of war and the systems of exchange that reward the fighter. All the goods in the world are not worth getting killed, Achilles contends. The one irredeemable possession a man has is his soul:

> For not
> worth the value of my life are all the possessions they fable
> were won for Ilium, that strong-founded citadel, in the old days
> when there was peace, before the coming of the sons of the
> Achaeans;
> . . .
> . . . Of possessions
> cattle and fat sheep are things to be had for the lifting,
> and tripods can be won, and the tawny high heads of horses,
> but a man's life cannot come back again, it cannot be lifted
> nor captured again by force, once it has crossed the teeth's barrier.
> (*Iliad* 9.400–403, 405–9)

Achilles emerges for many here as a model for one enduring permutation of the Western hero: a lone individual questions the assumptions of a dominant cultural system.

The emissaries depart with the understanding that Achilles might return once Hector sets fire to the Achaean ships (*Iliad* 9.649–55), but Achilles resumes fighting only after Patroclus dies. Incensed at the death of his companion, Achilles goes berserk on the battlefield (cf. *Iliad* 20.490–94), even fighting the river god, Scamander (*Iliad* 21.136–384), and showing no mercy toward the body of his nemesis, Hector (*Iliad* 22.395–404). And then another pivotal moment occurs in the development of the hero: Priam comes to Achilles' tent to ask him to return Hector's body, and the king and the warrior are soon grieving together:

> So he [Priam] spoke, and stirred in the other [Achilles] a passion
> of grieving
> for his own father. He took the old man's hand and pushed him
> gently away, and the two remembered, as Priam sat huddled
> at the feet of Achilles and wept close for man-slaughtering
> Hector
> and Achilles wept now for his father, now again
> for Patroclus.
>
> (*Iliad* 24.507–12)

Achilles recognizes the common bond between mortals – sorrow – as he tells the wretched Priam:

> There are two urns that stand on the doorsill of Zeus. They are
> unlike
> for the gifts they bestow: an urn of evils, an urn of blessings.
> If Zeus who delights in thunder mingles these and bestows them
> on man, he shifts, and moves now in evil, again in good fortune.
> But when Zeus bestows from the urn of sorrows, he makes a
> failure
> of man and the evil hunger drives him over the shining
> earth, and he wanders respected neither by gods nor mortals.
>
> (*Iliad* 24.527–33)

The Achilles of book 1 would never have presented such a sweeping vision of what it means to be human. With this knowledge Achilles is now ready to return to the community of men. He shares a meal with Priam (*Iliad* 24.618–27) and agrees to hold back the Achaeans while the Trojans mourn Hector (*Iliad* 24.656–70). Achilles participates in and reaffirms the value of two fundamental communal rituals: commensality and burial. Although reintegrated into the Achaean community, Achilles now shows his primary allegiance to the larger community of mortals. The narrative traced by this interpretation is seductive and recognizable: a character endures some formative crisis, changes for the better, and returns to the community from which he has been removed or estranged with a deeper understanding of the human condition.

Yet is it sufficient to cast Achilles as the great individual who alone questions the systems of exchange in which all the heroes participate?

One component of Donna Wilson's recent work on the *Iliad* offers new interpretative possibilities for those uncomfortable with treating Achilles as an alienated existentialist. Wilson traces the themes associated with exchange and compensation in the poem and finds that heroes will contest over assigning a particular theme to a given situation. Whereas Agamemnon in book 9 offers gifts to Achilles that are couched in language associated with the theme of ransom, Achilles portrays the situation as requiring the theme of reparation for a past wrong (which like ransom can take the form of material compensation). When he refuses to return to the fight Achilles above all resists Agamemnon's representation of the current state of affairs. He rejects Agamemnon's offer not out of a dawning awareness of the constraints of mortality or the insignificance of material possessions but because he does not think that Agamemnon has offered him proper compensation. Her analysis makes sense, for example, of the following passage in which one is hard pressed to understand what Achilles wants from Agamemnon:

> He cheated me and he did me hurt. Let him not beguile me
> with words again. This is enough for him. Let him of his own
> will
> be damned, since Zeus of the counsels has taken his wits away
> from him.
> I hate his gifts. I hold him light as the strip of a splinter.
> Not if he gave me tens times as much, and twenty times over
> as he possesses now, not if more should come to him from
> elsewhere,
> . . .
> not even so would Agamemnon have his way with my spirit
> until he has made good to me all this heartrending insolence.
> (*Iliad* 9.375–80, 386–7)

According to Wilson's model, Agamemnon can make "good all this heartrending insolence" if he offers Achilles gifts in the form of reparation.

Wilson goes on to suggest that Achilles returns to the fight to press a claim of reparation against Hector (represented as a desire to inflict physical harm in retaliation) and, in doing so, sets aside his claim of material reparation against Agamemnon. Returning to the battlefield, he exacts an overwhelming revenge for Patroclus' death that threatens the stability of the cosmic and social order. Yet he begins his reintegration into human society when he oversees the distribution of prizes at the funeral games in honor of Patroclus (*Iliad* 23.257–61) and is fully reintegrated when he accepts Priam's offer of material goods in exchange for Hector's corpse (*Iliad* 24.572–95), when, that is, he accepts a father's offer of ransom, a typical motif in the epic. Achilles' distinctiveness, then, stems from his ability to contest over and to manipulate to his own ends the themes of compensation that make up a significant part of the poem. He does not reject the systems of heroic exchange. He seeks to control them.

THE *ODYSSEY*

Odysseus achieves his *nostos* (return) by making his way back home to Ithaca and reclaiming his place as king from the suitors who have been courting his wife Penelope. Just as it is profitable to consider Achilles' participation in the dominant cultural systems of the *Iliad*, so it is worth focusing on Odysseus' return as a confrontation with the Other in two different guises. His travels among strange, violent, and sometimes magical people not only help to define what it means to be Greek but also threaten his ability and desire to return home. Further, he must regain his identity in the eyes of the people of Ithaca. Odysseus' return is incumbent not only upon his declaring himself but also upon his declaration's being accepted by those to whom he declares himself.

In his travels Odysseus encounters those who confound the unwritten rules of hospitality, or *xenia*, integral to the Greek social fabric. Telemachus' receptions at the houses of Nestor and Menelaus in the initial books of the poem show the proper way to treat a guest (e.g., *Odyssey* 3.29–74): welcome him, feed him and perhaps offer him a bath, and only then ask him who is he; let the guest depart when he desires and give him a parting gift when he does leave. In this way the aristocratic elites who travel in the Homeric world establish relationships of reciprocity. Odysseus meets a variety of figures that in one way or another transgress these norms. At the start of the poem, Odysseus is stuck pining away for home on Calypso's island, Ogygia (*Odyssey* 1.48–59). The goddess is keeping him against his will in violation of the laws of hospitality. Odysseus suffers far worse treatment at the hands of other hosts, who happen to be cannibals. Polyphemus, the Cyclops, traps Odysseus and his men in his cave and feasts on them (*Odyssey* 9.105–566). The Laistrygonians eat some of Odysseus' men before the rest escape (*Odyssey* 10.80–132). Circe does not eat Odysseus' men but slips a drug into their wine that makes them forgetful of their homes, before she turns them into pigs (*Odyssey* 10.233–43). In all four places Odysseus contends with hosts who do not adhere to the most basic etiquette associated with the civilized treatment of guests in the Greek world.

Just as big a threat to Odysseus' return comes during his time among the Phaeacians, exemplary hosts who are not irredeemably Other. Nausicaa, the Phaeacian princess, clothes the naked Odysseus when she finds him washed up on the shore (*Odyssey* 6.206–16). Her parents, Arete and Alcinous, receive him kindly and follow the rules for entertaining a guest (cf. *Odyssey* 7.155–96). Before this audience Odysseus tells of his travels and thereby becomes the agent behind the spreading of his own *kleos* (renown). In some sense Odysseus has reached the civilized world. But there is a major difference between Scheria and Ithaca. Walking into town, Odysseus chances upon Alcinous' garden, where fruits and vegetables grow of their own accord (*Odyssey* 7.112–32). The Phaeacians do not engage in agriculture, an activity integral to Greek self-definition. Thus when Odysseus comes upon an uninhabited island near where Polyphemus lives, he envisions cultivating the land and exploiting the island's natural resources:

> For it is not a bad place at all, it could bear all crops
> in season, and there are meadow lands near the shores of the gray
> sea,
> well watered and soft; there could be grapes grown there
> endlessly,
> and there is smooth land for plowing, men could reap a full
> harvest
> always in season, since there is very rich subsoil.
>
> (*Odyssey* 9.131–5)

As a fantasy island free from the toil of agriculture yet populated by those who practice *xenia*, Scheria represents a boundary between Ithaca and the outside world populated by Others. That liminality is why Nausicaa's desire to marry Odysseus (*Odyssey* 6.241–5) and Alcinous' offer of his daughter to Odysseus (*Odyssey* 7.311–15) pose a threat to the hero. He could stay on Scheria and live a life similar to that he left behind on Ithaca.

At the same time Odysseus is offered the possibility of forsaking his old life altogether. After he identifies himself to Circe and they make love (*Odyssey* 10.321–47), she turns his companions back into men (*Odyssey* 10.388–96). Odysseus then delays his homecoming:

> There for all our days until a year was completed
> we sat there feasting on unlimited meat and sweet wine.
> But when it was the end of a year, and the months wasted
> away, and the seasons changed, and the long days were
> accomplished,
> then my eager companions called me aside and said to me:
> "What ails you now? It is time to think about our own country,
> if truly it is ordained that you shall survive and come back
> to your strong-founded house and to the land of your fathers."
> (*Odyssey* 10.466–74)

Odysseus extricates himself from Circe only when his men grumble that he has forgotten the need to return home. Spending his days in the bed of a goddess (*Odyssey* 10.480) and not worrying about producing food sorely tempt the hero to embrace the life of the Other. Whereas the monsters he meets pose a physical threat to Odysseus, the Phaeacians and Circe present as great an obstacle to his return home by challenging Odysseus' sense of self.

The first half of the poem establishes a definition of Greekness in opposition to those Odysseus meets on his travels. Identity remains the focus of the second half of the poem, but attention shifts to Odysseus' assertion of his identity as king of Ithaca and husband of Penelope. There are thematic parallels between the poem's halves. Like the cannibals Odysseus meets in his travels, the suitors are figured as improper feasters. They eat nearly all the food in Odysseus' house and eat for too long, overstaying their welcome while courting the wife of a man not known to be dead. Nor do they offer the possibility of reciprocating the good treatment they have received as guests. In addition, when the disguised Odysseus shows up, several of the suitors mistreat him, violating, just like many characters he encounters abroad, the rule that guests and suppliants must be respected. Sheila Murnaghan argues that, throughout the poem, Odysseus can reveal himself when he is treated properly as a guest, as happens on Scheria. When Odysseus reveals himself to the suitors who have abused him as a guest, they fail to recognize him (e.g., *Odyssey* 22.1–47). The theme of the proper behavior of both guest and host, so important to the first half of the poem, is also vital to the second half.

I want to focus briefly on Murnaghan's concept of recognition as a two-way street. Much has properly been made of Odysseus' reclaiming his kingship and his wife. He tricks the suitors with his beggar disguise; he gradually reveals himself to his friends and family; he goes along with the contest of the bow in book 21 in order to prepare for the slaughter of the suitors. In achieving his *nostos* Odysseus emerges as a hero of *metis* (wisdom/cunning). Odysseus is the protagonist of the epic, but as Murnaghan notes, his return also depends upon the willingness and readiness of those to whom he reveals himself to accept his disclosures of identity. If they were not to accept his claim, Odysseus would be unable to achieve his homecoming. In particular, arguably the most important component of his homecoming, revealing himself to Penelope, entails gaining her recognition. How is he to win this assent?

The French sociologist Pierre Bourdieu contends that a speaker, such as a judge or a priest, is authorized to issue performative statements ("I sentence you to 10 years" or "I pronounce you man and wife") by the willingness of his audience to allow him to make such statements. In part this willingness is generated by the institutional trappings on display, such as a robe or the physical space of a courtroom or church, as well as by the official's references to the particular institution and its practices ("By the power vested in me by the state of Georgia . . . "). The presence of institutional apparatus authorizes the speaker, whereas one who attempted to perform the task of a police officer, for instance, without the proper trappings associated with the institution of law enforcement would be ineffective. Odysseus' task can be aligned with this formulation. His endeavors to state his name and thereby take a large step toward reclaiming his identity as king of Ithaca and husband of Penelope are attempts at performative speech. His interlocutors' acceptance of the tokens and the trappings of his identity that he presents authorizes Odysseus to make such statements. Melanthius and Eumaeus are convinced that Odysseus has returned home once he shows them his scar (*Odyssey* 21.221–5). Penelope tests Odysseus by suggesting that their bed can be placed outside the bedroom. The queen consents to recognize him as Odysseus only after he expresses indignation at the thought and reveals the secret that he shares with Penelope alone, that the bed is made from a rooted tree and cannot be moved (*Odyssey* 23.177–230). Laertes demands,

> If in truth you are Odysseus, my son, who has come back
> here, give me some unmistakable sign, so that I can believe you.
> (*Odyssey* 24.328–9)

In response Odysseus points to his scar and describes Laertes' orchard in detail (24.330–46). Finally, Odysseus cites the institution of parenthood to convince Telemachus to listen to him:

> Telemachus, it does not become you to wonder too much
> at your own father when he is here, nor doubt him.
> (*Odyssey* 16.202–3)

Odysseus is unable to walk into the palace and declare himself. He must first present himself to others and be granted by them the authority to make such statements. The *Odyssey*, then, not only depicts a dynamic hero of *metis* but also explores that hero's dependence on others.

Hesiod

The *Theogony* and *Works and Days* are the most famous poems of Hesiod, but others were attributed to him in antiquity too, such as the *Shield of Heracles*, an account of Heracles' battle with Cycnus, and the *Catalog of Women*, a continuation of the *Theogony* that tells of mortal women who bore children to gods. The previous discussion about the emergence of the Homeric poems pertains to those of Hesiod as well. In contrast to the Homeric poems, the *Theogony* foregrounds an "I" with the name of "Hesiod" in describing Hesiod's face-to-face encounter with the Muses: "And once they taught Hesiod fine singing, as he tended his lambs below holy Helicon. This is what the goddesses said to me first, the Olympian Muses" (*Theogony* 22–4). In the *Works and Days* an "I" (also conventionally called Hesiod[19]) points to a conflict over inheritance with his brother, Perses. Whereas a biographical school of criticism suggests that in both poems this "I" is the authorial "I," others think of it as the narrator's "I" that tells us nothing about the fashioning of the poems by one poet. Many treat Hesiod as a persona adopted by poets performing Hesiodic songs and the personal "I" as a generic component of Hesiodic poetry. Because these poems are oral and traditional,[20] the previous discussion of some of the interpretative tools relevant to the *Iliad* and *Odyssey* can also apply to Hesiod. The traditional nature of Hesiodic poetry is most significant. The *Theogony* shows clear affinities with cosmogonies (stories about the beginning of the cosmos) and theogonies (stories about the birth of a culture's gods and the establishing of order and hierarchies by and among them) from Near Eastern cultures. Instructional or wisdom poetry from the Near East and Egypt offers parallels for the didactic *Works and Days*.

The *Theogony*

Like the list of Achaeans and Trojans in book 2 of the *Iliad*, the *Theogony* is a catalog, this time of the Greeks' numerous gods and goddesses. Cataloging poetry is popular the world over and from a performative point of view stands out as a feat of memory. Particularly noticeable are the list of Nereids (*Theogony* 243–62) and the list of rivers (338–45) and nymphs (349–61) descended from Oceanus. But the poet must catalog what his audience values. Just as the *Iliad* and *Odyssey* are Panhellenic poems, the *Theogony* focuses on divinities worshiped by all the Greeks. Fittingly, the Muses move from the local Mount Helicon to the Panhellenic Mount Olympus at the start of the poem.[21] The poem also uses an account of the genealogy of the gods to chronicle Zeus' rise to power. That chronicle performs important political work, because the story of Zeus' ascension is a story of the emergence of the patriarchy.

Outwitted by their female consorts, Zeus' predecessors fail to stop one of their sons from taking over as supreme male god. Uranus, Zeus' grandfather, prevents his consort Gaea, "Earth," from giving birth (*Theogony* 155–9). On Gaea's urging, one of their children, Cronus, waits for Uranus to return to make love with Gaea and castrates him (*Theogony* 164–82). Once in power, Cronus tries to stop the cycle of generational succession by swallowing the children born from his consort Rhea (*Theogony* 459–67). Rhea tricks Cronus, however, into swallowing a stone instead of Zeus, who is spirited away to Crete (*Theogony* 468–91). Returning to claim his inheritance, the grown Zeus joins the Hundred-Handers to his side on Gaea's advice (*Theogony* 626) and wins a pitched battle against the Titans (his father's siblings; *Theogony* 664–735). Zeus then defeats the monster Typhoeus, the offspring of Gaea and Tartarus (*Theogony* 836–68). Gaea's birthing of Typhoeus, who "would have become king of mortals and immortals" (*Theogony* 837), is another attempt by a mother (or here grandmother) to overthrow the supreme male god. Once Zeus defeats Typhoeus, "on Earth's advice they [the other gods] urged that Olympian Zeus the wide-seeing should be king and lord of the immortals" (*Theogony* 883–4). Gaea skillfully remains kingmaker. In both generations the mother figure plays a pivotal role: Gaea and Rhea orchestrate or attempt to orchestrate the succession of rulers, and Gaea affirms the final ruler's prerogatives. Yet we might characterize Gaea as acquiescing to the rule of Zeus[22] and so begin to appreciate how Zeus solidifies his hold on power.

Zeus confronts the problem of succession by eliminating the mother figure most threatening to him. Upon learning from Gaea and

Uranus that the male child born to him and the goddess Metis will take his place, Zeus swallows Metis when she is about to give birth to Athena (*Theogony* 886–900) and himself gives birth to Athena from his head (*Theogony* 924–6). These two actions stop the cycle of succession of father by son. By internalizing the mother, Zeus does away with her threatening presence and the possibility that she will conspire against him with her children. Furthermore, Zeus stops Metis from having more children other than Athena. For her part, as she claims in Aeschylus' *Eumenides* (734–40), Athena always sides with the male, since she was born from one.

Zeus subordinates powerful female deities, especially those of an earlier generation, through diplomatic means as well, making sure that they are on his side and accede to his authority and dispensations. Although Zeus gives honors to all the gods, Hesiod pays close attention to his handling of Styx and Hecate. The river Styx, daughter of Oceanus and Tethys and Zeus' older cousin (Oceanus is Cronus' brother), begets a variety of powerful abstract forces, such as Might and Force, and so Zeus takes her and her children as allies. In particular, he makes Styx the entity the gods call to witness in swearing an oath (*Theogony* 397–401). Similarly, Zeus gives pride of place to the goddess Hecate, the sole child of the Titans Perses and Asteria. Prior to Zeus' ascension, Hecate had a position of honor among the gods, and, while making sure that Hecate remains a virgin lest she produce children who threaten him, Zeus "honored [Hecate] above all others, granting her magnificent privileges: a share both of the earth and of the undraining sea. From the starry heaven too she has a portion of honor, and she is the most honoured by the immortal gods" (*Theogony* 411–15). Zeus appeases but also subordinates this powerful goddess, whom Hesiod positions "as inheritor of the three cosmic realms, Pontus [sea], Gaea [earth], and Uranus [sky], a goddess who sums up in her person all of the cosmogonic processes that have preceded her."[23]

Zeus' control over Hecate's reproductive capabilities goes hand in hand with his appropriation of the female's part in reproduction when he gives birth to Athena. By bringing forth Athena "by himself" (*Theogony* 924), Zeus positions himself as equally as capable of childbirth as the female, if not more so. For when Hera counteracts Zeus' giving birth to Athena by creating a child on her own, she produces the crippled Hephaestus, who poses no threat to Zeus on account of his physical handicap (*Theogony* 927–8; cf. the *Homeric hymn to Apollo* 311–18). Zeus' assumption of a female role in reproduction is coupled with the subsequent valorization of his fecundity. To cement his power after swallowing Metis, he marries several goddesses and fathers immortals beholden to him (*Theogony* 901–23). His production of numerous offspring comes at the expense of one particularly powerful group of females: the Fates first appear as the daughters of Night (*Theogony* 218), but the trio are born again to Zeus and Themis (*Theogony* 904–6) and so subordinated to Zeus as daughters to father.

The Zeus of the *Theogony* ensures cosmic stability. He keeps tabs on male figures, such as the Hundred-Handers and the Cyclopes, but makes a special effort to control and appropriate the female forces around him. Fittingly, although the story of Pandora is told in both the *Theogony* (570–612) and the *Works and Days* (54–105), the version in the *Theogony* rehearses the anxieties over female sexuality and the female's role in reproduction evident in the story of Zeus. For the human race to survive man has no choice but to live with woman. She is a necessary evil, who threatens to eat a man out of house and home, while remaining the only means of perpetuating the household by begetting children. The *Theogony*, especially in its narratives about Zeus, makes a foundational contribution to the misogyny of the Greek world.

The *Works and Days*

The *Works and Days* (*WD*) divides into nine parts: 1. invocation (1–10); 2. the two types of Eris (11–41); 3. Prometheus and Pandora (47–105); 4. the five races of man (109–201); 5. the justice of Zeus (202–85); 6. moral precepts (286–382); 7. farmers' and sailors' calendars (383–694); 8. moral precepts (695–764); 9. days of the month (765–828). Whereas the *Theogony* focuses on Zeus' rise to power, the *Works and Days* discusses how mortals can live justly under Zeus' rule. Hesiod consistently links justice, a communal virtue, with the personal matter of feeding oneself. To this point we have been situating individual protagonists in the larger cultural systems in which they operate. The workings of a community can also be aligned with individual needs.

The beginning of the poem offers two related themes. Hesiod inaugurates the theme of *dike* (justice) by asking Zeus to "make judgment straight with righteousness (*dikei*)" (*WD* 9) and suggesting to Perses, "let us settle our dispute with straight judgments (*dikeis*)" (*WD* 35–6). Hesiod contrasts this exhortation with his contention that Perses bribed the *basileis* (kings/lords) who judged the case into allotting more of their father's inheritance to Perses than he warranted (*WD* 38–41). Justice is defined negatively: one should not take more than one's share, nor should judges make unfair allotments and grant someone more than his share. Hesiod presents the second theme in urging Perses "to work," by which he means to produce food: "For the gods keep men's food (*bion*) concealed; otherwise you would easily work even in a day enough to provide you for the whole year without working" (*WD* 42–4). In a world of scarce resources and requiring hard work, not taking more than one's share becomes even more vital to the concept of justice. The poem proceeds to fashion even stronger links between the themes of justice and work by discussing the present state of the world, in which justice is of paramount importance, through the motifs of food production and eating that food (the alimentary idiom).

Hesiod begins with a story about Prometheus and Pandora. Zeus grows angry because at the initial sacrifice at Mecone, Prometheus tricks him into taking the portion of fat and bones and leaving the meat for mortals. In response, "Zeus concealed it [food], angry because Prometheus' crooked cunning had tricked him" (*WD* 47–8). Zeus continues his assault upon man's ability to produce food by hiding fire (*WD* 50), with which men cook. When Prometheus steals fire back (*WD* 50–52), Zeus urges the gods to fashion Pandora (*WD* 60–82), some of whose attributes are presented in the alimentary idiom and whose arrival forces men to work. Aphrodite endows her with "limb-devouring (*guioborous*) cares" (*WD* 66; author's translation). The jar from which she lets out the various evils that plague humankind is a *pithos* (*WD* 94), a kitchen implement used to store wine in particular.[24] Prior to Pandora's arrival men "lived remote from ills, without harsh toil (*ponoio*) and the grievous sicknesses that are deadly to men" (*WD* 91–2). As Hesiod's discussion of the Golden Age makes clear, one of the benefits of living without toil (*ponos*) is that one need not labor at all for one's food (*WD* 116–18).[25] The version of the Pandora tale that appears in the *Theogony* specifies one of those generic evils unleashed by Pandora in the *Works and Days*: men have to feed women who remain at home like drones who "pile the toil (*kamaton*) of others into their own bellies" (*WD* 599). The *Works and Days* reasserts the connection between women and food in its latter half. The bad wife is described with the metaphor *deipnoloches* (*WD* 704), which the standard dictionary *Liddell, Scott, and Jones* defines as "fishing for invitations to dinner, parasitic," the implication being that one has to work to feed one's wife. And any wife is thought to *euei* (roast) her husband (*WD* 705). This first tale about Prometheus and Pandora ends with the moral "Thus there is no way to evade the purpose of Zeus" (*WD* 105). Perses should not only understand that he cannot avoid Zeus' retribution for transgressions but also adhere to Zeus' rules for human prosperity, namely a respect for justice in a world of scarce resources.

The section on the five races of men also links food production or eating with justice or the arrival of justice. Vernant envisions an alternation in the myth between justice and *hybris*, with the first race (just) being opposed to the second (hybristic) (*hybrin atasthalon, WD* 134) as the fourth (just) is to the third (hybristic) (*hybries, WD* 146). The fifth and current Iron Age exhibits justice and *hybris* and will become a site of pure *hybris*. Words for justice first appear in the discussion of the "more righteous (*dikaioteron*) and noble" (*WD* 159) race of heroes and in the description of the Iron Age: "one will sack another's town, and there will be no thanks for the man who abides by his oath or for the righteous (*dikaiou*) or worthy man, but instead they will honor the miscreant and the criminal" (*WD* 189–92). Vernant's interpretation suggests that, even though words related to justice are absent for the first three races, the *hybris* that defines the Silver and Bronze Age requires justice as an opposing term. Hesiod later opposes *hybris* to *dike* (*WD* 212), a juxtaposition also found in Homeric poetry (cf. *Odyssey* 6.120–2). In the particular context of the Silver and Bronze Ages *hybris* refers to taking more than one's share, a concept integral to Hesiod's definition of justice. The Silver race and the men of the Bronze Age attack one another in hopes presumably of gaining their opponents' lands or property (*WD* 134–5 and 152–4, respectively); the Silver Age's transgression of not sacrificing to the gods (*WD* 135–6), although they enjoy an unlimited supply of food, ultimately does them in. Conversely, some argue that justice appears with the advent of agriculture in the Heroic Age. Previously there was no need for justice, defined as the allotment of scarce goods, because resources were in such abundance.[26] Under either rubric, justice or its emergence plays a part in the myth of the five races, and so it is worth tracing the discussions of food production and/or eating in respect to each race.

Those who lived during the Golden Age were "remote from toil (*ponon*) and misery (*oizuos*)," as demonstrated by the fact that "they enjoyed themselves in feasting... All good things were theirs, and the grain-giving soil bore its fruits of its own accord in unstinted plenty" (*WD* 113, 116–18). The Silver race failed to sacrifice to the gods – a transgression against normal eating practices, because nearly every meal in the Greek world entailed some sort of sacrifice. Hesiod characterizes men of the Bronze Age as "no eaters of corn" (*WD* 146–7). By contrast, of the members of the Heroic Age, some were transferred upon dying to "the Isles of the Blessed Ones... fortunate Heroes, for whom the grain-giving soil bears its honey-sweet fruits thrice a year" (*WD* 171–3). Finally, men of the Iron Age "will never cease from toil (*kamatou*) and misery (*oizuos*) by day" (*WD* 176–7). This line recalls not only the earlier description of the lack of toil in the Golden Age that was characterized by abundance (see *WD* 113) but also the simile in the *Theogony* that compares women to drones eating up the toil (*kamaton*) of the worker bees (see *WD* 599). And of course the Iron Age is where Hesiod and Perses find themselves, having to work the land to produce food.

Discussions or references to justice in the so-called "justice of Zeus" section of the poem also make use of the alimentary idiom. In the fable of the hawk and the nightingale, addressed to the *basileis* (*WD* 202), the hawk contends that might makes right in his threat to eat the nightingale (208). Hesiod uses the epithet *dorophagoi*, "bribe-swallowers," to describe *basileis* who do not make just decisions (*WD* 39, 221, and 264). The fields of the cities of just and unjust men experience different fates. In the just city, "Neither does Famine attend straight-judging men, nor Blight, and they feast on the crops they tend. For them Earth bears plentiful food" (*WD* 230–2). For the inhabitants of the unjust city, "From heaven Cronus' son brings disaster upon them, famine and with it plague, and the people waste away" (*WD* 242–3). Finally, justice among men contrasts with the culinary practices of animals: "For this was the rule for men that Cronus' son laid down: whereas fish and beasts and flying birds would eat one another, because Right (*dike*) is not among them, to men he gave Right (*diken*), which is much the best in practice" (*WD* 276–80).

Articulating a connection between work and food production at the start and then presenting discussions of justice in the context of food production and eating allows Hesiod to devote most of the remainder of the poem to expanding on the injunction latent at its beginning.[27] A just man works. That is, a man acts justly by taking care of his farm, or sailing if need be, in order to maintain his livelihood and feed his family and retainers. He does not pursue the land or livelihood of others. Hesiod transitions into the section of the poem concerned with the actual mechanisms of farming and sailing by equating not working with injustice. The gods punish the man who does not work but attempts to gain wealth by going after another's property (*WD* 314–16, 321–6), just as Zeus "imposes a harsh return for his unrighteous (*adikon*) actions" (*WD* 333) on him who mistreats family members and guests. After presenting various instructions for working one's farm or sailing, Hesiod concludes the poem by emphasizing yet again the connection between work and justice: "Well with god and fortune is he who works with knowledge of all this, giving the immortals no cause for offence, judging the bird-omens and avoiding transgressions" (*WD* 826–8).

Homer and Hesiod

Homer and Hesiod were thought to have met in a poetic competition much like a modern rap duel. This traditional tale is preserved for us in the *Contest of Homer and Hesiod*, or *Certamen* – a second-century CE work, for which it is standard practice to evoke a fourth-century BCE model by a certain Alcidamas. The treatise hints at conceptions of epic in the classical period.

First, various parts of the contest echo "competitive" talk at symposia. Hesiod first asks Homer, "what is best (*phertaton*)?" and "what is most beautiful (*kalliston*)?" – standard prompts in sympotic competitions. When Paneides, the king who presides over the contest, asks the poets to recite their best lines, he requests *to kalliston* "the most beautiful bit." In another stage of the contest Hesiod speaks a one- or two-line sentence fragment that Homer has to complete with another line in order to make a coherent thought. This challenge recalls the verbal games requiring one symposiast to cap the line(s) of a previous speaker. By aligning the two poets with symposiasts, the treatise reaffirms epic as by and for men, because the proper symposium is a male-dominated affair. Second, the competition reveals a continued interest in, or at least acknowledgment of, the compositional mechanisms of epic. In the rapid back and forth of the verbal duel Homer is quick on his feet and responds with formulaic phrases or lines. In Plutarch's account of the contest, Hesiod wins after producing two lines *ek tou paratuchontos* "off the cuff" (*Banquet of the Seven Sages* 154a6). Furthermore, in the phase of the contest in which Homer needs to complete a couplet begun by Hesiod, each pairing is an exaggerated example of necessary enjambment, another of the tools essential to an oral poet.[28] Both poets compose as they perform, using phrases and techniques basic to their craft. The *Certamen* celebrates not the individuality of the poets so much as the traditions in and with which these two great culture heroes operated.

Notes

1 See Burgess 2001, 94–114.

2 Unless otherwise noted, all translations come, with emendation to the transliterations, from the following: the *Iliad* from R. Lattimore 1961; the *Odyssey* from R. Lattimore 1967; *Theogony* and *Works and Days* from M. L. West 1999.

3 As I will explain at the start of the section on Hesiod, the following two sections (Homeric Performance and Homeric Questions; Interpreting Traditional Oral Poetry) should be understood to apply to Hesiodic poetry as well.
4 Thalmann 1984, 132.
5 Stehle 1997, Chapter Four.
6 See Mastronarde 2002, ad loc.
7 Taplin 2000, 41–2.
8 See, e.g., Haslam 1997.
9 See Graziosi 2002, 92.
10 See Nagy 1996, 110–12.
11 See Wilson 2002, Segal 1971, and Muellner 1996, respectively.
12 See Foley 1990: Chapter 7 for a nuanced discussion of themes and type scenes.
13 Foley 2002, 121.
14 Foley 1999, 210.
15 Martin 1989, 65.
16 Bakker 1997, 43.
17 Minchin 2001, 14.
18 See Russo 1999, 165.
19 But see Stehle 1997, 208.
20 See Edwards 1971.
21 Clay 2003, 57.
22 See Clay 1989, 13.
23 Clay 2003, 23.
24 See *WD* 368 and Zeitlin 1996, 66–7.
25 See Vernant 1983, 9–10.
26 Clay 2003, 82.
27 See Thalmann 1984, 57 and 203 n. 70.
28 See Graziosi 2001 and Collins 2004: 187–91.

Bibliography and Suggested Readings

Translations

Lattimore, R. 1961. *The Iliad of Homer.*

______. 1967. *The Odyssey of Homer.*

West, M. L. 1999. *Hesiod Theogony Works and Days.*

On Gender and Performance

Doherty, L. E. 1995. *Siren Songs: Gender, Audiences, and Narrators in the Odyssey.*

Stehle, E. 1997. *Performance and Gender in Ancient Greece: Nondramatic Poetry in Its Setting.*

On the Fixation of the Homeric Poems

Janko, R. 1998. "The Homeric Poems as Oral Dictated Texts." *Classical Quarterly* 48(1): 1–13

Nagy, G. 1996. *Poetry as Performance: Homer and Beyond.*

______. 1996b. *Homeric Questions.*

West, M. L. 1995. "The Date of the *Iliad.*" *Museum Helveticum* 52: 203–19.

On the Type-Scene and the Theme

Edwards, M. W. 1992. "Homer and Oral Tradition: The Type-Scene." *Oral Tradition* 7: 284–330.

Foley, J. M. 1990. *Traditional Oral Epic: The Odyssey, Beowulf, and the Serbo-Croatian Return Song.*

Lord, A. B. 1960. *The Singer of Tales.*

Wilson, D. 2002. *Ransom, Revenge, and Heroic Identity in the Iliad.*

On Traditional Referentiality

Foley, J. M. 2002. *How to Read an Oral Poem.*

On Neoanalysis

Willcock, M. M. 1997. "Neoanalysis." In *A New Companion to Homer*. Eds. I. Morris and B. Powell. 174–89.

On Orality

Bakker, E. 1997. *Poetry in Speech: Orality and Homeric Discourse.*

Martin, R. P. 1989. *The Language of Heroes: Speech and Performance in the Iliad.*

Minchin, E. 2001. *Homer and the Resources of Memory: Some Applications of Cognitive Theory to the Iliad and the Odyssey.*

Parry, M. 1971. *The Making of Homeric Verse.*

Russo, J. 1999. "Sicilian Folktales, Cognitive Psychology, and Oral Theory." In *Contextualizing Classics: Ideology, Performance, Dialogue*. Eds. T. M. Falkner, N. Felson, and D. Konstan. 151–71.

On Hesiod

Clay, J. S. 2003. *Hesiod's Cosmos.*

Vernant, J. P. 1983. "Hesiod's Myth of the Races: An Essay in Structural Analysis." In *Myth and Thought among the Greeks*. 3–32.

West, M. L. 1997. *The East Face of Helicon: West Asiatic Elements in Greek Poetry and Myth.*

Zeitlin, F. 1996. "Signifying Difference: The Case of Hesiod's Pandora." In *Playing the Other: Essays on Gender and Society in Classical Greek Literature*. 53–86.

On the Contest between Homer and Hesiod

Collins, D. 2004. *Master of the Game: Competition and Performance in Greek Poetry.*

Graziosi, B. 2001. "Competition in Wisdom." In *Homer, Tragedy, and Beyond: Essays in Honor of P. E. Easterling*. Eds. F. Budelmann and P. Michelakis. 57–74.

Other Works

Bakker, E. 1990. "Homeric Discourse and Enjambement: A Cognitive Approach." *Transactions of the American Philological Association* 120: 1–21.

Bourdieu, P. 1991. *Language and Symbolic Power*. Ed. J. B. Thompson. Transls. G. Raymond and M. Adamson.

Burgess, J. 2001. *The Tradition of the Trojan War in Homer and the Epic Cycle.*

Clay, J. S. 1989. *The Politics of Olympus.*

Crotty, K. 1994. *The Poetics of Supplication.*

Edwards, G. P. 1971. *The Language of Hesiod in Its Traditional Context.*

Foley, J. M. 1999. *Homer's Traditional Art.*
Graziosi, B. 2002. *Inventing Homer: The Early Reception of Epic.*
Janko, R. 1982. *Homer, Hesiod, and the Hymns: Diachronic Development in Epic Diction.*
Haslam, M. 1997. "Homeric Papyri and the Transmission of the Text." In *A New Companion to Homer*. Eds. I. Morris and B. Powell. 55–100.
Mastronarde, D. 2002. *Medea Euripides.*
Muellner, L. 1996. *The Anger of Achilles: Menis in Greek Epic.*
Murnaghan, S. 1987. *Disguise and Recognition in the Odyssey.*
Segal, C. 1971. *The Theme of the Mutilation of the Corpse in the Iliad.*
Taplin, O. 2000. "The Spring of the Muses: Homer and Related Poetry." In *Literature in the Greek and Roman Worlds: A New Perspective*. Ed. O. Taplin. 22–57.
Thalmann, G. 1984. *Conventions of Form and Thought in Early Greek Epic Poetry.*

6: Archaic Greek Poetry

Leslie V. Kurke

The Proliferation of Lyric Voice

Not for me are the things of Gyges, rich in gold, a concern,
Nor has envy yet taken me, nor do I resent
The works of the gods, and I do not desire great tyranny;
For [these things] are far from my eyes.

Archilochus fr. 19 W [= 122 W^2]

Eros again the limb-loosener whirls me,
sweet-bitter, impossible, creeping thing. . . .

Sappho fr. 130 LP

Archaic Greek poetry confronts the reader with a sudden explosion of distinctive, individual voices from all over the Greek world, in contrast to what came before – the two great lone voices of the Greek epic tradition, Homer and Hesiod – and to what followed – the almost total dominance of Athens in the literary record of the classical period. Thus, in addition to Archilochus of Paros and Sappho of Mytilene on Lesbos (quoted above), the remains of Archaic poetry include verse composed by Hipponax of Clazomenae, Semonides of Amorgos, Xenophanes of Colophon, Solon of Athens, Theognis of Megara, Alcman of Sparta, Alcaeus of Mytilene, Stesichorus of Himera, Ibycus of Rhegion, Anacreon of Teos, Pindar of Thebes, and Simonides and Bacchylides of Ceos, spanning a period from roughly 700 to 450 BCE. More remarkably still, all of these poets were suddenly, insistently saying "I." Indeed, this explosion of confident, self-possessed lyric "I"s (in contrast to the Olympian objectivity and detachment of Homer, if not Hesiod) led many classical scholars of an earlier era to regard this period as the moment of the "discovery of the individual self or spirit" – thus, it has been said that Archilochus is the first "individual" on the stage of history.

I would like to approach this phenomenon from a different perspective and ask simply, where does this proliferation of lyric voices come from? What causes or motivates it? On one level, this sudden profusion of lyric voices saying "I" might be construed as merely a historical and generic mirage; on another level, the Archaic period does represent a moment of epochal break and innovation because of the convergence of different forces – technological, generic, and social/political. It is a mirage because it seems that lyric poetry had always existed – even before the Greeks became Greek, ca. 2200–2000 BCE. For, as scholars of comparative metrics have observed, one of the lyric meters used by Sappho and Alcaeus (ca. 600 BCE) is identical to one of the meters of the Sanskrit *Ṛg Veda*, the holy text of the Indian tradition, thought to have been orally composed between 1400 and 1000 BCE. This exact coincidence of meter in two kindred Indo-European traditions argues strongly for a common Indo-European poetic heritage reaching back to the third millenium BCE. Indeed, a couple of modern scholars have independently proposed that the hexameter – the meter of Greek epic poetry – developed out of common Indo-European lyric meters sometime in the second millenium BCE: so in this scenario, Greek lyric poetry is at least as old as epic poetry, and probably older. The appearance of a sudden profusion of lyric voices starting ca. 700 BCE is then a historical accident, resulting from the development of a new technology – the reintroduction of writing into the Greek world around 750–10 BCE. There had always been songs sung and verses recited, but now, for the first time, writing provided the means to fix poetry and song as text and thereby preserve them.

From another angle, the power and singularity of the lyric "I" might be regarded as a generic mirage. For lyric, in contrast to Greek epic poetry, never entirely shed its rootedness in a particular community and a particular context of utterance, which invariably necessitated an "I" addressing a "you." In contrast, Greek epic poetry as it comes down to us has the appearance of a tradition that has had most of its performance idiosyncrasies smoothed away, in order to make it as homogeneous and Panhellenic as possible. Thus if we were to remove the proem to Hesiod's *Theogony* (because epic *prooimia* were probably occasion-bound, the means of inserting a more universalizing mythic narrative into the here-and-now of particular performance), we would lose the single identification of Hesiod by name and the entire epic tradition would revert to the lofty anonymity of Homer.

More importantly, what we know of the exigencies of performance radically challenges the reading of the lyric "I" as the spontaneous and unmediated expression of a biographical individual. Archaic Greek poetry and song were always composed for public performance, marked off and enacted in a special space. This means that, even before the development of full-scale masked drama, the speaker or singer was always role-playing, assuming a character or persona, a more or less fictive position from which to speak. We can see this with particular clarity when occasional fragments of the male sympotic poets Alcaeus, Anacreon, and Theognis offer us first-person speakers in forms gendered feminine, but in fact we must always assume a gap or distance between the speaking persona and the poet as a historical individual. In this respect, the fragment of Archilochus quoted at the beginning of this chapter is a good object lesson. For we might be tempted to read its emphatic assertion of the "I"'s values, likes, and dislikes as the authentic voice of the historical Archilochus, but Aristotle tells us that this is the beginning of a poem spoken by "Charon the carpenter." Yet nothing in the four preserved lines of the poem would tell us that the "I" here is not Archilochus himself.

Indeed, there is much evidence that confirms not just role-playing, but that the roles played in lyric performance were traditional and generic. Thus, for example, we are told that the arch-conservative Athenian sophist and politician Critias (active in the last third of the fifth century BCE) said of Archilochus,

> If that one had not broadcast such an opinion concerning himself to all the Greeks, we would not know that he was the son of a slave woman named Enipo nor that having abandoned Paros because of poverty and resourcelessness he came to Thasos nor that having come there he became an enemy to those there nor that, indeed, he used to abuse his friends and enemies alike. And in addition to these things, he said, we wouldn't know that he was an adulterer, if we hadn't learned it from him, nor that he was lustful and arrogant, and the thing that is most shameful of all, that he threw away his shield.
>
> (Critias fr. B 44 DK)

Critias here offers us a perfect portrait of the generic blame poet (as we'll see), cast in the form of the poet's biography as derived directly from his poetic oeuvre. Our suspicion that genre characterization has here become biography is amply confirmed by the first "fact" cited by

Critias – that Archilochus' mother was a slave woman named Enipo. For Enipo is a proper name derived from the Greek word for "blame" or "abuse" (*enipe*), whereas her status as slave figures the blame poet's traditional role as marginalized and abjected outsider. We might wonder whether Critias at the end of the fifth century no longer understands the Archaic system of generic role-playing or whether (as I think more likely) he intentionally misrepresents and literalizes Archilochus' generic cues out of political motives. However that may be, Critias stands at the beginning of a long tradition of ancient literary criticism that developed in a literate era that no longer understood the conventions of oral performance culture, so that it extracted generic cues and traditional roles from Archaic Greek poetry and turned them into biographical "facts." Modern scholarship should not follow ancient literary criticism on this path, but instead attempt to excavate and reconstruct the complex and subtle system of generic cues and traditional role-playing that framed and informed Archaic Greek poetic production.

Another example of such traditional role-playing is the corpus of the sympotic elegiac poet Theognis. The transmitted corpus of Theognis appears to contain references to historical events ranging from the last quarter of the seventh century BCE to the Persian invasion of 480–79. Because this represents an impossibly long single lifespan, generations of scholars have attempted to fix a proper date for the poet and sort his corpus accordingly into "genuine" Theognis and (later, worse) accretions and intrusions into the text. But more recently, some scholars have suggested a different approach: that we should instead think of "Theognis" as a more or less fictive persona of the disaffected aristocrat at a symposium – a position to be occupied in performance for centuries by any number of singers from all over the Greek world.

Thus one scholarly position would doubt the real existence of any of the early poets whose names, fragments, and "biographies" come down to us, insisting that all this material derives from an extended oral tradition and that it is simply an accident of the invention of writing that lyric seems suddenly to appear and voice its confident individual "I." This is not my position, precisely because all Archaic poetry was composed for public (often ritual) performance, whether for a small group in symposium or for the entire city assembled. Given this significant embedding of poetry in its social context, we must assume that it accomplished some real social work in performance. This the poetry did by affirming – indeed, constructing anew on each occasion – the values and roles felt to be proper for the group, simultaneously inculcating them in singers and audience within the frame of performance. In this respect, we must imagine Archaic Greek poetry as akin to ritual or "social drama" in other premodern cultures.

But at the same time, as all the essays in this volume demonstrate, the Archaic period was one of tremendous ferment and upheaval, which witnessed the development of the *polis* (city-state), the rise of Panhellenism and the concept of a unified Greek ethnicity, the reinvention of writing, the surge of the colonization movement, the appearance of written law codes, the rise and fall of tyrants, the development of hoplite warfare, the breakdown of aristocratic hegemony, and the struggle for political representation by different groups within the cities. Precisely because Archaic Greek poetry was so integrally enmeshed in social life, it is impossible to imagine that the system of poetry remained rigid and impervious to such conditions of radical change. Instead, I would contend, the Archaic period shows us a traditional poetic system in dialectical interaction with a period of extreme social and political ferment. We might say that in the Archaic period everything was up for grabs and that these battles were partly fought through and in Greek poetry in performance. Thus we see in the poetry of this period a complex interaction of old and new, tradition and innovation. And although it may be impossible, given the form and system of Greek lyric, to extract biographical information about the "real lives" of individual poets, read differently, Archaic Greek poetry offers us a wealth of historical data. For it preserves a precious record of intense ideological contestation for this period of rapid and radical social and political change. And it is finally, I would suggest, the intensity of ideological contestation that accounts for the prominence of the assertive, individual "I" in Greek lyric at this particular moment. In this sense, the pervasive, self-assertive "I" is not merely a historical and generic mirage: it is rather an epiphenomenon of political and social contestation and resistance. But to see this more clearly, we must lay out synchronically the complex system of Archaic Greek genre and occasion as they relate to performance contexts and sociopolitical interests.

Genre, Occasion, and Ideology

What we conventionally call Greek "lyric" in fact comprises three distinct categories of poetry, differentiated by formal features as well as by social context and occasion of performance. These are:

(1) *Iamboi*: A category that included, but was not limited to iambic meter; *iamboi* were also composed in trochaic meters, and in

epodes, which combined iambic or trochaic with hexameter lines. The defining feature of *iamboi* in this period seems to have been their coarse, "low class" content, sexual narratives, animal fables, and use for blame. There is dispute about their performance context, but many scholars take *iamboi* to be a kind of dramatic monologue performed at public festivals, perhaps originally associated with fertility rituals. *Iamboi* were apparently spoken, not sung. The main Archaic composers of *iamboi* were Archilochus of Paros (traditional dates ca. 700–640 BCE), Semonides of Amorgos (trad. floruit 664–1 BCE), Solon of Athens (trad. floruit 594/3 BCE), and Hipponax of Clazomenae (trad. floruit 540–37 BCE).

(2) Elegy: Poetry composed in elegiac couplets (a dactylic hexameter followed by a dactylic pentameter). All the elegy we have preserved from the Archaic period shows a marked Ionic dialect coloring, suggesting that the genre of elegy developed originally in East Greece. Although in later antiquity elegy was strongly associated with funeral lament, there is no good evidence for this function in the remains of early elegy. Instead, there seem to have been two different genres of elegy: brief paraenetic and/or erotic poems probably performed at the symposium, and longer historical narrative elegies or poems of military exhortation probably performed at public festivals or on campaign. In style, elegy tended to be more decorous than iambic, but not as elevated as melic poetry. It appears to have been recited or sung, perhaps to the accompaniment of the *aulos* (a double-piped reed instrument). The most important Archaic elegists were Mimnermus of Colophon and Smyrna (trad. floruit 632–29 BCE), Callinus of Ephesus (trad. dated first half of the seventh c.), Tyrtaeus of Sparta (trad. dated seventh c.), Theognis of Megara (ca. 625–480 BCE), Solon of Athens (trad. floruit 594/3 BCE), Xenophanes of Colophon (trad. dates ca. 565–470 BCE), and Simonides of Ceos (trad. dates ca. 556–468 BCE).

(3) Melic: Composed in lyric meters properly so called, melic is conventionally divided into monody (performed at the symposium) and choral poetry (performed in public for the civic community). Monody was sung by a solo performer, accompanying him- or herself on the lyre; choral poetry by an entire chorus singing (and dancing) in unison, to the accompaniment

of a lyre (and sometimes perhaps also an *aulos*). Monody tended to be shorter and simpler in its metrical structure; choral poetry longer and more elaborate, both in diction and meter. The language of monody tended to be closer to (though not identical with) the local dialect of the composer, whereas choral poetry exhibited an elaborate *Kunstsprache* (an artificial poetic dialect; cf. chapter 5) with a marked Doric coloring. By the Hellenistic period, a fixed canon of nine "great lyric poets" had already crystallized – all of them active in the Archaic period: Alcman of Sparta (trad. floruit 654–11 BCE), Sappho and Alcaeus of Mytilene (trad. floruit ca. 600 BCE), Stesichorus of Himera (trad. dates ca. 632–556 BCE), Ibycus of Rhegion (trad. dated mid-sixth c.), Anacreon of Teos (trad. floruit 550–20 BCE), Simonides and Bacchylides of Ceos (trad. dates ca. 556–468 and ca. 520–?430, respectively), and Pindar of Thebes (trad. dates 518–438 BCE).

Because Archaic Greece was a "song culture" in which performance was very much a living part of every aspect of social life, song and poetry figured in all kinds of contexts – there were (for example) marriage songs, war songs, harvest songs, grinding songs, and songs to accompany children's games. But, as the preceding summary of iambic, elegy, and melic makes clear, two very important contexts for the performance of verse and song were the symposium and the *agora* or center of the city. To some extent, these two performance sites were opposed to each other. For public performance in the *agora* (notionally) spoke to and for the entire city assembled, whereas the symposium took shape as a small elite gathering where no more than fifteen to thirty participants forged their own group loyalties and group values, which often contravened the emerging egalitarian values of the city. Thus, in a sense, the symposium was always a political gathering, in which a "band of companions" (*hetaireia*) constituted itself in opposition to other sympotic groups and to the city as a whole.

Within the fragmentary remains of Archaic poetry, these two opposed venues of performance tend to align with two opposed ideological positions, characterized by Ian Morris as "middling" and "elitist." The "elitist" position (which tends to be expressed in monody and other symposium poetry) celebrates *habrosyne*, luxury strongly associated with the Greeks' Eastern neighbors the Lydians, in the form of long flowing garments, elaborately coiffed hair, perfumes, gold ornaments, and sensuality, whereas the "middling" position rejects such luxuries as "useless" for the city. The valorization of luxury tends to pattern with a self-identification by these same poets with the gods, the mythical heroes of the past, and the fabulously wealthy East, whereas again the middling anti-*habrosyne* position abjures such external sources of authority for the modest community of citizens. Finally, for the former position, aristocratic birth and status are the most important thing, trumping even gender difference, whereas for the latter, citizen status becomes the most important thing and so (because throughout the Greek world citizenship was exclusively a male prerogative) gender difference becomes proportionately more significant. As in our own society, such "culture wars" are not just about what you wear, how you smell, and how you do your hair; they are ultimately political. In a context where everything is up for grabs, these two different lifestyles, enacted in practice and articulated in poetry in performance, contest the culture's most fundamental values: who should be in charge? what are the proper sources of authority?

We can see the celebration of sympotic luxury and sensuality, for example, in the monodic poetry of Anacreon. Thus Anacreon frequently sings of love, often associated with flowers and Eastern finery, as in the lines "For I am concerned to sing of Eros, the luxurious one (*habron*), teeming with flowering headbands" (fr. 505d *PMG*). In another three-line fragment, Anacreon manages to incorporate many of the elements of sympotic *habrosyne*:

> I breakfasted, having broken off a little bit of delicate honey-cake, and I drained my vessel of wine. But now I delicately pluck the lovely *pektis*, celebrating the *komos* with a dear and dainty girl.
>
> (fr. 373 *PMG*)

In contrast to Homeric heroes, who "breakfast" on whole sheep, Anacreon's speaker nibbles on "delicate honey-cake"; we may be tempted to take this line as a metapoetic characterization of his own "delicate" verse in contrast to the scale and themes of martial epic. The fragment goes on to mention wine, music produced on the Eastern lyre or *pektis*, and a female companion described in the same language used for male sympotic companions (*phile*). With it all, the poet includes two forms of the buzzword *habros* ("luxurious, delicate") in as many lines.

But we should not read Anacreon's jewel-like lyrics celebrating wine, women (or boys) and song as simple hedonism, for his fragments also offer us several examples of scathing abuse directed at gauche outsiders trying and failing to ape the exquisite lifestyle of elitist *habrosyne*.

More to the point: The political program that undergirds this sympotic sensuality is more explicitly formulated in the monodic lyrics of Alcaeus and the elegiacs of Theognis. Alcaeus' lyrics address and attempt to rally a counterrevolutionary aristocratic faction amid the political upheavals of sixth-century Mytilene, where tyrants rise and fall and the Mytilenean *demos* (the citizens at large) seems unexpectedly to be asserting its own will and authority. Thus in a long papyrus fragment,

> . . . the Lesbians once founded this great conspicuous precinct as a common one, and in it they established altars of the blessed immortals, and they named Zeus Antiaos, and you, glorious Aeolian Goddess, the mother of all, and third, this one they named Kemelios, Dionysus, eater of raw flesh. Come, hear our prayers, holding your spirit well-disposed, and save us from these toils and from grievous exile. But let the Furies of those men pursue the child of Hyrrhas [Pittacus], since once we swore, cutting . . . never to [betray or abandon(?)] anyone of the companions, but either to lie clothed in earth, dead at the hands of the men who then [held power], or, having killed them, to save the *demos* from griefs. Of these men Fatty [= Pittacus] did not speak sincerely, but easily mounting upon the oaths with his feet, he devours our city. . . .
>
> (fr. 129 LP)

Here the speaker and perhaps his sympotic companions have been driven out of the city, and, instead of "saving the *demos* from griefs" (what the speaker clearly regards as the rightful prerogative of his aristocratic faction), they are themselves forced to pray to the gods to "save [them] from grievous exile." Or more briefly, in a fragment preserved by Aristotle that sounds like a howl of rage and surprise:

> [The Mytileneans] established the baseborn Pittacus as tyrant of the gutless and ill-fated city, praising him greatly all together.
>
> (fr. 348 LP)

The political struggles Alcaeus' lyrics chronicle with great specificity and detail are echoed in more generalizing and schematic form in the elegiac verses of Theognis. Thus Theognis, whose poetry makes constant reference to the symposium, sympotic companions, drinking, love, and song, often speaks about "the citizens" but never to them, instead advising "companions" (*philoi* or *hetairoi*) on the proper running of the city. The speaker often announces his alienation or disaffection from the state of affairs in the city, as for example when he predicts the rise of a tyrant (ll. 39–52) or bemoans the fact that uncivilized outsiders "are now the good" (*agathoi*, ll. 53–60).

Sappho's monodic song also participates in the same elitist cult of *habrosyne*, often asserting the speaker's close connection with the gods, the heroes, and the East through luxury objects and lyrics of sensuous beauty. For example, a cletic hymn to Aphrodite imagines the goddess herself present "serv[ing] nectar delicately (*habros*) mixed with festivity in golden cups" (fr. 2 LP, ll. 14–16). The dissolution of literal and figurative ("nectar mixed with festivity") conjures up a magical landscape in which this divine epiphany occurs, whereas the mention of golden cups and nectar (the drink of the gods) in place of wine collapses the distance between divinity and worshipper. Sappho's participation in this milieu is complicated by her gender (as we shall see); nonetheless, much in her lyrics conforms to the cult of Eastern luxury as we find it articulated in other Archaic monody. Thus, in another fragment, the speaker passionately affirms, "I love *habrosyne* . . . and it is love (*eros*) that has allotted to me the brightness and beauty of the sun" (fr. 58 LP, ll. 25–6). We might read these lines as programmatic for all Sappho's poetry, for it is precisely this elitist culture of luxury and sensuality (*habrosyne*) that opens up a space for Sappho to pursue love (*eros*) and love poetry, and to achieve thereby a kind of poetic immortality ("the brightness and beauty of the sun"). (And all this applies whether or not we take these lines to be the beginning of a new poem, as papyrus fragments of Sappho newly published in 2004 seem to suggest.)

That *habrosyne* is indeed a lifestyle and not merely a literary theme is confirmed by another domain of evidence – images on Attic drinking cups. In almost fifty representations that range in date from 530 to 470 BCE, we find groups of male symposiasts dressed in long flowing garments, with elaborate headbands or turbans, occasionally sporting parasols and even earrings (the latter two accoutrements strongly marked as Eastern exotica; see Figures 16 and 17). These vase representations look like perfect illustrations of the poetry of Anacreon, and indeed we find a figure labeled "Anacreon" on three of them, confirming the intimate association of this lifestyle with the poet of sympotic luxury and love. The archaeologist Keith De Vries has pointed out that the dress of these figures is almost identical with fifth-century representations of Lydians in friezes at the Persian palace of Persepolis, whereas these same friezes show the parasol as a mark of honor for high dignitaries in the East. Based on these parallels, he suggested that the vase paintings represent fantasy scenes of Lydians at the symposium, or (East Greek) Ionians imitating them, or elite Athenians imitating Ionians imitating Lydians. Beyond his identification of the source of these costumes, De Vries' interpretation has the virtue of capturing something of the phantasmatic play-space the symposium seems to have provided, with its dizzying regress of dress-up and role-playing.

At the same time, we find vigorous opposition to this elitist culture of luxury and refinement voiced in the reasoned cadences of public elegy and the scabrous parodies of iambic. Thus a fragment of Xenophanes, probably derived from publicly performed historical elegy, casts a jaundiced eye on the affectations of the Colophonian elite:

> Having learnt useless *habrosynai* (plural) from the Lydians, as long as they were free of hateful tyranny, they went to the *agora* wearing purple cloaks, no less than a thousand in general, boastful, glorying in their beautiful hair, drenched in unguents curiously wrought in scent.
>
> (fr. B 4 DK)

That Xenophanes' standard of "uselessness" here is civic is suggested by the brief hexameter aphorism credited to the poet Phocylides (sixth century?): "And this of Phocylides: a small *polis* on a rock, inhabited in orderly fashion, is better than witless Nineveh" (fr. 4 Diehl).

Finally, we may see parody of the lifestyle of *habrosyne* and the links it cultivated with the empires of the East in publicly performed iambic poetry, in the scurrilous, picaresque narratives of Hipponax. Much of Hipponax' poetry seems to characterize the "I" of iambic as a debased and marginal figure – a scapegoat, whose invective paradoxically gives him the power to scapegoat and destroy others. Thus, one fragment of Hipponax describes the speaker having his genitals beaten in a privy as a cloud of dung-beetles whirs around, by a woman "talking Lydian" (*lydizousa*, fr. 92 W), in a scene whose sordidness seems deliberately to undermine the elitist fetishization of things Lydian. Another fragment (apparently giving directions) bathetically juxtaposes royal monuments of the East with the too-vivid intrusion of an individual body:

> [Go?] . . . straight through the Lydians beside the tomb of Alyattes and the monument of Gyges and the stele of Sesostris and the memorial of Tos, sultan for Mytalis, having turned your belly toward the setting sun.
>
> (fr. 42 W)

In light of all this, we can recognize in the iambic lines of Archilochus quoted at the beginning of this chapter a systematic rejection of the elitist lifestyle and its claims to authority – Gyges, Eastern gold, "the works of the gods," tyranny, all that, in the speaker's view, is "far from [his] eyes." It is significant then that Aristotle attributes these lines to "Charon the carpenter" as speaker; that is, to a humble working man and middling citizen. The middling posture of iambic may also explain the late fifth-century Critias' maliciously literal reading of Archilochus. As an arch-conservative opponent of Athenian democracy (and prime mover of the oligarchic coup of 404 BCE), Critias had every reason to undermine Archilochus' authority and reject the middling values espoused in his poetry. This he did by reading iambic poetry's generic declarations literally as "facts" about the poet.

It bears emphasizing that, in all likelihood, all the poets whose fragments we possess come from an elite of birth, wealth, and status, and this applies as much to Xenophanes, Archilochus, and Hipponax as to Sappho, Alcaeus, and Anacreon. Thus this is not a battle fought between "aristocratic" and "middle-class" poets, but an ideological contest of paradigms over what constitutes the good life and the proper sources of authority within the highest echelon of society. And this fact in turn makes clear that it is less about the speaker than about the audience – the characterization of the persona as a proponent of elitist luxury or as a modest, middling citizen crucially responds to and shapes in turn audience expectations and ambient ideology in performance. In this respect, it is striking how closely the two divergent ideological positions represented in the poetic remains correlate with the two different performance venues independently derived from formal features, later reports, and the internal evidence of the fragments: the developing, pervasive egalitarianism of the civic sphere shapes the middling persona of iambic and publicly performed elegy, whereas the elitist identification with Eastern luxury, the gods, and heroes takes shape as the oppositional voice of sympotic elegy and monody.

It is worth noticing the prominence of the "I" in many of the fragments quoted: Anacreon says "*I* am concerned to sing of Eros"; Sappho declares "*I* love *habrosyne*"; Archilochus (in the persona of Charon) asserts "*I* do not desire great tyranny." This "I" is passionate – vividly expressing its wants and desires, its hates and frustrations – so that modern readers, accustomed to post-Romantic models of subjectivity, are easily seduced into seeing the self-assertion of real individuals as the point of these poetic utterances. But in all these cases, the confident voicing of "I" serves a different purpose. The "I" stiffens and takes shape on the edge of ideological conflict; indeed, it demarcates the lines of social and political contest.

This is nowhere clearer than in the Greek poetic form of the priamel. In rhetorical terms, the priamel is a focusing device that adds weight and emphasis to a particular point by introducing it contrastively. In terms of content, however, the priamel often represents ideological contestation in its most concentrated and explicit form, while demonstrating how such contestation generates the speaking "I" at (and as) the point of resistance. Thus in an extended priamel in one of Tyrtaeus' elegies, which is presumably a poem of military exhortation:

> I would not mention, nor would I put in account a man
> neither for the virtue of his feet nor for wrestling,
> nor if he should have the size and strength of the Cyclopes
> nor if he should beat Thracian Boreas at running,
> nor if he should be lovelier in form than Tithonus,
> or richer than Midas or Cinyras,
> nor if he should be more kingly than Pelops, son of Tantalus,
> or have the honey-voiced tongue of Adrastus,
> nor if he should have every glory except thrusting courage.
> For he would not be a man good in war
> unless he could endure seeing bloody slaughter,
> and fight, taking a firm stand near the enemies.
>
> (fr. 12 W, lines 1–12)

Here the speaker rejects a whole series of culturally valued qualities and possessions (including athletic prowess; mythic speed, strength, and beauty; and the wealth and royal power of Eastern dynasts) in order to valorize the ideal of the hoplite warrior who stands his ground fighting for his city (see Chapter 2). And in this context, the "I" takes shape with – and as a byproduct of – the promulgation of this civic ideal. Thus the composers of Archaic poetry are indeed men and women "in the active voice," though in very different terms from what is conventionally understood by moderns as the literary construction and representation of individual subjectivity. These are voices actively engaged in fierce political and ideological contestation – contestation from which the Greek *polis* in its classical form emerges.

Against this backdrop, we can also see with particular clarity how old and new interact; how a traditional poetic system of genre and occasion adapts to new social and political pressures and contingencies. This is perhaps most conspicuous in the public poetry of Solon and the generic developments of choral lyric. Solon, who was supposedly made archon (chief magistrate) by the Athenians in 594/3 BCE with a mandate to resolve the tensions within the city and construct a new law code, was also credited with the composition of poetry in elegiac and iambic meters. And Solon's poetry seems to work and achieve its political purposes through the interaction of traditional elegiac and iambic personae. From elegiac poetry, Solon derives his stance as authoritative advisor and lawgiver for the city (a posture that also resonates through the elegiacs of Theognis). But whereas Theognis' poetry limits its address to other aristocrats within the elite symposium, Solon's seems to speak to and for the whole community, even on occasion using the festive and orderly sacrificial banquet (*dais*) as an image for proper civic behavior:

> And the mind of the leaders of the *demos* is unjust, for whom it is ready
> to suffer many griefs from their great hybris.
> For they do not know how to restrain excess nor, when festivity
> is present, to adorn the feast in peace and quiet.
>
> (fr. 4 W, lines 7–10)

Indeed, it is tempting to imagine that the performance venue for this poem might be a citywide festival and sacrifice, which would in a sense merge the settings of banquet and public sphere.

At the same time, Solon's iambic fragments, although they seem more decorous and solemn than those of Archilochus and Hipponax, still exploit characteristic iambic elements such as beast fable and the representation of the iambic poet as an isolated or marginalized scapegoat figure. Thus in the concluding lines of a long fragment in which the speaker defends his political program:

> But if another had taken the goad, as I did,
> an evil-plotting and avaricious man,
> he would not have restrained the *demos*. For if I had willed
> what things then pleased the opposing side
> and what things in turn the other side thought,
> I would have widowed the city of many men.
> On account of these things, defending myself from every side
> I was turned like a wolf among many dogs.
>
> (fr. 36 W, lines 20–27)

Here the speaker segues abruptly in the last lines to the image of a lone wolf. The single wolf, turning and defending himself from a pack of dogs attacking on all sides, figures both the cunning and the isolation of the scapegoated iambic persona. But in this case, the "I" does not assume this characteristic iambic position in order to scapegoat and drive out another individual (as is the dynamic of Archilochus' and Hipponax's iambic abuse); instead the dramatic isolation of the "I" serves to carve out a middle space that will become the common political space of the city. This figuration of voluntary and suspended isolation is even more sharply delineated in a few iambic lines preserved by Aristotle:

> But I, just like a boundary stone in the no-man's-land
> between these parties, took my stand.
>
> (fr. 37 W, lines 9–10)

Here the "I" describes himself as a boundary stone set in the no-man's-land between two enemy armies. As Nicole Loraux points out, this image collapses the opposition (so essential to Greek thought) between civil and foreign war, while it strands and freezes the "I" between two hostile camps in what can only be a temporary lull before combat. In this impossible space, the "I" as a single boundary stone incarnates "the middle" (*to meson*) – the space that makes possible political activity, common to everyone because it belongs to no one. In a final interaction of elegiac and iambic personae, Solon makes this middle space available to the whole city by vacating it. For in the traditional biography of Solon, we are told, he bound all the citizens on oath to accept his laws for ten years without change, and then consigned himself to ten years of exile to obviate any appeals to his personal authority as lawgiver. In this tradition of his decade-long voluntary exile, the figure of Solon fuses the elegiac role of civic sacred ambassador (*theoros*) with that of iambic scapegoat (*pharmakos*).

If Solon's verse weaves together elements of elegy and iambic to forge a new public space and a statesman's voice to speak in it, choral lyric poetry seems to provide a medium for negotiating and reconciling within the public sphere different interests and claims, both those of individual and community and those of middling and elitist ideological positions. A tantalizing fragment of Stesichorus suggests that this work of mediation already characterized choral poetry of the seventh century, for a three-line fragment neatly combines the discourse of *habrosyne* with the claims of the public or common sphere:

> It is fitting for those who have found a Phrygian strain to hymn such things belonging to the *demos* (*damomata*) delicately (*habros*) when spring comes on.
>
> (fr. 212 *PMG*)

Yet the remnants of early choral poetry are so fragmentary that we cannot say much more; only when we get to the fully preserved poems of Bacchylides and especially of Pindar at the end of the Archaic period can we trace this choral work of mediation in any detail.

The corpus of these two poets also shows us in fully developed form a relatively new genre of choral poetry – the *epinikion* or epinician ode to celebrate an athletic victory, normally won at one of the great Panhellenic games (Oympian, Pythian, Isthmian, Nemean). These poems seem to have been commissioned by the victor or his family for performance by a chorus of the victor's fellow citizens on his return home from the games. In its elaborate performance of praise of an individual by a citizen chorus at the center of the city, *epinikion* represents an anomalous hybrid form. For, as far as we can tell, the traditional context for choral poetry was communal and religious; the performance of a chorus (male or female) represented the whole community in hymns to the gods and religious festivals (e.g., the various choral forms of *partheneion*, paean, dithyramb, and hymn itself). *Epinikion* appropriates and transfers that choral form to the praise of a single mortal individual (what had traditionally been the purview of sympotic encomium).

And this generic hybridity correlates with complexity of social interests served, because athletic competition and victory were themselves ideologically contested, with participation almost entirely limited to an elite of birth and wealth, whereas the value of such pursuits was frequently questioned by middling, civic voices (as in the priamel of Tyrtaeus, quoted above). Epinician poetry (at least in the form we have it) deployed its generic hybridity in the service of reconciling in performance individual and community, elitist and middling values. By going off to the site of the games and winning, the elite athletic victor isolated and singled himself out from his community, returning with exceptional status and charismatic authority. The epinician ode in performance worked to reintegrate the isolated and exceptional victor back into his various communities – his household, his city, and the Panhellenic network of the aristocracy.

The rhetoric of such reintegration varied from city to city and, crucially, with the status of the victor – poems composed for tyrants diverge significantly from those composed for private citizens. The latter regularly assert that athletic victory served the common good, glorifying the whole city, while they work to reassure the victor's fellow citizens that he does not aim at excessive political power through the prominence and charismatic authority gained by athletic victory. These poems for private citizens carefully craft a portrait of the victor as an ideal middling citizen whose values are often expressed through a generalizing first person, as in these lines from *Pythian* 11:

> I would desire beautiful things from god,
> Striving for things that are possible within my age class.
> For finding the middle ranks blooming with more enduring
>   prosperity throughout the city,
> I blame the lot of tyrannies;
> And I am strained over common achievements. And the envious
>   are fended off,
> if a man, having taken the peak of achievement, plies it in peace
>   and avoids dread hybris. . . .
>
> (Pindar, *Pythian* 11.50–58)

The "I" here is nominally the poet's persona, but the values and choices it espouses, sung in unison by a chorus of the victor's fellow citizens, are meant to represent or mirror the victor's own. Thus the victor's civic contribution is affirmed and the envy of his fellow citizens allayed.

In contrast, the *epinikia* composed for victorious tyrants and dynasts make no effort to allay envy; in one poem addressed to Hieron, tyrant of Syracuse, for example, Pindar asserts "envy is better than pity" (*Pyth.* 1.85). Instead, they emphasize all that is exceptional about the victor's wealth, military prowess, athletic success, and scope of rule. These poems simultaneously laud the victor's political virtues, fashioning a portrait of him as an ideal ruler – a portrait aimed both at the victor's own citizen–subjects and at the wider community of the Panhellenic elite. In the tyrant odes, the poet's "I" takes a different form, assimilating itself to the exceptional status of the victor so that the poet can address and advise him as an equal. Thus, for example, at the end of *Olympian* 1:

> The furthest height caps itself
> for kings. No longer look further.

May it be for you [Hieron] to tread aloft for this time,
As for me to the same extent to keep company with victors,
being preeminent in poetic skill throughout all Greece.
(Pindar, *Olympian* 1.113–15b)

In all of Archaic poetry, there is no more prominent and assertive "I" than that of Pindar's *epinikia*. But this "I" is prominent precisely because it does the work of mediating and finessing the divergent interests and claims of individual and community, elitist and middling values, and for this reason, there is no more mercurial and unstable "I" than that of the *epinikia*. We cannot derive Pindar's politics, or values, or religious commitments from the shifty, evanescent "I" of the victory odes – only those of the patrons who commissioned, the choruses who sang, and the audiences who heard his songs.

Sappho: Gender and Lyric Subjectivity

I have thus far emphasized the necessity of understanding the lyric "I" in terms of the social work it does in performance, and I have considered at some length the dialectic of tradition and innovation in the poetic remains of the Archaic period. When we turn to the poetry of Sappho, we confront both these issues again, but with a difference. For the latter: What seems crucially to inflect Sappho's interaction with traditional forms is her gender and the gender of her audience. For the former: One has the feeling reading Sappho that no sociological account does justice to the power of her lyric "I"; even in fragments (and in translation) it is hard to resist the compelling lyric subjectivity that seems to infuse Sappho's poetry. I want to try to account for this latter phenomenon and suggest that the two issues are, in fact, intimately related.

Sappho may well be the only female voice preserved from the Greek Archaic period, and we know next to nothing for certain about her milieu and the social conditions for the composition and performance of her poetry. We are told that she belonged to an aristocratic family of Mytilene on Lesbos, was married, and had a daughter named Cleis. Later sources also report that she went into exile for some period, presumably for the same political reasons that motivated the repeated exiles of her aristocratic contemporary Alcaeus. Sappho's poetic production was reported in antiquity to fill nine books or papyrus rolls, but because of her ancient reputation as a "lover of women," her work fell into disfavor in the Christian era; it ceased to be read and therefore ceased

FIGURE 1. Scene from a Protocorinthian aryballos, ca. 690–680 BCE, from the Lechaion Cemetery near Corinth. Corinth Museum CP 2096. [From Eliot and Eliot, "The Lechaion Cemetery near Corinth," *Hesperia* 37 (1968) plate 102,2.]

FIGURE 2. Attacking warrior. Formerly part of a vessel. Greek bronze statuette, from Dodona, ca. 510–500 BCE. H.: 12.8 cm. Photograph Johannes Laurentius. Antikensammlung, Staatliche Museen zu Berlin, inv. Misc. 7470. Photograph credit: Bildarchiv Preussischer Kulturbesitz/Art Resource, NY.

FIGURE 3A. The "Chigi Vase": a Protocorinthian olpe from Veii (Rome, Villa Giulia 22679). Ca. 640 BCE. Photograph credit: Jeffrey M. Hurwit.

FIGURE 3B. Scene from the "Chigi Vase." [Drawing in E. Pfuhl, *Malerei und Zeichnung der Griechen* (Munich 1923) no. 59].

FIGURE 4. Scene from the Protocorinthian "Macmillan Aryballos", ca. 655 BCE, from Thebes (British Museum 1889.4-18.1) [Drawing in *Journal of Hellenic Studies* 11 (1890) pl. 2.].

FIGURE 5. Scene from a Protocorinthian aryballos, ca. 675 BCE, from Perachora [Drawing in T. J. Dunbabin, *Perachora* vol. 2 (Oxford 1962) pl. 57, no. 27].

FIGURE 6. Scene from the Nereid monument, ca. 390-380 BCE. London, British Museum GR 1848.10–20.51 (Sculpture 872). Photograph courtesy of the Trustees of the British Museum.

FIGURE 7. Scene from the North Frieze of the Siphnian Treasury at Delphi, ca. 525 BCE. Delphi, Museum. Photograph courtesy of the Archives of the American School of Classical Studies, Alison Frantz Collection.

FIGURE 8. Scene from a Protocorinthian aryballos, ca. 650 BCE. Paris, Musee du Louvre CA 1831. [Drawing from K. Friis Johansen, *RevArch* 13 (1921) 8 fig. 1.]

FIGURE 9. Scene from a Protocorinthian aryballos from Gela, ca. 650 BCE. Syracuse. [Drawing from *MontAnt* 17 (1906) 157–158 fig. 116.]

FIGURE 10. Attic black-figure drinking vessel depicting *erastes* and *eromenos*, ca. 530 BCE. Courtesy, Museum of Fine Arts, Boston. Gift of E.P. and Fiske Warren. Accession Number 08.292.

FIGURE 11. Greek Scaraboid with an archer testing an arrow, ca. 500 BCE. Attributed to Epimenes. Courtesy of Metropolitan Museum of Art, Fletcher Fund, 1931 (31.11.5) Image © The Metropolitan Museum of Art.

FIGURE 12. Scene of a chorus of young women, on an Attic black-figure lekythos, ca. 550 BCE. Attributed to the Amasis Painter. Courtesy of Metropolitan Museum of Art, Purchase, Walter C. Baker Gift, 1956 (56.11.1). Photograph, all rights reserved, The Metropolitan Museum of Art.

FIGURE 13. Scene of a bridal procession, on an Attic black-figure lekythos, ca. 550 BCE. Attributed to the Amasis Painter. Courtesy of Metropolitan Museum of Art, Purchase, Walter C. Baker Gift, 1956 (56.11.1). Photograph, all rights reserved, The Metropolitan Museum of Art.

FIGURE 14. Scene of a *prothesis*, on an Attic black-figure loutrophoros, late sixth century. BCE. Courtesy of Metropolitan Museum of Art, Funds from various donors, 1927 (27.228). Photograph, all rights reserved, The Metropolitan Museum of Art.

FIGURE 15A–B. The Blinding of Polyphemus, on a Protoattic amphora from Eleusis, ca. 660 BCE. Courtesy of the German Archaeological Institute, Athens; photograph: Eva-Maria Czakó, D-DAI-ATH-Eleusis 546, 547.

FIGURE 15B.

FIGURE 16. Anacreontic symposiasts on an Attic red-figure cup by the Briseis Painter (Side A). Ca. 490–80 BCE. Courtesy of the J. Paul Getty Museum, Villa Collection, Malibu CA (86.AE.293).

FIGURE 17. Anacreontic symposiasts on an Attic red-figure cup by the Briseis Painter (Side B). Ca. 490–80 BCE. Courtesy of the J. Paul Getty Museum, Villa Collection, Malibu CA (86.AE.293).

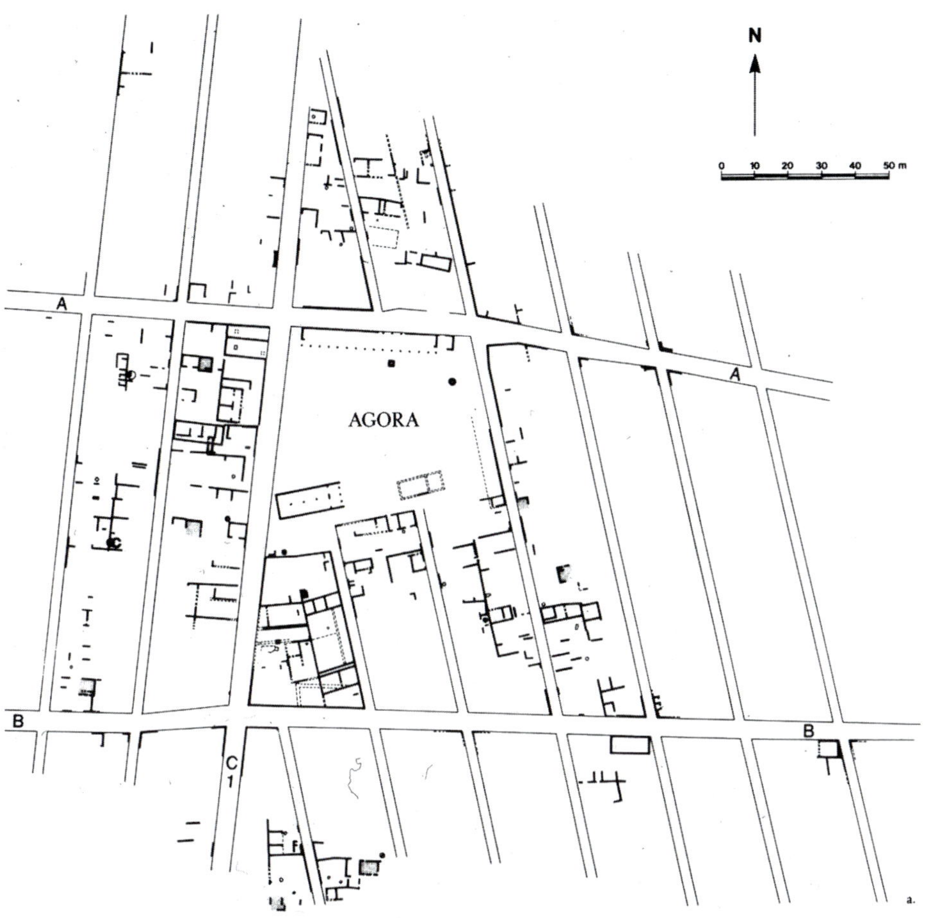

FIGURE 18. Plan of Megara Hyblaia. [From Giovanni Pugliese Carratelli, ed., *The Western Greeks: Classical Civilization in the Western Mediterranean* (1996) 266.]

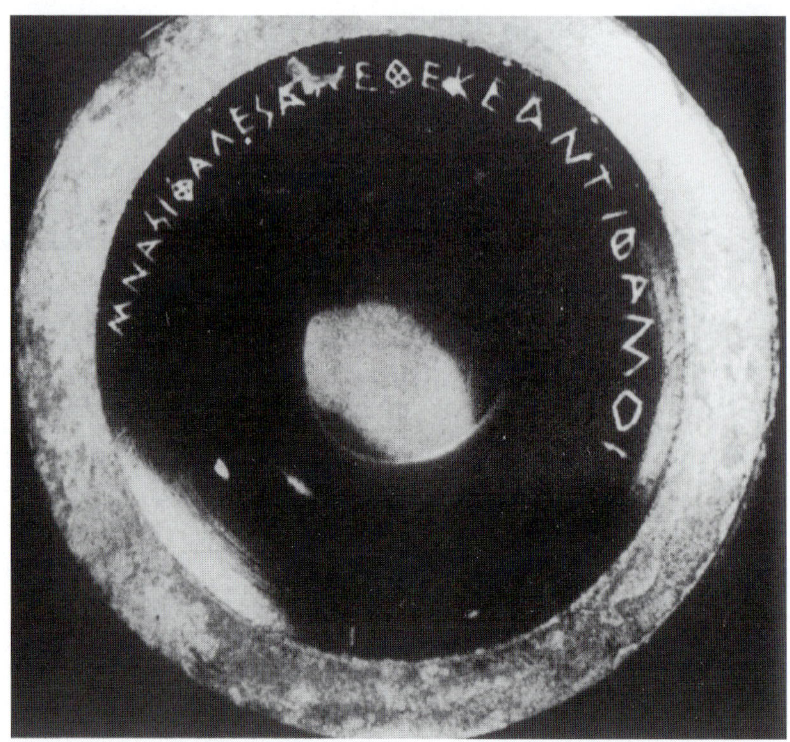

FIGURE 19. Dedication to Antiphemus, founder of Gela, on Attic kylix. [From *Annuario della Scuola archeologica di Atene* n.s. xi–xiii (1949–51) 108.]

FIGURE 20. Deinomenid dedication base at Delphi. Photograph Carla M. Antonaccio.

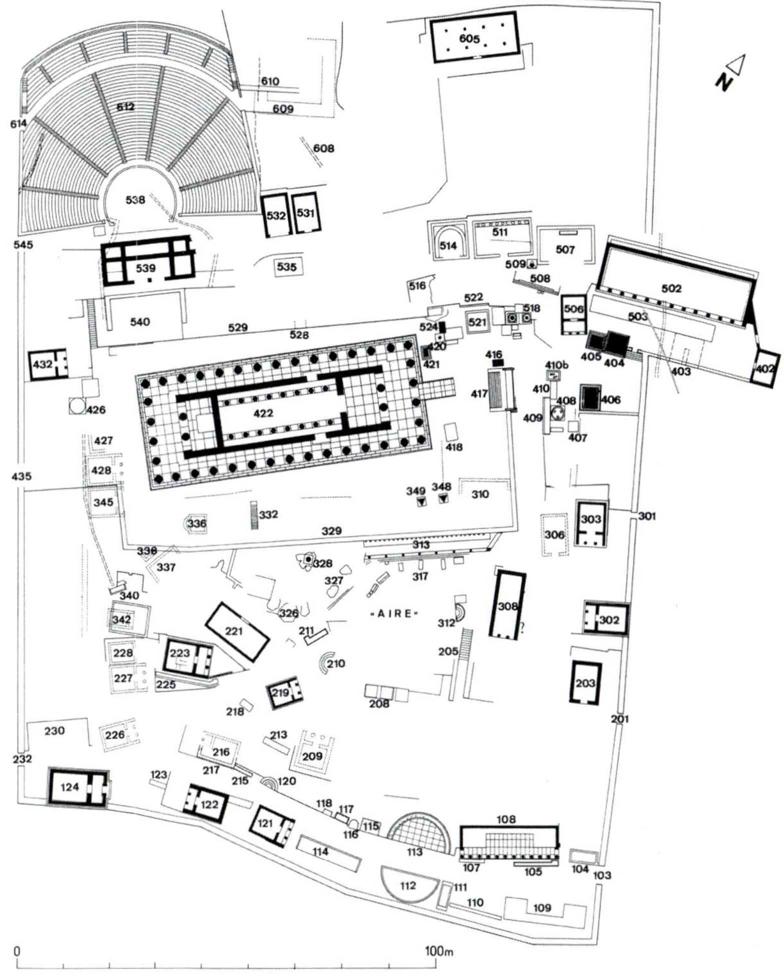

104 Base of the Bull
of the Corcyreans
105 Base of the Arcadians
108 Anonymous Stoa
109 Base of the Navarchs (Admirals)
110 Site of the Miltiades Monument
111 Base of the Argive Horse
112 Base of the Seven and the Epigonoi
113 So-called Niche of the Argive Kings
114 Base of the Tarentines "Below"
121 Treasury of the Sicyonians
122 Treasury of the Siphnians
123 Base of the Liparians
124 Treasury of the Thebans
203 Anonymous *Oikos*
205 Dolonia Stairs
209 Anonymous Treasury
211 Base of the Boeotians
215 Base of the Aetolians
216-217 Treasury and terrace
of the Megarians
219 Treasury of the Cnidians?
221 Council House?
223-225 Treasury of the Athenians
and Marathon Base
226 Treasury of the Boeotians
227 Anonymous Treasury
228 Anonymous *Oikos*
302 Treasury of the Cyreneans
303 Treasury XVI (of Brasidas and
the Acanthians?)
306 Anonymous Treasury
308 Treasury of the Corinthians
313 Stoa of the Athenians
317 Base of Attalus II
326 Rock of the Sybil?
328 Column of the Sphinx
of the Naxians
329 Retaining wall and terrace
of the Temple
332 Fountain (of the Muses?)
336 *Oikos* XXIX (shrine of Ge?)
337-338 Anonymous *Oikoi* (XXVII and XXII)
340 Fountain of the Asclepius shrine
342 Treasury X (Etruscan?) beneath (342)
the shrine of Asclepius
345 Anonymous Treasury (XXI)
348 Approximate site of the Messenian Pillar
349 Presumed site of the pillar on the black stone
402-503 Terrace of Attalus I
404 Pillar of Eumenes II
405 Pillar of Attalus I
406 Pillar of the Rhodians
407 Tripod of Plataea?
408 Base of the Crotonates
409 Base of the Tarentines "Above"
410b Site of the Apollo of Salamis
416 Aetolian Pillar of Eumenes II
417 Altar of Apollo
422 Temple of Apollo
427 Anonymous *Oikos* (XXX)
428 Anonymous Treasury (XX)
432 Anonymous Treasury (XXXI)
506 Anonymous Treasury (XVII)
507 Unfinished enclosure and base
508 Base of the Corcyreans
509 Base of the column of the acanthus
511 Base of Daochus
514 Horseshoe base
518 Offering of the Deinomenid tyrants
521 Square base (Apollo Sitalcas?)
524 Pillar of King Prusias
528 Foutain niche
531-532 "Treasuries of the Theater"
(XVIII-XIX)
538-612 Theater
540 Niche of Craterus
605 Lesche of the Cnidians

FIGURE 21. Site plan of Delphi. [From J.-F. Bommelaer, *Guide de Delphes: Le Site* (1991) pl. V.]

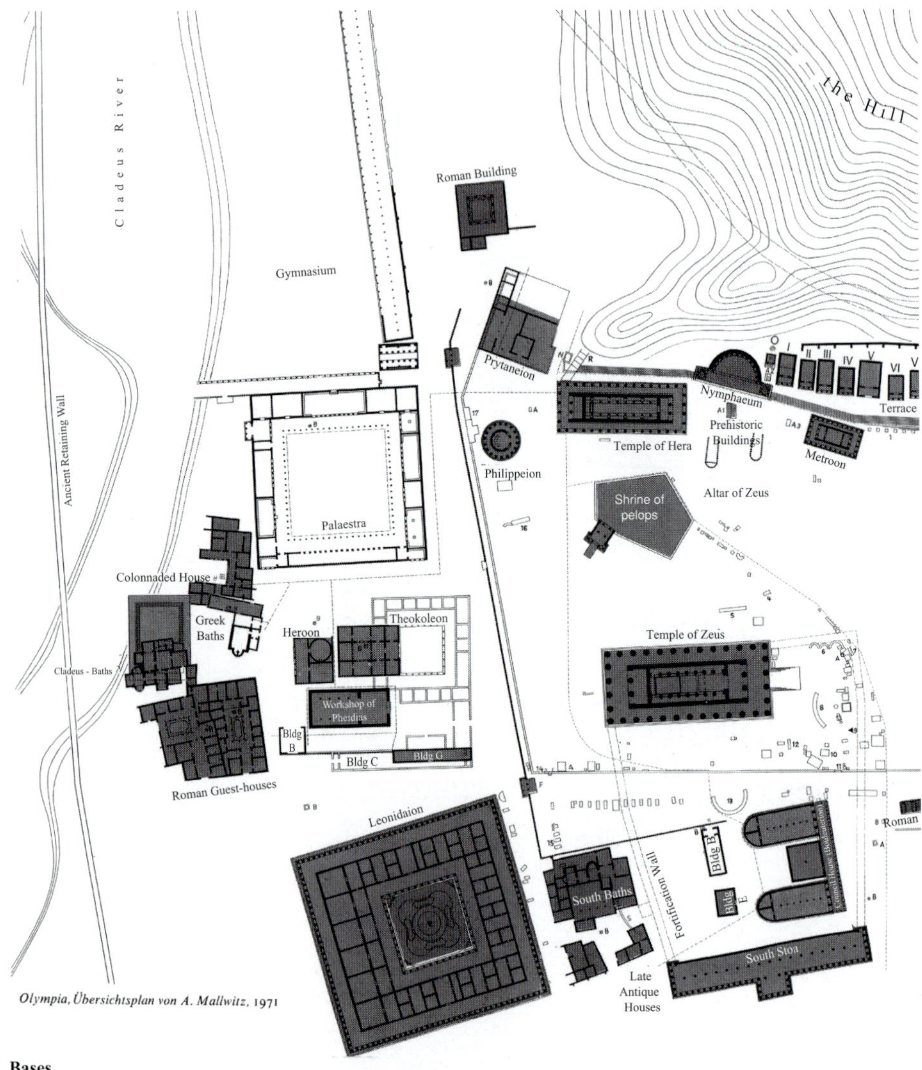

Bases

1. Older "Zanes" bases
2. New "Zanes" bases
3. Ptolemy and Arsinoe
4. Base for Dropion statue
5. Dedication of Micythus
6. Eleian Semi-circular Bases
7. Bull of Eretria
8. Archaic Dedication
9. Nike of Paeonius
10. Zeus in Memory of the Victory at Plataea
11. Base of Telemachus
12. Dedication of Praxiteles
13. Dedication of Apollonia
14. Base of Philonides
15. Base of M.M. Rufus
16. Dedication of Phormis
17. Base of Callicrates

Altars

A unknown altars
A1 Altar of Hera
A2 Altar of Heracles
A3 Altar of the Mother
A4 Altar of Artemis

FIGURE 22. Site plan of Olympia. [From A. Mallwitz, *Olympia und seine Bauten* (1972) 313.]

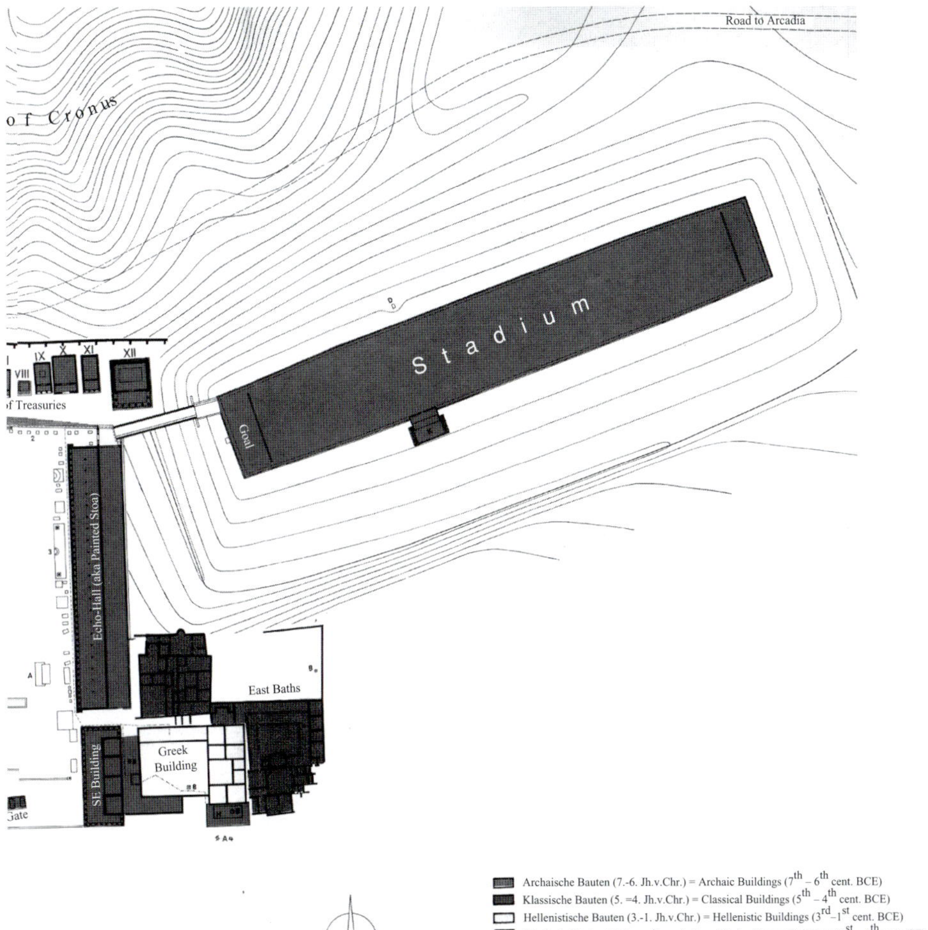

Buildings of the Treasuries Terrace

O Oikos
I Treasury of Sicyon
II Treasury of Syracuse
III Treasury of Epidamnus
IV Treasury of Byzantium
V Treasury of Sybaris
VI Treasury of Cyrene
VII Unknown Treasury
VIII Altar?
IX Treasury of Selinous
X Treasury of Metaponto
XI Treasury of Megara
XII Treasury of Gela
B Well
D The Seat of the Priestess of Demeter
F Roman Festival Gate
H Classical Stoa Foundation
K Platform for Judges
R Gaion Ramp
S Retaining Wall
W Tank for Water Storage
_ _ _ Greek Gutters

FIGURE 23. Helmet of Miltiades, Olympia, ca. 490 BCE. Courtesy Deutsches Archäologisches Institut, Athens (No. D-DAI-ATH-1976/558). Photograph Gëjta Hellner.

FIGURE 24. Nike of Kallimakhos, Athens, ca. 490 BCE. Courtesy Deutsches Archäologisches Institut, Athens (No. D-DAI-ATH-2001/878). Photograph Hans Rupprecht Goette.

FIGURE 25. Deinomenid charioteer, Delphi. Ca. 466 BCE. Photograph courtesy of the Archives of the American School of Classical Studies, Alison Frantz Collection.

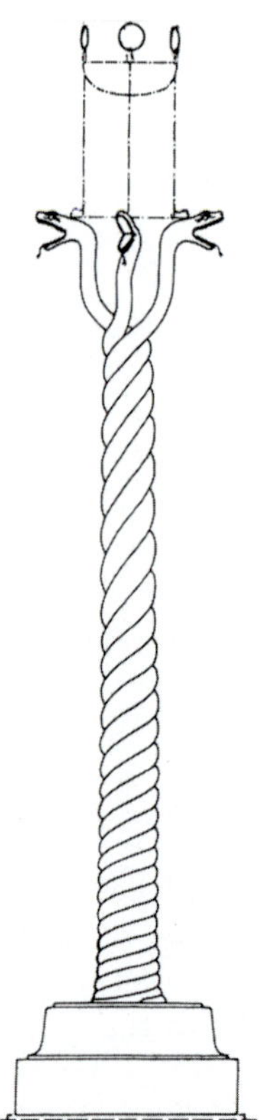

FIGURE 26. Reconstruction of Serpent column, Delphi. [From J.-F. Bommelaer, *Guide de Delphes: Le Site* (1991) fig. 69 left.]

FIGURE 27. Sicyonian metope with *Argo*, Delphi. Early sixth century BCE. Photograph courtesy of the Archives of the American School of Classical Studies, Alison Frantz Collection.

FIGURE 28. East pediment, Archaic Temple of Apollo, Delphi. Late sixth century BCE. Photograph courtesy of the Archives of the American School of Classical Studies, Alison Frantz Collection.

FIGURE 29. Athenian Treasury, Delphi. Ca. 490–80 BCE. Photograph courtesy of the Archives of the American School of Classical Studies, Alison Frantz Collection.

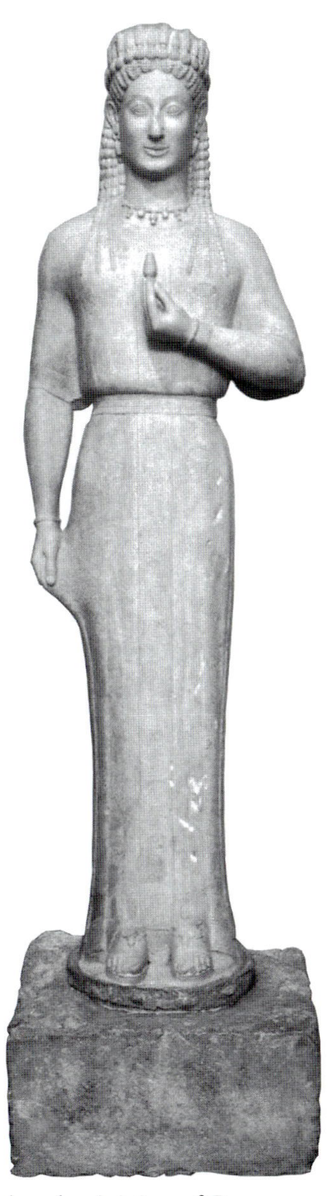

FIGURE 30. Phrasikleia *kore*, by Aristion of Paros, ca. 550–540 BCE. National Archaeologcal Museum, Athens (Inv. No. 4889). Photograph Jeffrey M. Hurwit.

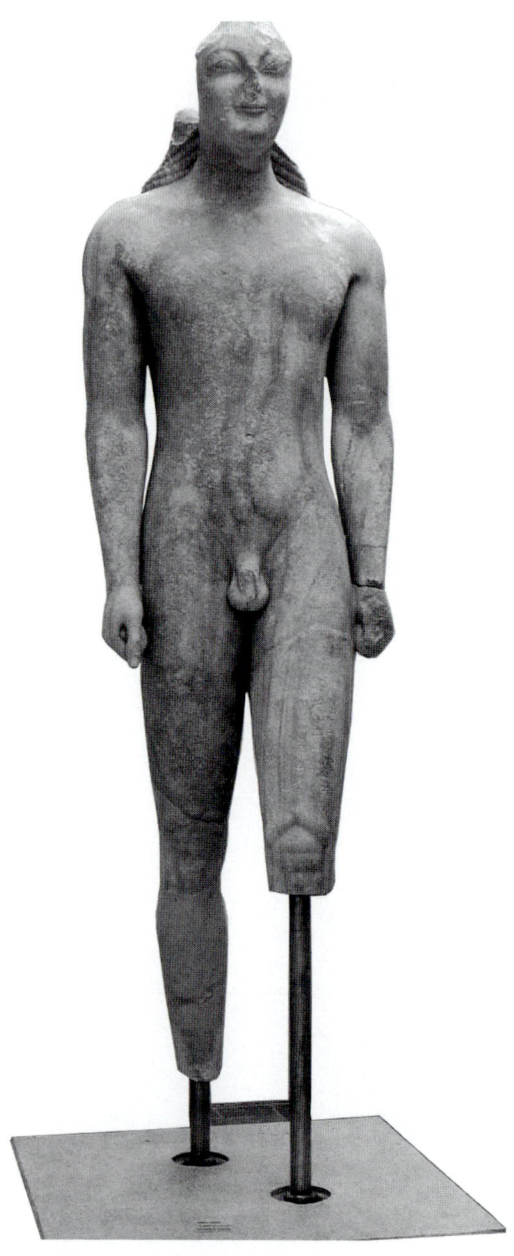

FIGURE 31. Isches *kouros*, ca. 580 BCE. Samos Museum. Photograph Jeffrey M. Hurwit.

FIGURE 32. Black Figure amphora by Exekias, ca. 530 BCE. Vatican Museums 344. Photograph courtesy of Hirmer Fotoarchiv, Munich.

FIGURE 33. *Kore*, Acropolis Museum 685, ca. 510 BCE. Photograph Jeffrey M. Hurwit.

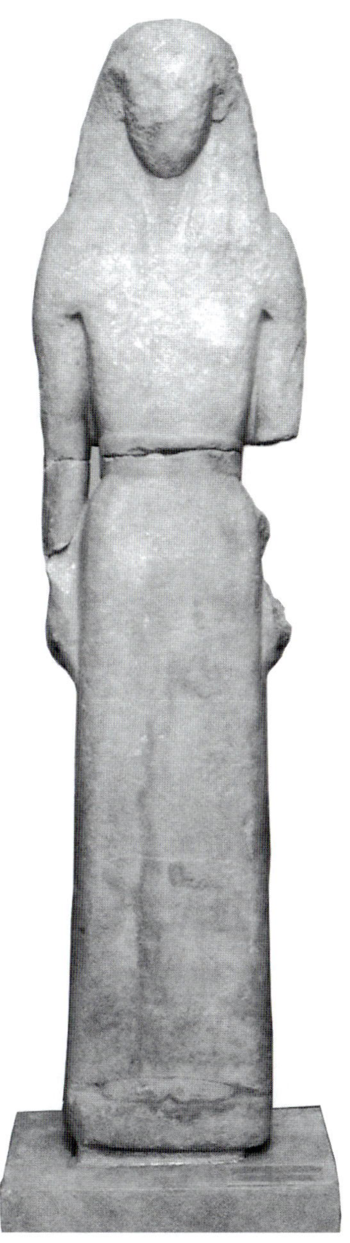

FIGURE 34. Nikandre *kore*, from Delos, ca. 650 BCE. National Archaeological Museum, Athens (Inv. No. 1). Photograph Jeffrey M. Hurwit.

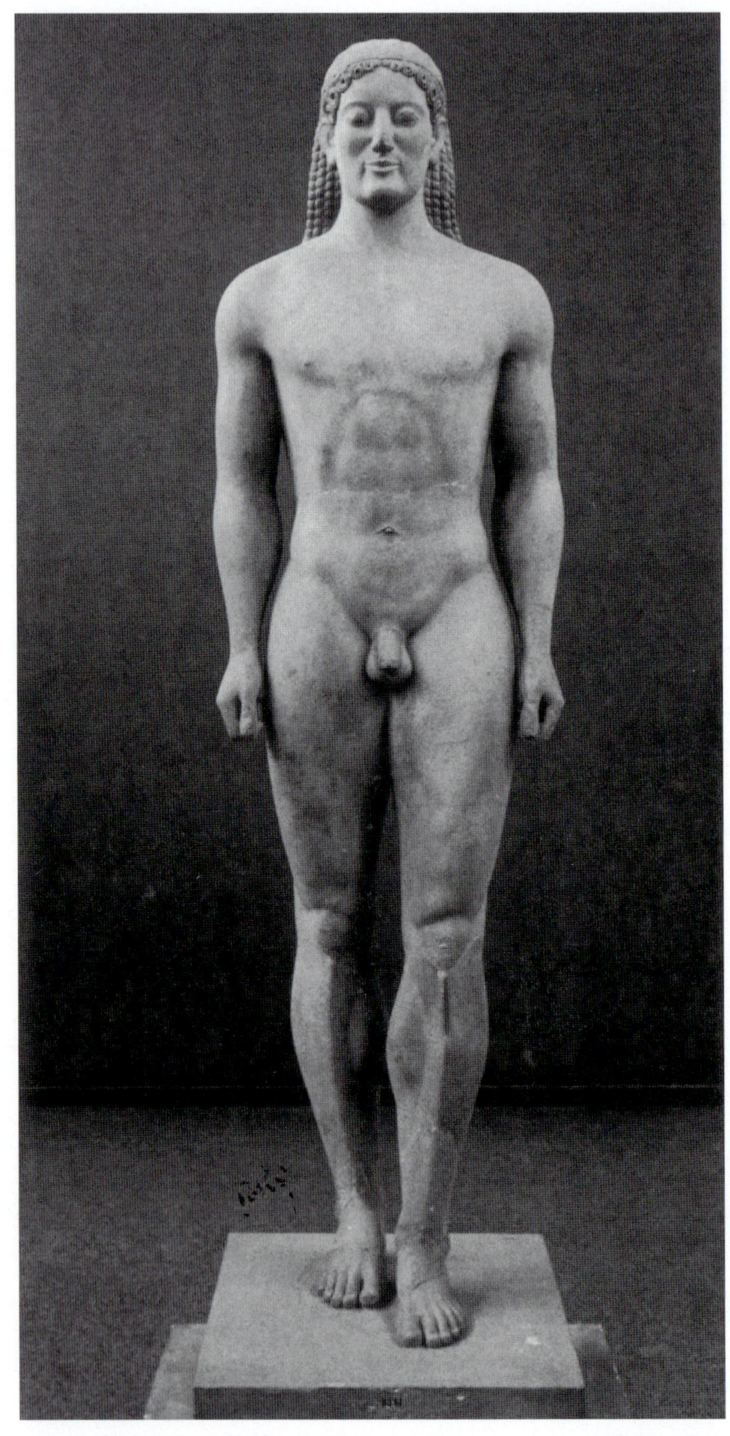

FIGURE 35. *Kouros* from tomb of Kroisos at Anavyssos, ca. 530 BCE. National Archaeological Museum, Athens (Inv. No. 3851). Photograph Jeffrey M. Hurwit.

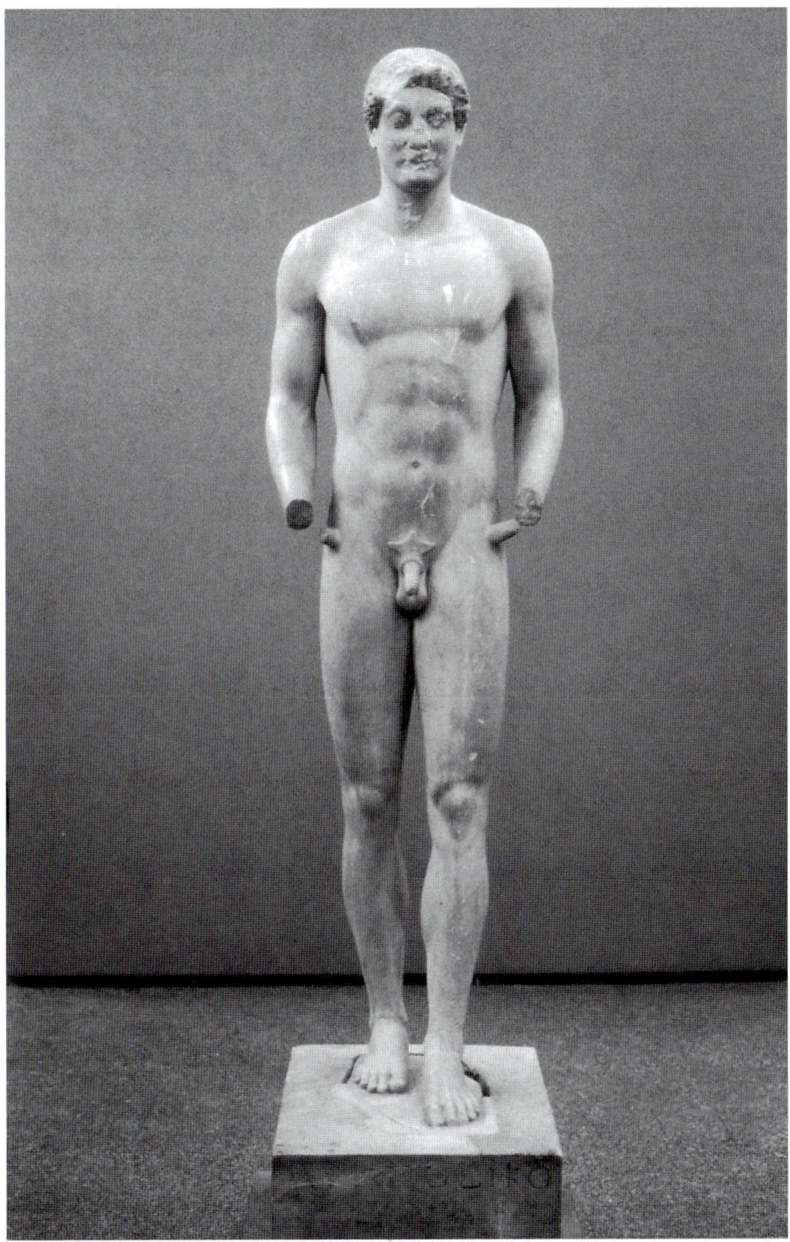

FIGURE 36. *Kouros* from tomb of Aristodikos, ca. 510–500 BCE. National Archaeological Museum, Athens (Inv. No. 3938). Photograph Jeffrey M. Hurwit.

FIGURE 37. Base of *kouros* from Themistoclean wall, ca. 510–500 BCE. National Archaeological Museum, Athens (inv. No. 3476). Photograph courtesy DAI, Athens.

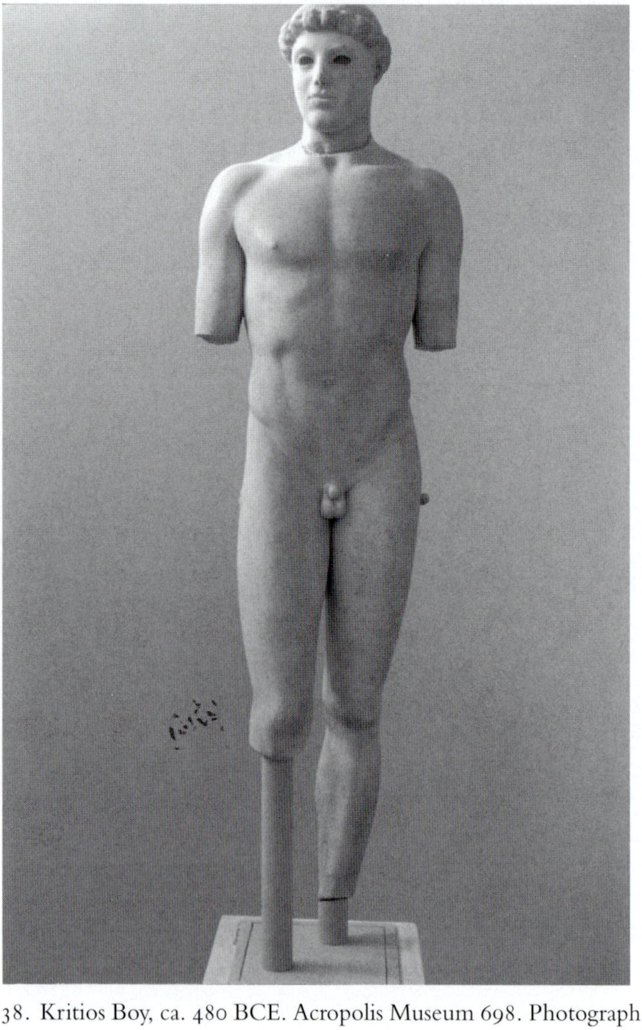

FIGURE 38. Kritios Boy, ca. 480 BCE. Acropolis Museum 698. Photograph Jeffrey M. Hurwit.

FIGURE 39. Funeral scene from Late Geometric amphora by Dipylon Master, ca. 750 BCE. National Archaeological Museum, Athens (Inv. No. 804). Photograph Jeffrey M. Hurwit.

FIGURE 40. Red Figure amphora by Euthymides, ca. 510 BCE. Munich Antikensammlungen 2307. Photograph courtesy of Hirmer Fotoarchiv, Munich.

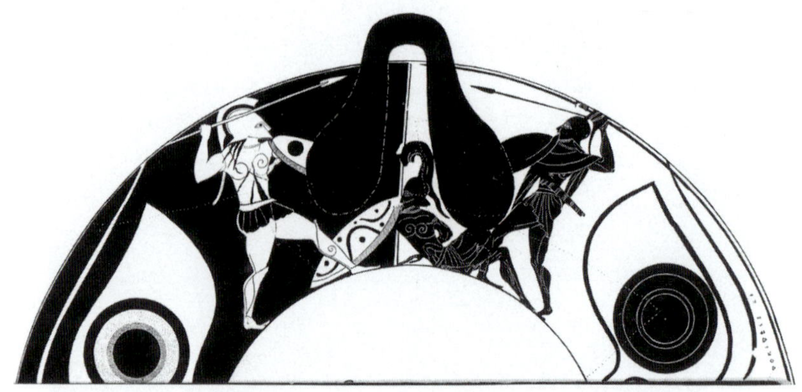

FIGURE 41. Detail of bilingual cup by Andokides Painter, ca. 525–520 BCE. Palermo V 650. [From *JdI* 4 (1889), pl. 4.]

FIGURE 42. Fragment of Red Figure cup by Psiax ca. 520 BCE. Munich. Drawing by K. Ibach, after Williams 1991b, fig. 2.

to be copied and recopied, and so never made the crucial transition from papyrus to vellum. As a result, her poetry disappeared almost entirely, until ancient papyri unearthed at the turn of the previous century gave us back many poems, though in tattered and fragmentary form.

As we have it, Sappho's poetic production seems to have split between choral ritual songs such as *epithalamia* (marriage songs) and what look like more intimate poems of erotic pursuit, love, and loss between women. Scholarly debate currently rages over what we should understand as the milieu and audience for these latter poems – are they sung for a female sympotic group akin to Alcaeus' *hetaireia*? Or a group of young girls Sappho is educating? Are they monodic or, in fact, choral and publicly performed? Or are they instead the products of a new, intimate technology of writing, not performed at all, but given as private gifts between women? Bearing in mind that any reconstruction is conjectural, I regard the most likely scenario to be that Sappho led some kind of organized school for aristocratic girls, both from Lesbos and mainland Asia Minor, perhaps with some religious or cult affiliation. For there is evidence in the fragments that Sappho addressed young women, and several poems chronicle the loss or departure of these young women (in one instance, at least, apparently for marriage).

The fact that Sappho participated in the elitist subculture of luxury and refinement (as discussed above) is by no means accidental to the existence and ancient preservation of her lyrics. In a sense, Sappho's poetry could only have been produced and preserved within the milieu of *habrosyne*, where, as we noted, elite status trumped gender. And yet, we know very little about the status of women – even aristocratic women – in seventh- and sixth-century Lesbos. Scholars conjecture (mainly on the basis of Sappho's poetry) that they had more freedom in this place and era than in fifth- and fourth-century Athens, where women were largely excluded from the public sphere, except for certain religious rites (which were the women's duty). It is noteworthy, then, that the contexts for Sappho's poems fall very much within the same narrowly defined boundaries: either poems for some kind of ritual that included female participants (e.g., marriage, Adonia festival), or private poems addressed to other women. It is in this sense that gender complicates Sappho's participation in the cult of *habrosyne* and inflects her interaction with the poetic tradition. For what we see in Sappho's poetry is a consistent turning inward – the construction in song of a private women's space that inverts and sometimes engulfs a male, public space. We might say that Sappho is thereby making a virtue of necessity: she seems to have been consigned by her culture to an enclosed sphere of women's activities and shut out from the larger world of the *polis* that is such a concern to Alcaeus. But in that situation, she finds a way to make that private sphere expand to embrace everything else.

To demonstrate this, I would like to follow the reading of John J. Winkler and consider several poems as Sappho's dialogue with Homer and the Homeric tradition. We assume that in this period, Homeric epic was performed at public festivals, so that both in its performance and its subject matter, the *Iliad* endorsed the public, political world as a male space. We might then read Sappho fr. 1 LP (her only poem preserved complete from antiquity because quoted by a later writer) as Sappho's response to the *Iliad*:

> Deathless Aphrodite of the spangled mind
> child of Zeus, who twists lures, I beg you
> do not break with hard pains,
> O lady, my heart
>
> but come here if ever before
> you caught my voice far off
> and listening left your father's
> golden house and came,
>
> yoking your car. And fine birds brought you,
> quick sparrows over the black earth
> whipping their wings down the sky
> through midair –
>
> they arrived. But you, O blessed one,
> smiled in your deathless face
> and asked what (now again) I have suffered and why
> (now again) I am calling out
>
> and what I want to happen most of all
> in my crazy heart. Whom should I persuade (now again)
> to lead you back into her love? Who, O
> Sappho, is wronging you?
>
> For if she flees, soon she will pursue.
> If she refuses gifts, rather she will give them.
> If she does not love, soon she will love
> even unwilling.
>
> Come to me now: loose me from hard
> care and all my heart longs

to accomplish, accomplish. You
be my ally.

(trans. Anne Carson)

Notice the martial language of the last line ("be my ally"). In fact, this poem (a cletic hymn to Aphrodite) contains many echoes of the *Iliad*, specifically of *Iliad* book 5, Diomedes' great day in battle and his prayer to Athena. The elaborate chariot sequence here (which spans three strophes of this short poem) echoes the descent of Athena and Hera in a chariot to assist Diomedes in *Iliad* 5. In that context, Athena gives Diomedes the power to recognize the gods in their true form – a power that the rampaging hero wields to wound Aphrodite on the wrist, mockingly driving her from the field of battle:

"Yield, daughter of Zeus, from war and battle.
Or is it not enough that you lead astray weak women without warcraft?"

(*Iliad* 5.348–9)

We can read fr. 1 LP as Sappho's (and Aphrodite's) revenge for *Iliad* 5, for Aphrodite appears here as a great and powerful goddess whose activities appropriate the language of epic, the world of war, for a private erotic sphere. This ironic appropriation works both ways and colors our experience of both poems. On the one hand, it validates Sappho's private world and private concerns; it asserts that her erotic pursuits are just as important as war and epic. On the other hand, it introduces the private and erotic in retrospect into the world of *Iliad* 5. Why does Diomedes so desperately need to banish Aphrodite from the battlefield? Is he in a sense trying to exorcise an erotic element in combat itself?

The same question hovers over the opening strophe of fr. 16 LP (a fragmentary poem recovered on papyrus in the early twentieth c.):

Some men say an army of horse and some men say an army on foot
and some men say an army of ships is the most beautiful thing
on the black earth. But I say it is
what you love.

Easy to make this understood by all.
For she who overcame everyone
in beauty (Helen)
left her fine husband

behind and went sailing to Troy.
Not for her children nor her dear parents
had she a thought, no –
] led her astray

] for
] lightly
] reminded me now of Anactoria
who is gone.

I would rather see her lovely step
and the motion of light on her face
than chariots of Lydians or ranks
of footsoldiers in arms. . . .

(The poem may continue for four more, extremely fragmentary strophes; trans. Anne Carson)

The opening priamel juxtaposes three masculine pronouns ("some men . . . some men . . . some men") with Sappho's emphatic "I" to suggest that men think the instruments of war are beautiful. The speaker opposes this view, offering as her own opinion a very general statement that "the most beautiful thing is whatever anyone passionately desires" (here using the verb that goes with the noun *eros*). Thus the speaker subsumes the whole male world to her own realm of desire and erotics; men think weapons are beautiful, but they don't realize that their attraction to weapons is itself erotic. Then, notice the mythic example Sappho chooses to prove her claim: Helen, who gave up everything and caused the Trojan War because of her desire for Paris. But, as far as we can tell from the poem's fragmentary remains, Sappho does not blame Helen for this (as the *Iliad* does, frequently putting the words of reproach into Helen's own mouth; and as Sappho's contemporary Alcaeus does even more vituperatively). Instead, Sappho appears to valorize Helen (and simultaneously take her back from the world of epic) as a paradigm of all-powerful Eros and of a woman desiring.

A third example of Sappho's revisionary response to epic is fr. 96 LP (another poem recovered from papyrus, and therefore fragmentary at beginning and end):

] . . . Sardis
] . . . often holding her mind here. . . .

When we . . . -ed, she honored you
like a far-conspicuous goddess,
and she used to rejoice most of all in your song.

But now she is conspicuous among
the Lydian women, as, when the sun
has set, the rosy-fingered moon

surpasses all the stars; and her light spreads
equally upon the salt sea
and on the much-flowering fields,

And dew pours down in beauty,
and roses bloom and soft chervil
and flowering melilot.

And wandering much, remembering
gentle Atthis, with longing
she consumes, I suppose, her delicate heart [at your fate].

But for us to come there . . . this is not
]mind . . . much
] sings . . . [in the] middle . . . .

We might describe this (at least what we have of it) as a very short poem with a bulge in the middle. For – unusually, for the spare form of monodic lyric – this poem contains a simile that, like an epic simile, starts off from a single point of contact (the woman in Lydia is like the moon) and expands, apparently gratuitously, until it fills up the middle third of the poem. And, in case we had any doubt that this is Sappho's version of an epic simile, it starts with an epic epithet – the "rosy-fingered moon" of line 8 features the same epithet as Homer's "rosy-fingered Dawn." We can take the dawn and the day as emblematic of the public world of men, the world of business, the world of the assembly and the lawcourts. In opposition to that world, Sappho appropriates the fixed Homeric epithet of the dawn to characterize a moonlit landscape where dew falls and roses bloom in the middle of the night. This is then a magical, unreal landscape; and in this lush, flowering, dream landscape, Sappho creates a space where the two women – the one with Sappho on Lesbos and the other now married in Lydia, missing each other – can be together, just as they contemplate the same moon. Thus the Homeric simile becomes a private reality and expands at the center of the poem because it is a space conjured by Sappho where the two women can, at least in imagination, be reunited. I suspect that this is the significance of line 20, "sings ... in the middle"; Sappho sings "in the middle" and thereby creates this magical space "in the middle" for the two women.

Clearly, there is more to say about these poems than their engagement with (and difference from) Homeric epic. All three poems exhibit a typically Sapphic play of time and thematics of memory, whereas frr. 1 and 16 also illustrate with particular clarity the fluid instability or multiplicity of point of view and position within Sappho's lyrics. For the former: Over and over again, Sappho's poems start from a present condition of loss or sorrow and conjure an image of past happiness and fullness through the controlled exercise of memory. Thus the speaker of fr. 16 is reminded of the "lovely gait and glinting face" of Anactoria "who is not present" (presumably by the exemplum of Helen), whereas in fr. 96, she reminds Atthis of another woman's regard, conjuring an image of the other "wandering to and fro remembering Atthis."

Fr. 1 exhibits the most complex play of time, because it stages a moment "now" wherein the speaker prays to Aphrodite to come as she had before, and then, within the recreation of that earlier epiphany, Aphrodite herself gestures toward at least one earlier occasion when she had come to "Sappho's" aid. This temporal regress, marked by the thrice repeated "now again" (*deute*) within the poem, also produces a proliferation of different "I"s: there is the poet who has composed this exquisitely controlled song, the present "I" who moves from desperation to confidence through the invocation of Aphrodite, and at least two temporally earlier "I"s discernable through the prism of Aphrodite's epiphany. More remarkably still: the shift from indirect to direct speech in the midst of Aphrodite's remembered epiphany causes "I" and "you" to shift in the midst of the poem, so that suddenly anyone voicing it is speaking from the position of Aphrodite to "Sappho." From this perspective, it is not at all surprising that, after ventriloquizing the serene words of the goddess, the present "I"'s tone has shifted from abjection to confidence (from "do not break me" to "be my ally").

We can chart the same shiftiness or instability of position in fr. 16. This poem is generally read (as I have read it above) as a valorization of Helen against the epic tradition, as a positive exemplum of an active, desiring woman. This reading undeniably captures part of the song's effect, but not the whole. After all, the poem begins with an uncompromising general claim about the relativity of beauty (the "most beautiful" is "what you love"), then goes on almost immediately to identify Helen as "she who overcame everyone in beauty." But from whose perspective? The opening lines have taught us that beauty is in the eye of the beholder (and desirer), so that the second strophe's emphatic superlative characterization of Helen requires location in a consciousness, in a desiring subject. The positive description of Menelaus ("her fine husband") and the wistful moment at which the speaker, left behind, remembers Anactoria as she flits out of the poem suggest sympathy and identification simultaneously with the abandoned husband and with the woman pursuing her own desire at all costs. And this doubled focalization or point of view is confirmed by the representation of Anactoria's beauty in the final legible strophe. It is not just that her gait and face are juxtaposed to an Eastern army of chariots and foot soldiers, but that the terms used (*bama, amarygma*) more appropriately characterize the march of soldiers and the glinting of armor. Like Helen's, hers is a terrible beauty, a beauty that sets armies in motion, poignantly captured by an "I" who sees both beauty and terror.

I have indulged in more extensive reading of these fragments, because both their thematics of time and memory and their proliferation of subject positions seem unique and distinctive within the fragmentary remains of Archaic poetry. John J. Winkler attributes both these phenomena, especially the latter (which he characterizes as Sappho's "many-mindedness"), to her position as a woman within ancient Greek culture. We do not find the same emphasis on loss, longing, and memory in the male lyric poets, nor do we find such complex and multiple shifts in focalization or position within their preserved remains. This is not to argue for Sappho's participation in some kind of ahistorical, essentialized *écriture feminine*, but instead to suggest that these distinctive elements in her lyrics arise from the conflict or rift (for her and her female audience) between elite status and their abject – or at least marginalized – role as women. It is this that produces the poetic thematics of loss, separation, memory, and longing among agents not entirely in control of their social positioning and movement, whereas Winkler explicates what he calls Sappho's "many-mindedness" as akin to the double consciousness of disempowered bilingual speakers within a hegemonic monolingual culture. Being women within this culture forces Sappho and her female audience into more marginalized, enclosed, and interiorized spaces and subject positions, even as her status as a member of the aristocratic elite opens up a space for Sappho's poetic voice. Paradoxically, this division in status and enforced exclusion from the public sphere generate in Sappho's lyrics forms of interiorized subjectivity that seem much more akin to our modern notions of self and self-formation. This is partly also a result of the reception of Sappho's lyrics, which, especially through the citation of fr. 1 by the first/second-century CE author on style Longinus, have contributed to our own Romantic and post-Romantic notions of what lyric voice and lyric subjectivity should be. In any case, we might say that her poems still function as remarkably efficient engines for the production of lyric subjectivity.

In comparative terms: the only other Archaic poet whose persona approximates Sappho's shifty, evanescent, and labile "I" is Pindar, but the difference between them is also instructive. Perhaps because Sappho sings for an audience of the socially disempowered or irrelevant (women), her rapidly mutating "I" seems socially gratuitous in contrast to Pindar's; we can detect no obvious political or ideological work these poems perform within the forms of hegemonic culture. For this reason, Sappho's "I" seems to exist for itself and its shifts come to seem like the flicker of pure subjectivity.

I would like to end this discussion of Sappho's distinctiveness with an anecdote reported by the second- to third-century CE anthologist Aelian (presumably taken by him from some older source):

> Solon son of Execestides of Athens, when his nephew sang some song of Sappho's at the drinking, was delighted with the song and bid the young man to teach it to him. When someone asked him why he was so eager about this, he said, "so that I may learn it and die."
>
> (Aelian, quoted in Stobaeus *Florilegium* 3.29.58 = Sappho *Test.* 10 Campbell)

This tradition, true or not, had a plausible ring to it in antiquity. As such, it sheds light on the mechanism by which Sappho's lyrics may have survived, through ongoing reperformance within the male space of the symposium. The complexity and density of subject positions these lyrics offered meant that anyone could play the "I" and that there was great emotional appeal in doing so within the play-space of the symposium. But at another level, we might read this anecdote as a kind of Foucauldian allegory, acknowledging both a synchronic unevenness and an epochal rupture in the forms of subjectivity. According to their traditional dates, Solon and Sappho were exact contemporaries; their synchronicity figures the coexistence of two very different models of subjectivity – public and hegemonic with marginalized and interiorized. But paradoxically, the marginal form will eventually come to look normative within a very different *episteme*. Thus, taken at face value Solon's answer means, "Once I learn this extraordinary song, I can die happy"; but we might (perversely, tendentiously) take Solon's response literally – in these terms, the full inhabiting of Sappho's lyric subjectivity would mark the death of the Archaic public persona Solon here represents.

BIBLIOGRAPHY AND SUGGESTED READINGS

In the interests of readability, I have entirely eschewed footnotes in this chapter. For full citation of the work of scholars mentioned in the text (as well as recommendations for further reading), see below.

Translations

Bing, P. and R. Cohen. 1991. *The Games of Venus*. (Bing and Cohen provide excellent translations of the major fragments of Sappho.)

Campbell, D. A. 1982–93. *Greek Lyric*. 5 vols. (Part of the Loeb Classical Library, these volumes offer the original Greek and prose translations, and include Bacchylides.)

Carson, A. 2002. *If Not, Winter: Fragments of Sappho*. (Carson provides a compelling recent poetic translation of all the fragments of Sappho.)

Nisetich, F. J. 1980. *Pindar's Victory Songs*. (For Pindar, this is the most readable translation.)

West, M. L. 1993. *Greek Lyric Poetry*. (West provides verse translations of all archaic poetry down to 450 BCE, excluding Pindar and Bacchylides.)

Other editions of the Greek texts are listed on p. xiii.

General Treatments of Archaic Poetry in Context

Gentili, B. 1988. *Poetry and Its Public in Ancient Greece from Homer to the Fifth Century*.

Kurke, L. 1999. *Coins, Bodies, Games, and Gold: The Politics of Meaning in Archaic Greece*.

Morris, I. 2000. *Archaeology as Cultural History*. (Esp. chapters 4 and 5.)

Nagy, G. 1979. *The Best of the Achaeans*: Concepts of the Hero in Archaic Greek Poetry

______. 1990. *Pindar's Homer: The Lyric Possession of an Epic Past*.

Stehle, E. 1997. *Performance and Gender in Ancient Greece: Nondramatic Poetry in Its Setting*.

Archilochus, Hipponax, Iambic

Miralles, C. and J. Portulas. 1983. *Archilochus and the Iambic Poetry*.

______. 1988. *The Poetry of Hipponax*. (In this and the preceding book, Miralles and Portulas argue that the generic persona of the iambic poet is an abject outsider who paradoxically has the power to scapegoat others.)

Elegy, Theognis

Bowie, E. L. 1986. "Early Greek Elegy, Symposium and Public Festival." *Journal of Hellenic Studies* 106: 13–35. (On the performance contexts of archaic elegy.)

Figueira, T. and G. Nagy, eds. 1985. *Theognis of Megara: Poetry and the Polis*. (See especially Nagy's essay for a reading of "Theognis" as a mask or generic persona; the elegist as civic advisor/ lawgiver.)

West, M. L. 1974. *Studies in Greek Elegy and Iambus*. (West is the foremost modern proponent of the traditional theory that there was a real Theognis, whose remains are identifiable within a corpus filled with later accretions.)

Solon

Anhalt, E. 1993. *Solon the Singer: Politics and Poetics.*

Loraux, N. 1984. "Solon au milieu de la lice." In *Aux origines de l'Hellénisme: La Crète et la Grèce.* Hommage à Henri van Effenterre. 199–214.

(And I must acknowledge here a debt to Tim Pepper, who suggested public sacrifice as a plausible context for performance of Solon's poems.)

Pindar, Bacchylides, Choral Poetry

Burnett, A. P. 1985. *The Art of Bacchylides.*

Kurke, L. 1991. *The Traffic in Praise: Pindar and the Poetics of Social Economy.*

Sappho

DuBois, P. 1995. *Sappho is Burning.*

Greene, E., ed. 1996. *Reading Sappho: Contemporary Approaches.* (A good selection of modern essays on Sappho; for debate about performance context, see the essays by Calame and Lardinois in Greene; for Sappho's responses to Homer, see Winkler's essay in Greene.)

Robbins, E. 1995. "Sappho, Aphrodite, and the Muses." *The Ancient World* 26(2): 225–39.

A Newly Discovered Poem of Sappho

West, M. L. 2005. "A New Sappho Poem." *Times Literary Supplement,* June 24: 8.

West, M. L. 2005. "The New Sappho." *Zeitschrift für Papyrologie und Epigraphik* 151: 1–9.

Sappho's Reception

Greene, E., ed. 1996. *Re-Reading Sappho: Reception and Transmission.* (A good selection of modern essays on Sappho's reception; for further debate about her original performance context, see Parker's essay in the volume.)

Prins, Y. 1999. *Victorian Sappho.*

The Symposium

De Vries, K. 1973. "East Meets West at Dinner." *Expedition* 15: 32–9.

Lissarrague, F. 1990. *The Aesthetics of the Greek Banquet: Images of Wine and Ritual.*

Murray, O., ed. 1991. *Sympotica: A Symposium on the Symposion.*

Neer, R. 2002. *Style and Politics in Athenian Vase-Painting: The Craft of Democracy, ca. 530–460 B.C.E.*

7: The Philosophers in Archaic Greek Culture

Andrea Wilson Nightingale

In his *Lectures on the History of Philosophy*, Hegel claims that there is a paradox inherent in the very notion of a "history of philosophy":

> The thought which may first occur to us in the history of Philosophy is that the subject itself contains a contradiction. For Philosophy aims at understanding what is unchangeable, eternal, in and for itself: its end is Truth. But history tells us of that which has at one time existed, at another time has vanished, having been expelled by something else. Truth is eternal; it does not fall within the sphere of the transient, and has no history.[1]

Although few scholars would now endorse Hegel's solution to the problem of philosophy's "development in time,"[2] the tension between philosophy and history still remains. For, if the notion of an atemporal and transhistorical truth is no longer in vogue, scholars who work in the "history of philosophy" nonetheless analyze philosophic texts in abstraction from the historical and cultural contexts that ground these discourses. Certainly this has been the dominant approach to the Archaic Greek thinkers, who have generally been treated as detached intellectual theorists since the time of Aristotle and Theophrastus (who wrote the first "histories" of philosophy). At the end of the nineteenth century, John Burnet famously characterized Archaic philosophy as "The Greek Miracle" – the extraordinary creation of a rational mode of thinking radically distinct from the discourse and "mythic" mentality of Greek culture. The Archaic thinkers, according to Burnet, transcended their culture and miraculously produced the discipline of philosophy. Though

Burnet's severance of Archaic philosophy from poetic and "mythic" thinking has been widely contested, even scholars who argue that philosophic *logos* developed from traditional mythic discourse have rarely analyzed the Archaic thinkers in the sociopolitical context of Archaic Greece.

In the mid- to late twentieth century, a group of French scholars (Gernet, Detienne, Vernant) challenged this approach to Archaic philosophy, claiming that the early thinkers should be interpreted in the context of the political, social, and technological developments of Archaic Greece.[3] In particular, they argued, we should analyze the emergence of philosophy in relation to the greatest sociopolitical achievement of this period, namely, the institution of the Greek city-state. Vernant, in fact, links philosophy directly to the development of the *polis*:

> The advent of the *polis*, the birth of philosophy – the two sequences of phenomena are so closely linked that the origin of rational thought must be seen as bound up with the social and mental structures peculiar to the Greek city. Thus restored to its historical setting, philosophy casts off the character of pure revelation. . . .[4]

According to Vernant and Detienne, the Archaic city-state was predicated on and constituted by a particular mode of discourse – what they call the "secularization of speech." In Vernant's formulation, "positivist" and "secular" thinking replaced "mythical thought" in the political life of the city-state. Detienne constructs a similar dichotomy, claiming that the "dialogue-speech" of public affairs in the *polis* supplanted the "magico-religious discourse" of the earlier period. It was the discourse of desacralized thinking, these scholars claim, that generated the discipline of philosophy. The origin of philosophy is thus directly tied to the formation of the city-state and its particular discourses and ideologies.

There can be little doubt that what we now call "philosophy" developed, in part, in response to the sociopolitical transformations taking place in Archaic Greece. But it is too simple to view this intellectual development as a move from "myth" to "reason" or from "religious" to "secular" thinking. In fact, in articulating these claims, these French scholars join ranks with many traditional interpreters who have identified philosophy with "reason" and designated poetic and mythic modes of thinking as nonrational ("un-reason").[5] Whether arguing for a gradual or sudden emergence of "rational" thinking, scholars have often reached for extreme formulations that conceal the true complexity of the early Greek thinkers. To some extent, this reflects the sheer difficulty of articulating the precise ways in which early "philosophic" thinking differed from traditional discourses and modes of thought. There most certainly are some clear points of difference, but the distinction between "mythic" and "rational" discourse (or between "religious" and "secular" thought) has proven unwieldy. Indeed, as many scholars now agree, the early Greek philosophers did not abandon or transcend mythic or poetic discourse, and all of them set forth serious theological claims.[6]

In this essay, I will not attempt to explain the "birth of philosophy" in the Archaic period (indeed, I believe that the specialized discipline of philosophy was constructed in the fourth century BCE). Rather, I will examine both the intellectual and practical activities of the Archaic Greek thinkers and attempt to understand their ideas in the context of Archaic Greek culture.[7] As we will see, the development of new modes of thinking directly responded to the social and political changes that transformed Greek culture in the Archaic period. Consider, first, the dramatically increased cultural interaction in Greece generated by trade, colonization, travel, and war. We have ample evidence that the Greek thinkers encountered and responded to many different cultures and ideologies. Consider, for example, the city of Miletus, which was the center of intellectual activity in sixth-century Ionia. Miletus bordered on the Lydian and, later, the Persian empires and had extensive dealings with these cultures.In addition, it had trading relations all over the Mediterranean and sent out numerous colonies to Egypt and Thrace. The Milesian thinkers thus encountered ideas and practices from all over the "known" world. In the Archaic period, the interaction of different peoples from Greece, Italy, Egypt, and the Near East created a cultural ferment that had a profound impact on Greek life and thought.

Many other cultural factors in Archaic Greece influenced the development of philosophic thinking. Let me briefly mention the most important of these:

(1) *The discovery and (slow) spread of the technology of an alphabetic system of writing*: There can be no doubt that written texts played an important role in the development of the tradition of philosophy. Written texts enabled thinkers to articulate – and readers to study – abstract and intricate systems of thought. In addition, the mobility and durability of written texts made it possible for thinkers living in different places and times to participate in an ongoing intellectual dialogue.[8]

(2) *The development of codes of law, which aimed (at least in principle) at impersonal and impartial forms of justice*: The codification of

laws offered standards of judgment that were higher and more universal than those adopted by any single individual or party. As we will see, the development of the notion of an impersonal, impartial, and lawful dispensation of justice in the Archaic *polis* directly informed philosophic theories of cosmic order.

(3) *The adoption and development of systems of coinage, which enabled the Greeks to (progressively) conceptualize the notion of a universal equivalent*: The move from the personalized exchange of goods in a gift economy to the impersonal exchange of conventionally accepted coins marked a development from private and personal valuations to a higher, more universal system of value. The notion of a universal equivalent or standard of measure finds its way into the philosophic theories of exchange and valuation in the cosmic economy.

(4) *The development of Panhellenic sanctuaries and festivals, which instituted religious and sociopolitical practices that brought disparate (and, often, hostile) Greeks together in a single, shared space*: Panhellenic religious centers represented a move toward a unified Greek religion, which operated above and beyond local cults and rituals. The Panhellenic festivals and oracles, though sponsored by individual cities, operated in a "space" that transcended the culture or ideology of any single *polis* (see Chapter 9); Panhellenic ideology articulated and affirmed the notion of a single "Greek" identity. This move toward a broader, more universal sense of human identity encouraged the Archaic thinkers to place human beings in the larger context of the earth and, indeed, the cosmos.

In examining the Archaic Greek thinkers, we must rely on evidence provided by much later sources. In fact, the history of philosophy, as a genre, did not emerge until the later part of the fourth century BCE (following, as one would expect, the creation of philosophy as a specialized discipline in the first half of the century). Aristotle offers the earliest systematic attempt to organize and analyze the doctrines of his predecessors, and is thus identified as the first historian of philosophy. Although Aristotle offers precious evidence of certain ideas articulated by Archaic thinkers, his historical accounts in the *Metaphysics* and *Physics* are highly tendentious (as scholars have long recognized). For Aristotle constructs his "history" as a discussion of the evolution of the ideas that he himself sets forth, for the first time, in a full way (especially the doctrine of the four causes). The only early wise men who qualify as "philosophers" are those who appear to have apprehended at least one of Aristotle's four causes and who articulated this in relatively "clear" discourse (which included, in some cases, poetic texts).[9] The labels that Aristotle uses for the early philosophic thinkers are revealing: in particular, he identifies most of the early thinkers as "natural philosophers" (*physikoi*; *physiologoi*), in contrast to poetic "theologians" (*theologoi*) such as Homer and Hesiod. In fact, all of the "physicalist" philosophers of the Archaic period identified the first principle(s) of the cosmos or the cosmos itself as divine: for these thinkers – as for the poets – *physis* was not at odds with divinity. To be sure, the Archaic thinkers departed from the poetic conception of the gods as personal, anthropomorphic deities; but they hardly dispensed with divine beings.[10] Aristotle's categorization is thus misleading: it privileges the materialist aspects of the Archaic cosmologies, while downplaying if not occluding their radical theories of divine essence.

Let me emphasize that Aristotle's "history" of philosophy is an extraordinary achievement that had a powerful impact on Western thinking. In the modern period (beginning with Hegel), scholars have generally accepted Aristotle's claim that the Archaic Greeks invented philosophy and that the first philosopher was Thales. They have also tended to view the history of philosophy in the developmental terms that Aristotle used: they treat the earliest philosophers as beginners at (analytic) philosophy rather than mature thinkers in their own right. Although this approach has generated some superb scholarship, it tends to obscure the fact that Archaic thinkers did not set out to invent analytic philosophy but rather to articulate new ideas of the world and new conceptions of the relation of word and world. In addition, the Archaic thinkers were not mere intellectual theorists (and certainly not contemplatives); most of them engaged in a variety of practical and political activities. We need to attend to the pragmatic and polymathic nature of these individuals if we are to understand their unique brands of wisdom.

Sophia in the Sixth and Fifth Centuries BCE

In the sixth and fifth centuries BCE, the term *sophoi* ("wise men") had a wide range of application (including poets, prophets, doctors, statesmen, astronomers, scientists, historians, inventors, and various kinds of artisans): it did not pick out a specific kind of wisdom or expertise.[11]

Although, in this period, different kinds of wise men were seen to be practicing distinct activities, there was nonetheless a generalized competition among the different groups for the title of "wise man." It was not until the late fifth century that intellectuals began to construct boundaries between disciplines such as philosophy, history, medicine, rhetoric, and various other *technai*.[12]

What, then, identifies a certain set of Archaic *sophoi* as "philosophers"? To be sure, some Archaic thinkers – as well as certain poets, doctors, and historians – engaged (at times) in a mode of thought that we now recognize as "philosophical"; philosophic *thinking* existed well before philosophy constituted itself as a distinct and specialized discipline. But the Archaic thinkers did not call themselves "*philosophoi*," nor did the people of their day refer to them as such. Strictly speaking, it is anachronistic to identify the Archaic thinkers as philosophers (*sophoi* or *sophistai* would be the correct terms). But even if we bow to convention and use the term "philosopher," it is difficult to identify the precise criteria that distinguish the "philosophic" thinkers from other sages in this period. Consider, for example, Thales of Miletus, who was ranked by posterity as both a Sage (one of the elite Seven) and a Philosopher. According to Aristotle, Thales was the first philosopher because he said that all things are water: in making this claim, Aristotle suggests, Thales was the first to identify the material substrate of the universe in philosophic terms. This (proto-) cosmology – if indeed it is that – separates Thales from your run-of-the-mill sage.

But other sources depict Thales as a typical Archaic sage. Herodotus, for example, claims that Thales predicted an eclipse and engineered the diversion of the river Halys (when Croesus attempted to invade Persia). In addition, when the Ionians in Asia Minor were being subdued by the Persians, Thales fought to create a confederation of Ionian city-states and to institute a supreme deliberative council for the alliance (Herodotus 1.74–5, 170; see also Diogenes Laertius [hereafter D.L.] 1.25). Indeed Aristotle himself relates a story about Thales' "cunning intelligence": Thales, foreseeing that it would be a good season for olives, rented all the oil-presses and obtained a monopoly on the proceeds (Aristotle *Politics* 1.4, 1259a; see also D.L. 1.26). These stories about Thales portray a man of great wisdom. In addition to astronomical and cosmological expertise, he possessed a wide range of practical and technical skills (including engineering, politics, agriculture, and commerce). Why, then, should we identify Thales as a philosopher rather than a *sophos* whose métier included cosmological speculation?

We run into the same problem in the figure of Pythagoras, who emigrated from Samos to southern Italy in the second half of the sixth century.[13] Pythagoras almost certainly did not publish any writings, though he did lay down a complete system of doctrines and rules. He was a highly practical and performative sage who founded a religious society in the city of Croton. The members of this society, which included women as well as men, lived a life of austerity and discipline that featured a vegetarian diet, the practice of self-examination, obedience to specific precepts, and a strict code of silence about Pythagorean doctrine and practice. Pythagoras and his followers, then, performed an entire way of life: their ideas and doctrines translated directly into daily *praxis* (for example, their belief in the immortality of the soul and its transmigration into animals led them to abstain from meat). Insofar as Pythagoreanism offered its members hidden knowledge that could not be divulged, it resembled the mystery religions, which promised to benefit initiates by the revelation of secret wisdom. In addition to these private and secret practices, however, Pythagoras participated fully in political life; in fact, he and his followers are said to have taken over the government of Croton.

Although his fellow Greeks no doubt identified Pythagoras as a guru and a sage, it was his (alleged) creation of the "number theory" that later earned him the title of philosopher. It is impossible to know the extent to which Pythagoras had worked out this theory (which granted ontological status to numbers). According to recent scholars, it was the fifth-century followers of Pythagoras who developed this theory, having inherited very rudimentary ideas from the master.[14] It seems likely, in fact, that Pythagoras laid down only the most basic principles for the number theory. His true contribution lies in the fact that he developed a particular mode of living and thinking that generated a long train of followers. A mystic, sage, ascetic, and proto-metaphysician, Pythagoras defies easy characterization.

In the Archaic period, then, the boundaries between philosophy and other modes of wisdom were far from firm. Heraclitus, for example, attacks a wide range of *sophoi* in his efforts to exalt his own wisdom: the poets Homer, Hesiod, and Archilochus; the guru Pythagoras; the proto-historian Hecataeus (who wrote in prose); and the poetic philosopher Xenophanes (DK B40, 42, 57). Clearly, Heraclitus conceived of himself as rivaling disparate wise men rather than the specialized group of intellectuals later called philosophers. The fact that Heraclitus' opponents include poets and prose writers as well as a religious/political guru such as Pythagoras gives us a good idea of the milieu in which he was working.

He and other early thinkers did, then, seek to distinguish themselves from other "wise men." But these attacks were *ad hominem* and should not be mistaken for the explicit and systematic differentiation of a new genre or discipline from other genres.

THE PERFORMANCE OF WISDOM IN EARLY GREEK CULTURE

As Richard Martin has persuasively argued, the Archaic "sage" was not identified according to a given field of expertise (e.g., poetry, politics) but rather by the exemplary "performance" of one or another kind of wisdom. The sages "performed wisdom" by *displaying* or *enacting* it in a public context.[15] I believe that this notion of "performing wisdom" captures a central fact about the nature and dissemination of *sophia* in the Archaic period. In this era, there were no schools of higher learning conferring authority or credentials. In addition, the vast majority of Greeks did not communicate via the written word, because literacy was not widespread in this period.[16] In order to gain the title of *sophos*, an individual had to make himself known by exhibiting some exceptional action or exceptional discourse in a public context.

All claimants to *sophia* performed their wisdom, including the early philosophic thinkers (though the venues of their performances no doubt varied in nature and in size). As Schofield observes, the Archaic thinkers "had to create their own audiences (in the literal sense of the word), without the aid of such institutions as the university or the publishing industry, and without the possibility of relying upon a practice of book reading; each was an example of purely individual and local enterprise."[17] Some thinkers opted to disseminate their wisdom by way of poetic texts, whereas others opted for prose. Importantly, none wrote more than one or two short treatises until the later fifth century (when literacy and book production began to increase): this indicates that writing and publishing formed only a small part of their intellectual activities. Even the thinkers and sages who did commit discourses to writing, we may infer, relied in large part on the spoken word to disseminate their wisdom.

Clearly, a number of these thinkers packaged their "philosophical" ideas to reach a nonspecialized public. Xenophanes wrote elegiac and hexameter poems and (according to tradition) "rhapsodized" his own works (D.L. 1.18); Heraclitus constructed quotable aphorisms that emulate the discourse of the Delphic oracle; and Parmenides rivaled

Homer and Hesiod by writing hexameter poetry. I am not suggesting that these thinkers achieved the kind of popularity enjoyed by more traditional poets; the point is that they exploited traditional forms of poetry and authoritative discourse in an effort to attract audiences and gain a hearing.[18] No doubt all of the early "philosophic" thinkers worked privately, at times, with a few close associates, but the need to achieve authority and (at least local) fame were basic features of the life of an intellectual in this period.

Let me emphasize that the wisdom of the Archaic thinkers was not just discursive: many of these men were able performers of practical and political wisdom. For example, of the Ionian thinkers, Thales played a leading role in Ionian politics, and Anaximander led a colony from Miletus to Apollonia on the Pontus (he also made the first map of the world). Pythagoras created a religious society (complete with practical and political regulations) and also functioned as a politician in Croton. Parmenides served as a lawmaker in the city of Elea. As several recent scholars have suggested, these individuals were not only practicing theoretical speculation but were also engaged in political, poetic, salvific, and theological projects akin to those of nonphilosophical *sophoi* of the Archaic period.[19]

Defining the Archaic "Philosopher"

Although our evidence for the Archaic sages and thinkers is far from adequate, we must nonetheless attempt to locate them in their contemporary intellectual and cultural context. In doing this, we may find it a bit difficult to distinguish them from other wise men of the period. On what grounds, we must ask, can we isolate these figures and treat them as philosophers? Barnes claims that the philosophers can be identified by their use of reason and argumentation: "the theories which they advanced were presented not as *ex cathedra* pronouncements for the faithful to believe and the godless to ignore, but as the conclusions of arguments, as reasoned propositions for reasonable men to contemplate and debate."[20] But the traditional poets did not speak in a dogmatic fashion to a group of the "faithful." And, even more importantly, the "pre-Socratics" offered almost nothing resembling an analytic argument until Parmenides. It was the Archaic thinkers – rather than the poets – who spoke *ex cathedra* to the "faithful," articulating thoughts that are far from "reasoned propositions" (indeed, Barnes himself speaks of their "precocious intoxication"[21]).

Rather than forcing the Archaic thinkers into reductive (and anachronistic) categories, we should acknowledge their extraordinary polymathy and their remarkable diversity. To be sure, a tradition of critical thinking – a tradition that later became a specialized discipline – developed out of the work of these diverse thinkers. But the Archaic thinkers initially acted as ambitious individuals staking a claim to *sophia* rather than as members of a new and collective discipline. By offering powerful responses to alternative modes of wisdom – poetic and "philosophical," Greek and non-Greek – these thinkers created an enduring tradition of intellectual thinking that could be studied, criticized, and improved upon. In addition, the Archaic thinkers engaged in projects that were not only rational, but also "transformative and perhaps even salvational": the cultivation of true *logos*, they claimed, would lead to a better life.[22]

I cannot begin to discuss all the Archaic thinkers in this brief essay. I will therefore focus on three central figures: Anaximander of Miletus, Heraclitus of Ephesus, and Parmenides of Elea. Each used a different mode of discourse, and each offered a different conception of reality. An investigation of these thinkers will not do justice to Archaic "philosophy" or its cultural context. But I hope it will offer a sense of the complexity of philosophic wisdom in this period and the ways in which the early thinkers responded to the discourses and practices of the Archaic *polis*.

Anaximander

Anaximander of Miletus (first half of the sixth century BCE) wrote the first prose treatise on cosmological and philosophical issues.[23] The decision to write in prose represented a radical break with Greek literary discourse and inaugurated a tradition that came to full flower in the classical period. Because we have such a tiny number of fragments of the Milesian thinkers, it is difficult to speak with confidence about their style. As I would urge, we should not assimilate Anaximander's discourse to the philosophic prose of the fifth century. Simplicius, in fact, says that Anaximander "articulated his theories in rather poetic language" (DK A9). Certainly Anaximander's discourse was informed, at least in part, by the poetic tradition (as well as by discourses that had currency in the city-state of Miletus). But he opted for prose rather than poetry in a deliberate effort to find words that would match his new conception of the world.

Anaximander claimed that the first principle of the cosmos was an entity called the Boundless (*to apeiron*). In Archaic usage, the word *apeiron* means "indefinite" rather than "infinite": the Boundless, then, is either "spatially indefinite," "indefinite in kind," or (more likely) both.[24] At first glance, the Boundless resembles Hesiod's Chaos in being a primary and undifferentiated cosmic entity. But Anaximander's theory radically diverges from Hesiod's *Theogony*: for the Boundless not only gives birth (in some sense) to the cosmos, but also governs it according to strict laws. The Boundless, as it seems, is both a divine (pro)creator and a political regulator. As Aristotle states:

> Of the Boundless there is no beginning . . . but this seems to be the beginning of other things, and to encompass all things and steer (*kubernan*) all things. . . . And this is the divine; for it is immortal and indestructible. . . .
>
> (Aristotle *Physics* 3.4, 203b)

Although it is difficult to know to what extent Aristotle is imposing his own terminology on Anaximander, the suggestion that the Boundless is some sort of divine principle that both generates and governs all things seems genuine.

How, then, does the Boundless generate the cosmos, and in what sense does it "govern" the universe? According to Anaximander's theory, the elemental opposites – hot, cold, wet and dry – were "ejected" (*apokrinomenon*) from the Boundless (DK A9). The word *apokrinesthai* generally refers to the secretion or ejection of a seed: Anaximander's use of this term indicates that the primal products of the Boundless were, in some sense, its offspring.[25] Anaximander, then, conceived of the formation of the cosmos in terms of procreation: "something *generative* (*gonimon*) of the hot and cold was ejected from the eternal [Boundless] at the genesis of this world." This notion of a divine being "generating" things may seem to derive from Hesiod's *Theogony*, which claimed that a divinity called Chaos "came first" and gave birth to several lesser gods, thus generating certain – but by no means all – components of the cosmos (116–23). In the *Theogony*, Earth "came to be" right after Chaos, and she gave birth to the greater part of the cosmos. There was no single god who created or gave birth to the entire cosmos (see Chapter 5 on Hesiod and the *Theogony*). Anaximander's Boundless is a more complex sort of principle. First, it is the primary principle of the *entire* cosmos, not just some of its parts. Second, and even more importantly, the Boundless not only generates the cosmos but also serves to regulate it according to strict and abiding "natural" laws. This does not mean that the Boundless intervenes in the cosmic motions and processes: in stark contrast to the traditional Greek gods, the *apeiron* is not an anthropomorphic despot but an impersonal ruling principle that "encompasses" the cosmos and safeguards its lawful order.[26] Anaximander, then, set forth a radically new conception of the divine (pro)creator: the Boundless governs the universe not by personal whim but by natural laws.

In attempting to understand Anaximander's discourse and ideas in their sociopolitical context, we must give special attention to the famous "Anaximander fragment," which contains the only extant sentence of Anaximander. As Simplicius reports:

> Anaximander said that the principle and element of things . . . is neither water nor any other of the so-called elements, but some different, boundless (*apeiron*) nature, from which all the heavens arise and the worlds within them; out of those things from which there is generation for existing things, into these again does their destruction take place, "according to necessity; for they pay the penalty (*diken*) and recompense (*tisin*) to one another for their injustice (*adikias*), according to the ordinance of time."
>
> (DK B1)

The elements in the cosmos – which are generated by the Boundless – engage in an ongoing battle for power: hot and cold, wet and dry attempt to increase themselves and destroy their opposites. But, in spite of this endless struggle, a balance of powers is preserved overall. None of the opposites ever fully prevails: one or another gains ascendancy for a time, but will eventually "pay the penalty and recompense" to the others for its "unjust" claim to sole power. This language of justice and recompense clearly derives from the legal and political sphere. Nature follows the "laws" of political justice (even as justice, in turn, is naturalized). The cosmos, in short, operates according to laws that reflect those of the *polis*.

As Vernant observes, in Anaximander's cosmology, "*monarchia* was replaced by *isonomia*."[27] In this scheme, no single element possesses sole primacy or power – as water does in Thales and air in Anaximines. Rather, a divine entity outside the cosmos generates a system whose elements rule and are ruled in turn according to principles of justice. This stands in stark contrast to Hesiod's rule of Zeus, which is patterned on the monarchies of the ancient Mycenean and Near Eastern kingdoms. Anaximander's cosmos, in fact, reflects the (emerging) systems of the city-state in Greece, many of which were exploring ways to achieve *isonomia*. Though Anaximander's "opposites" do struggle for power, they are ultimately limited and, in some sense, equalized by the laws of justice. The result is a cosmos whose elements are, over the duration of time, equal and balanced. Although the opposites and elements "naturally" struggle for dominance (like the elites in the Archaic *polis*), the cosmos as a whole preserves equality and justice.[28]

As many scholars have observed, Anaximander's cosmos operates according to mathematical rules and ratios (indeed, his cosmology reflects his direct debt to Babylonian mathematics and astronomy).[29] In Anaximander's scheme, the cosmos exhibits a very definite and, indeed, mathematical symmetry. As Anaximander claimed, the earth is located precisely at the center of the heavenly sphere:

> The earth is aloft, not dominated (*kratoumenen*) by anything; it remains in place because of the similar distance from all points [of the celestial circumference].
>
> (DK A11)

The earth maintains its position because it is at the center of the heavens. In making this claim, Anaximander inaugurates the geometrical approach to astronomy that (beginning in the fourth century BCE) dominated philosophic and scientific thinking until Copernicus. But note that Anaximander's claim reflects political as well as mathematical principles: the earth is not "ruled" (*kratoumenen*) by any one of the opposites or elements because the cosmos is based on principles of equality and equilibrium. According to Aristotle, Anaximander claimed that an entity "in the middle" (*epi tou mesou*) that exhibits a "like relation" (*homoiotes*) to all points of the celestial circumference will maintain a stable position within the equilibrium (*De Caelo* 295b).

This use of the discourse of *meson* and *homoiotes* (which Aristotle may have taken directly from Anaximander) clearly derives from the civic and political sphere. As Morris has shown, in the Archaic city-state a "middling" ideology emerged that conceived of citizens as equal and "like" (*homoios*) one another; these "equals" rule the city by placing power "in the middle" (*es meson*), that is, in a position that is shared.[30] To get a sense of this ideology and its discourse, consider Herodotus' account of the political changes in Samos in the late sixth century (3.142): when Maeandrius inherited power in Samos after the death of the tyrant Polycrates, he claimed that it was wrong for Polycrates "to lord it over men who were his equals (*homoioi*)." Maeandrius, by contrast, opted to place the power "in the middle" (*es meson*) and to institute "equality before the law" (*isonomia*). Anaximander's placement of the earth *epi meson*, then, has a clear ideological valence: his earth is not "dominated" by any single element, but possesses a "like relation" (*homoiotes*) to all sides of the celestial sphere. The structure and organization of Anaximander's cosmos directly reflects the "middling" ideology that was developing (in opposition to traditional aristocratic ideology) in the Archaic *polis*. Anaximander, then, utilizes both mathematical and political notions of harmony, bringing these different modes of thinking together in a dazzling and original synthesis.

Anaximander and the Milesians set forth a number of ideas not found in the previous Greek tradition. In particular, they offered a new conception of god: an impersonal, nonanthropomorphic divine principle that generates and subtends the laws of the physical cosmos. This radical conception of deity clearly breaks with traditional cultic practices, but it does not, as some scholars have suggested, represent a move from religious to secular modes of thinking. In addition, the Milesians (following the Babylonians) studied the astral cycles and their numerical measurements, which led to new ways of thinking about the cosmos (Anaximander took this the furthest, developing a geometric model of the heavens). Finally, these thinkers reconceived physical change in terms of the conflict of elemental powers, a conflict that generated a cosmos characterized by reciprocity and equilibrium. This new conception of the world created a tradition of mathematical and empirical inquiry that progressively refined and corrected the early theories. For example, Anaximander's claim that the earth was a flat disk soon gave way to the theory of a spherical earth. Likewise, the Milesian theories of lunar and solar eclipses were improved upon by the Italian thinker Parmenides and successfully corrected by Anaxagoras of Clazomenae in the fifth century BCE. This reveals an extraordinary level of cross-cultural dialogue and interaction, beginning with the Greek response to Babylonian astronomy.

Heraclitus

Heraclitus lived and worked in Ephesus (on the coast of Asia Minor) in the late sixth/early fifth century. For much of this period, Ephesus was part of the Persian empire; but the city retained its Ionian character and was fully embedded in the social, political, and economic life of Greece. Like Miletus, Ephesus interacted with many different cultures, both East and West. As we will see, Heraclitus reflects the cross-fertilization that characterized Archaic Greece in this period. He explicitly refers to figures as disparate as Homer, Hesiod, Archilochus, Bias of Priene, Pythagoras, Xenophanes, and Hecataeus (denouncing all except Bias as ignorant fools!). And, implicitly, he responds to the Milesian cosmological theories and to various non-Greek ideas.[31] Like other Archaic thinkers, Heraclitus asserts his unique possession of wisdom while objecting to all other accounts of physical and human life: he stakes his claim to wisdom by way of direct opposition to acclaimed wise men and their ideas.

According to Diogenes Laertius, Heraclitus inscribed his discourses in a book which he offered as a dedication in the temple of Artemis so that he could hide his writings from all but the select few (D.L. 9.5). Did Heraclitus really opt for the written word as a way of avoiding mass audiences? The very survival of the fragments indicates that he achieved a degree of fame comparable to (at least minor) poets. Certainly the aphoristic style of the extant fragments lends itself to oral delivery, and this may have been his preferred mode of dissemination. No doubt Heraclitus also inscribed his aphorisms in a book.[32] But if he dedicated this book in the temple, he was not trying to keep the book hidden from the masses; on the contrary, this kind of dedication was a public display that would have given Heraclitus' book an extraordinary status.

Even more boldly than the other Archaic thinkers, Heraclitus set out to "do things" with his words. Using an oracular form and voice, Heraclitus makes paradoxical and enigmatic pronouncements. As he says in fragment DK B93, "the lord whose oracle is in Delphi neither speaks nor conceals, but gives a sign." Because Heraclitus himself uses language in precisely this way, we may infer that he was deliberately adopting a Delphic mode of discourse. He did this, no doubt, because the riddling discourse of the oracle was well suited to conveying his provocative and unorthodox claims: that the cosmos is a unity consisting of warring opposites; that the knower (the soul) can be discovered in the intelligible cosmos (and vice versa). According to Heraclitus, the world is not as it appears, and the wise person must therefore find a new language in which to articulate its deep and divine structure.

Heraclitus attempts to describe the world in objective terms, that is, in terms of its "hidden" structure, while also acknowledging the difference between this hidden truth and the phenomenal world as it appears to the subjective human percipient. As Long claims, "by writing in riddling discourse, Heraclitus wants to signal the gap between appearance and deep structure."[33] Because of the direct correlation between the human soul and the cosmos (both at the rational and physical levels), humans can adopt an objective, god's-eye perspective on the world: they can and, indeed, should identify with the cosmos and its *Logos* by abandoning their private and subjective opinions and entering into the cosmic perspective. In order to reveal this objective perspective to human beings mired in subjectivity, Heraclitus composes a riddling discourse that "juxtaposes surface and hidden meanings, human and god's-eye viewpoints."[34]

In adopting the riddling style, Heraclitus also adopts the voice of divine authority that was associated with oracular discourse. Heraclitus speaks from on high to confused mortals:

> Although the *Logos* holds forever, men prove to be uncomprehending, both before they have heard it and when once they have heard it. Although all things come into being in accordance with the *Logos*, men are like inexperienced people, even when they experience such words and deeds as I explain, distinguishing each thing according to its nature and declaring how it is; but other men fail to notice what they do when awake just as they forget what they do when asleep.[35]
> (DK B1)

When encountering such a statement, one may imagine that Heraclitus addressed himself to only a few intelligent initiates, because the mass of men are too stupid to get the point. But, as Heraclitus explicitly asserts here, ordinary men have indeed heard his account of the truth (though they generally do not understand it). This seems to indicate that his work was not confined to an audience of a few elite associates. Indeed, one could argue that this passage is a clever piece of rhetoric that invites the ordinary man to remove himself from the common herd by using his reason and tapping into the *Logos*. In short, it divulges to the public a knowledge that it proclaims to be unavailable to the majority. In addition, it places its audience in the role of the interpreter of an oracle (a not unfamiliar role for ancient Greeks): it invites people to aspire to wisdom by solving enigmas, and to act on this wisdom in their daily lives. We must remember that Heraclitus does not simply exhort people to achieve intellectual understanding: true wisdom, he claims, will lead them to act piously and virtuously in practical affairs – to live good lives. Heraclitus' urgent message is simultaneously ethical, religious, and intellectual.[36]

What, then, does Heraclitus mean by the *Logos*? Clearly, he does not simply refer to his own discourse. Indeed, as himself asserts, "although the *Logos* is common (*xunou*), most men live as though they have wisdom that is private" (DK B2). The *Logos* is something that is "common" (*xunos*) in several different ways. First, it is common to all men because they possess rationality. At times, in fact, Heraclitus seems to suggest that the human soul or mind is more or less coextensive with the *Logos* (DK B45).[37] But the *Logos* is not simply a matter of language and rationality. For it also serves as a cosmic principle: "all things come into being (*ginomenon)* in accordance with the *Logos*" (DK B1). Here, Heraclitus identifies the *Logos* as the organizing principle of the *genesis* of everything in the physical world. It is "common," then, not just to humans but indeed to the entire cosmos. In another fragment, Heraclitus compares the *Logos* to the civic law, indicating that it functions as the lawful regulator in the macrocosm:

> Speaking with understanding, they must hold fast to what is common (*xunos*) to all [i.e., the *Logos*], as a city holds to its law (*nomos*) and even more firmly. For all human laws are nourished by a divine one.
>
> (DK B114)

The *Logos*, then, functions as the common law of the cosmos (including its inhabitants) just as a legal code serves the community of the *polis*. In addition, *Logos* as "divine law" is not just parallel to human law, but its very creator and nurturer. The *Logos*, then, is a divine principle that pervades the physical cosmos, the human mind, and the civic community.

Not surprisingly, Heraclitus' riddling discourse has generated profoundly different interpretations. In particular, scholars have debated the question of whether Heraclitus offered a physicalist cosmology (as Aristotle and Theophrastus believed), or whether his discourse offered not a literalist account of the physical cosmos but a metaphorical account that set forth a metaphysical philosophy. The majority of scholars have followed the Aristotelian tradition and view Heraclitus' philosophy as offering a physicalist cosmology that responds to but also corrects the Milesian theories. These scholars focus on Heraclitus' discussions of Fire, which they identify as both the material principle that generates the cosmos (like Water in Thales, Air in Anaximines) as well as one of the elements within it.

Is Heraclitus' Fire a physical or a metaphysical entity? Consider the following enigmatic fragment: "The cosmic-order, the same for all, no god nor man has made, but it always was and is and will be: everliving fire, kindled in measures and going out in measures" (DK 30). Here, Heraclitus echoes the Milesians in claiming that the cosmos is characterized by the opposition and transformation of opposites in accordance with some sort of measure and balance.[38] Fire is "everliving" and possesses a divine status, but it also generates the cosmos as an element within it. As Heraclitus claims, this immanent divine element serves as the organizing principle of the cosmos: Fire "steers" all things (DK B64).[39] Paradoxically, however, this divine principle of Fire is "kindled in measures and goes out in measures." What sort of "everliving" and eternal divinity waxes and wanes in this fashion? As Kahn rightly suggests, Heraclitus offers us "the double paradox of a world order identified with one of its constituent parts, and an eternal principle embodied in the most transitory of visual phenomena."[40] This is very different from the physicalist theories of the Milesians.

We may articulate this paradox as follows. On the one hand, the cosmos is characterized by flux. Heraclitus asserts the doctrine of flux in numerous fragments – most famously in the statement that "you can't step in the same river twice" (DK B12, B91). The point here is not simply that the river is flowing and changing. Rather, the river – and, indeed, the water in it – is a process rather than a single element or entity.[41] Heraclitus also expresses the notion of flux in terms of the war of opposites: "war" (like *Logos*) is "common" (*xunon*) to all things (DK B80) and is the "father and king of all" (DK B53). In saying that war is "common," Heraclitus means that the strife between opposites pervades all things to such an extent that the opposites themselves have no lasting, substantial status.

Fire and war may seem to conjure chaos rather than cosmos (order). Heraclitus, however, not only identifies fire and war with the cosmos, but claims that this fiery cosmos is governed by laws and "measures" (DK B30, B31, B90, B94). This results in the provocative claim that "conflict is Justice" (DK B80). Conflict does not lead to some future just requital, but is *itself* justice. Here and elsewhere, Heraclitus borrows the political language of the city-state and its laws to describe a cosmos that is very different from the *polis*. On the one hand, the strife and flux that characterize the cosmos actually break down the boundaries between different elements and substances: the Heraclitean cosmos is not constituted by a group of "like" (*homoioi*) powers that enjoy some sort of equality, but rather by a continuous process that never settles into stable, separate entities. Instead of equality, Heraclitus insists on unity: "listening to the *Logos* it is wise to agree that all things are one" (DK

B50).[42] But if all things are in flux, then how can Heraclitus speak of unity? The assertion of a "unified" cosmos sits uneasily with the claim that the cosmos is characterized by the war of opposites (perhaps the very lack of differentiation between individual substances and elements allows Heraclitus to see the cosmic process itself as *one thing*).

The ultimate paradox is yet to come: the suggestion that Fire *is* the *Logos* that regulates the world order. As we have seen, Heraclitus identifies Fire with the entire, everlasting cosmos: Fire is more than an element operating within the material world. If we interpret Heraclitus' references to Fire in exclusively physicalist terms (following the Aristotelian tradition), we may lose sight of the fact that Fire has a symbolic as well as a material status. The dual status of Fire is well captured in the following fragment: "All things are an equal exchange (*antamoibe*) for fire, and fire for all things, as goods for gold and gold for goods" (DK B90). Here, Heraclitus refers to the "interchange" of material opposites in the cosmos while also identifying Fire as the universal standard against which all things are measured. Fire is both one of the interchangeable material opposites and also an abstract "coin" that measures the value of everything else.

This reference to monetary exchange directly reflects the socioeconomic conditions of the developing Greek *polis*. The Greeks first began to develop systems of coinage in the sixth century (following the Lydians); by the turn of the century, a number of *poleis* were minting their own coinage for local, civic use.[43] Given that the city of Ephesus was under Persian power for much of Heraclitus' lifetime, he would have encountered both Persian and Greek systems of coinage. Whereas Lydian and Persian coins came only in very large denominations and operated in select, large-scale transactions, the Greeks (progressively) developed a system that covered transactions of smaller values, using coins of varied denominations, including small change. The Greek coinage systems, then, had a much broader range of measure and reflected the evolving Greek understanding of the notion of a universal equivalent.[44] Just as the institution of a law code provided an impersonal and (within its own domain) universal system of judgment, the institution of a coinage system created an impersonal and (within each *polis*) universal medium of exchange. The development of systems of law and monetary exchange were central features of the evolving *polis* in the Archaic period. Heraclitus turns to both legal and monetary practices in his efforts to articulate a system in which *Logos* and Fire function as universal regulators and equivalents. Both *Logos* and Fire operate at a universal level, beyond "private" opinions, values, and transactions.

Heraclitus' monetary metaphor is especially revealing: just as gold is both a concrete object and an abstract standard of measure (it has a physical use value as well as a supersensible exchange value), Fire is both a concrete, material entity within the cosmos and an abstract cosmic standard. Just as gold and other precious metals have value in themselves but can also be minted in the form of coins, Heraclitus' Fire is both "naturally" valuable (a precious metal) and a "conventional" form of currency (a coinage). As Kurke has shown, aristocratic ideology in the Archaic period set precious metals in opposition to coinage: gold and other metals were identified as possessing an essential and unchanging value, and their possession demonstrated the "natural" superiority of the aristocracy. Coinage, by contrast, undermined this essentialist claim to "natural" value, because currency (*nomisma*) operated according to civic conventions. As Kurke observes,

> the aristocratic monopoly on precious goods within a closed system of gift exchange guarantees an absolute (naturalized) status hierarchy. Coinage represents a double threat to that system, for it puts precious metal into general circulation, under the symbolic authority of the *polis*. As stamped civic tokens, coinage challenges the naturalized claim to power of the aristocratic elite.[45]

To put it another way, coinage represented a triumph of the ideology of *nomos* over *physis* (even though coinage was initially rooted in the "natural" value of precious metals).

Heraclitus' reference to Fire as a unique precious metal that also functions as a coin in a system of exchange undermines the aristocratic distinction between "naturally" precious metals and "conventional" currency. Indeed Heraclitus' whole philosophy challenges the opposition between *nomos* (including *nomisma*) and *physis*.[46] In Heraclitus' philosophy, Fire is a "naturally" valuable entity that possesses the highest power and status in the cosmos – indeed it is unique and divine. At the same time, Fire functions as a conventional form of currency in the cosmic economy – as a coin that can be exchanged for other "goods." One might argue that Heraclitus believed that Fire-as-*nomisma* is completely dependent on the *physis* of Fire: the essential value of Fire (like gold) provides the "natural" ground for a system of exchange in which Fire functions as a symbolic, abstract counter. But this reading, I think, should be resisted, because it privileges the physicalist conception of Fire-as-matter/*physis* over the symbolic conception of Fire-as-*nomos*.

As I have tried to suggest, these two notions of Fire operate simultaneously in Heraclitus' thinking. Indeed, one could say that his entire philosophy attempts to efface the boundary between *physis* and *nomos*: hence the claim that the *Logos* and the laws of the cosmos are identical to (or coextensive with) its material processes. For Heraclitus, *physis is Logos* (and vice versa).

Because Fire has this dual status, it has led interpreters in divergent directions, with some treating Heraclitus as a physicalist philosopher, and others as a (proto-) metaphysician. But we must note that the Archaic thinkers (with the possible exception of Parmenides) did not think in terms of a distinction between physics and metaphysics: in interpreting these philosophers, we must attempt to grasp a mode of thinking that preceded philosophic dualism. Heraclitus sets forth a philosophy that exhibits the conceptual tension between the laws of *Logos* and the flux of the physical cosmos while insisting that they are identical. The abstract and the concrete, the supersensible and the sensible, *nomos* and *physis* are conceived *as a unity*. Heraclitus does not, then, create a logical division between physics and metaphysics – this was a move made by later philosophers. Rather, he sets forth a monistic philosophy that finds the principles of law and justice in the flux of material opposites. In interpreting Heraclitus, we must honor this provocative paradox.

PARMENIDES

By the time of Heraclitus at the end of the sixth century, the tradition of philosophical inquiry had begun to spread from Miletus to neighboring cities (Samos, Colophon, Ephesus, Clazomenae) and had also been exported to the distant west by Ionian refugees. In the second half of the sixth century, Pythagoras migrated from Samos to Croton; perhaps a bit later, Xenophanes left Colophon and, after much wandering, settled in Sicily. The great thinker Parmenides, born around 515 BCE in Elea (a city founded in southern Italy in 540 BCE), was the beneficiary of this broad-ranging intellectual interchange. He responded with yet another radical new theory. Like Heraclitus, Parmenides explored the gulf between appearance and reality, rejecting ordinary human perceptions and opinions. But Parmenides went further than Heraclitus in questioning the world of appearance. In particular, his poem features a goddess who claims that because Being can only be itself, and can never be anything else, it therefore must be unitary, homogeneous, and unchanging. Because the phenomenal world features plurality and change, it must be "other" than Being, that is, nonbeing. The entire phenomenal world, then, does not exist. In sum, there is no change or motion in the cosmos. How are we to interpret the Goddess's discourse? This question is more difficult than it may at first appear, for the poem has a highly complex literary structure and contains a number of difficult paradoxes. Although most philosophers focus on the Goddess's arguments rather than on dramatic or narratological issues, this has the effect of abstracting Parmenides from his literary and cultural context. In grappling with Parmenides, we need to attend to all aspects of the poem.

Parmenides chose to write in hexameter, thus setting himself up as a rival to the great epic poets. Like Homer and Hesiod, Parmenides invokes the authority of a goddess who plays the role of a Muse. But Parmenides makes a very different use of the *topos* of the muse. First, the Goddess in Parmenides' poem does not – like Hesiod's muses in the *Theogony* (30–34) – "breathe a divine voice" into the poet.[47] Once the poet encounters the Goddess, she does all the talking, and he remains voiceless. To be sure, the poet – whom the Goddess addresses as "boy" (*kouros*) rather than by name – narrates the whole event in the first person: here is what the Goddess said "*to me*." The poet does, then, have a voice, but he speaks only as a narrator, not as an authority. In some sense, we never hear Parmenides speaking for himself (except insofar as he tells the story of his journey). Note also that the poet describes the revelation as an event that happened in the past (presumably, when he was a very young man): who, we may ask, is this present person who has assumed the role of a messenger?

If the status of the author's voice raises questions in our minds, so also does that of the Goddess. She tells the poet that she will speak both "truthful" and "deceptive" *logoi* (echoing Hesiod's Muses). Although she is careful to mark the exact moment when the false account begins, we must ask why the Goddess articulates this falsehood at all. What is the status of these divinely stated deceptions, and how do these affect the message of the poem as a whole? In Parmenides' poem, the Goddess weighs in as a divine authority that (at least in principle) cannot be questioned or denied. But she sets forth a detailed logical argument that invites assent by the sheer force of reason (indeed the Goddess herself tells the poet to "judge by reason my much-contested argument" [DK B7.5–6]). The inscrutable and unquestionable authority of the Goddess thus jostles with the dictates of reason, which can be inspected and understood by the human mind.

Let us look first at the dramatic proem (DK B1), which depicts the poet as being fetched from the human world by the daughters of the

Sun, who escort him on a divine chariot to the abode of the Goddess. From the very beginning, the poet plays a completely passive role in the drama: he is "carried" to this remote place (rather than traveling there on his own), and functions thereafter as the privileged but mute recipient of a divine *Logos*. The daughters of the Sun lead the poet along the "resounding road of the Goddess" to the threshold of the "gates of day and night." Here, a divinity opens the doors, and the chariot passes through. At this point, the reader may expect that the poet will now see the Goddess. Instead, he hears her speak. After he enters the gates, there is no description of the appearance of the Goddess and, indeed, no visual detail at all (except a reference to a "yawning chasm"). Surprisingly, from our post-Platonic vantage point, the poet journeys out of – rather than into – the light: the sun maidens venture out of the "House of Night" and "into the light" in order to fetch the poet, and they then escort him back to the "gates of the paths of day and night."[48] What the poet encounters when he passes through these gates, then, is not a sunlit realm of vision but rather the voice of an unseen goddess. "Come now, and I will tell you," she says, "and, when you have heard me (*akousas*), carry my account away" (DK B2.1).

The proem, then, depicts a dramatic journey out of the phenomenal world and into the realm of a remote and hidden Truth. To be sure, the poet does not transcend the temporal realm entirely, for his journey takes place in and through language. But he does depart from the light of day and from the multiplicity of phenomenal things which "appear" because of light. In making this journey, the philosopher completely cuts himself off from the social world in order to apprehend truth – he travels "far from the steps of men" (DK B1.27). But the proem hints at a return journey, for the Goddess instructs the poet to "carry [her] account away" to other humans (and the poem itself enacts this mission). Clearly, the Goddess occupies a place "outside" the city and its affairs. How does the world look from this position? The Goddess begins by setting forth two ways or "paths" of thinking about existence and reality. According to the first, the "Way of Truth," "[what-is] is and cannot not be"; according to the second, "[it] is not, and it is necessary that [it] not be." The Goddess rejects the latter path altogether: it is "wholly unlearnable," because we can neither know nor refer to what does not exist. Later, the Goddess refers to a third path – the "Way of Seeming" – which is wrongly taken by ignorant, "two-headed" mortals who conflate "what is" with "what is not." This path represents what ordinary humans believe who trust in their senses (rather than reason) and attribute existence to unreal phenomena (DK B6, 7). The first and the third paths serve to structure the poem as a whole: the first part of the poem outlines the Way of Truth, and the second the Way of Seeming.

After differentiating the three paths, the Goddess offers an account of what-is. She identifies what-is as (a) ungenerated and unperishing; (b) single, undivided, and continuous; (c) unmoving; and (d) perfect and free of all deficiency. The Goddess, then, rejects the notion of an interplay of opposites – which characterized earlier thinking – and claims that reality is completely uniform. Where, we may ask, does this leave human beings? As Long has persuasively argued, the Goddess links the human mind to what-is by identifying thinking with being: "it is the same to think (*noein*) and to be (*einai*)" (DK B3; see also B8.34–6).[49] Human thinking – when it is true and correct – is identical with what-is: the human knower exists insofar as it thinks true thoughts. But what about other aspects of human identity? What about our social and bodily lives? To answer this question, we must turn to the "Way of Seeming." As I have suggested, the Goddess rejects this mode of thinking about reality, which is wrongly adopted by "two-headed" mortals. Yet she opts to describe this path and to account for the error that has led people that way. As the Goddess states at the end of the "Way of Truth":

> Here I end my trusty *logos* and my thought concerning truth;
> henceforth learn the opinions (*doxas*) of mortals, hearing the
> deceitful (*apatelon*) ordering of my verse.
>
> (DK B8.50–2)

The Goddess explains that she will explicate this "deceitful" and "implausible" path (DK B130, B8.50, B8.52) so that no one will "outstrip" Parmenides in discussing reality (DK B8.61).[50] Many scholars have suggested that this part of the discourse sets forth the best possible account of the phenomenal world, that is, better than any others on offer. But why should any deceitful account be better than others?

Before the Goddess sets forth her deceitful account of the physical cosmos, she explains how the illusion of such a cosmos presents itself to human beings. As she claims, humans have erred by making one simple mistake: "they decided to name two forms, one of which it is not right [to name] – and here they go astray; they distinguish these [forms] as opposite in appearance . . . " (DK B8.53–5). As she goes on to say, humans have "separated" and "named" light and night, and this division creates a world of sensible appearances, presumably in the eyes of the perceiver (DK B8.55–9; B9, B10). In short, the act of identifying two things instead of one has led humans to "be borne along, blind and deaf" DK (B6.6–7). Not surprisingly, there are a number of different ways to interpret these claims. I follow Popper and Sedley, who argue that the initial mistake was the addition of "light" to the darkness of Being. In other words, what-is lacks light (which introduces phenomenal distinctions) – Being is "full," "continuous," and dark, lacking in all differentiation.[51] This reading is supported by the drama of the proem, in which Parmenides leaves the realm of light to go to a place where he can hear (but not see) the Goddess.

The identification of two things in the world – light and night – creates the illusion of a phenomenal realm. Having explained how this illusion came about, the Goddess proceeds to give an account of the earth, the heavens, and the generation of human beings. This account falls squarely within the cosmological tradition inaugurated by the Milesians. Yet the Goddess insists that it is a false view, because the phenomenal world does not exist. Clearly, most men believe that it does, and thus possess a false conception of reality. What, then, is the status of their lives and thoughts? Do their erroneous beliefs relegate them to the nullity of nonbeing? This seems hard to accept, especially because the drama of the poem represents an individual moving from ignorance to knowledge. In addition – and even more tellingly – the Goddess's truth itself is communicated in language, which features a plurality of signifiers and unfolds sequentially in time. As Morgan observes, "at the heart of the goddess's revelation lies the dream of language denying itself, an unshaken kernel where Being is uniform and there is no distance between the referring word and that to which it refers."[52] Ultimately, the Goddess (and, after her, the poet) operates at the threshold between Being and Seeming – she (and he) translates Being into the language of Seeming (hence her frequent use of the language of opposites, even in the Way of Truth). Paradoxically, her discourse opens up a third space – a space where the Way of Truth intersects the Way of Seeming. It is no coincidence that the drama of the poem takes place at the gates that separate night and day. Although the Goddess speaks of two different paths, the poem hovers at the crossroads.

As this all-too-brief summary reveals, Parmenides' poem is highly ambiguous. In particular, it confronts us with the paradox of a Goddess who endorses radical monism in a plurality of words; who posits an atemporal being in the temporal sequence of language; who says not only that she *can* lie and tell the truth, but that she *is* doing just that. Finally, the poet journeys away from the phenomenal world to learn the truth, but he is told to "carry it away" to mortals who dwell (we may infer) in the realm of appearances: he must bring this *logos* into the light! Interpreters may flatten out these paradoxes in an attempt to derive a (more or less) logical account. But this seems to me to miss the extraordinary provocation of this text.

In the late Archaic period, certain intellectuals began to quarrel with traditional political and religious "wisdom" and to develop new modes of knowledge. Although many of the early Greek thinkers (including Parmenides) participated in political affairs, their turn toward cosmic and universal "truths" – together with their critique of social and religious practices – encouraged intellectuals in later centuries to challenge traditional forms of political activity and, in some cases, to turn their backs on civic life. The Archaic attacks on the world of appearance and opinion offered challenges to the *polis* and its ideologies. Although the Archaic thinkers certainly made use of the discourse and practices of the Greek civic life, their philosophies raised serious questions about traditional cultural practices.

NOTES

1 Hegel 1892, 7–8.
2 Hegel 1892, 32.
3 Gernet 1955, 1981; Vernant 1982, 1983; Detienne 1996; Detienne and Vernant 1991.
4 Vernant 1982, 130.
5 The phrase "un-reason" is used by Kirk, Raven, and Schofield 1983 (hereafter KRS), 72.
6 On the Archaic thinkers' use of myth and poetry, see Detienne 1986; Lloyd 1987, chapter 4 and *passim*; Most 1999; and Morgan 2000, Chapter 3 and *passim*.
7 Although it is difficult to date some of the early Greek thinkers, I would locate thinkers such as Empedocles and Anaxagoras (whose floruit came after 480 BCE) in the classical rather than the Archaic period.
8 Lloyd 1987, 70–83.
9 Mansfeld 1990, 22–83,126–46.
10 For examples of theologizing in the Archaic thinkers: Anaximander (DK B2, B3), Xenophanes (DK B23, B24, B25, B26), and Heraclitus (DK B67, DK B30). See Broadie 1999 on theological ideas in early Greek thinkers.
11 Lloyd 1987, 83–103.
12 Thomas 2000, 31 and *passim*; see also Nehamas 1990; Vegetti 1999.
13 On Pythagoras and the early Pythagoreans, see Burkert 1972; Kahn 2001, chapters 1–3.
14 Kahn 2001.
15 Martin 1993, 115–16.
16 Harris 1989; Thomas 1989 and 1992.
17 Schofield 1980, 29.

18 Of course, even as they made use of popular poetic forms to gain a hearing, they engaged in a specialized discussion of the nature of the universe, of change, and of reality.
19 Long 1999a, Broadie 1999, Lesher 1999, and Most 1999.
20 Barnes 1982, 4–5.
21 Barnes 1982, 4.
22 Long 1999b, 9, 13–14.
23 So far as we know, Thales did not commit his ideas to writing.
24 KRS 109–110.
25 Kahn 1960/1994, 156 and KRS 129–30.
26 Vlastos 1947/1970, 81.
27 Vernant 1982, 122–3; see also Vlastos 1947/1970, 75–6.
28 Cf. chapter 2 on the *polis* and friction among elites; chapter 6 on expressions of such struggles in lyric poetry.
29 On Anaximander's use of Babylonian ideas, see Kahn 1960/1994, 91–8.
30 Morris 1996.
31 See West 1971, chapters 4–6 and (more persuasively) Kahn 1979, appendix on Heraclitus' response to ancient Indian and Iranian thinking.
32 Kahn 1979; cf. Barnes 1983, who argues that Heraclitus' fragments were not aphoristic, but came from a continuous prose treatise.
33 Long 1992, 268. See DK B 54 and B123 and on the "hiddenness" of the deep structure of the cosmos.
34 Long 1992, 268.
35 I follow Kahn's reading of fr. B1 (1979, 28–9, 96–100); cf. KRS 187–8.
36 Heraclitus believed that the human misunderstanding of the cosmos and its deities led to impious religious behavior (see, e.g., DK B5, B14, and B15).
37 See also DK B113, "thinking is common (*xunon*) to all," which parallels the claim in DK B114 that the *Logos* is "common" (*xunos*) to all.
38 See also DK B31 ("The reversals [*tropai*] of fire: first sea; but of sea half is earth, half lightning storm"), as well as frs. B36, B90, B126.
39 It also "discerns and grasps all things" (DK B66).
40 Kahn 1979, 23.
41 Guthrie 1962, 449–54; Popper 1998, 18–20; cf. KRS 193–197.
42 See also DK B10: "Things taken together: wholes and not wholes, something brought together and brought apart, in tune and out of tune; out of all things a unity, and out of a unity all things."
43 Kraay 1976. On the sociopolitical aspects of coinage economy, see Seaford 1994, 199–234; von Reden 1995, 171–217; Kurke 1999; and Kim 2002.
44 Of course the Greek city-states developed different systems of coinage at different times in the sixth and fifth centuries. There was no single model or standard of measure in the Archaic period.
45 Kurke 1999, 47.
46 Heraclitus does not use the terminology of *nomos* and *physis*, but he is clearly operating with these categories.
47 On Parmenides' Muse-goddess, see Morgan 2000, 74–5.
48 See KRS; Furley 1989; Popper 1992; and Sedley 1999.
49 On this difficult fragment, I follow the interpretations of Long 1996 and Sedley 1999, 120.

50 The deceitful Way of Seeming, however, is "plausible" or "likely" (*eoikota*) to ordinary humans (B8.60).

51 Popper 1992, 72; Sedley 1999, 124.

52 Morgan 2000, 85.

BIBLIOGRAPHY AND SUGGESTED READINGS

Austin, S. 1986. *Parmenides: Being, Bounds, and Logic.*

Barnes, J. 1982. *The Presocratic Philosophers.* Revised ed.

______. 1983, "Aphorism and Argument." In *Language and Thought in Early Greek Philosophy.* Ed. K. Robb. 91–109.

Broadie, S. 1999. "Rational Theology." In *Long 1999b.* 205–24.

Burkert, W. 1972. Lore and Science in Ancient Pythagoreanism.

Burnet, J. 1908. *Early Greek Philosophy.* Second ed.

Cartledge, P. 1998. *Democritus.*

Cornford, F. M. 1912. *From Religion to Philosophy: A Study in the Origins of Western Speculation.*

______. 1952. *Principium Sapientiae: The Origins of Greek Philosophical Thought.*

Coxon, A. H. 1986. *The Fragments of Parmenides.*

Detienne, M. 1986. *The Creation of Mythology.* Transl. M. Cook.

______. 1996. *The Masters of Truth in Archaic Greece.* Transl. J. Lloyd.

Detienne, M. and J.-P. Vernant. 1991. *Cunning Intelligence in Greek Culture and Society.* Transl. J. Lloyd.

Diels, H. 1909. *Herakleitos von Ephesos, griechisch und deutsch.* Second ed.

______. 1952. *Die Fragmente der Vorsokratiker.* Sixth ed., revised with editing and index by W. Kranz.

Dougherty, C. and L. Kurke, eds. 1993. *Cultural Poetics in Archaic Greece.*

Furley, D. 1987. *The Greek Cosmologists.* Vol. 1, *The Formation of the Atomic Theory and Its Earliest Critics.*

______. 1989. *Cosmic Problem: Essays on Greek and Roman Philosophy of Nature.*

Furley, D. J. and R. E. Allen, eds. 1970. *Studies in Presocratic Philosophy.* Vol. 1.

Gernet, L. 1955. *Droit et société dans la Grèce ancienne.*

______. 1981. *The Anthropology of Ancient Greece.* Transls. B. Nagy and J. Hamilton.

Guthrie, W. K. C. 1962. *A History of Greek Philosophy.* Vol. 1. *The Earlier Presocratics and the Pythagoreans.*

______. 1965. *A History of Greek Philosophy.* Vol. 2. *The Presocratic Tradition from Parmenides to Democritus.*

Harris, W. V. 1989. *Ancient Literacy.*

Havelock, E. A. 1963. *Preface to Plato.*

Hegel, G. W. F. 1892. *Lectures on the History of Philosophy* vol. 1, trans. E. S. Haldane.

Humphreys, S. C. 1978. *Anthropology and the Greeks.*

Inwood, B., ed. 2001. *The Poem of Empedocles.* With transl. and comm.

Jaeger, W. 1947. *The Theology of the Early Greek Philosophers.*

Kahn, C. 1960/1994. *Anaximander and the Origins of Greek Cosmology.*

______, ed. 1979. *The Art and Thought of Heraclitus.* With transl. and comm.

______. 2001. *Pythagoras and the Pythagoreans.*

Kim, H. S. 2002. "Small Change and the Moneyed Economy." In *Money, Labour and Land: Approaches to the Economies of Ancient Greece*. Eds. P. Cartledge, E. Cohen, and L. Foxhall. 44–51.

Kirk, G. S., J. E. Raven, and M. Schofield. 1983. *The Presocratic Philosophers*. Second ed.

Kraay, C. M. 1976. *Archaic and Classical Greek Coins*.

Kurke, L. 1999. *Coins, Bodies, Games, and Gold*.

Lesher, J. "Early Interest in Knowledge." In *Long 1999b*.225–49.

Lloyd, G. E. R. 1987. *The Revolutions of Wisdom: Studies in the Claims and Practice of Ancient Greek Science*.

______. 1990. *Demystifying Mentalities*.

Long, A. A. 1992. "Finding Oneself in Greek Philosophy." *UIT Tijdschrift voor Filosofie* 2: 255–79.

______. 1996. "Parmenides on Thinking Being." *The Boston Area Colloquium in Ancient Philosophy* 12: 125–51.

______. 1999a. "The Scope of Early Greek Philosophy." In *The Cambridge Companion to Early Greek Philosophy*. Ed. A. A. Long. 1–21.

______, ed. 1999b. *The Cambridge Companion to Early Greek Philosophy*.

______. 2001. "Ancient Philosophy's Hardest Question: What to Make of Oneself?" *Representations* 74: 19–36.

Mansfeld, J. 1990. *Studies in the Historiography of Greek Philosophy*.

Martin, R. 1993. "The Seven Sages as Performers of Wisdom." In *Cultural Poetics in Archaic Greece*. Eds. C. Dougherty and L. Kurke. 108–28.

Morgan, K. 2000. *Myth and Philosophy from the Presocratics to Plato*.

Morris, I. 1996. "The Strong Principle of Equality and the Archaic Origins of Greek Democracy." In *Ober and Hedrick*. 19–48.

Most, G. W. 1999. "The Poetics of Early Greek Philosophy." In *Long 1999b*. 332–62.

Mourelatos, A. P. D., ed. 1993. *The Presocratics. A Collection of Critical Essays*. Reprint.

Nehamas, A. 1990. "Eristic, Antilogic, Sophistic, Dialectic: Plato's Demarcation of Philosophy from Sophistry," *History of Philosophy Quarterly* 7: 3–16.

Nightingale, A. W. 1995. *Genres in Dialogue: Plato and the Construct of Philosophy*.

______. 2000. "Sages, Sophists, and Philosophers: Greek Wisdom Literature." In *Literature in the Greek and Roman Worlds*. Ed. O. Taplin. 56–91.

______. 2004. *Spectacles of Truth in Classical Greek Philosophy: Theoria in its Cultural Context*.

Ober, J. and C. Hedrick, eds. 1996. *Demokratia. A Conversation on Democracies, Ancient and Modern*.

Popper, K. R. 1992. "How the moon might shed some of her light upon the two ways of Parmenides." *CQ* 42:12–19.

______ 1998. *The World of Parmenides: Essays on the Presocratic Enlightenment*. Eds. A. Petersen with J. Mejer.

Primavesi, O. 1998. *Empedokles-Studien. Der Strassburger Papyrus und die indirekte Überlieferung*.

Schofield, M. 1980. *An Essay on Anaxagoras*.

Sedley, D. 1999. "Parmenides and Melissus." In *Long 1999b*.113–33.

Seaford, R. 1994. *Reciprocity and Ritual: Homer and Tragedy in the Developing City-State*.

Thomas, R. 1989. *Oral Tradition and Written Record in Classical Athens*

______. 1992. *Literacy and Orality in Ancient Greece*.

______. 2000. *Herodotus in Context*.

Vegetti, M. 1999. "Culpability, Responsibility, Cause: Philosophy, Historiography, and Medicine in the Fifth Century." In *Long 1999b*. 271–89.

Vernant, J.-P. 1982. *The Origins of Greek Thought.*

______. 1983. *Myth and Thought Among the Greeks.*

______. 1991. *Mortals and Immortals.* Ed. F. Zeitlin.

Vlastos, G. 1947/1970. "Equality and Justice in Early Greek Cosmologies." In Furley and Allen. 56–91.

______. 1952/1970. "Theology and Philosophy in Early Greek Thought." In Furley and Allen. 92–129.

Von Reden, S. 1995. *Exchange in Ancient Greece.*

West, M. L. 1971. *Early Greek Philosophy and the Orient.*

Zeller, E. 1920–23. *Die Philosophie der Griechen in ihrer geschichtlichen Entwicklung.* Ed. W. Nestle. Vol. I.1, seventh ed.; Vol. I.2, sixth ed.

Part Three

HISTORY AND MATERIAL CULTURE

8: Colonization: Greece on the Move, 900–480

Carla M. Antonaccio

A tension between two views of the Archaic period, one emphasizing the emergence of the individual, the other stressing the importance of the community, is as dominant in approaches to colonization as in everything else. Colonization, on the one hand, is viewed as a kind of protocapitalist enterprise of self-starting, pioneering risk-takers and entrepreneurs as well as the castoffs of society (and an individual affair). Alternatively, colonization is seen as a protoimperialist movement that established Hellenism in foreign territory, secured trade for the mother city, and inscribed the *polis* by means of the spatial allocations of city and country that some of the earliest colonies created. Thus establishing a colony was an official activity of an established state, or city-state (*polis*). In encounters between Hellenes and indigenes, moreover, Greek colonization could be seen to prefigure the classic trope of Greek and Other, which was fully expressed in the struggles with the Persians that unfolded in the late Archaic period. Indeed, the definition and redefinition of Hellenic identity, of Greekness or "Hellenicity," was ongoing and continued right through the end of Greek hegemony and on into the ascendancy of Rome.

In recent years, as programs of archaeological investigation have expanded and borne fruit, and as comparative perspectives in colonial studies have gained hold, the centrality of the colonial movement to Greek identity and experience has become clear. The early Greek colonies were innovators that not only created distinctive identities (civic, cultural, and even ethnic), but also were perhaps responsible for the formation of what are commonly regarded as crucial aspects of core Greek identity, including forms of cult. An emergent view in recent scholarship suggests that the colonial world was a productive "middle ground" between Greeks and non-Greeks in which the mode of interaction was accommodative, rather than conflictive. Approaches using comparative methods employed by historians studying colonial encounters in other places and times have also been influential, emphasizing models of acculturation and culture contact. More recently, creolization and hybridity have begun to displace the older idea of "Hellenization" as a model for colonial experience for both the colonized and the colonizers.

As Robin Osborne has remarked, the last generation of the eighth century BCE was responsible for the establishment of a new settlement in Sicily and south Italy about every two years. The intensity of this activity in the several areas permanently settled by Greeks hardly abated in the Archaic period, and indeed, new settlements continued to be founded in various forms through virtually all of what can be called Greek history. The pace of Greek emigration and permanent settlement "abroad" merits the phenomenon usually called Greek colonization a chapter in any study of the Archaic period.

Home Away from Home

The seemingly continuous and uniform development implied by Osborne, however, is not entirely either. Cities were founded for a variety of reasons, by a wide range of individuals and groups, and had a variety of fates. Polities on the island of Euboea dominated early colonial efforts in the West and in the North Aegean as well, but were not alone: Corinthians, Megarians, Spartans, and Achaeans also founded early colonies. The distribution of colonies, as well as their character, is not as uniform as Osborne's assessment would suggest, either (see Map 3). Nor was early colonization confined entirely to south Italy and Sicily. Moreover, settlements were not evenly distributed in these regions. Colonies on the eastern and south coasts of Sicily and in south Italy were all founded within a relatively short period, ca. 730–650 BCE. Cities were founded in Sicily well into the sixth century BCE and beyond, however, and, new cities were being founded in south Italy until the mid-fifth century.

Before we can examine further what we conventionally call Greek colonization, however, it is important to try to discern how it both resembles and differs from other historical movements that go by the same name. At the close of the Bronze Age, for example, migrations of displaced Mycenaeans are cited to explain the depopulation of some regions (like Messenia) and the apparent increase of population in places like Cyprus after the fall of the mainland palaces. Indeed, the broad movement of Mycenaean refugees from Greece eastward is the context, according to many historians, for the foundation of East Greek settlements in the early Iron Age.

Yet most historians also draw a distinction between this kind of foundation, in the pre- or protohistorical period of "migration," and two other phenomena. The first is the establishment of trading posts, *emporia*, whether in prehistory or in ensuing periods. We know of several *emporia* that were not independent Greek communities, but settlements with populations of non-Greeks and often with good evidence for manufacturing or shipping of varied commodities and finished goods. Two are particularly noteworthy, though controversial: Al Mina in Syria, and Pithekoussai on the island of Ischia. They are controversial because there is disagreement among scholars as to whether these places were "founded," or controlled, by Greeks as opposed to locals or Phoenicians. It seems clear that the inhabitants of such places were of different origins, if we accept pottery and some graffiti in different languages as evidence of different groups living and working together. Transfers of styles, forms, and technologies (including, probably, the Semitic writing system that was adopted and adapted some time in the eighth century into the alphabet used to write Greek) resulted from these kinds of encounters. Their background, though, was the older networks of trade and exchange that seem never to have entirely ruptured after the Bronze Age. One indicator of this is the establishment of a settlement on Kerkyra (Corcyra) by Eretria (soon supplanted by Corinthians), right on the route west toward the Adriatic and the south coast of Italy, and on to Sicily. Indeed, Corinth and the communities of Euboea dominate both early, precolonial encounters and some of the earliest colonial activities.

The second phenomenon is the permanent settlement of Greeks "overseas," in independent communities (*poleis*, or city-states) consisting of an urban center and a dependent territory, which comes under the rubric of colonization. The English word "colony" derives from the Latin *colonia*. Neither the Roman form of population movement and settlement, and certainly not the Greek, correspond particularly well to the category of "colony" or "colonialism" in world history – especially since the period of European expansion beginning about half a millennium before the present. Despite the application of the Latin-derived term to refer to both Roman and Greek colonies, there was in fact more than one type of Roman colony. The earliest were formed of Roman citizens and located within Roman territory. The so-called Latin colonies, however, were independent communities that served as political and military instruments of the Roman state, although the formal distinctions between citizen and Latin colonies ended by the early second century BCE. Colonies after this period were founded to provide settlements for landless citizens and veteran soldiers. In the late Republican period, large-scale settlements of veterans were established throughout the Mediterranean beyond Italy.

The Greek word that we translate as colony, however, was *apoikia*, "[home] away from home." This captures well the fact that Greek colonies were founded not in totally alien territories, but in lands bordering the Mediterranean, Adriatic, and Black, and even the very Aegean, seas. The landscapes and environments, and thus the agricultural economies and trade and transportation networks, were in many cases remarkably similar to those of colonies' *metropoleis* ("mother cities"). Moreover, interactions with the inhabitants of colonized territories may have run the gamut from violent aggression to alliance, but in the Archaic period at least there is some reason to believe that the severely polarized categories of Greek and Barbarian, so familiar in the Classical period, were not operative. Greeks and indigenes may have operated more at the level of partners, whether in hostilities or in the reciprocal obligations of friendship called *xenia* (both highly ritualized, in Greek society at any rate).

At the heart of the term *apoikia* is *oikos* or *oikia*, the notion of household or family, as well as the built house that can be indicated by the same words. In colonial traditions the founder, *oikister* or *oikistes* (sometimes rendered awkwardly in English as "oikist" or even "oecist"), establishes the colony, canonically with an oracle from Delphic Apollo that directs the founder to act and indicates the territory in which the new community should be established. Apollo, the god of purification and of prophecy, was honored as Apollo Archegetes ("leader of the foundation") with an altar set up by the founder, Thucles, at Naxos, and thus a founder could also be called *archegetes* (e.g., Battus, founder of Cyrene; he is also, exceptionally, named king – see ML 5.26) The act of foundation is termed a *ktisis*, from the verb *ktizo*, which connotes the action of creation in a very concrete sense. Indeed, the founder (also occasionally called *ktistor*) is credited with establishing the topography of the new community, from the *agora* (city center or marketplace) and cult places to housing lots and distributions of farmland. That these activities were the regular circumstances and procedures of foundation are often illustrated with Megara's colony in Sicily, called Megara Hyblaia

(Figure 18), one of the earliest founded on the island in the last third of the eighth century. The site of this colony has been extensively excavated and published and provides a handy illustration – however, it may not be typical.

It is indisputable that Greek and Roman colonies were different in character, despite the application of the same English term to both. All Greek colonies were politically independent of their mother cities (*metropoleis*) from the start, even if various contradictory claims could be made – and were. For example, claims of close religious ties were common, symbolized in the notion that colonists brought sacred fire from the communal hearth of the *metropolis* to kindle new fire abroad. A quasi-political tie is suggested by Thucydides' description (1.24.2) of "ancient custom" (*palaion nomon*): sending to the original *metropolis* in the case where a colony wished to itself found a colony, as when Kerkyra sent to Corinth when founding Epidamnos (possibly in the later seventh century; see below on "secondary colonization"). It was usually the involvement of *metropoleis* and colonies in each others' affairs centuries later that is the context for such reports, as in the Epidamnian affair at the start of the Peloponnesian War (mid-fifth century BCE) that Thucydides is narrating.

None of these claims, however, militates against political independence.[1] Although the original community might be directly and collectively – "officially" – responsible for a colony's founding, as in the case of Cyrene, this was not necessarily a rule. The earliest were established before the communities that founded them might even have been considered *poleis*, or at least before they were urbanized communities (not necessarily the same thing). Others were founded by *ethne*, an alternative form of political organization somewhat akin to a federation of communities centered on a common assembly, and a shared sense of regional identity, articulated by common cults (see Chapter 2 on *poleis* and *ethne*). Because colonies were independent communities themselves founded by relatively small and independent polities (even *ethne*, which could have rather large populations, can be thus characterized), the Greek experience of colonization cannot be said to have participated in the kind of imperialism that operated in other times and places. Greek colonies were not put into place to claim territory for a distant ruler or state, or to secure resources for the same, or with any of the other justifications of imperial expansion in history. Indeed, the early Greek colonies are, to some extent, a natural outgrowth of two processes operating in the Iron Age. Population growth is the first, a development that also led to what has been called the "internal colonization" of the territories surrounding Iron Age communities, or the "infilling of the landscape" by settlers from existing groups from nearby settlements. The second is Greek trading activities, some of which used old Bronze Age routes to south Italy, Sicily, and the East that broke the paths to settlement (see below). Finally, although colonies were founded throughout Greek history, they appeared and, in some regions, reached their apogee in the period that forms the focus of this book – a time when a Greek empire simply did not exist.

It is interesting to note that although *ethne* could found *poleis*, *ethne* did not, apparently, found *ethne* away from home. Something about the process that established a new community, and seems to stand behind the notional figure of the oikist and the *ktisis* stories in our literary sources, resulted in the establishment of city-states from the first, and no other kind of community, in the Archaic period.

A Brief Outline of Greek Colonization

Many summaries of the order of Greek colonization are available, but no reference work can do without at least the basic outline. A brief summary, then, of who, what, when, and where in the earliest phase of colonization is set forth below. (The Greek colonial movement in detail through three centuries is beyond the possibilities for this essay, however, and the reader is referred to the sources in the bibliography for further reading.) Leaving aside trading posts or *emporia*, for the moment, the earliest permanent settlements were founded nearly within a generation in several parts of the Aegean world: Naxos and Leontinoi, within five years of each other (according to Thucydides) by the same oikist, Thucles of Chalcis, and then Catane by another Chalcidian, Euarchus. Meanwhile, the Corinthian Archias had founded Syracuse within a year of Naxos. (Another founder, Chersicrates, supposedly left with him on the same voyage but stopped to found Kerkyra, later resettled by Corinthians, and which figured in the Peloponnesian War). Within the decade, Megarians settled Megara Hyblaia, after several failed attempts at setting up permanent shop, including cooperation with the Chalcidians at Leontinoi. All were on the east cost of Sicily. Finally, Zankle and its satellite, Mylai, on the straits of Messina, founded probably by Chalcidians and other Euboeans, as well as settlers from Kyme (pirates, according to Thucydides), round out the eighth century.

Almost simultaneously, colonies in south Italy were also founded: Rhegium again by Chalcidians together with Messenians, securing the other side of the Straits of Messina; Sybaris by Achaeans and possibly settlers from Troizene as well; Croton, by Achaeans reportedly led by Myscellus of Rhype; and Taras, by Laconians from Amyclae under the leadership of Phalanthus. All were in existence by the close of the eighth century BCE. These foundations would seem to follow on what we know of the traffic westward in the early Iron Age, but many of the colonial sites were chosen with an eye toward arable plains, as well as maritime trade. The Greeks had arrived to stay, and the rich territories commanded by most would be the basis for the great wealth and prestige of many, which rivaled any community of the homeland.

In the seventh century new colonies joined those of south Italy: Metapontion (Metaponto), probably early in the century by Achaean settlers, and Siris, reputedly by Ionians from Colophon, right around 700. Locri founded Locri Epizephyri in the early seventh century. These last two foundations were an exception to the Achaean domination of this coast. On the south coast of Sicily, Rhodians from Lindos, together with Cretans, founded Gela in the first quarter of the century. In this century, too, new areas were settled – the north Aegean region of the Chalcidice; the island of Thasos and the mainland coast opposite; the far western Mediterranean (Marseilles and sites in Spain), especially by Phocaeans, first trading and then fleeing the Persians. The Sea of Marmara (or Propontis) and the Black Sea (or Pontus) were settled by many colonies sent primarily from the Ionian city of Miletus, but also from far-flung *metropoleis*, including especially Megara and Athens. At the same time, the original colonies of Sicily and south Italy were joined by others sent from homeland *metropoleis* and also themselves effectively became *metropoleis*, sending out secondary colonies that extended Greek settlement to the south and west of Sicily and filled in the south and west Italian coasts. Given the frequent invocation of overpopulation and land-hunger that is used to explain the initial colonizing movement, it is interesting that some of the earliest colonies themselves immediately underwent fission. Syracuse led the way with foundations of Heloros and Akrai early in the seventh century, and Camarina around 600. Megara Hyblaia jumped to the far west of Sicily and founded Selinous in the second quarter of the seventh century, which in turn founded Herakleia Minoa ca. 580. Gela founded Akragas early in the sixth century as a response to the Megarian expansions. Zankle founded Himera in the last quarter of the seventh century This happened not only in the west; Thera, an early colony of Sparta, founded Cyrene in North Africa, which in turn spread settlements throughout the Cyrenaica (modern Libya).

In Asia Minor, the situation is similar in some ways, but less fully documented archaeologically or historically. Although the Greeks who settled in the west had both the Etruscans and the Phoenicians or Carthaginians already established in their new territories, the Greeks of Asia Minor and the "old country" also had to contend with several non-Greek groups on their margins. These were bona fide empires: Assyrians, Lydians, and Persians in turn. These imperial powers and the ambitions of their rulers presented conditions different from any confronted by Greeks in the West. The resources that colonization made available to trade in the Aegean and Mediterranean, moreover, were particular to this part of the world, including fish and timber. In colonization, Miletus dominated, but Megara was also very active, and Samos and Athens were players as well. Indeed, Megara founded some very important colonies in the seventh century, including Chalcedon and Byzantium, as well as Selymbria. Miletus, however, outpaced all others; its status as a *metropolis* was, indeed, proverbial. It founded Abydos with the cooperation of the Lydian tyrant Gyges in the early seventh century, Berezan, Olbia, Istrus, in the mid-seventh century, and Sinope, which in turn founded Trapezous, sometime in the sixth. Aside from the late colony of Thurii, founded in the mid-fifth century by Athens on the site of the destroyed Sybaris, all of Athenian colonial activity was confined to this region: Athens had settled Sigeion as early as the sixth century and also put *klerouchies* in Lemnos and Imbros around 500. Athens' large territory may be a reason for this, but it is not at all clear that land was the primary motivation for colonization.

Sources and Representations

Several sources, some of them mentioned already, provide the basis for the survey outlined above. Foundation stories, a bona fide theme (if not a genre) in Greek literature, are alluded to in an oft-cited reference of Plato's *Hippias Maior* (285d). The passage speaks of the delight of the Spartans in hearing "the origins of both heroes and men, and of settlements – how cities were founded in antiquity, and in short, concerning all the discourse of antiquity (*archaiologia*)." Our knowledge of Greek colonization comes from three main sources, each of which has its own modes of discourse and inquiry.

The first is literary–historical, that is, texts that provide chronological frameworks, including the order of foundations, the names of founders and their original communities, and absolute dates. (There are a few inscriptions that belong in this category, but see below.) There is information that bears on colonization even in Homer: the *Odyssey* features two episodes that have a distinctly colonial flavor. In the encounter with the Cyclopes, a description of an ideal site for a colony occurs, and in the Phaeacia episode, a founder's actions are echoed in the description of Nausithous' establishment of Scheria. For the late Iron Age and archaic periods, Thucydides' history is of crucial importance (see below), and Herodotus runs a close second. Other sources include the archaic poet Archilochus, the geographer Strabo, writing around the turn of the era, and the chronographer Eusebius, writing in the fourth century CE.

The second we might call mythological–ethnographic: poetry, especially, that conveys myths and other narratives that account for the indigenous groups already on the ground and the interactions with the first Greek arrivals. Epinician poetry, especially Pindar's, is particularly important here (on which see also Chapter 6). All these sources, of whatever date and type, and referring to a very wide variety of foundations, have been used to build up a composite picture of colonization, although it is not clear that such a procedure is legitimate.

The third category of information is archaeology, which supplies the material record that provides a crosscheck to the chronologies derived from other sources and recovers the built environment and material culture of the earliest settlers. Archaeological data also provide independent chronological criteria, but for this purpose must be used with caution. The dates of early Greek pottery styles are themselves derived in part from the Sicilian colony dates as transmitted especially in the texts of Thucydides, and thus the danger of circular arguments about dating is high. Archaeology also creates a discourse of things that must be read against the written sources.

It is possible in many cases to compare the written record and the archaeological data to good effect (Thucydides' dates, to speak only of chronology, actually hold up rather well). Archaeology is especially suited to providing information about settlement patterns, cult, and interactions with local populations. In addition, archaeological excavation and survey of sites not much mentioned or discussed in written sources provide the only information available for them. Finally, archaeology provides information on interactions between Greeks and non-Greeks, both in the period before colonization proper, that is, the earlier Greek Iron Age, and once permanent settlements are established. The dynamic of precolonial encounters is trade or exchange and the alliances that go with it, and is epitomized in the oft-cited story of Damaratus, a seventh-century Corinthian who traded with Etruria and eventually settled among the Etruscans, becoming the progenitor of the Etruscan kings, the Tarquins. But even before this, Homer knows about Sicily and south Italy, as well as the coast of North Africa. Hesiod speaks of seafaring and trading, as well as the economic hardships that might lead a Greek of the late Iron Age, such as Hesiod's own father, to seek a better lot somewhere else.

Such stories hint at the multiple reasons and mechanisms by which Greeks moved out of their native territories. The motivations for leaving Greece and settling permanently "abroad," like the communities and regions from which colonists set out, are as varied as the individuals who left. Taras was reputedly founded by illegitimate sons of Spartan mothers; Syracuse by a Corinthian of the ruling Bacchiad clan; Cyrene because of famine; and (a little later) Gela practically by accident, by two oikists from different regions, Rhodes and Crete.

It seems likely that trade and exchange and the relationships that undergirded them blazed the trail for the permanent settlements that colonization brought. Why trade changed to settlement has been endlessly debated. Ancient sources speak of famine, civil disturbances and exile, and personal tragedy. Modern scholarship has tended to generalize the causes not as famine, but as "land-hunger," and to see colonization as a kind of safety valve for societies under pressure. Alternatively, colonization is seen as a state-sponsored enterprise aimed at securing lucrative resources (grain, metals, timber, fish, and so on) or trade with native populations (as seen especially in pottery imports).

In this early period (ninth and early eighth century BCE), the Euboeans seem to be the Greek participants in these ventures, as they were in voyages and outposts in the north Aegean, for example. Mende and Torone, in the north Aegean, were founded by Eretria and Chalcis, respectively, paralleling the early Euboean movement westward, and probably reflecting similarly continuous connections eastward. As we shall see directly, Euboeans were also among the first colonists in the early Greek settlements of Sicily. Meanwhile, Thera is said to have been colonized by Sparta, sometime in the early Iron Age, and then to have sent a colony to North Africa – the only Greek state to do so. (Among major *poleis*, only Sparta colonized so little; aside from Thera, the only colony was Taras. Athens presents a special exception to the picture, wholly absent from early colonial activity though apparently participating in eastern trade from at least the ninth century.)

The origins of the colonies are varied and generalization is probably unwise, but colonization does represent a fissioning of existing populations into permanent and independent new settlements. Carol Dougherty has well described the "emplotment" of colonial foundation narratives in the Archaic period as follows: Delphic Apollo, consulted during a crisis either collective or personal, directs the foundation of a colony, which resolves the original situation and is (literally) enshrined in a hero cult to the founder. The Apollo who purifies is called upon to support an endeavor that is sometimes framed as expiation for literal or metaphorical murder. The resolution of the original crisis is not really effected, nor is the transition to political independence, until the death of the founder – an event that, canonically, engenders a hero cult dedicated to the founder. (The choice of the name of Naxos for the first Euboean colony may point to the Cyclades and the Apollo of Delos rather than to the Apollo of Delphi.)

Dougherty has convincingly argued, however, that this pattern is invented to deal with the crisis of permanently leaving home (for whatever reason) and the unfamiliar experience of creating a new community ex nihilo. Indeed, despite much ink spilled to demonstrate the contrary, colonies are not very tightly bound to their mother cities by religion, military alliance, or other ties. The decision to send out a colony as a corporate act has been preserved epigraphically in a few so-called foundation charters. Only one of them belongs firmly to the period under consideration here: the founding of Cyrene in North Africa by Thera in the late seventh century BCE. The authenticity and accuracy of this document are an issue, and it should be regarded as a representation from the fourth BCE of imagined origins, though it may be based on the terms of the original resolution of the Theran polity to action. Indeed, as noted by Dougherty, there is little evidence for a genre of archaic *ktisis* literature, although stories about colonization abound in many kinds of texts. The figure of the founder, the *oikistes*, should therefore be particularly scrutinized. He would seem to be the *sine qua non* of colonization: the community's choice, approved by Apollo at Delphi, who had total responsibility over all aspects of creating the new city. This view has been defended even though many recorded early oracles are unlikely to be genuine, and many founders' names are attested only late, if at all. Nevertheless, early planned cities are founded in which the allotment of sacred, public, domestic space can be archaeologically documented. How land was allocated is a matter of greater dispute, because there is little evidence from the preclassical period for either procedures or actual allotments, and the presumption of equal shares that may have governed house plots in the city cannot be assumed to have applied in the countryside. Finally, despite the extraordinary powers ascribed to the *oikistes*, there is little information about how power devolved after the initial colonization, or after the death of the founder.

There is some archaeological evidence to support the idea of instantaneous foundation, at least some of the time, in the form of orthogonal urban grids, with comparable house lots and houses with shared party walls and similar plans. The textbook illustration is Megara Hyblaia, where, however, the evidence points to multiple grid plans in different parts of the site, which may mirror neighborhoods consisting of clusters of houses at places like Corinth and Athens in the old country (see Figure 18). The houses themselves are extremely simple, and small. Megara Hyblaia had an *agora* from the first, even though public buildings did not appear immediately. This general, conceptual framework stands in stark contrast to the built domestic and public environments of old cities like Athens, Corinth, or Sparta, which grew by accretion and whose polities were formed by the synoecism (*synoikismos* or political unification) of smaller settlements, punctuated by deliberate reorganization. These towns only saw grid plans, if at all, later in their histories. In cities such as these, public spaces had to be carved out at a particular stage, whereas sacred places were sometimes of considerable antiquity. Although urban forms do not necessarily express political structure directly, corporate decisions are represented by monumental construction and by forms that affect large parts of the population, even if a founder (or tyrant) makes them with popular consent and the willingness to mobilize labor and resources necessary. Thus, it may not take a *polis* to found a *polis* (we hear that the founder of Syracuse came from the village of Tenea, not from Corinth itself). It may take a *polis* to found a *metropolis*, however, in two senses: a colony that founds other colonies itself becomes a *metropolis*, and a colony makes the *metropolis* as much as the foundation of the colony does.

It is easier in most cases to document the layout of an urban plan than to understand the organization of the countryside and access to its resources. The model of a *polis* calls for political unity between the *asty*, or central place in the community, and its territory. Metapontion has been important in demonstrating that colonization might be more of a process than an event and in challenging canonical notions about the division of the territory and the importance of sanctuaries in marking that territory. The material culture of the earliest settlement in the seventh century is a mix of local and Greek. The territory was not reorganized until the second half of the sixth century, with a major increase in the number of farmsteads, and the regular land division still visible in the countryside was not accomplished until ca. 500, when olive cultivation was also introduced. At the same time, there was a major reorganization of civic space, including a massive structure interpreted as an *ekklesiasterion* (assembly place), indicating that both civic and rural space were ordered in a "colonial" manner only nearly a century after the first Greek settlers arrived. Thus, the division of the territory into plots still visible at Metapontion (and from the later site of Chersonesus in the Crimea) is not usually preserved to the present time. It is very unclear if equal division of the territory from the earliest period parallels the equal division of the urban space into house lots – or that either signifies political *isonomia*, or equality before the law. The emphasis has been on arable land and its division, but other resources, for example pasture, water rights, and perhaps the harvesting of timber or extraction of raw materials such as clay, or hunting rights, were also considered. A very late sixth century inscription documenting the foundation by Locrians of a new community or apportionment of new territory makes provision for the division of both public and private land, as well as inheritance of land or of rights to pasture (ML 13).

The lack of consistent evidence for an "instant *polis*" may also explain the relatively scanty archaeological evidence for hero cult. A building fronting on Megara Hyblaia's *agora* is cited as a probable heroön, as is a feature of the *agora* at Cyrene, and an archaic kylix dedicated to Antiphemus, one of the founders of Gela, is also known (Figure 19). The Sicilian tyrants sought heroic honors in founding new settlements (see below). But even so, we are left with the many instances in which a founder's name is not preserved. It seems likely that hero cult may be a back-formation from a later period in which colonial origins were being investigated – but also a particularly colonial focus of identity, more so than heroic cults in the homelands from which colonists originated.

Barbarians and Hybrids

Another way in which foundation is murder (in addition to that in the foundation myth; see above) regards the indigenes who were already living on the sites and in the territories to which Greeks emigrated. In Sicily, starting with the foundation of Syracuse, where the Sicels are said to have been driven out and the earliest Greek buildings appear to directly replace Sicel structures, interactions between Greeks and local people could be adversarial and violent. Some native populations apparently became subjugated (at Syracuse, they were called the Killyrioi), but others cooperated with Greek settlers (e.g., Hyblon, ruler of the

Sicels in east Sicily, who allowed Megarians to settle the colony that carried his name, Megara Hyblaia). Still others remained in independent settlements in the interior for centuries (see below). In south Italy, the record is mixed; although the founder of Taras was urged to his task as a "scourge to the [native] Iapygians" by the Pythia, there is good evidence for the coexistence of natives in and around Metapontion at least early in the colony's history. In the Black Sea area, "natives" are probably more collaborators in the colonial enterprises of the Greeks than anywhere else, and there are many indications, in the form of local types of pottery and of housing, for the Greek adoption of local forms of material culture.

Often the Greeks represented themselves as moving into *eremos chora*, empty territory, when they colonized. Indeed, the description of "goat island" in the *Odyssey*, noted above, remarks that this ideal land is uninhabited and consequently undomesticated. Yet we know very well that almost all territories colonized by the Greeks were occupied when the Greeks arrived. This brings us to consider the inhabitants of the lands colonized in the eighth century and later, some of whom had been trading partners of the Greeks before they came to stay. Indeed, the background to the surge of settlements in the eighth century BCE is the trade, elite gift-exchange, warfare, and migration between the inhabitants of the prehistoric Aegean and those living on its margins that characterized the entire Bronze Age and even earlier periods.

The presence of traders and craftsmen from the East and of permanent settlements of Levantines in the Aegean and Aegean Greeks in the east, for example, seems assured in the late Bronze Age in particular. The impetus for the entire westward movement was probably the metal-bearing region of central Italy; the establishment of Kyme (Cumae) on the mainland of Italy, directly opposite Pithekoussai, is a good illustration of this. On the Aegean side, the site of Lefkandi in Euboea (succeeded in the eighth century by its possible successor, Eretria, as well as Chalcis) looks more eastward, but the burial customs – including cremation burials in bronze receptacles – show up at Kyme. Voyaging Euboeans may have been responsible for the adaptation of the alphabet; one of the earliest Greek inscriptions turns up at Pithekoussai, the so-called "Nestor's Cup" from tomb 168 in the Valle di San Marzano cemetery. This is often cited as evidence for the dissemination of the Homeric poems already in the eighth century in the context of sympotic drinking (a krater was found with the cup, as well as a set of Early Protocorinthian aryballoi). Despite its allusion to the aged Nestor and the gifts of Aphrodite, however, the drinking vessel, an imported Rhodian kotyle, was actually found in the grave of a young boy.

A variety of impulses, sponsors, and participants for early traveling and trade are probable, however. In the aftermath of the Bronze Age, trade may have been in the hands of an elite, but not exclusively so, and not entirely in Greek hands, either. Thus the colonial experience is important in challenging the firmly established polarity of barbarian versus Hellene. With this model in mind, the concomitant process by which indigenous barbarians were acculturated and assimilated was formulated as "Hellenization." As implied by the root, Hellene/Hellas, the process was conceptualized as becoming Greek, aided by intermarriage between native women and Greek men. The mechanisms and expressions of Hellenization included adoption of Greek material culture, technologies, foodstuffs, social forms (such as the symposium), religion (including architectural frameworks for cults as well as divinities), language (starting with the alphabet to write native languages), and civic forms (coinage, fortifications). The term conveyed very well the import of the operation: loss of native identity, along with political independence, in a very unidirectional process. Although philhellenic chauvinism among scholars may underlie both the terminology and the assumptions of cultural, social, and military superiority that made it obvious that Greekness would win out, it is a fact that there is less evidence for the influence of indigenous cultures on colonists than vice versa. Thus, although the term has been (justly) criticized, the facts remain that everywhere, Greek replaced local languages, Greek material culture came to dominate, and local groups were caught up in, and overtaken by, the Greeks in their territories.

Nevertheless, having defined a sharp dichotomy between Greeks and Others, epitomized by the Persian struggle but applicable to all encounters with non-Greeks, scholars have recently been engaged in breaking it down. This has implications for our understanding of the colonial experience from both the Greek perspective and the native, and even for how to frame the very question of what it was to be Greek in the late Iron Age, when the colonization movement began to intensify. How Greeks would have perceived themselves, and non-Greeks, and how they would have interacted with others, are at the heart of the matter. It is common to regard Greek identity as a kind of ethnic identity, and to define ethnicity as culture plus lineage. The cultural definition of ethnicity, however, may have only emerged in the fifth century. Before this, ethnic identity among those we call the Greeks, but who did not themselves self-identify as Hellenes until the end of the Archaic period, was perhaps expressed in terms of fictive kinship, as related in the mythological genealogies that produced the ethnic eponyms of Dorus, Aeolus, Ion, and so forth. According to this view, Greek colonists would not therefore have seen themselves as partaking in a Greek identity, encountering wholly other natives. Instead, the culturally and technologically similar Greeks and natives would have been relatively evenly matched.

The presence of and relations with local populations also affected the secondary colonization that took place in some cases almost immediately. Syracuse expanded fairly rapidly and came to dominate the southeastern part of the island, founding Kasmenai and Akrai in the early seventh century. Important Sicel sites such as Pantalica had been abandoned already in the eighth century, and these subcolonies did not displace or destroy indigenous settlements. On the other hand, in the same period the lately founded Gela fought a series of wars with the local populations, the Sikans. Meanwhile, the thoroughly Hellenizing Elymians at Segesta had close relations with the Selinuntines, including the right of intermarriage. We know less about the relations of Himera, one of the latest colonies to be founded, and the indigenes from literary sources, but the material culture of Himera includes a discernable admixture of native objects and ceramics – an unusual state of affairs in a Greek colony. It may be that Himera's relative isolation on the north coast, bordered by the Punic territory immediately to its west and somewhat removed from other Greek colonies, created a different kind of cultural hybridity. Himera, in any case, was among the least durable of all the Greek colonies, existing for a mere 200 years.

Indeed, colonization in all times and places has produced literally mixed results – hybrid, or "Creole," societies, populations, and cultures. In the discourse of domestication, the term "hybrid" is a cross of two distinct varieties to produce something new that combines both. (It has had negative connotations, as when invoked with the pejorative "mongrel.") Cultures, persons (bodies), ethnicities, languages, and all forms and manifestations of identity are thus analogous to plants and animals; lineages can be crossed to produce something new.

Although such categories have entered classical studies through the discourse of Postcolonial Studies, there is a longer history of such concepts in anthropology and culture history. In these literatures hybridity was employed in the 1950s to describe the literally mixed results of culture contact (for example, in Native North America). In addition, as pointed out by Jonathan Hall, as early as 1930 Sir John Myres traced the "becoming of the Greeks," a process that took place over time and was the result of the mixing of many population "stocks," with their different qualities and characteristics. In connection with this, it is important to acknowledge that ethnic identity is often used interchangeably with biological and cultural identity, but that recent work has sought to distinguish ethnicity very precisely as an identity based on criteria including (notional) common descent, shared history, and ancestral territory. Culture, biologically inherited features, language, and so on are sometimes indicators of ethnic identity as so defined, but not its essential, constitutive elements. In this view, the criteria are conveyed in written and spoken discourses, without which archaeology cannot discern ethnicity per se, rather than some other identity. Thus, it is not sufficient to simply identify "Greek" or "indigenous" material culture (or language) and then proceed to trace how its features change, meld, or disappear over time, and thereby trace a specifically ethnic identity. Individuals using Greek pottery in the colonial world, for example, may have self-identified as indigenes, and even if they give their children indigenous names, these individuals may have been members of a Greek *polis*. Because it is very unclear whether Greek colonists brought wives and children with them, intermarriage between colonists and locals is clearly one route by which hybridity in one sense may have come about.

Although the querying of basic concepts has been productive, it also raises the question of what the category of "Greek" itself means. If Hellenicity is a discourse solely about descent before the formation of a specifically "Hellenic" cultural consciousness in the fifth century (as argued by Jonathan Hall), then it is meaningless to speak of "Greek" colonization, or of "Hellenization." Yet, at the same time, the arrival of emigrants had definite effects on the landscapes and inhabitants that they encountered. The built and created environment, which came to incorporate aspects of both new and existing objects, practices, foods, rituals, and so on, cannot be held of no account in discussing the lived experiences of ancient colonial spheres. Although we do have information from Greco-Roman sources (see above) about the criteria for native ethnicity assigned by colonists or their descendants, we do not know if indigenes would have accepted these notions. Nor do we know whether native stories of their origins are responsible, for example, for the information in Thucydides that a Sicel king named Italus gave his name to the Italian peninsula (6.2.4). Nor do we know for certain if native ethnicity per se was expressed through distinctive forms of dress, material culture, language, foodways, ritual, and domestic space. We cannot say if a Sicel (for example) would have considered him- or herself to be a member of that ethnic group by virtue of a putative ancestor, an ancestral homeland, and a shared history, whether or not he or she was using Greek pottery or carrying a Greek name.

Thus, what archaeologists frequently discuss as evidence for ethnic identity should perhaps be viewed more broadly: material culture as the material expression symbolic of distinctiveness. This distinctiveness might be local (i.e., one community defining itself against another), civic (a community of citizens versus another), class, gender, age, or ethnic. For the purposes of studying colonization, we can propose that the previously loosely bounded cultures of the *metropoleis* were redeployed in a colonial setting both in the colonies themselves and in the surviving indigenous populations. In the former, mixtures of pottery, architectural styles, and experiments in urbanism and religion were undertaken; the latter accepted selected aspects of Greek culture (material and immaterial) over time and without entirely giving up local ways of doing, making, and being. That is to say, both "native" and "Greek" colonials were hybrids with regard to their persons, their cultures, and their built environments, and in the end all gave way relatively quickly to other Others, such as the Carthaginians in Sicily or the Lucanians in south Italy, who overturned the colonial worlds sometimes in very short order.

BECOMING GREEK, STAYING GREEK: COLONIES AND SANCTUARIES

Perhaps the most salient form of material expression of colonial identity can be seen in sanctuaries, both in the colonies themselves, and at home. The colonies are remarkable for their temple-building activities, on a scale and with a frequency that often surprises modern visitors. Perhaps the best examples are Akragas, with its chain of temples in the so-called "Valley of the Temples" at the edge of the city, and Selinous, with its profusion of temples in addition to the extramural sanctuary of Demeter the Apple-Bearer (Malophoros). This activity bespeaks the incredible, if short-lived, wealth of these places. Selinous, Metapontion, and indeed nearly any colony are good places to see at work the varieties of being Greek at a time when the Greeks were still in the process of becoming (as they always were, in fact), expressed through "noncanonical" forms, proportions, and uses of the orders. Colonial innovation is on view in the early temple of Apollo at Syracuse, rivaling the second temple of Apollo at Corinth with its monolithic columns and dedication inscribed on the stylobate, or the mixed Ionic and Doric orders of the temple of Athena at Posidonia (Paestum), a colony of Sybaris. This is to say nothing of such unique categories as the clay dedicatory plaques of Locri Epizephyri (the so-called Locrian *pinakes*) and the sculpture that decorated many of the temples.

As noted above, there is no Panhellenic, or "Pansicilian," sanctuary on the island, and indeed the focus of most of the colonial regions is on the Panhellenic sanctuaries of the homeland (on which, see Chapter 9). Indeed, an oft-remarked feature of relations of the colonies with the old communities and territories is the close connections and considerable investments of the former in the major sanctuaries. The most conspicuous of these investments is the many treasuries dedicated by colonies at Delphi and especially at Olympia. Leaving little trace in the archaeological record is the concomitant participation in the Panhellenic games, celebrated so eloquently in the poetry of Pindar and Bacchylides. The material manifestations of these victories are nearly all lost, with the occasional exception such as the bronze statue from Delphi often referred to simply as "The Charioteer" (see Figure 25). This is the sole surviving figure from a chariot group that included the groom and the horses, and commemorates a victory by Polyzalus of Gela perhaps in 466. Although the late archaic tyrants and their circle are perhaps the most famous victors, colonial participation in the games can be traced in victor lists and the dedications of celebratory monuments back to the seventh century Like many other Greek, and non-Greek, communities, colonies also staged their military victories and displayed their prestige through dedications at Delphi and Olympia. One example is the golden tripod dedication of the Deinomenid tyrants Gelon and Hieron on the Sacred Way and close to the terrace of the Temple of Apollo at Delphi (Figure 20; see also no. 518 on the plan of Delphi, Figure 22). Adjacent to the snake column and tripod that was the allied Greek monument commemorating the defeat of the Persians at Salamis (see Figure 26 and no. 407 in Figure 21), this monument proclaimed the local identities of both the dedicator (Syracusan) and the artist (Milesian) in a venue back "home."

Although investment at Delphi, the site of the oracle that sanctioned many of the foundations, may be thought to be natural in some way, Olympia seems to have been a virtual western Greek cult center – both cause and explanation for why the Sicilian Greeks never had a shared sanctuary of their own (for a plan of the sanctuary, see Figure 22). Nearly all the treasuries at Olympia were constructed by colonies (principally west Greek). The prestige of competing in the other games seems to have been an end in itself, a claim of equal standing with the *metropoleis* and peer communities back home, as well as a vehicle for the tyrants of the late Archaic period in particular. We may also note the presence in Hellenic sanctuaries of dedications originating both east and west that pre-date colonial activity, or are coeval with it. Often thought to be booty or souvenirs dedicated by Greeks, it is also possible that sanctuaries like Olympia and Delphi attracted investment by non-Greeks as early as the ninth century, prefiguring the interest of such figures as Gyges in making dedications in the Archaic period.

Tyrants and Patronage

Whereas Cyrene, like its grandmetropolis Sparta, was ruled by a hereditary kingship, the political systems of other colonies are less easy to map out. Tyranny constitutes a notable feature of Archaic colonialism, but one that came late to the western colonies. It was the fifth century, not the seventh or sixth, that witnessed the ascent of the Emmenid tyrants of Akragas and the Deinomenids of Gela and Syracuse. Indeed, most of the colonies were ruled by landowning oligarchies, and the western tyrannies may be considered against this background. The earliest tyrant we know of, however, was Panaetius at Leontinoi, who held power at the end of the seventh century; an early predecessor of the two clans was Phalaris of Akragas, who came to power during the generation after the colony's founding in the early sixth century. A dizzying alternation of tyrannies and oligarchies forms the backbone to the histories of many of the Sicilian and south Italian cities, though with Hippocrates of Gela we have the beginning of a more stable succession. Hippocrates, at the beginning of the fifth century, marched through the center of Sicily on a quest for power and territory that ended with his death fighting Sicels near Etna, but he inaugurated an era of instability in the colonial west. Indeed, conflict and instability, both internally generated and caused by the exodus of the Ionian Greeks fleeing from Persian oppression, and by confrontation with the Carthaginians, mark the end of the Archaic period.[2]

The activity of many of the tyrants and their circles as competitors in the Panhellenic games has already been noted. They were also patrons of the arts and of artists from the mainland – Bacchylides and Pindar being two, but sculptors and other artists were also in their employ. As also noted, one feature of western Greek tyranny is the activity of the tyrants as movers of populations and founders of new cities. Thus, Aitnia was founded by Hieron, as celebrated by Aeschylus in his nearly lost play

Aitnissai. But the west had long been a home for poets and other cultural figures. The philosopher Pythagoras, originally from Samos, made his home at Croton at the end of the sixth century, the poet Ibycus was born at Rhegium and spent some of his life in Sicily, and the lyric poet Stesichorus was likely born at Himera in Sicily (although south Italy also claims him).

The relatively late efflorescence of tyranny in the west contrived to put the tyrants at the center of the Persian conflict as well as their own with Carthage. Thus Gelon, tyrant first in Gela and after 485 in Syracuse, proposed to the Greeks planning the defense of the homeland against the Persians that he should not just send help, as asked, but should lead the entire combined force. This was rejected, but Gelon was soon to triumph over the Carthaginians in a major battle on the north coast, at Himera, in 480. Not only was this the same year as the definitive Greek victory over the Persians at Salamis, but also the two battles were soon said to have happened on the very same day.

Conclusion: The Shortness of Greekness

The boundary for this volume and the Archaic period is 490/480, which is a high-water mark in the west as well as the old country. This decade, which has structured history of the Archaic Period for generations in terms of the epic struggle with Persia, pivots in the west around the defeat of the Carthaginians at Himera – defeated by a Greek force led by Gelon, whose leadership in place of the Spartans the Greeks had rejected. The unlikely synchronism is rich with symbolism. Although the colonies were often regarded as upstarts and their ruling classes as nouveaux riches, the experience of the Greeks in the Archaic period cannot be fully understood without them. Indeed, the early extension of Greek settlement and its immediate success and reproduction of itself in new territories is testament to the integrality of the colonies to what we must consider Greece and Greekness. Thus, although study of the cities of Old Greece usually sets the pace for history, it may be argued that the cities founded "abroad" are as typical and important.

There is a caveat to this, however, and that is the instability of colonial settlements. The fifth century would see almost constant warfare in Sicily, which was inaugurated by the campaigns of Hippocrates. The preface to the Sicilian Expedition was the displacement and resettling of populations by the Emmenid and Deinomenid tyrants and continuing conflict with communities who still considered themselves, and were considered, non-Greek (particularly the Sicels). The fifth century ends with catastrophic conflict with Carthage, especially for the cities of the south coast of the island. War also came, and earlier, to south Italy, most notoriously the destruction of Siris just after the middle of the sixth century at the hands of Sybaris and Metapontion. Then Croton destroyed Sybaris close to the end of the century. Thus two of the most wealthy and important of the colonies came to an end after only 200 years of existence. The instability of Italian Greek societies ultimately resulted in the elision of Greek identity and the ascendance of new Italic groups, such as the Samnites, Bruttians, and Lucanians.

Greek colonization in the Archaic period was limited to the coastal regions of the Mediterranean, Aegean, Propontis, and Black Seas. These limits were, in part, determined by the limited aims of colonizing movement. No Greek *metropolis* set out to conquer a new empire, to bring religion to the natives, or to secure tribute from subject foreign peoples for the *metropolis*. It was not until the Athenian hegemony of the fifth century that a de facto empire of tributary, mostly Greek, communities was created. This included Athenian colonies established in the north Aegean and Bosporus and *klerouchies*. Syracusan expansion and extraction of tribute from the Sicels is a close parallel; nothing is known of the status of early Syracusan foundations such as Akrai and Kasmenai, though Kamarina both is regarded as a separate *polis* and yet had to fight for its independence ca. 50 years after its foundation. But it was not until the Hellenistic period and the ambitions of Alexander and his successors that wide swaths of very distant territory were secured with the foundations of Greek cities – and an imperial model of colonization can be discerned.

Notes

1 It was this independence that also distinguished a colony from a *klerouchy* (or cleruchy), another form of Greek settlement in foreign territory. In this case, however, the inhabitants remained citizens of the original *metropolis*. This term derives from the Greek term for allotment, *kleros*, and *ekhein*, to have or hold – hence, the allotment of land held by each settler. *Klerouchies* are a peculiarly Athenian institution before the Hellenistic period.

2 For more on tyrants, see Chapter 1.

Bibliography and Suggested Readings

Aubet, M. E. 2001. *The Phoenicians and the West. Politics, Colonies and Trade* (2nd ed.) (Important corollary to studies of Greek settlement.)

Boardman, J. 1999. *The Greeks Overseas. Their Early Colonies and Trade* (2nd ed.). (Indispensable summary of the Greek expansion abroad, both east and west.)

______, and N. G. L. Hammond, eds. 1982. *The Expansion of the Greek World, Eighth to Sixth Centuries B.C.* [*The Cambridge Ancient History* (2nd ed.), Vol. III, Pt. 3]. (Basic chapters by A. J. Graham and J. M. Cook on colonization.)

d'Agostino, B. and D. Ridgway, eds. 1994. *Apoikia: I più antichi insediamenti greci in Occidente: funzioni e modi dell'organizzazione politica e sociale [Scritti in onore di G. Buchner; AION archaeol. 1].* (Fundamental set of papers on early Greek colonization in the western Mediterranean.)

Descœudres, J.-P., ed. 1990. *Greek Colonists and Native Populations.* (Groundbreaking collection of papers focusing on interactions between Greeks and indigenes.)

Dougherty, C. 1993. *The Poetics of Colonization. From City to Text in Archaic Greece.* (Important reconsideration of the literary and cultural representations of colonization.)

______. 2001. *The Raft of Odysseus. The Ethnographic Imagination of Homer's Odyssey.* (The Mediterranean world in the Greek mind just before and on the cusp of colonization.)

Dunbabin, T. J. 1948. *The Western Greeks. The History of Sicily and South Italy from the Foundation of the Greek Colonies to 480 B.C.* (Still the unsurpassed and indispensable study, though the archaeology is out of date.)

Gosden, C. 2004. *Archaeology and Colonialism. Cultural Contact from 5000 BC to the Present.* (Comparative study of colonialism, including but not limited to classical antiquity, with emphasis on material culture and social relations.)

Graham, A. J. 1964. *Colony and Mother City in Ancient Greece.* (Though much reconsidered by later scholars' work, this is still a basic study.)

______. 2001. *Collected Papers on Greek Colonization. Mnemosyne.* Suppl. 214. (Convenient volume of publications by a prominent scholar.)

Hall, J. 2002. *Hellenicity. Between Ethnicity and Culture.* (Important chapters on method and theory in studying identity and on encounters with non-Greeks in the Archaic period.)

Hurst, H. and S. Owen. 2005. *Ancient Colonizations. Analogy, Similarity and Difference.* (Collection of papers by Greek and Roman archaeologists and historians providing broad overviews with comparative perspective on ancient colonialism.)

Leighton, R. 1999. *Sicily before History.* (Up-to-date handbook on precolonial and early colonial Sicily.)

Lomas, K., ed. 2003. *Greek Identity in the Western Mediterranean.* Proceedings of an International Conference in Honour of Professor B. B. Shefton, F.B.A. (Collection of papers by archaeologists and historians focusing on Sicily, south Italy, and Spain.)

Lyons, C. and J. Papadopoulos, eds. 2002. *The Archaeology of Colonialism. Issues and Debates* 9. (Comparative perspectives on colonization, including several papers on the Greek case.)

Malkin, I. 1987. *Religion and Colonization in Ancient Greece.* (Important book on this fundamental topic, arguing for close connection of mother city and colony in ritual practice.)

______. 1994. *Myth and Territory in the Spartan Mediterranean.* (Sparta's role in early colonization focusing on but not exclusively considering Taras and Cyrene.)

______. 1998. *The Returns of Odysseus. Colonization and Ethnicity.* (Provocative volume on the background to Greek colonization and cultural and ritual borrowings between Italy and Greece.)

Osborne, R. 1996. *Greece in the Making, 1200–479 B.C.* (Recent handbook on Archaic Greek history, with many sections on the colonial experience.)

Pugliese-Caratelli, G. (ed.) 1996. *The Greek World. Art and Civilization in Magna Graecia and Sicily.* (Massive exhibition catalog with essays on all aspects of Greek colonization from the earliest precolonial contacts to the Roman period. Richly illustrated and with useful bibliography.)

Redfield, J. 2003. *The Locrian Maidens. Love and Death in Greek Italy.* (Not only a major study of Locri Epizephyri, but also a long meditation on the western Greeks and their distinctiveness.)

Ridgway, D. 1992. *The First Western Greeks.* (Best summary of precolonial period and of Pithekoussai.)

Smith, C. and J. Serrati, eds. 2000. *Sicily from Aeneas to Augustus.* (Papers on a variety of topics from the pre-Greek populations to the Roman period.)

Tsetskhladze, G., ed. 1998. *The Greek Colonisation of the Black Sea Area. Historical Interpretation of Archaeology. Historia* Einzelschriften 121. (Wide range of papers on the colonies of this region by various specialists.)

______, ed. 1999. *Ancient Greeks East and West. Mnesmosyne* Suppl. 196. (Major and varied collection of contributions encompassing both the western Mediterranean and the eastern world.)

______, ed. 2006. *Greek Colonisation. An Account of Greek Colonies and Other Settlements Overseas- vol. 1 Greek Colonisation.*

______, and F. De Angelis, ed. 1999. *The Archaeology of Greek Colonisation.* (Important Papers on Early Greek Colonization Especially in the West and Black Sea Regions.)

______, and A. M. Snodgrass, eds. 2002. *Greek Settlements in the Eastern Mediterranean and the Black Sea. BAR* International Series 1062. (Papers ranging from first millennium contacts of Greeks and easterners to Greek identity in the Hellenistic period.)

9: Delphi, Olympia, and the Art of Politics

Richard T. Neer

For Froma Zeitlin

From the eighth century onwards, the history of inter-state sanctuaries, including the two most prestigious, Olympia and Delphi, was the history of the establishment of a state framework for pilgrimage.
– Catherine Morgan, *Athletes and Oracles*, 234.

Panhellenic Sanctuaries and Archaic Ideology

The "Panhellenic" sanctuaries of Delphi, Olympia, and Delos are astonishingly complex, and their importance for the history of early Greece can hardly be overstated. To consider even the most exiguous remains from one of these sites is, immediately, to find oneself enmeshed in an intricate web of economic, social, artistic, literary, and religious histories. The present discussion, accordingly, does not attempt to be in any way systematic, nor does it offer detailed histories of the sites themselves. Instead, it will knit together a few of these remains, tracing their interconnections and their underlying patterns. The daunting complexity of these sites has one benefit: their inscriptions, statues, and buildings are mightily overdetermined, threaded through with cross-cutting political and ideological strands. They are, for that very reason, at once difficult and fascinating. Individual monuments both demand and reward close attention; hence this chapter will move from the relatively general and schematic to the relatively specific and concrete, from secondary literature to the close reading of poems and sculptures.

But first, a bit of definition. For present purposes, the term "Panhellenic" implies a major shrine in Greek territory that is not under the control of a single, strong *polis* or *ethnos*. Zeus' sanctuary at Olympia was governed by Elis, but Elis was weak and, in the early period, had to vie for control of the site with the equally insignificant Pisa. Delphi was in theory an independent *polis*, but the sanctuary of Apollo was controlled by a council of interested cities, known as the Amphictyony; some members, such as Athens, were quite far removed from the shrine itself. Isthmia and Nemea, by contrast, were effectively large state sanctuaries: even though they took their place alongside Delphi and Olympia on the circuit of great quadrennial games, they were under the control of Corinth and Argos, respectively. Indeed, they were smaller and less cosmopolitan than major Ionian centers such as the Heraion on Samos or the Artemision at Ephesus. Delos presents a more complex case. It was dominated variously by Naxos and Athens in the sixth century; in the fifth it was firmly controlled by the latter, and utterly politicized; in the Hellenistic period it was famously independent. It may be, therefore, that a site could be functionally "Panhellenic" at one point in its history and not at others. As a simple rule of thumb, I take the threshold criterion for Panhellenic status to be whether the shrine permitted outside cities to build on its premises. It would, for instance, have been unthinkable for the Athenians to allow another city to raise a building on the Acropolis or at Eleusis, even though both sites attracted pilgrims from all over the Greek world. At Delphi, Olympia, and Delos, by contrast, there are many instances of other states building large, elaborate structures – most notably treasure-houses, or *thesauroi*, for holding costly dedications. At Delphi, even the Etruscans of Agylla (Caere) were welcome to build one. A truly Panhellenic shrine was, in Pindar's phrase, a *pandokos naos*, an "all-welcoming temple" (Pindar *Pythian* 8.61–2): it was open, in theory at least, to everyone. In this respect, the Panhellenic shrine is the literal antithesis of a *polis*. It is Greek, not barbarian; civilized, not wild; but it stands in the place *where the polis is not*. Limiting as it may be, this definition reveals just how distinctive Delphi, Olympia, and (to a lesser extent) Delos actually were.

Catherine Morgan has argued, in a series of brilliant studies, that such shrines arose for essentially two reasons: they provided venues for conspicuous consumption by aristocrats, via athletics and votive offerings; and they helped to resolve internal conflicts in emergent states by means of their oracles. In the case of Olympia (see Figure 22 for the site plan), votive deposits of ca. 800 BCE suggest that the shrine began as a neutral site for petty chiefs of Arcadia and Messenia to meet, to vie with one another in games and in the dedication of offerings, and to consult the oracle of Zeus. The formalization of athletic contests, traditionally dated to 776 BCE but more likely occurring over the course of the century, spurred development; the conquest of Messenia by Sparta actually led to more diverse patronage from around the Peloponnese. As competition increased and visitors came from farther afield, offerings became more elaborate. Bronze tripods, for instance, developed into an important class of prestige good. By the seventh and sixth centuries, some form of participation at Olympia was a *sine qua non* of elite status: in this way, the shrine was integral to the self-definition of a Peloponnesian aristocracy as such. With the development of more centralized political communities during the same period, however, a potential conflict opened up between elite self-aggrandizement at the distant shrine and the interests of the *polis* community. As will become clear, this conflict was a driving force behind much of the activity at the site in the remainder of the Archaic period.

Delphi had a similar history of gradual expansion in the eighth century, with the signal difference that its oracle was always more important than its games (see Figure 21 for the site plan). Although musical contests seem to have been a fixture from early times, there were no athletic contests at Delphi until 583 BCE. The oracle was the shrine's real attraction. As Robert Parker has argued, its essential function was not to predict the future but to provide divine sanction for potentially divisive political decisions. States would appeal to the oracle in moments of internal crisis, typically asking yes-or-no questions on matters of policy. The god's response would legitimize one or another course of action, thereby paving the way for consensus. Classic examples of such "binding arbitration" include the ratification of constitutions at Sparta and Athens and the use of the oracle to legitimate risky and divisive colonial expeditions. The neutrality of the oracle was crucial to this mediatory task, and required protection: when the nearby town of Crisa attempted to seize control of the sanctuary in the early years of the sixth century, a coalition of nearby states formed to reassert its independence. This First Sacred War reveals the depth of state involvement at Delphi. The shrine did not lack for private visitors and was as much a center of elite display as Olympia; the oracle, likewise, addressed individual queries. Still, Delphi always had a stronger connection with civic governments. The results are visible in the topography itself. Olympia, for all its wealth, had far less monumental architecture than Delphi; Zeus probably did not even have a temple before the fifth century. Delphi, by contrast, was dotted with small buildings from the middle of the sixth century at least.

The oracle may have been a useful and effective way to paper over disagreement – even violent disagreement – in particular cases. But it cannot often have addressed the root material causes of such disagreements, which will have had more to do with the exercise of power and the allocation of resources than with divine mandates. The issue becomes, if anything, more acute with time, as internal divisions within the Greek aristocracies become more visible. Morgan argues persuasively that, in the eighth century, costly dedications at Olympia "served a domestic political purpose by reinforcing the position of the elite within the emerging state."[1] One might add, simply, that claims to prestige tend to call forth counterclaims; there is no reason to assume that "the elite" in question was monolithic. At the Kerameikos cemetery in Athens, for instance, there is good evidence for intra-elite competition from the ninth century at least: competing ways of disposing of the body (inhumation versus cremation), of making offerings (in the grave or in separate trenches), even of pottery style (Middle versus Late Geometric, or Late Geometric versus Protoattic). Because the graves in question are all relatively well furnished, the implication is that these disparate modes of funerary display track social rivalries *within* an emerging Athenian elite. There is every reason to suppose that similar rivalries played out in other communities. As much as interstate sanctuaries reinforced the position of elites within the state, as much as they provided useful meeting points for upper-class interaction, they will also have provided venues for political infighting and for competition within local aristocracies. The consensus in question is merely conflict deferred, or repressed.

Ian Morris and Leslie Kurke have emphasized the importance of such internal divisions within the Greek cities. Synthesizing archaeological and literary evidence, they have described a broad division in *polis* society between two constellations of images, texts, values, and claims to power. The resulting model is, of its nature, schematic, and both authors spend much of their time tracing the nuances and complexities of individual cases. But the basic distinction is between those aristocrats who identified themselves first and foremost as members of a local, civic community, and those who identified themselves as part of a larger aristocracy above and beyond petty local concerns. Morris terms the first group *middling*, the second *elitist*. "The elitists," he writes, "legitimated their special role from sources outside the *polis*; the middling poets rejected such claims. The former blurred distinctions between male and female, present and past, mortal and divine, Greek and Lydian, to reinforce a distinction between aristocrat and commoner;

the latter did the opposite."[2] This division resulted naturally from the ongoing process of state formation: that is, from the gradual movement of power from persons to institutions, from clans to communities. Crucially, however, the operative distinctions are ideological and cultural, not reductively economic. Both "elite" and "middling" name *upper-class* systems of value (cf. Chapter 6 on expressions of these ideologies in Archaic lyric poetry).

In this account, interstate shrines were crucial to elitist ideology. Part of the appeal of these sanctuaries was, precisely, the fact that they were not under the control of any single city. Situated "in the interstices of the *polis* world,"[3] they provided elites with a venue for competitive display through athletics and large-scale dedications. Investing in ostentatious, self-aggrandizing behavior at an interstate shrine could be a way of asserting solidarity with one's fellow aristocrats in other *poleis*: to claim that wealth, or birth, or a special relationship with the gods was of greater significance than membership in a particular citizen community. In some cases, as Anthony Snodgrass has suggested, local pressures may have prevented elites from displaying their wealth too conspicuously at home, leading them to invest more heavily elsewhere. Forms of behavior that were unseemly in the eyes of one's fellow citizens could be admirable at Delphi or Olympia. In other cases, however, the reverse may have been true: the weakness of local forces may have allowed elites greater freedom for expenditures away from home. But whatever the specific, precipitating cause, costly displays at interstate shrines all shared one feature: they were all investments in a sphere of exchange outside the home *polis*, and potentially opposed to it.

An especially clear instance of these competing tendencies is visible in the layout of the Ptoön sanctuary in Boeotia. Although controlled directly by Thebes from ca. 480, the Ptoön flourished in the second half of the sixth century, during a time when Delphi seems to have been partially closed for repairs following a disastrous fire in 548. Not normally considered "Panhellenic," the Ptoön was, briefly, Delphi's understudy. The sanctuary complex consisted in fact of two distinct shrines: one, an oracle of the hero Ptoös; the other, a temple to Apollo. These two shrines served different constituencies. The oracle was patronized more often by cities, and the dedications to Ptoös were most often state-sponsored and collective, with a special emphasis on bronze tripods. The sanctuary of Apollo, by contrast, contained almost exclusively private offerings, including a spectacular quantity of nude marble youths or *kouroi*, the veritable icons of the interstate aristocracy.[4] The distinction was not absolute – *kouroi* were offered to Ptoös, and tripods to Apollo – but the overall pattern is clear. The oracle of Ptoös corresponds well with Morgan's account: it seems to have functioned primarily as a place for communities to legitimize potentially divisive decisions. The sanctuary of Apollo, on the other hand, fits equally well with the view of Kurke and Morris. A sort of anti-*polis*, it provided a venue for upper-class display; significantly, the series of *kouroi* died out around the time it lost its independence decisively to Thebes. Although it would be premature to call Ptoös "middling" and Apollo "elite," still the dramatic bifurcation of this site does suggest that ideology could map easily enough onto cultic topography.

The handling of athletic victors reveals the political and ideological complexities of such sanctuaries. The earliest and most prestigious games were those at Olympia. But in the first half of the sixth century, Delphi, Nemea, and Isthmia instituted or expanded their own quadrennial games. The result was a cycle or circuit of contests: in any given year there was a major event at one of these four sites. These games had no reward but prestige: victors received a crown of twigs. Especially at Olympia, victors were allowed, but not required, to erect statues of themselves in the shrine. What the Panhellenic victor left behind was not his prize, but a replica of himself. These statues are securely attested at Olympia from 544 BCE, but the practice may go back much earlier at the site. The image could be life-sized or smaller; the earliest were of wood, but bronze soon became the favored material. Although few traces survive, in the Archaic period most victor-statues will inevitably have been variants of the *kouros*-type, the all-purpose icon of the aristocracy (cf. Pausanias 8.40.1; cf. Figure 35, a funerary *kouros* from ca. 530 BCE). It follows that Olympia, and to a lesser extent Delphi, must have been crowded with dozens or even hundreds of more or less identical male figures. At Olympia, the statues clustered on the south side of the sanctuary, or Altis, an arrangement that, as Federico Rausa has noted, will have emphasized their homogeneity. So far from appropriating the victor's prize, the Panhellenic sanctuary invited him to participate, via his image, in this assembly of the generically best and brightest: to become one of the *homoioi*, the "peers" or "interchangeables," dwelling permanently in the shrine. Uniting past victors and present ones, Greeks from the mainland and those from distant colonies, the army of *kouroi* is a veritable instantiation of the imagined community of the Hellenic elite.

For the home community, the prestige of victory could translate into real, and potentially destabilizing, power. More than a few leaders of Greek colonial expeditions were former athletic victors in the great games, as were more than a few would-be tyrants – a fact that reveals not just the prestige of victory, but also the difficulty of accommodating the winners in the existing political framework. Better, perhaps, to send them overseas than to keep them at home. Kylon of Athens is the classic example of a subversive victor: having won the double-length footrace at Olympia in 640 BCE, he used the occasion of a subsequent festival to launch a *coup d'état*. The timing, as Thucydides observes (1.26), was "appropriate to an Olympic victor." Kylon failed, but his attempt to use Olympic prestige to personal advantage was naked. For just this reason, as Kurke has argued, the custom arose in some *poleis* that the victor would dedicate his crown on the altar of his city's tutelary deity. Through this ritual of "crowning the city," the glory of victory became communal. In exchange, the city would shower the victor with *civic* honors. In some instances the city even erected a second victor-statue at home, a local counterpart to the one in the Panhellenic shrine. To honor the victor is, in this sense, to reassimilate him into the city (cf. Kurke in Chapter 6 for the role of epinician poetry in this process). Rather less subtly, but to similar effect, in the mid-sixth century the Athenian tyrant Peisistratos pressured his rival Kimon to "hand over the victory" when his horses won the chariot race at Olympia for the second time in a row (Herodotus 6.103). The heralds announced the victory in the tyrant's name. When, in the next Olympiad, Kimon's horses won yet again, he was deemed too dangerous to live, and was killed.

One may usefully contrast the situation at ethnic or regional centers, such as the oracle of Triopian Apollo outside Cnidus. The site seems to have started out as a state sanctuary: standing on a peninsula between Cnidus and the mainland, it helped to define the city's territory. Its oracle may well have acquired stature in mediating local disputes, and eventually it became a meeting place for the local Dorian cities. By the sixth century, if not earlier, the Triopeion evolved into an ethnic center, governed not by Cnidus alone but by a federation of six Dorian towns, known as the Hexapolis or "Six Cities." Offerings came in from Etruria, Cyprus, and Phoenicia. Yet the Triopeion never attained the prestige of its Pythian counterpart. One likely reason is that it was closely associated with the institutional activities of the Dorian federation. Although notionally an interstate shrine, the Triopeion was effectively civic in nature. Its civic overseers maintained strict control over the dedicatory practices of its patrons in the local aristocracy. Herodotus (1.144) tells how his own city, Halicarnassus, was expelled from the governing board in the second quarter of the sixth century. The story usefully illustrates the stakes of aristocratic dedication.

> The Dorians of what is now the country of the "Five Cities" – formerly the country of the "Six Cities" – forbid admitting any of the neighboring Dorians to the Triopian temple, and even barred from using it those of their own group who had broken the temple law. For long ago, in the games in honor of Triopian Apollo, they offered certain bronze tripods to the victors; and those who won these were not to carry them away from the temple but dedicate them there to the god. Now when a man of Halicarnassus called Agasicles won, he disregarded this law, and, carrying the tripod away, nailed it to the wall of his own house. For this offense the five cities – Lindus, Ialysus, Camerius, Cos, and Cnidus – forbade the sixth city – Halicarnassus – to share in the use of the temple.

The Triopian shrine provided a venue for local aristocrats to appear before a broader, interstate community, even as its bylaws made it effectively impossible for them to turn their victories to personal ends. Victors were forced to leave their tripods in the communal, collective sanctuary; their glory remained civic (or federal), not exclusively personal. This short-circuiting of elitist display may explain why Agasicles took the extraordinary measure of nailing his tripod to the wall of his own house. If his goal was to keep the glory of victory for himself, then neither leaving it at the Triopeion, nor dedicating it at a public shrine in Halicarnassus, would do the job. The regulations of the sanctuary left him no choice but to take the tripod home. They boxed him in, which, presumably, was just their intent.

The laws of Triopian Apollo represent a triumph of middling regulation over elitist self-assertion. Delphi and Olympia, by contrast, had no such rules. Access was open to all, and some of the offerings were extraordinarily lavish. For elites, in other words, there was a real difference between a dedication at a home or regional sanctuary and one at a Panhellenic shrine. Precisely because they were relatively remote, standing outside the control of any strong, local state, Delphi and Olympia could function as venues for elitist aristocrats to assert their independence from their home communities. And the cities responded, setting up offerings and built monuments, even, in the case of Argos, submitting publicly owned horses to compete at Olympia (winning twice in the early fifth century). The drama of sites such as Delphi and Olympia comes from the fact that they were scenes of ideological contest as well as athletic: places where cities, tyrants, and aristocrats of all political persuasions made their offerings and jockeyed for position.

The Politics of Dedication

One place to see the politics of dedication "in action" is in the rhetoric of dedicatory inscriptions. These short, formulaic texts are exercises in self-presentation, and it is revealing to see how Greek aristocrats chose to announce themselves to the wider world. Sometime around 550 BCE, for instance, a noble Athenian named Alkmaionides gave a *kouros* to Ptoian Apollo. The statue is lost, but its inscribed base survives:

> I am a beautiful delight for Phoebus, son of Leto.
> Alkmaion's son, Alkmaionides,
> Dedicated me after the victory of his swift horses,
> Which Knopiadas the [...] drove
> When in Athens there was a festive gathering for Pallas.

Given the elitist connotations of chariot racing, it is significant that Alkmaionides should identify himself by his patronymic, not his ethnic: by his noble birth, not his citizenship. His father Alkmaion was famous as an Olympic victor in the chariot race, and his clan was among the most prestigious in Greece. For such a one, it was apparently not enough to be famous at Athens, and Athenian citizenship was not worth proclaiming. The *polis* does not figure into the equation at all, even when the victory in question occurs at Athens itself. This emphasis is all the more striking given that the "festive gathering for Pallas" is presumably the great Panathenaic festival, a spectacular display of Athenian civic identity. Reorganized in the 560s, just after the final consolidation of the four-year circuit of "crown" games, the Panathenaia was in one sense a "middling" counterpart to those contests. Alkmaionides saw fit to compete in the Panathenaia and to receive acclaim from the Athenian *polis*. But he also felt it necessary to disseminate his deeds and parentage within an *interstate* community. In this venue, Athens became a mere pretext for aristocratic display.

At the opposite extreme stands a victor statue that Pausanias saw at Olympia (2.2.9): "The inscription on the Samian boxer says that his trainer Mykon dedicated the statue and that the Samians are the best among the Ionians for athletes and at naval warfare – but it tells us nothing at all about the boxer himself!" In this case, the *polis* gets all the attention, eclipsing even the victor's own name. The anonymous Samian participated in the Olympic games, thereby making a bid for status; but he appears as the very antithesis of an ostentatious elitist. It may even be significant that boxing requires less of a financial outlay than chariot racing, and that naval warfare – in so far as it placed military power in the hands of the common citizens who manned the oars – was often a specialty of tyrannical and democratic regimes. Be that as it may, the boxer is in every way subordinate to his civic community. Where Alkmaionides failed to mention his homeland, the Samian fails to mention himself. The result is an extreme instance of the "middling" position. These two dedications may stand as limit cases: two radically different modes of aristocratic self-presentation.

Three Athenian offerings from the Persian Wars further clarify the distinction. Soon after leading the Athenians to victory at Marathon in 490, the general Miltiades sent a helmet to Olympia (Figure 23). The inscription is simple: "To Zeus, from Miltiades." One might contrast the inscription on a helmet that the Athenian state sent to the same shrine during the same period. Here, as on most public offerings, there is no mention of individual commanders: "The Athenians [dedicated this] to Zeus, having taken it from the Medes." Miltiades does the opposite: he omits all mention of the Athenian soldiers and personalizes the victory. Like Alkmaionides, he does not even mention that he is from Athens. Unlike Alkmaionides, however, Miltiades also omits his patronymic: given that he claimed descent from Zeus via the hero Aiakos, he may have deemed such details superfluous. But in fact the omission is unremarkable – many dedications are equally laconic – and it may be better to see such texts as addressing a restricted audience. Quite deliberately, the text speaks only to the knowledgeable: "If you've got to ask," as Louis Armstrong put it, "you ain't never going to know." In this way, the Athenian general uses the occasion of a communal military victory to assert a special relationship with the mightiest of the gods; he simply freezes his home *polis* out of the transaction. In the event such self-aggrandizement was unsustainable in democratic Athens. Miltiades' high-handed conduct after Marathon (specifically, his advocacy of a punitive expedition to the enemy island of Paros) resulted in a trial in 489; after being fined fifty talents for "misleading the people," he died of gangrene from a wound incurred on campaign.

Miltiades was the hero of Marathon, but the actual commander-in-chief was Kallimakhos, who fell in the battle. A posthumous offering in his name on the Athenian Acropolis makes a telling contrast with the two helmets at Olympia (Figure 24). The choice of venue is revealing in itself: Kallimakhos' votive addresses an Athenian, local audience, not a "Panhellenic" one. The iconography makes this point nicely. Atop a tall column, Nike ("Victory") or Iris appears in a whirligig running pose, carrying the staff of a herald. The conceit is that the goddess is just arriving on the Acropolis, bearing a message – news, no doubt, of the Athenians' victory. If Alkmaionides' *kouros* proclaims victory at Athens to the wider Greek world, Kallimakhos' goddess literally brings victory at Marathon home to Athens. The dedicatory inscription works to similar effect (*GHI*[3] 33–4 no. 18):

> Kallimakhos of Aphidna dedicated me to Athena – I am the messenger of the immortals who have their home on Olympus – because he was victorious, when he was commander-in-chief, in the festival of the Athenians. And fighting most bravely of them all he won fairest renown for the men of Athens and a memorial for his own valor.

Here all is civic: the text identifies Kallimakhos by his township, not his ancestry, and it specifies that he earned glory "for the men of Athens," not himself. Where Miltiades uses his role in the battle to assert his own special prerogatives in the wider world outside Athens, the family of Kallimakhos defines his glory in terms of the local *polis* community. The difference between the two encapsulates neatly the elite/middling opposition. Kallimakhos and Miltiades are both wealthy and well-born, but they take very different stances relative to their home community. The only truly anonymous and collective offering in this set is the helmet that the state itself sent to Olympia.

In the case of the Marathon dedications, Olympia stands as the virtual antithesis of the Athenian Acropolis. It does not follow, of course, that any dedication at an interstate shrine was intrinsically elitist, nor that any dedication at home was intrinsically middling. Both Alkmaionides and Miltiades also made dedications at Athens at one time or another, and the Athenian state sent offerings to Delphi and Olympia. Such complexities only underscore the need to take offerings as much as possible on a case-by-case basis. Delphi and Olympia should not serve as ideological pigeonholes. So far from determining in advance the political tenor of dedications, the interstate shrines were more often sites of complex negotiation between elite and middling. Offerings, accordingly, require close reading. Statistical studies of fluctuations in the number and quality of offerings are invaluable, but we should not lose sight of the trees for the forest.

Such complexity is especially evident in dedications by tyrants. The typical tyrant was a populist aristocrat, holding sole power by leading the commons against the rest of the upper class. It was in the interest of such men to present themselves as open-handed elitists, spending more lavishly than any of their elite rivals, even as they maintained the fiction that their expenditure was made on behalf of, or in tandem with, the broader *polis* community. As a result, tyrants tended to finesse the elite/middling distinction. A dedication by Miltiades the Elder, uncle of the hero of Marathon and himself an Olympic victor in the chariot-race, is fairly typical in this regard. This elder Miltiades held the tyranny in the Gallipoli peninsula, or Chersonesus, in the later sixth century. Following a military victory, he dedicated an ivory horn, said to be that of the ram Amaltheia, at Olympia. Pausanias (6.19.6) gives the inscription:

> To Olympian Zeus was I dedicated by the men of Chersonesus
> After they had taken the fortress of Aratus.
> Their leader was Miltiades.

The Syracusan tyrant Hieron made a similar offering in 474, after his ships defeated the Etruscans off Cumae. Two helmets from Olympia read: "Hieron, son of Deinomenes, and the Syracusans [dedicated this] to Zeus, [taken from the] Tyrrhenians from Cumae." Such texts strike a balance between the pure self-aggrandizement of the younger Miltiades and the anonymity of the collective state offering. It is noteworthy, for one thing, that they mention the "leaders" at all: contrast the Athenian helmet at Olympia, which follows standard practice in attributing victory to the citizenry as an anonymous collective. Yet if the mere mention of the tyrant's name is revealing, still both Hieron and Miltiades appear in a broader political framework. In the case of the ivory horn, "the men of Chersonesus" make the dedication, and capture the fortress of Aratus, whereas Miltiades himself comes last in the inscription even as he comes first in the army. Significantly, perhaps, Miltiades requires neither introduction nor identification, and the very grammar of the inscription assures his preeminence: his name is the only nominative singular noun in the entire text. Hieron, on the other hand, comes first in the inscription, identified by his patronymic, and appears as co-dedicant with the Syracusans as a whole: in this case, and rather more assertively, the tyrant is "first man" of the *polis*. Both dedications, however, imply that the tyrant's position does not come at the cost of the broader community. It is not a zero-sum game.

For Hieron, such tact was in fact the exception rather than the rule. He and his brothers, known collectively as the Deinomenids, ruled much of eastern Sicily for a generation or more in the early fifth century. So far from suggesting reciprocity between tyrant and *polis*, they more often presented themselves as superelitists: more aristocratic, more ostentatious, and more disdainful of communitarian pressures than anyone else. As if to literalize the elitist's claim to transcend the local community, the Deinomenids actually changed cities on more than one occasion, calling themselves Geloans, Syracusans, or Aetnans as the political situation required. They encouraged similar behavior in their henchmen. Hieron, notoriously, suborned the athlete Astylos of Croton into shifting allegiance and becoming Syracusan; the Crotonates responded by tearing down his victor statue at Croton and turning his house into a prison (Pausanias 6.13.1). Just so, a man named Phormis, who served both Gelon and Hieron, made lavish offerings at Delphi and Olympia, describing himself as "an Arcadian of Maenalus, now Syracusan" (Pausanias 5.27.2). Both Astylos and Phormis set up monuments at Olympia, parading their changes of allegiance for all to see. In these instances, the imagined community of Panhellenic aristocrats actually became a reality, as ties of friendship between the Deinomenids and the elites of other cities resulted in literal renunciations of citizen identity.

The Deinomenids' own offerings were fully consistent with this practice. They erected several multifigure bronze chariot groups at Delphi and Olympia (see Figure 20). The so-called Delphi Charioteer comes from one such ensemble and gives a clue as to their appearance (see Figure 25). Dedicated in 466 by the last of the dynasty, Polyzalos of Gela, the monument commemorated earlier victories by his late brother Hieron: two in the horse race and one in the chariot race. Reconstructions suggest a chariot with four horses and charioteer, flanked by an additional two horses, each with a boy jockey. This is ostentation on an unparalleled scale; Alkmaionides' *kouros* in the Ptoön pales in comparison. The accompanying inscription was in this instance recut after the fall of the tyranny in 466. Although the text is only partially preserved and remains controversial, the original version went something like this:

> [A memorial for a brother:] lording over [*anasson*] Gela, [Polyzalos] dedicated it. Make this man prosper, O honored Apollo.

Later, the Geloans changed it to read:

> Polyzalos dedicated me. Make this man prosper, O honored Apollo.

It is revealing to note what the Geloans chose to erase. The first version mentions Gela, but only as the object of the verb *anasson*, "lording." Polyzalos presents himself to his peers as a *wanax*, or "Lord," a Bronze Age word redolent of epic. Such vaunting rhetoric is fully consistent with the way that Pindar had praised Hieron as a *basileus*, "King," and a *tyrannos*, "tyrant" (Pindar *Olympian* 1.23, *Pythian* 3.70, *Pythian* 3.85; cf. Bacchylides 3.11–12). The second version retains Polyzalos' name, and (somewhat ironically under the circumstances) the prayer for his prosperity. But it removes the offending phrase *Gelas anasson*, "lording over Gela." This second version effectively transforms the dedication from an arrogant assertion of power into a splendid, but relatively innocuous, piece of upper-class glory-mongering.

As with athletic victories, so with victories under arms: the Deinomenids personalized military success to an unparalleled degree. When, for instance, a coalition of Sicilian Greeks defeated the Carthaginians at Himera in 480, Gelon of Syracuse dedicated a column at Delphi surmounted by a golden Nike and tripod (see Figure 20). The text on the base, beautifully carved in Syracusan characters, reads:

> Gelon, son of Deinomenes, of Syracuse, dedicated [this] to Apollo. The tripod and the Nike were made by Bion son of Diodoros of Miletus.

Gelon does identify his home city, but only to overshadow it: he may be from Syracuse, but the Syracusans did not make this dedication. When, in 474, Hieron defeated the Etruscans off Cumae, he set up a matching column: the inscription, though fragmentary, suggests that he too made the offering in his own name. The inscription was, it seems, at first even longer and more vainglorious than it appears today: two additional lines were deliberately effaced after the fall of the Deinomenids in 466. In each of these texts, the Deinomenids described military victories with formulae more appropriate to athletic ones: not only did their allies disappear, but so did the actual citizen-soldiers who did the fighting. The result is an elitist rhetoric of massive hyperbole. Not surprising, therefore, that Bacchylides (3.17–22) cites these very tripods as examples of the extraordinary ostentation of the Deinomenids: Hieron, he says, "knows how not to hide his towering wealth in black-cloaked darkness.... [G]old shines with flashing light from the high elaborate tripods standing in front of the temple where the Delphians tend the great sanctuary of Phoebus by the waters of Castalia."

Such stratagems were not always successful, and the failures can be instructive. Following their great victory over the Persians at the battle of Plataea in 479, the Greek allies made offerings at Delphi and Olympia. The monument at Delphi consisted of three bronze serpents, twisted together to form a single pillar some twenty-five feet high; at the top, a gold tripod rested one foot on each of the serpents' heads (see Figure 26). The column is still visible today in the Hippodrome at Istanbul, whither it was removed under the emperor Constantine; the tripod, however, is lost, as are two of the serpents' heads. The third was knocked off during a wild party in 1700 CE by a member of the Polish embassy; it is now in the Istanbul Museum. When the monument first went up, the Greek commander-in-chief, Pausanias of Sparta, tried a familiar ploy. He inscribed the column with his own name and neglected to mention any of the allied *poleis* (Thucydides 1.132):

> Pausanias, supreme commander of the Greeks, when he had destroyed the host of the Medes, dedicated to Phoebus this memorial.

When the allies protested, the inscription was changed: visible on the column in Istanbul is a simple list of all the states that participated in the battle. On the tripod itself was inscribed, "This is the gift the saviors of far-flung Hellas upraised here, having delivered their *poleis* from loathsome slavery's bonds" (Diodorus 11.33.2). From *polis* as a category on the tripod to the list of cities on the column, the contrast with Pausanias' epigram was pointed; as extreme, in its own way, as the difference between Alkmaionides and the Samian boxer. Not long after Pausanias himself was accused of colluding with the Persians and endeavoring to set himself up as a tyrant. He was starved to death in the temple of Athena-of-the-Brazen-House at Sparta.

Architectural Self-Presentation

Short and formulaic, dedicatory inscriptions present a vivid but schematic picture of ideological positioning. It is only in larger, more elaborate structures that a more nuanced picture emerges. Indeed, one way to think of monumental sculpture and architecture at these sites is as the visual counterpart to the inscriptions: more or less combative or conciliatory modes of self-presentation, subject to subsequent contestation and revision. In these cases, however, the dedicants in question tend to be civic, not private. Architecture was, for the most part, beyond the means of even the wealthiest elites. What is preserved, in the form of foundation courses and fragments of sculpture, is the civic response to private dedications.

An especially interesting class of buildings, in this respect, is the treasure-house, or *thesauros*: small, temple-like buildings, built by individual states to hold the offerings of their wealthy citizens. There were nearly thirty such buildings at Delphi, from every corner of the Greek world. At Olympia, eleven (possibly twelve) stood in a row overlooking the Archaic stadium. Most of the latter examples were built by Western colonies, leading to the skewed impression that colonies favored Olympia over Delphi. In fact, however, there were nearly as many Western treasuries at Delphi. Their remains are exiguous – terracotta roofing elements – but the colonial bias in favor of Olympia is a mirage (if anything, mainland cities *avoided* Olympia).[5] At Delos the situation is more complex. Hellenistic inscriptions mention a number of *oikoi*, "houses," used for storage purposes and dedicated by the peoples of Andros, Delos, Carystus, Ceos, and Naxos. Six buildings west of the Temple of Apollo have been associated with these *oikoi*. The three earliest examples are rather grander than treasuries elsewhere. It is uncertain whether they were all originally used for storage; the oldest, the seventh-century *oikos* of the Naxians, may well have been an early temple of Apollo. The three later buildings, dating from 475–50, do resemble the treasuries at Delphi and Olympia. The cities with which they were later associated were all members of the Delian League; if those cities did in fact build them, then one might easily imagine that, in the early years of the alliance, some member states could have set up stronghouses to hold their contributions. But the matter is desperately uncertain, and the Delian *oikoi* have been neglected in the archaeological literature.

Delos aside, the basic function of a treasury is to hold costly dedications. But mere storage, mere practicality, cannot explain the existence of such buildings. Many large, powerful cities, whose wealthy citizens made lavish offerings, never saw fit to build treasure-houses: there has got to be more to the matter.[6] The politics of dedication suggests another explanation. We can compare two roughly comparable sets of prestige offerings from Olympia and the Heraion on Samos. The travel-writer

Polemon saw a silver siren, a wooden triton holding a silver cup, a silver kylix, a golden oinochoe, and three gilt offering-plates in the Byzantine and Metapontine *thesauroi* at Olympia (in Athenaeus 11.479f–480a). The list finds an echo in a late sixth-century inscription recording the offerings of two Perinthians to Samian Hera: a silver siren, a gold gorgon, a silver phiale, and a bronze lampstand. Although there is little difference between the two sets of offerings, there is a marked difference in their presentation. When placed on view in a treasury, such offerings were *recontextualized*: they still reflected well on their dedicants, to be sure, but they also glorified the *polis*. The Perinthians, by contrast, glorified no one but themselves (and, of course, Hera). It is significant in this regard that many treasuries were built in part or in whole from stone imported at great expense, and to no "practical" purpose, from the home territory. In the most literal way possible, the treasury brought a little bit of the *polis* into the heart of a Panhellenic shrine, so that when it was placed in a treasury, a dedication, in a way, never really left home at all. I would suggest that the purpose of such a building was not just to store votives but to nationalize them, and with them a dedicant's privileged relationship to the gods. These buildings transform upper-class extravagance into civic pride. A *thesauros* is not just a storeroom: it is a frame for costly dedications, a way of diverting elite display in the interest of the city-state.

The Cnidian Treasury at Delphi presents these issues in condensed form. If its role at the shrine of Triopian Apollo is any indication, Cnidus set considerable store by the regulation of aristocratic display. It invested heavily in Delphi, raising two separate buildings in the sanctuary. The first, a treasury, went up shortly before the city's capture by the Persians in 544; the second, a meeting house for citizens, went up after its liberation early in the 460s. The Archaic building bore a boustrophedon inscription on the architrave, "The [Cnid]ian [people dedicated to Apollo] Pythios, as a tithe, the treasury and the votive statues [*agalmata*]." The treasury was built of Island marble; it was perhaps the first in mainland Greece to employ the Ionic order, and the first to employ caryatides in an architectural setting: the two columns in the entryway take the form of well-dressed, bejeweled women, each extending one hand to make an offering. The meaning of such figures is controversial. Although many scholars have argued that all caryatides possess chthonic, eschatological, or political significance, there is no visual evidence to support such claims – no feature of the statues themselves that could count for or against a hidden, symbolic meaning. Whether we believe in the symbolism or not, the statues represent the same thing: women making offerings. It would be more prudent, therefore, simply to take them at face value: caryatides look exactly like wealthy female dedicants, so that is probably what they are. That said, their structural function does register visually and is therefore at least potentially significant. In a sort of visual metaphor, the caryatid type equates a dedicant with a column. Circumstantially it is good to know that this very trope turns up in fifth-century literature: for Aeschylus, Agamemnon is "the firm-based pillar of a lofty roof" (*Agamemnon* 898); for Euripides, "male children are the pillars of a house" (*Iphigenia in Tauris* 57); and so on. Caryatides, so far from conveying religious allegories, probably represent one version of this familiar conceit. It is fully consistent with their overall appearance. They are servants, *therpontes*, of the deity: as votaries, they serve by making offerings; as "pillars of the community," they serve by bearing weight. It is a simple and utterly concrete metaphor.

These figures relate cogently to the treasury's function. As prominent, aristocratic dedicants, the caryatides model the building's ideal user: the wealthy Cnidian who offers up a tithe to the god. Yet these figures do not simply *represent* gift-giving. They are themselves gifts, offerings to Apollo, perhaps even the "votive statues," *agalmata*, mentioned in the dedicatory inscription; and they stand in the entryway of a building that exists to hold gifts. For all their ostentation and prominence, therefore, these figures are part of a larger, state-sponsored system of offering and display. As such the caryatides are at once sumptuous statues and load-bearing columns, ideals of the good Cnidian and functional elements within a civic edifice. The result is a remarkably effective political icon: a way to imagine the integration of upper-class display into the fabric of the *polis*. In this instance, to be a conspicuous dedicant *just is* to support a civic building; to be structurally useful *just is* to be elaborate and ostentatious. There is no need to posit hidden meanings. Simply by being what they are, the caryatides clarify the logic of the treasury itself: the way it frames gifts in order to reconcile elite glory-mongering with civic pride. Sculpture, in other words, provides a set of literal and tangible terms for thinking the political. With hindsight, it is not surprising that architectural caryatides should first appear at Delphi, nor that Cnidus should be the city that set them up. The town that helped to punish Agasicles also invented an elegant iconographic formula for figuring the integration of a city and its wealthy inhabitants; and it did so at the very place in which those wealthy inhabitants were most likely to assert their independence from, and opposition to, the *polis*.

The Sycionian Tyrants at Delphi and Olympia

If the function of a treasury was indeed to "frame the gift," then it is not surprising that many of the earliest examples were built by tyrants. The oldest treasury at Olympia was built by Myron of Sicyon; that at Delphi, by Kypselos of Corinth. Gelon of Syracuse built one treasury at Olympia and modified another, and it is even possible that the Peisitratids raised a predecessor to the Athenian treasury at Delphi. The antagonism of tyrants to elite display is well attested and easily understood: even as some, such as the Deinomenids, presented themselves as superelitists, they jealously guarded their own preeminence. Kypselos, in fact, inscribed his treasury with his own name, subsequently effaced by the Corinthians after the fall of the regime; the Eleans refused a similar request (Plutarch *De Pythiæ oraculis* 13). In these early instances, we might see the treasuries as none too subtle attempts by rulers to keep tight control on the activities of rival aristocrats.

Sicyon provides a useful case study. From the mid-seventh to the mid-sixth century, the city was ruled by tyrants of the Orthagorid family.[7] The founder of the dynasty, Orthagoras, parlayed his hereditary role as sacrificial butcher (*mageiros*) on embassies to Delphi into a tyranny; he may have used it as a springboard to the office of *basileus* or sacral king. The last Orthagorid tyrant, Aiskhines, was not expelled until circa 520. Under Kleisthenes, ruler from ca. 600 to 570, Sicyon flourished as a naval, and perhaps a mercantile power. As noted earlier, such an arrangement placed military power in the hands of a tyrant's natural allies: the poorer citizens who could not afford armor and therefore manned the oars. Sicyon's ships played an important role in the First Sacred War; after the destruction of Crisa, Kleisthenes probably derived substantial income by extracting protection money from shipping in the Gulf of Corinth.

The Orthagorids adopted very different stances toward Delphi and Olympia. In 648, following a chariot victory, Myron built the first treasure house in the Altis. The proximate cause was to commemorate a chariot-victory; but there is some irony to the fact that the tyrant chose to commemorate his own triumph with a building in which to lock away the offerings of others. It contained two "chambers" (*thalamoi*) made of bronze that was said in Pausanias' day to have been brought from Tartessos in far-off Spain. The tradition is very likely to be ancient, and might suggest that the tyrant was flaunting his city's growing maritime power. The inscription on these chambers stipulated that they had been dedicated by Myron and the *demos*, or commons, of Sicyon (Pausanias 6.19). Thus the lower classes and the ruler unite to constrain the dedicatory practices of the wealthy: a virtual diagram of the workings of Archaic tyranny. At Delphi, by contrast, the Orthagorids did not build a treasury. Instead they made a pair of exceptionally lavish offerings: a small, round building, or *tholos*, and a rectangular pavilion. Both were found in the foundation of a later Sicyonian treasury (on which more below) and are identified with the city on that basis. They date to the second quarter of the sixth century and are usually associated with Kleisthenes; his successor Aiskhines is, however, just as likely on chronological grounds. The function of the *tholos* remains a mystery, but the pavilion seems designed for the display of a large offering, presumably to glorify the tyrant. In short, whereas the Orthagorids built a cell for costly dedications at Olympia, at Delphi they made lavish and prominent offerings to Apollo. The discrepancy may be related to the fact that the tyrants had ancestral ties with Delphi via the position of *mageiros*. At the root of their prominence was a personal connection with the Pythian shrine; so Pytho was theirs. It is probably no coincidence that Kleisthenes also built a new temple to Apollo in the agora of Sicyon and established a local version of the Pythian Games. Such local versions of the Panhellenic contest had counterparts elsewhere. As celebrations of Apollo Pythius, they are usually understood as unambiguous honors to the Delphic shrine. That they did honor Delphi is indisputable, but the politics of the local Pythia were doubtless complex. At the very least, local Pythian games and cults blurred the distinction between *polis* and sanctuary; that they existed all suggests that cities must have found the ambiguity congenial. Kleisthenes' gesture is perhaps a subtler version of a ploy attempted in the seventh century by Pheidon, tyrant of Argos, who is said to have tried to seize control of the Olympic games themselves (Strabo 8.3.33).

The interaction between the Orthagorids and the interstate shrine thus emerges as a delicate negotiation, whereby the tyrant simultaneously recognized the importance of the sanctuary, permitted aristocratic display, and appropriated all the glory for himself. The trick, it seems, was to channel elitist display into venues and formats acceptable to the tyrant, either by framing costly gifts with a treasury, or by overwhelming them with impossibly expensive offerings while bringing the Pythian festival to Sicyon. It is a policy of containment, not confrontation, and it accords well with accounts in Herodotus and Aristotle stressing the moderation of Orthagorid rule.

It is possible, however, to be more specific. We can see some traces of this process in the sculptural decoration of the square pavilion, or *monopteros*, at Delphi. Its metopes, running 3 × 4 around the building, were unusually prominent: each panel bridged the entire distance between two columns, so that the intercolumnar triglyph was omitted. Spanning three entire metopes (hence one short side of the building) was a depiction of the ship *Argo*; matching it on the other short side were three panels depicting the Calydonian boar hunt (Figure 27). Other surviving panels depict Phrixos on the ram of the Golden Fleece, Europa on the bull, and the Dioskouroi rustling cattle. These metopes are among the earliest in mainland Greece to bear sculpture; they may even be *the* earliest. Discounting some controversial fragments from Mycenae, demonstrably earlier examples all come from the West, notably from Temple Y at Selinous in Sicily. This fact has led some scholars to wonder if the pavilion is really Sicyonian at all, and not Sicilian; but the reasoning is dangerously circular, and there are some connections between the architecture and that of the Apollo temple at Sicyon itself. It might be better to compare the pavilion's metopes with Myron's Tartessian chambers at Olympia. Just as the earlier tyrant had emphasized Sicyon's maritime power by importing (or claiming to import) bronze from distant Spain, so a later Orthagorid adopted a characteristically Western sculptural device. The tyrants emphasize, whenever possible, the connections between Sicyon and long-distance travel. It is thus fitting that a ship should occupy one entire side of the building.

Within this framework, the surviving *Argo* panel warrants closer consideration. Flanking the ship are the Dioskouroi, mounted on horseback; between them, on the ship itself, stand Orpheus and a comrade, each playing the lyre. The oft-remarked clumsiness of this arrangement, slapping frontal, upright figures against the long lateral plane of the ship, is usually explained as stylistic immaturity – a sort of primitivism. But the pertinent factor may be less stylistic than ideological. The panel may be crowded and difficult to read, its figures may relate unclearly to one other, its sculptural space may be incoherent. But this awkwardness only underscores the strangeness, and the stakes, of its iconography. Ships and horses do not come together often in Archaic art, less for aesthetic reasons than for political and social ones. For they embody the military functions of the highest and the lowest classes of a Greek city-state. Where navies gave power to the people, horse ownership was the defining characteristic of the Greek aristocracy (in

Athens, for instance, the second highest property class was the *hippeis*, the "horsemen"). More to the point, the Orthagorids relied on naval power even as they presented themselves as haughty elitists. On the metope, however, the two are basically equivalent. The Dioskouroi are also Argonauts, that is, oarsmen: social realities notwithstanding, there is *no contradiction* between horse and ship, cavalry and navy. Pindar figures this same interchangeability in his version of the myth. "Instead of short-finned dolphins," says his Medea, "they will have swift horses, and reins instead of oars, and they will drive storm-footed chariot teams" (*Pythian* 4.17–18). Compositionally it is the role of the lyre-players to effect this equation: occupying the center of the frame, they are upright and frontal like the horsemen, but they stand in the background, inside the ship itself. Their instrument is, of course, Apollo's own, and is appropriate to his foremost shrine, site of the most prestigious musical contest in the Greek world (Pindar notes that the oracle itself mandated the *Argo*'s voyage, and that Apollo sent Orpheus to participate: *Pythian* 4.163–4, 176–7). In the space of the lyre, which is the space of Apollo, high and low come together. Just as the Orthagorids sought to reconcile elitist practice with a tyranny based on sea power, so the *Argo* metope presents a harmonious world in which cavalrymen and oarsmen are the same thing, and Apollo's music floats over all.

The fate of the Orthagorid offerings is instructive. Following the collapse of the tyranny around 550, an oligarchic regime came to power (Aristotle *Politics* 1316a). For the next twenty years or so, Delphi was undergoing substantial renovation in the wake of the fire of 548, and there was no large-scale building at the site. But when activity resumed in the 520s, the Sicyonians promptly built a treasury. It was in the substructure of this *thesauros* that the remains of both the *tholos* and the pavilion were discovered. Both structures had been carefully dismantled: perhaps after the fire, perhaps later. Regardless of when the older buildings were taken down, however, their burial and reuse as the foundation of a new civic building are political theater of the highest order. The treasury at Olympia, on the other hand, remained in place for a generation or more. But sometime around 480 it, too, was dismantled; its blocks were dispersed throughout the sanctuary. A new treasury took its place: it was in this later building that Pausanias saw the bronze chambers of "Myron and the *demos*." As at Delphi, placing the tyrant's frame for offerings inside yet another, more acceptable structure dramatizes the changed political situation. Just as the Geloans and the Syracusans reinscribed the Deinomenid votives, so the Sicyonians literally built new monuments on the tyranny's ruins.

Athenians at Delphi

A series of buildings at Delphi provides a final, extended example of such political negotiation. The first is the late Archaic temple of Apollo at Delphi. We know neither the date nor the size of the first large temple (or temples) on the site, but fragments of a large marble sima of the second quarter of the sixth century have been plausibly associated with Apollo's temple and suggest, at the very least, a substantial renovation in that period. The sima has close parallels with examples from the Athenian Acropolis that are regularly associated with the tyrant Peisistratos. The similarity is not especially surprising – Peisistratos was on the winning side in the First Sacred War for control of the Delphic sanctuary – and it is just possible that he contributed to Apollo's temple as well. Be that as it may, a disastrous fire destroyed the building in 548. Over the following decades the Delphic authorities overhauled the entire sanctuary, constructing a series of terraces suitable for large-scale offerings and laying out the course of the present Sacred Way (it was during this interim period that the Ptoön flourished, and Alkmaionides made his dedication). The Amphictyony paid three-quarters of the cost, and the remainder was to be supplied by the Delphians. They sought contributions throughout the eastern Mediterranean; the pharaoh Amasis (r. ca. 570–26) was said to have been especially generous (Herodotus 2.180). By the end of the 510s, the time had come to rebuild the temple itself. At this time the Alkmaionid clan was in exile from Athens, where Peisistratos' son Hippias held the tyranny. The Alkmaionids acquired (or perhaps already possessed) the commission to rebuild the temple of Apollo. They did so, but, in a gesture that would become famous, they exceeded the terms of the contract. Although the agreement called for a temple of limestone, the Alkmaionids built the east façade in costly Parian marble. The splendid pedimental decoration of this building, dated circa 510, is in the Delphi Museum (Figure 28). On the east was an epiphany of the god Apollo in a chariot, flanked by youths, maidens, and wild beasts; on the west, a battle of Gods and Giants, centering on Zeus in his chariot. The metopes on the long flanks were apparently undecorated. Those on the short sides were sculpted: part of a multipanel sequence depicting Heracles stealing the cattle of Geryon survives from the east façade, whereas Euripides mentions scenes of Heracles fighting Hydra and Bellerophon fighting Chimaera on the west.

In a significant and striking innovation, the sculptor used statues of the *kouros* and *kore* types for the east pediment. Such figures were normally reserved for votive or mortuary use; *korai* could be adapted to serve as caryatides, as we have seen, but *kouroi* do not appear elsewhere in an architectural setting. Standing frozen and immobile, such figures are in fact ill-suited to narrative scenes. Their presence in the pediment, odd as it may be, clearly aligns the Alkmeonid temple with aristocratic dedicatory practice. Indeed, the pedimental group essentially adopts the compositional formula of a monument for a chariot victory. As Manolis Korres has shown, such monuments – like Polyzalos' later dedication at Delphi – typically combined a single figure in the car with standing ones on either side. In effect, the sculptor – often thought to be Antenor of Athens – simply adapted the most characteristic types of elite votive statuary to a new setting. He found an appropriate way to integrate the demands of pedimental sculpture with the fact that the east façade was, in effect, a votive offering of the Alkmeonid clan. The result, however, is that the temple proclaims unmistakably its semiprivate, semivotive character. Just as the Deinomenids conflated military victories and athletic ones, so the Alkmaionids conflated votive and architectural sculpture; just as Agasicles sought to evade the collectivizing tendencies of the Triopian shrine, so the Alkmaionids upstaged all the cities that contributed money to the temple. The result was one of the most striking examples of aristocratic ostentation that the Greek world ever saw.

Such lavish expenditure at an interstate shrine could be a direct or indirect challenge to the authority of the home *polis*. In this case, the challenge was especially blunt. With the completion of the new temple, the Delphic Oracle launched into a series of pro-Alkmaionid, anti-Peisistratid pronouncements that led indirectly to Hippias' ouster. The Alkmaionids returned home; after further vicissitudes, their leader Kleisthenes wound up granting unprecedented concessions to the Athenian commons in return for a share of power. The result was the beginning of the Athenian democracy. In short, prestige gained at the interstate shrine led to a coup at home. Although the sums in question are larger, and the results more dramatic, the basic situation does not differ all that much from the Kylonian conspiracy over a hundred years earlier.

Even after the fall of the tyrants, the Alkmaionid temple remained something of an embarrassment to the Athenian government. Kleisthenes soon faded from the scene, and the democracy embarked upon a fairly systematic program to outdo his family's extravagant gesture. Almost immediately, the Athenians built a new temple to Athena on the north side of their Acropolis. Although there were doubtless many motives behind this project, it is significant that the new temple was of almost identical proportions to the one at Delphi, had a similar iconographic program (a Gigantomachy in one pediment, a frontal chariot group in the other), and was constructed entirely (not partially) of Parian marble. Precisely because it owed its very existence – albeit indirectly – to Alkmaionid extravagance at Delphi, the Athenian democracy had good reason to build a temple of even greater ostentation in the heart of the *polis*.

A few years later, the Athenians constructed a small treasure-house at Delphi, immediately below Apollo's great temple (Figure 29). The building's exact date has long been uncertain, but recent excavations seem to confirm Pausanias' statement that it was a thank offering for victory at Marathon. As the battle occurred in the autumn of 490 BCE, work could have begun as early as 489, though 488 is more likely. The treasury was built entirely of Parian stone. That Athens was in fact at war with Paros at the time – the island had assisted the Persians at Marathon, and Miltiades the Younger had attacked it unsuccessfully after the battle – can only have delayed matters. Be that as it may, the Parian marble makes a clear visual counterpart to the famous east end of the "Alkmaionid" temple. Its sculptural program makes the allusion explicit. Like the temple, it combined an epiphany in the east pediment with a Gigantomachy in the west (in this instance, however, the epiphany was that of Athena, the civic patron, not Pythian Apollo). More strikingly still, the treasury mimicked the temple by depicting the fight of Heracles and Geryon over several metopes along one side. This scene is rare in architectural sculpture and relates the treasury unmistakably to the nearby temple.

That temple was not built by the Athenians: it was built by the Alkmaionids, which was by no means the same thing. When the treasury was under construction in the 480s, the clan's relationship to the state was in the forefront of public discourse. The Alkmaionids were suspected – justly or not – of having tried to betray Athens to the Persians at Marathon, and in 486 their leader, Megakles, was ostracized as a "Friend of the Tyrants." By asserting a connection to the Alkmaionid temple, the Athenian treasury effectively reintegrates the clan's ostentatious gesture into the fabric of Athenian public life. The similarities of material and iconography seem intended to remind pilgrims, as they mount the Sacred Way, that the Alkmaionids are citizens of Athens. The treasury makes the temple of Apollo, if not quite an Athenian dedication, then at least *a dedication by Athenians*.

Supporting evidence for this assertion comes from the response it elicited. Pindar's seventh Pythian ode was composed in the summer of 486 BCE to commemorate the victory of Megakles – the Alkmaionid leader, who had been ostracized only a few months before – in the chariot race at the Pythian games at Delphi. The poem reads as follows:

> The great city of Athens is the fairest prelude to lay down as a foundation course of songs [*krepid'aiodan*] to the clan of the Alkmaionids, broad in strength, for their horses. What fatherland, what house [*oikon naion*], will you inhabit and name with a more conspicuous renown in Greece?
>
> For the reputation of the townsmen of Erechtheus holds discourse with all cities, O Apollo, how they made your dwelling in divine Pytho a marvel to see. Five Isthmian victories lead my song forward, and one outstanding triumph at Zeus' Olympian games, and two from Cirrha,
>
> O Megakles, belonging to your family and ancestors. I rejoice at this new success; but I grieve that fine deeds are repaid with envy. Yet they say: the abiding bloom of good fortune brings a man now this, now that.

Pindar refers to the Alkmaionid temple in lines 9–11, "For the story of the townsmen of Erechtheus holds discourse with all cities, O Apollo, how they made your dwelling in divine Pytho a marvel to see." Significantly, however, the poet attributes this temple not to the Alkmaionids specifically, but to the "townsmen of Erechtheus," that is, the Athenians as a whole. As Leslie Kurke has observed, Pindar here suggests a model of "reciprocal advantage" between the noble clan and the city-state. On the one hand, the city of Athens is a "foundation-course" for Alkmaionid glory; on the other, the Alkmaionid temple allows the reputation of "the townsmen of Erechtheus" to keep company with all cities.

There is, however, another architectural metaphor in the poem: the "foundation-course of songs" in the opening lines. When Megakles won his victory, and when Pindar wrote his ode, there was of course a real Athenian foundation-course at Delphi: that of the Athenian Treasury, begun in 489 or later. Could Pindar be referring to the partially completed building? The phrase *krepid'aoidan*, "foundation of songs," certainly echoes the *hymnon thesauros*, the "treasury of songs," of *Pythian* 6.7–8. Moreover, the placement of this "foundation-course" at the beginning of the poem, as a "prelude" to Alkmaionid glory, replicates the topography of Delphi itself, where the pilgrims of 486 would pass the partially completed *thesauros* en route to the Alkmaionid temple. If Pindar is indeed referring to the unfinished treasury, then it at once becomes clear that *Pythian* 7 provides a simple and elegant account of the economy linking Athens to Alkmaionids, treasure-house to temple. The first two sections construct a model of reciprocity. In the strophe, the work in progress of the treasury is a conduit linking the great city of Athens with the Alkmaionids "broad in strength." Pindar asserts that the Treasury, although a civic, Athenian foundation, also glorifies the clan. Then, in the antistrophe, the clan reciprocates, as their temple comes to glorify "the townsmen of Erechtheus." In the stand, however, the cycle breaks down, and "fine deeds are repaid with envy." The reference is of course to Megakles' recent ostracism. The two halves of the relationship are left disconnected at the end, as the poet concludes with a remark more aporetic than gnomic: "the abiding bloom of good fortune brings a man now this, now that."

Conclusions

The "establishment of a state-framework for pilgrimage" was a political and ideological process (indeed, words such as "politics" and "ideology" have no meaning outside such practical activities as placing an offering in a treasury or nailing it to the wall of one's house). Dedications, inscriptions, buildings, stones, statues, anecdotes, and poems are the material traces of this process. As such, they repay our close attention, for their complexities and equivocations are, tangibly and concretely, those of Greek social life. Strident propaganda is not often apparent in such remains, for the simple reason that they tend to present a world devoid of conflict, devoid of contradiction – a world in which horses and ships are interchangeable, in which rich women serve the city just by being the extravagant creatures they are, in which anything written in stone can always be erased and revised.

But there comes a time when the process is effectively at an end. The civic colonization of Delphi and Olympia continued apace in the fifth century. The Persian Wars heralded an explosion of treasury-building at Delphi; the last one, the treasury of Cyrene, went up just before the Macedonian conquest. The Sacred Way was lined with state offerings during this same period. At Olympia there were no more treasuries, but here too there was an increase in the number of monumental public offerings: statues, armor, columns, and, of course, the Temple of Zeus with its chryselephantine statue by Pheidias. In the same period there was, as Anthony Snodgrass has shown, a dramatic decline in the number of private votives, not just at the great interstate centers but throughout Greece. Dedication as such was becoming a less significant venue for private display, even as cities dedicated with increasing ostentation; even the wealthiest elites could not compete with the enormous, multifigure ensembles of the late fifth and fourth centuries. Many aristocrats turned to new modes of self-presentation. The increasing importance of rhetorical training in the fifth century is an oft-cited example. As interstate competition lost some of its cachet, demonstrations of verbal prowess could take its place; the rise of sophists, expensive teachers of such skill, may be seen as an investment in this new form of upper-class display. Investment of this kind could translate directly into political power: to be a successful speaker was, by definition, to win over an audience. At Athens, the democracy harnessed old practices of elite display to new, civic ends through the institution of liturgies: massive expenditures by wealthy citizens on public projects. Underwriting the production of a tragedy for the civic competition, or outfitting a warship, were examples of such eminently acceptable modes of display (indeed, Athenian tragedy sometimes seems like an institutionalized, state-sponsored performance of the same conflicts visible "on the ground" at Delphi and Olympia). To be sure, the great sanctuaries remained important, and the old practices did not entirely disappear. The ambitious Spartan admiral Lysander directly challenged the authority of his home city by celebrating victory in 404 with a huge statue group at Delphi that showed himself being crowned by Poseidon before an audience of gods and men. Such appropriation of civic victory is familiar enough: like Pausanias and Miltiades before him, Lysander ended badly, and for similar reasons. It is significant nonetheless that few treasuries were built in the fourth century, and none at all after the Macedonian conquest. People continued to consult the Pythian Oracle, and the Olympic games would not disappear for nearly a millennium. But for cities of the later Classical and Hellenistic periods, there was no reason to be overly concerned about the dedicatory practices of their elites. Delphi and Olympia were, first and foremost, theaters of political drama; when the political situation changed irrevocably, that drama lost much of its urgency.

Notes

1 Morgan 1990, 102.
2 Morris 1996, 35–6.
3 Morris 1996, 36.
4 For a discussion of the *kouros* sculpture type, and its female counterpart the *kore*, see Chapter 10.

5 For more on the activities of Greek colonies in the homeland sanctuaries, see Chapter 8, *Becoming Greek, Staying Greek: Colonies and Sanctuaries.*

6 It is often said that Greek colonies built treasuries to reaffirm their connections with the motherland. They may have done so; but then one is entitled to wonder why some of the largest and most important colonies, such as Akragas, Leontini, Rhegium, and Taras (Taranto), never built. The colonial situation may be relevant but is neither necessary nor sufficient for the decision to build.

7 See also Chapter 1, *The Orthagorids of Sicyon (ca. 620/610–520/510)*, for a family tree and further discussion of the activities of this family.

Bibliography and Suggested Readings

Not Site-Specific

On Greek Sanctuaries in General

Alcock, S. and R. Osborne, eds. 1994. *Placing the Gods: Sanctuaries and Sacred Space in Ancient Greece.*

Bergquist, B. 1967. *The Archaic Greek Temenos: A Study of Structure and Function.*

De Polignac, F. 1995. *Cults, Territory, and the Origins of the Greek City-State.* Transl. J. Lloyd.

Dillon, M. 1997. *Pilgrims and Pilgrimage in Ancient Greece.*

Graf, F. "Gli dèi greci e i loro santuari." In *I Greci. Storia Cultura Arte Società.* Ed. S. Settis. Vol. 2.1: 342–80.

Hägg, R. ed. 1996. *The Role of Religion in the Early Greek Polis.*

______, ed. 1998. *Ancient Greek Cult Practice from the Archaeological Evidence.*

Hägg, R., N. Marinatos, and G. Nordquist, eds. 1988. *Early Greek Cult Practice.*

Jantzen, U. ed. 1976. *Neue Forschungen in griechischen Heiligtümern.*

Marinatos, N. and R. Hägg, eds. 1993. *Greek Sanctuaries: New Approaches.*

Pedley, J., 2005. *Sanctuaries and the Sacred in the Ancient Greek World.* (The best general introduction.)

Schachter, A. ed. 1992. *Le sanctuaire grec* (Fondation Hardt 37).

Valavanis, P. 2004. *Games and Sanctuaries in Ancient Greece: Olympia, Delphi, Isthmia, Nemea, Athens.* (Lavishly illustrated overview.)

Panhellenism and the Great Sanctuaries

Morgan, C. 1990. *Athletes and Oracles: The Transformation of Olympia and Delphi in the Eighth Century BC.* (A classic study.)

______. 1993. "The Origins of Panhellenism." In *Greek Sanctuaries: New Approaches.* Eds. N. Marinatos and R. Hägg. 18–44.

Rolley, C. 1983. "Les grands sanctuaires panhelléniques." In *The Greek Renaissance of the Eighth Century B.C.: Tradition and Innovation.* Ed. R. Hägg. 109–14. (Stressing discontinuity with Mycenaen period.)

Snodgrass, A. 2006. "Interaction by Design: The Greek City-State." In *Archaeology and the Emergence of Greece.* 234–58.

Ethnic/Regional Sanctuaries

Bowden, H. 1996. "The Greek Settlement and Sanctuaries at Naukratis: Herodotos and Archaeology." In *More Studies on the Ancient Greek Polis* (Historia Einzelschriften 108). Eds. M. H. Hansen and K. Raaflaub. 17–37.

Morgan, C. 2003. *Early Greek States beyond the Polis*. 107–63.

Sinn, U. 1996. "The Influence of Greek Sanctuaries on the Consolidation of Economic Power." In *Religion and Power in the Ancient Greek World* (Boreas 24). Eds. P. Hellström and B. Alroth. 67–74. (Arcadian border sanctuaries.)

Offerings, General

De Polignac, F. 1996. "Offrandes, mémoire et compétition ritualisée dans les sanctuaires grecs à l'époque géometrique." In *Religion and Power in the Ancient Greek World* (Boreas 24). Eds. P. Hellström and B. Alroth. 59–66.

De Polignac, F. and P. Schmitt-Pantel, eds. 1998. *Public et privé en Grèce ancienne: Lieux, conduits, pratiques* (Ktèma 23).

Linders, T. and G. Nordquist, eds. 1987. *Gifts to the Gods: Proceedings of the Uppsala Symposium 1985* (Boreas 15).

Ideology of Offering

Hintzen-Bohlen, B. 1992. *Herrscherrepräsentation im Hellenismus. Untersuchungen zu Weihgeschenke, Stiftungen und Ehrenmonumenten in den mutterländischen Heiligtümern Delphi, Olympia, Delos, und Dodona.*

Kurke, L. 1993. "The Economy of *Kudos*." In *Cultural Poetics in Archaic Greece: Cult, Performance, Politics*. Eds. C. Dougherty and L. Kurke. 131–63.

______. 2003. "Aesop and the Contestation of Delphic Authority." In *The Cultures within Ancient Greek Culture: Contact, Conflict, Collaboration*. Eds. C. Dougherty and L. Kurke. 77–100.

Appropriation of Elite Types (Tripods) by Cities

Amandry, P. "Trépieds de Delphes et du Péloponnèse." *Bulletin de correspondance hellénique* 111: 79–131.

Dedicatory Inscriptions

Ebert, J. 1972. *Griechische Epigramme auf Sieger an Gymnischen Agonen* (Abhandlungen der sächsischen Akademie der Wissenschaften zu Leipzig 63.2).

Lazzarini, M. 1976. "Le formule delle dediche votive nella Grecia arcaica." *Memorie. Atti della Accademia nazionale dei Lincei, Classe di scienze morali, storiche e filologiche* 19: 47–354.

Schachter, A. 1994. "The Politics of Dedication: Two Athenian Dedications at the Sanctuary of Apollo Ptoieus in Boeotia." In *Ritual, Finance, Politics: Athenian Democratic Accounts Presented to David Lewis*. Eds. R. Osborne and S. Hornblower. 291–306.

Placement of Offerings

Linders, T. 1987. "Gods, Gifts, Society." In *Gifts to the Gods: Proceedings of the Uppsala Symposium 1985* (Boreas 15). Eds. T. Linders and G. Nordquist. 115–22.

Van Straten, F. 1992. "Votives and Votaries in Greek Sanctuaries." In *Le sanctuaire grec* (Fondation Hardt 37). Ed. A. Schachter. 247–84.

Fifth-Century Decline

Kyle, D. G. 1997. "The First Hundred Olympiads: A Process of Decline or Democratization?" *Nikephoros* 10: 53–76.

Snodgrass, A. 2006. "The Economics of Dedication at Greek Sanctuaries." In *Archaeology and the Emergence of Greece*. 258–68.

"ELITE" VERSUS "MIDDLING"

Kurke, L. 1991. *The Traffic in Praise: Pindar and the Poetics of Social Economy.*

______. 1999. *Coins, Bodies, Games, and Gold: The Politics of Meaning in Archaic Greece.*

Morris, I. 2000. *Archaeology as Cultural History*. 109–91.

POLITICS OF ATHLETICS

Kurke, L. 1991. *The Traffic in Praise: Pindar and the Poetics of Social Economy.*

Pleket, H. W. 1975. "Games, Prizes, Athletes, and Ideology." *Stadion* 1: 49–89.

PRIZES AND VICTOR-STATUES (SEE ALSO UNDER OLYMPIA, "VICTOR STATUES")

Kyle, D. 1996. "Gifts and Glory: Panathenaic and Other Greek Athletic Prizes." In *Worshipping Athena*. Ed. J. Neils. 106–36.

Lattimore, S. 1989. "The Nature of Early Greek Victor Statues." In *Coroebus Triumphs: The Alliance of Sport and the Humanities*. 245–56.

Rausa, F. 1994. *L'immagine del vincitore: L'atleta nella statuaria greca dall'età arcaica all'ellenismo.*

TREASURIES IN GENERAL

Mari, M. 2006. "Sulle tracce di antiche ricchezze. La tradizione letteraria sui thesauroi di Delfi e di Olimpia." In *Stranieri e non cittadini nei santuari greci. Atti del convegno internazionale*. Ed. A. Naso. 36–70.

Neer, R. 2001. "Framing the Gift: The Politics of the Siphnian Treasury at Delphi." *Classical Antiquity* 20: 273–336.

Partida, E. 2000. *The Treasuries at Delphi: An Architectural Study.*

Rups, M. 1986. Thesauros: A Study of Treasury Building as Found in Greek Sanctuaries. Dissertation, The Johns Hopkins University.

TYRANTS AT DELPHI AND OLYMPIA

Catenacci, C. 1992. "Il tiranno alle Colonne d'Eracle: L'agonistica e le tirannidi arcaiche." *Nikephoros* 5: 11–36.

De Libero, L. 2001. "Delphi und die archaische Tyrannis." *Hermes* 129: 3–20.

Hansen, O. 1990. "On the Helmets Dedicated by Hieron to Zeus at Olympia." *Hermes* 118: 498.

Krumeich, R. 1991. "Zu den goldenen Dreifüssen der Deinomeniden in Delphi." *Jahrbuch des Deutschen Archäologischen Instituts* 106: 37–62.

KOUROI AND *KORAI*

Fehr, B. 1996. "Kouroi e korai. Formule e tipi dell'arte arcaica come espressione di valori." In *I Greci. Storia Cultura Arte Società*. Ed. S. Settis. Vol. 2.1: 745–46.

Karakasi, K. 2003. *Archaic Korai.*

Osborne, R. 1994. "Looking On, Greek Style. Does the Sculpted Girl Speak to Women Too?" In *Classical Greece: Ancient Histories and Modern Archaeologies*. Ed. I. Morris. 81–96.

Stewart, A. 1986. "When Is a Kouros Not an Apollo? The Tenea 'Apollo' Revisited." In *Corinthiaca: Studies in Honor of Darrell A. Amyx*. Eds. M. del Chiaro and W. Biers. 54–70.

Zinserling, V. 1975. "Bedeutungsgehalt des archaisches Kuros." *Eirene* 13: 19–33.

Delphi

Popular Account

Dossiers d'archéologie 151 (1990).

Useful Guides to the Site, the Finds, and the Scholarly Literature

Bommelaer, J.-F. 1991. *Guide de Delphes: Le Site.*

Bommelaer, J.-F. 1991. *Guide de Delphes: Le Musée.*

Bommelaer, J. F. 1997. *Marmaria: Le sanctuaire d'Athéna à Delphes.*

Oracle

Arnush, M. 2005. "Pilgrimage to the Oracle of Apollo at Delphi: Patterns of Public and Private Consultation." In *Seeing the Gods: Pilgrimage in Graeco-Roman and Early Christian Antiquity*. Eds. J. Elsner and I. Rutherford. 97–110.

Fontenrose, J. 1978. *The Delphic Oracle: Its Responses and Operations, with a Catalogue of Responses.*

Parker, R. 1985. "Greek States and Greek Oracles." In *Crux: Essays in Greek History Presented to G. E. M. de Ste. Croix on His 75th Birthday*. Eds. P. Cartledge and F. Harvey. 298–326.

Price, S. 1985. "Delphi and Divination." In *Greek Religion and Society*. Eds. P. Easterling and J. Muir. 128–54.

Mythical Origins

Sourvinou-Inwood, C. 1991. *"Reading" Greek Culture.* 192–243.

Amphictyony

Lefèvre, F. 1998. *L'amphictionie pyléo-delphique. Histoire et institutions.*

Pythian Games

Brodersen, K. 1990. "Zur Datierung der ersten Pythien." *Zeitschrift für Papyrologie und Epigraphik* 82: 25–31.

Fontenrose, J. 1988. "The Cult of Apollo and the Games at Delphi." In *The Archaeology of the Olympics*. Ed. W. Raschke. 121–40.

Votives

Felten, F. 1982. "Weihungen in Olympia und Delphi." *Mitteilungen des Deutschen Archäologischen Instituts, Athenische Abteilung* 97: 79–97.

Jacquemin, A. 1999. *Offrandes monumentales à Delphes.*

Mass, M. 1992. "Fruhe Weihgaben in Delphi und Olympia als Zeugnisse für die Geschichte der Heiligtümer." In *Delphes. Centenaire de la "Grande Fouille" réalisée par l'École française d'Athènes (1892–1903)*. Ed. J.-F. Bommelaer. 85–93.

Monument of Plataea

Laroche, D. 1989. "Nouvelles observations sur l'offrande de Platées." *Bulletin de correspondance hellenique* 113: 183–98.

Stichel, R. H. W. 1997. "Die Schlangensäule im Hippodrom von Istanbul. Zum spät- und nachantiken Schicksal des delphischen Votivs der Schlacht von Plataiai." *Istanbuler Mitteilungen* 47: 315–48.

"Delphi Charioteer" and Chariot Groups:

Korres, M. 2000. "Anathematika kai timetika tethrippa sten Athena kai tous Delphous." In Delphes cent ans après la Grande fouille. Essai de Bilan. Bulletin de correspondance hellénique Suppl. 36. Ed. A. Jacquemin. Paris: 293–329.

Nicholson, N. 2003. "Aristocratic Victory Memorials and the Absent Charioteer." In *The Cultures within Ancient Greek Culture: Contact, Conflict, Collaboration*. Eds. C. Dougherty and L. Kurke. Cambridge: 101–28.

Rolley, Cl. 1990. "En regardant l'Aurige." *Bulletin de correspondance hellenique* 114: 285–97, with earlier bibliography.

West Greek Involvement

Ioakimidou, Ch. 2000. "Auch wir sind Griechen! Statuenreihen westgriechischer Kolonisten in Delphi und Olympia." *Nikephoros* 13: 63–94.

Jacquemin, A. 1992. "Offrandes monumentales italiotes et siciliotes à Delphes." In *Magna Grecia e i grandi santuari della madrepatria. Atti del trentunesimo Convegno di studi sulla Magna Grecia, Taranto, 4–8 ottobre 1991*. 193–204.

Le Roy, C. 1967. *Les terres cuites architecturales* (Fouilles de Delphes 2.10).

Mertens-Horn, M. and L. Viola 1990. "Archaischer Tondächer westgriechischer Typologie in Delphi und Olympia." *Hesperia* 59: 235–50.

Treasuries (Architecture)

Laroche, D. and M. Nenna 1993. "Etudes sur le trésors en poros à Delphes." In *Les grands ateliers d'architecture dans le monde égéen du VIe siècle av. J.-C.* Eds. J. des Courtils and J.-C. Moretti. 227–45.

Partida, E. 2000. *The Treasuries at Delphi: An Architectural Study.*

Treasury of Agylla/Caere

Laroche, D. and M.-D. Nenna. 1992. "Deux trésors archaïques en poros à Delphes." In *Delphes. Centenaire de la "Grande Fouille" réalisée par l'École française d'Athènes* (1892–1903). Ed. J.-F. Bommelaer. Leiden: 109–24.

Cnidian Treasury, Inscription

Salviat, F. 1977. "La dédicace du trésor de Cnide à Delphes." BCH Suppl. 4: 23–36.

Cnidian Treasury, Caryatides

De La Coste-Messelière, P. and J. Marcadé. 1953. "Corés delphiques." *Bulletin de correspondance hellenique* 77: 346–76.

Langlotz, E. 1975. *Studien zur nordostgriechischen Kunst*. 59–61.

Caryatides, General

Ridgway, B. S. 1999. *Prayers in Stone: Greek Architectural Sculpture (ca. 600–100 B.C.E.).* 145–50.

Corinthian Treasury

Østby, E. 2000. "Delphi and Archaic Doric Architecture in the Peloponnese." In *Delphes cent ans après la Grande fouille. Essai de Bilan. Bulletin de correspondance hellenique Suppl.* 36. Ed. A. Jacquemin. 239–62.

Sikyon, Delphi, and the Orthagorids

Oost, S. I. 1974. "Two Notes on the Orthagorids of Sicyon." *Classical Philology* 69: 118–20. (on the office of sacrificial butcher, or *mageiros*)

Parker, V. 1994. "Some Aspects of the Foreign and Domestic Policy of Kleisthenes of Sicyon." *Hermes* 124: 404–24.

Sikyonian Structures at Delphi

Laroche, D., and M.-D. Nenna. 1990. "Le trésor de Sicyon et ses fondations." *Bulletin de correspondance hellenique* 114: 241–84.

Østby, E. 2000. "Delphi and Archaic Doric Architecture in the Peloponnese." In *Delphes cent ans après la Grande fouille. essai de bilan. Bulletin de correspondance hellenique* Suppl. 36. Ed. A. Jacquemin. 239–62.

Roux, G. 1992. "La tholos de Sicyone à Delphes et les origins de l'entablement dorique." In *Delphes. Centenaire de la "Grande Fouille" réalisée par l'École française d'Athènes (1892–1903).* Ed. J.-F. Bommelaer. 151–66.

Sikyonian Metopes

De La Coste-Messelière, P. 1936. *Au musée de Delphes.* 77–95.

Knell, H. 1990. *Mythos und Polis. Bildprogramme griechischer Bauskulptur.* Darmstadt: 18–23.

Ridgway, B. S. 1993. *The Archaic Style in Greek Sculpture.* Second ed. 339–43, 361–2 n. 8.15.

Salviat, F. 1984. "Le navire Argo sur les metopes sicyoniennes à Delphes." *Archaeonautica* 4: 213–22.

Apollo Temple, Pre-548

Billot, M.-Fr. 1977. "Note sur une sima en marbre de Delphes." *Bulletin de correspondance hellenique Suppl.* 4: 161–77.

"Alkmaionid" Temple of Apollo, Architecture and Date

Childs, W. 1993. "Herodotos, Archaic Chronology, and the Temple of Apollo at Delphi." *Jahrbuch des Deutschen Archäologischen Instituts* 108: 399–441.

De La Coste-Messelière, P. 1946. "Les Alcméonides à Delphes." *Bulletin de correspondance hellénique* 70: 271–87.

"Alkmaionid" Temple of Apollo, Pedimental Sculpture

Stewart, A. 1990. *Greek Sculpture: An Exploration.* 86–9.

"Alkmaionid" Temple of Apollo, Metopes

Bookidis, N. 1967. *A Study of the Use and Geographical Distribution of Architectural Sculpture in the Archaic Period: Greece, East Greece and Magna Graecia.* Dissertation, Bryn Mawr. 189–92.

Athenian Treasury, Basic/Technical

Audiat, J. 1933. *Le Trésor des Athéniens. Fouilles de Delphes 2.3.*

Büsing, H. 1994. *Das Athener Schatzhaus in Delphi. Neue Untersuchungen zur Architektur und Bemalung* (Marburger Winckelmann-Programm 1992).

Athenian Treasury, Date

Amandry, P. 1998. "Le 'socle marathonien' et le trésor des Atheniens." *Bulletin de correspondance hellénique* 122: 75–90.

Athenian Treasury, Sculpture

De La Coste-Messelière, P. 1957. *Sculptures du Trésor des Athéniens. Fouilles de Delphes* IV.4.

Hoffelner, K. 1988. "Die Metopen des Athenerschatzhauses: Ein neuer Rekonstruktionsversuch." *Mitteilungen des Deutschen Archäologischen Instituts, Athenische Abteilung* 103: 77–117.

Athenian Treasury, Politics

Neer, R. 2004. "The Athenian Treasury at Delphi and the Material of Politics." *Classical Antiquity* 22: 63–93.

Athenian Treasury, Second Example in Sanctuary of Athena?

Gauer, W. 2000. "Die Spuren eines ungesühnten Mordes, der Zorn des Zeus und zwei Schatzhäuser der Athener in Delphi." *Ktèma* 25: 75–85.

Olympia

Popular Account

Sinn, U. 1996. *Olympia. Kult, Sport, und Fest in der Antike.*

Site

Herrmann, H.-V. 1972. *Olympia. Heiligtum und Wettkampfstätte.*

Mallwitz, A. 1972. *Olympia und seine Bauten.*

Layout of the Early Sanctuary

Brulotte, E. 1994. "The 'Pillar of Oinomaos' and the Location of Stadium I at Olympia." *American Journal of Archaeology* 98: 53–64.

Archaic Temple and Possible Cult-Statue

Arafat, K. W. 1995. "Pausanias and the Temple of Hera at Olympia." *Annual of the British School at Athens* 90: 461–73.

Mallwitz, A, 1966. "Das Heraion von Olympia und seine Vorgänger." *Jahrbuch des Deutschen Archäologischen Instituts* 81: 310–76.

Sinn, U. 2001. "Die Stellung des Hera-Tempels im Kultbetrieb von Olympia." In *Archaische griechische Tempel und Altägypten*. Ed. M. Bietak. 63–70.

Treasuries

Herrmann, K. 1976. "Beobachtungen zur Schatzhaus-Architektur Olympias." In *Neue Forschungen in griechischen Heiligtümern*. Ed. U. Jantzen. 321–50.

______. 1992. "Die Schatzhauser in Olympia." In *Proceedings of an International Symposium on the Olympic Games*. Eds. W. Coulson and H. Kyrieleis. 25–32.

Schilbach, J. 1984. "Untersuchung der Schatzhausterrasse südlich der Schatzhauses der Sikyonier in Olympia." *Archäologischer Anzeiger* 1984: 225–36. (stratigraphy).

Athletics

Coulson, W. and H. Kyrieleis, eds. 1992. *Proceedings of an International Symposium on the Olympic Games*. 25–32.

Raschke, W., ed. 1988. The Archaeology of the Olympics. Madison.

Argive Public Horses

Moretti, L. 1957. "Olympionikai. I vincitori negli antichi agoni olimpici." *Memorie Accademia nazionale dei Lincei* Ser. 8.8: Nos. 207 and 233, with Nos. 204, 210, and 222.

Connections with Western Greece

Herrmann, H.-V. 1983. "Altitalisches und Etruskisches in Olympia. Neue Funde und Forschungen." *Mitteilungen des Deutschen Archäologischen Instituts, Athenische Abteilung* 61: 271–94.

Philipp, H. 1992. "Olympia, die Peloponnes und die Westgriechen." *Jahrbuch des Deutschen Archäologischen Instituts* 109: 77–92.

Connections with Aegean

Mallwitz, A. 1980. "Kykladen und Olympia." In *Stele. Tomos eis mnemen Nikoalou Kontoleontos*. 361–79.

Oracle

Parke, H. W. 1967. *The Oracles of Zeus: Dodona, Olympia, Ammon.*

Offerings

Felten, F. 1982. "Weihungen in Olympia und Delphi." *Mitteilungen des Deutschen Archäologischen Instituts, Athenische Abteilung* 97: 79–97.

Himmelmann-Wildschütz, N. 2001. "La vie religieuse à Olympie: fonction et typologie des offrandes." In *Olympie*. Ed. A. Pasquier. 153–80.

Mallwitz, A. and H.-V. Herrmann. 1980. *Die Funde aus Olympia.*

Mass, M. 1992. "Fruhe Weihgaben in Delphi und Olympia als Zeugnisse für die Geschichte der Heiligtumer." In *Delphes. Centenaire de la "Grande Fouille" réalisée par l'École française d'Athènes (1892–1903)*. Ed. J.-F. Bommelaer. 85–93.

Siewert, P. 1991. "Staatliche Weihungen von Kesseln und anderen Bronzegeräten in Olympia." *Mitteilungen des Deutschen Archäologischen Instituts, Athenische Abteilung* 106: 81–4.

Sinn, U. 1998. "Die architektonischen Weihgeschenke im Zeusheiligtum von Olympia. Perspektiven des Zusammwirkens von Archäologie und Bauforschung. Zusammenfassung." In Bericht über die 39. Tagung für Ausgrabungswissenschaft und Bauforschung, Leiden 15.-19. Mai 1996. Bonn: 17–19.

Victor Statues

Hyde, W. W. 1921. *Olympic Victor Monuments and Greek Athletic Art.*

Herrmann, H.-V. 1988. "Die Siegerstatuen von Olympia." *Nikephoros* 1: 119–83.

Peim, O. 2000. "Die Siegerstatuen von Schwerathleten in Olympia und ihr Zusammenstellung durch Pausanias." *Nikephoros* 13: 95–100.

Victor Lists

Bilik, R. 2000. "Die Zuverlässigkeit der frühen Olympionikenliste. Die Geschichte eines Forschungenproblems in chrologischen Überblick." *Nikephoros* 13: 47–62.

Moretti, L. 1957. "Olympionikai, I vincitori negli antichi agoni olimpici." *Memorie Accademia nazionale dei Lincei* Ser. 8.8: 55–198.

______. 1970. "Supplemento al catalogo degli Olympionikai." *Klio* 52: 295ff.

______. 1987. "Nuovo supplemento al catalogo degli Olympionikai." *Miscellanea Greca e Romana* (Studi publicati dall'Instituto Italiano per la storia antica, Fasc. 39) 12: 67ff.

The Horn of Amaltheia

Graham, A. J. 1993. "A Dedication from the Chersonese at Olympia." In *Nomodeiktes: Greek Studies in Honor of Martin Ostwald.* Eds. R. M. Rosen and J. Farrell. 331–8.

Helmet of Miltiades

Krumeich, R. 1996. "Namensbeischrift oder Weihinschrift? Zum Fehlen des Miltiadesnamens beim Marathongemälde." *Archäologischer Anzeiger* 43–51.

Mallwitz, A., and K. Herrmann 1980. *Die Funde aus Olympia.* 95–6 No. 57, with bibliography.

Sikyonian treasury

Herrmann, K., A. Mallwitz, and H. van de Löcht 1980. "Bericht über Restaurierungsarbeiten in Olympia. Schatzhaus der Sikyonier." *Archäologischer Anzeiger* 1980: 351–67.

Schilbach, J. 1984. "Untersuchung der Schatzhausterrasse südlich des Schatzhauses der Sikyonier in Olympia." *Archäologischer Anzeiger* 1984: 225–36.

See also under ***Delphi*** for Orthagorids.

Delos

General

Bruneau, P., and J. Ducat. 1983. *Guide de Délos.*

Etienne, R. 2002. "The Development of the Sanctuary at Delos: New Perspectives." In *Excavating Classical Culture: Recent Archaeological Discoveries in Greece* (British Archaeological Reports 1031). Eds. M. Stamatopoulou and M. Yeroulanou. 285–93.

Gallet de Santerre, H. 1958. *Délos primitive et archaïque.*

Vallois, R. 1944. *L'architecture hellénique et hellénistique à Delos I: Les Monuments.*

______. 1978. *L'architecture héllenique et hellénistique à Delos 2: Grammaire historique de l'architecture delienne.*

Oikoi

Roux, G. 1973. "Salles de banquets à Delphes." *Bulletin de correspondance hellénique Suppl.* 1: 525–54.

Tréhaux, J. 1987. "L"Hiéropoion et les oikoi du sanctuaire à Delos." In *Stemmata: Mélanges Jules Labarbe.* 377–90.

Naxian Oikos

Kalpaxis, A. E. 1990. "Naxier-Oikos I und andere Baugerüste." *Archäologischer Anzeiger* 1990: 149–53.

Gruben, G. 1997. "Naxos und Delos. Studien zur archaischen Architektur der Kykladen." *Jahrbuch des Deutschen Archäologischen Instituts* 112: 261–416.

Isthmia

Gebhard, E. 1993. "The Evolution of a Pan-hellenic Sanctuary: From Archaeology towards History at Isthmia." In *Greek Sanctuaries: New Approaches.* Eds. N. Marinatos and R. Hägg. 154–77.

______. 1998. "Small Dedications in the Archaic Temple of Poseidon at Isthmia." In *Ancient Greek Cult Practice from the Archaeological Evidence.* Ed. R. Hägg. 91–115.

Morgan, C. 1994. "The Evolution of a Sacral Landscape: Isthmia, Perachora, and the Early Corinthian State." In *Placing the Gods.* Ed. R. Osborne and S. Alcock. 105–142,

______. 1999. The Late Bronze Age Settlement and the Early Iron Age Sanctuary. Isthmia 8.

Nemea

Miller, S. G. 1988. "Excavations at the Panhellenic Site of Nemea." In *The Archaeology of the Olympics: The Olympics and Other Festivals in Antiquity.* Ed. W. J. Raschke. 141–51.

Miller, S. G. 1990. *Nemea: A Guide to the Site and Museum.*

Miller, S. G. 2002. "The Shrine of Opheltes and the Earliest Stadium of Nemea." In *Olympia 1875–2000. 125 Jahre Deutsche Ausgrabungen.* Ed. H. Kyrieleis. 239–50.

Cnidus and Triopian Apollo

Bankel, H. 2004. "Knidos. Das Triopion. Zur Topographie des Stammesheiligtums der dorischen Hexapolis." In *Macht der Architektur, Architektur der Macht.* Eds. E. Schwander and K. Rheidt. 100–113.

Berges, D. 1994. "Alt-Knidos und Neu-Knidos." *Istanbuler Mitteilungen* 44: 5–16.

______. 1995/1996. "Knidos und das Heiligtum der dorischen Hexapolis." *Nürnberger Beiträge zur Archäologie* 12: 103–20.

Berges, D., and N. Tuna. 1990. "Ein archaisches Heiligtum bei Alt-Knidos." *Archäologischer Anzeiger* 1990: 19–35.

______. 2000. "Das Apollonheiligtum von Emecik. Berichte über die Ausgrabungen 1998 und 1999." *Istanbuler Mitteilungen* 50: 171–214.

______. 2001. "Kult-, Wettkampf-, und politische Versammlungsstätte. Das Triopion, Bundesheiligtum der dorischen Pentapolis." *Antike Welt* 32: 155–66.

Parke, H. W. 1985. *Oracles of Apollo in Asia Minor*.

The Ptoön

Ducat, J. 1971. *Les kouroi du Ptoion: Le sanctuaire d'Apollon Ptoieus à l'époque archaïque* (Bulletin des Écoles françaises d'Athènes et de Rome 219).

Schachter, A. 1994. "The Politics of Dedication: Two Athenian Dedications at the Sanctuary of Apollo Ptoieus in Boeotia." In *Ritual, Finance, Politics: Athenian Democratic Accounts Presented to David Lewis*. Eds. R. Osborne and S. Hornblower. 291–306. (Alkmaionides.)

Athens

Burials and Intra-elite Competition

Morris, I. 1987. *Burial and Ancient Society: The Rise of the Greek City-State*.

Whitley, J. 1992. *Style and Society in Dark Age Greece*.

______. 1994. "Protoattic Pottery: A Contextual Approach." In *Classical Greece*. Ed. I. Morris. 51–70.

Acropolis Votives, General

Keesling, C. 2003. *The Votive Statues of the Athenian Acropolis*.

Raubitschek, A. 1949. *Dedications from the Athenian Acropolis*.

Nike of Kallimakhos

Harrison, E. 1971. "The Victory of Kallimachos." *Greek, Roman, and Byzantine Studies* 12: 5–24.

Korres, M. 1994. "Recent Discoveries on the Acropolis." In *Acropolis Restoration: The CCAM Interventions*. Ed. R. Economakis. 174–9, at 178.

Acropolis Temple and Delphi

Childs, W. 1994. "The Date of the Old Temple of Athena on the Athenian Acropolis." In *The Archaeology of Athens and Attica under the Democracy*. Eds. W. D. E. Coulson, O. Palagia, T. L. Shear Jr., H. A. Shapiro, and F. J. Frost. 1–6.

Stähler, K. 1972. "Zer Rekonstruktion und Datierung des Gigantomachiegiebels von der Akropolis." In *Antike und Universalgeschichte. Festschrift H. E. Stier zum 70. Geburtstag am 25.5.1972*. 88–112.

Stähler, K. 1978. "Der Zeus aus dem Gigantomachiegiebel der Akropolis?" *Boreas* 1: 28–31.

Liturgies

Wilson, P. 2000. *The Athenian Institution of the Khoregia: The Chorus, The City and the Stage*.

Samian Heraion

Kienast, H. J. 2002. "Topography and Architecture of the Archaic Heraion at Samos." In *Excavating Classical Culture: Recent Archaeological Discoveries in Greece* (British Archaeological Reports 1031). Eds. M. Stamatopoulou and M. Yeroulanou. 317–325.

Klaffenbach, G. 1953. "Archaische Weiheninschrift aus Samos." *MdI* 6: 15–20. (Perinthians.)

Kyrieleis, H. 1993. "The Heraion at Samos." In N. Marinatos and R. Hägg 1995: 125–53. (Overview.)

Dodona

Cabanes, P. 1988. "Les concours des Naia de Dodone." *Nikephoros* 1: 49–84, with earlier bibliography.

Parke, H. W. 1967. *The Oracles of Zeus: Dodona, Olympia, Ammon.*

10: The Human Figure in Early Greek Sculpture and Vase Painting

Jeffrey M. Hurwit

Phrasikleia

In a year probably not long after 550 BCE, one of Athens' leading families lost a daughter and buried her in a rural cemetery at Myrrhinous (Merenda) in eastern Attica. The girl was named Phrasikleia, and her family commissioned Aristion (a sculptor who came from the marble-rich island of Paros but who made his reputation in Attica) to carve a statue in Parian marble to mark her grave (see Figure 30). To judge from its nearly perfect state of preservation, the statue did not mark the grave for very long: rather, it was apparently removed for its own protection and was buried (together with a statue of a nude youth) in a pit, where it was discovered in 1972 CE.[1] The image is over life size – if we assume most women in the middle of the sixth century stood less than 1.79 m (or about 5′10″) tall. It shows a girl standing upright and frontally, wearing a long-sleeved dress, belted at the waist, with a zigzag hem that flares gently over close-set, sandaled feet. The dress is incised with ornaments (rosettes, stars, swastikas, meanders) and was originally painted in deep red, yellow, and other bright colors (the skin may have been painted white or cream): the effect would strike the modern eye as garish, but the Greeks were in many ways different from us, and the practice of vividly painting marble sculpture was the ancient Greek norm. The girl pinches her dress with her right hand, but the unresponsive cloth remains sheathlike: from the front there is no hint of her form beneath – no curve of thigh, no bulge of knee, no depression between the legs. Her left hand is brought before her pubescent breasts and holds a single closed lotus bud exactly between them. She wears bracelets, a necklace (adorned with pomegranates or, perhaps, poppies), and lotus-bud earrings. Three long beaded tresses begin to curve over each breast; around her forehead the hair is coiffed in waves. Enigmatically she smiles – a sign not of joy or happiness, but of transcendence. This "Archaic smile" (found on many Archaic faces, both carved and painted) is a device that in effect removes her (and all other figures who wear it) from the uncertain flux of mortality, that deflects any attempt to search for emotion or thought behind the surface of the face, but that may also intimate a life-force that ancient statues were often supposed to possess. Finally, she wears a crown of (again) lotus, this time buds alternating with flowers that have just begun to open, just as the girl seems on the verge of opening up into womanhood.

The statue was, however, just one part of Phrasikleia's memorial. It stood atop a base that has been known since 1729 or 1730 CE and has long been famous for its poetic inscription, neatly carved in five short lines on the front:

> Marker (*sema*) of Phrasikleia.
> Maiden (*kore*) shall I be called
> forever, given instead of marriage
> this name from the gods
> as my lot.

In this ensemble each element, statue and text, image and elegy, complements and fulfills the other. Phrasikleia means something like "She Who Pays Attention to Fame" or "She Who Draws Attention to Fame,"[2] and the inscribed text enlists the viewer as the vehicle of her renown. In the Archaic period, written Greek was typically read aloud: a text – any text – was a prompt to speak. Anyone who approached the *sema* (marker, sign, tomb) of Phrasikleia and saw the inscription on its base would thus have given voice to it, and in so doing assumed the first person identity of the maiden herself: "I shall be called *kore* forever. . . ."[3] The reader stated aloud Phrasikleia's compensation for death – according to the inscription it is not the statue but the title, Maiden (Forever) – thus conferring fame (*kleos*) upon "She Who Draws Attention to Fame," giving speech to a statue that itself claims the power of speech, and so seems active or animate. At the same brief moment, the reading/speaking spectator, male or female, impersonated or "became" the virgin whom death took before marriage and sexual maturation, a woman unfulfilled, a flower plucked, like the bud she holds, before it could blossom. The reader/speaker played a role, imitating Phrasikleia, proclaiming her *kleos* as he or she sounded her name, just as the statue itself in some sense acted as a replacement for, and a semblance of, the richly adorned, marriageable, but eternally unmarried daughter of a wealthy clan, a colorful marble memory.[4]

The Isches Colossos

Several decades before Aristion of Paros created Phrasikleia's *sema* for a rural Attic funeral plot, across the Aegean on the island of Samos a man named Isches commissioned a sculptor whose name we do not know to carve a huge marble statue of a man or youth that he then dedicated in the great sanctuary of the goddess Hera (see Figure 31).[5] Carved out of richly veined Samian marble, the statue is a completely nude colossos almost three times life size (4.81 m, or over 15′6″, tall). If it dates as early as 580 BCE (as its excavators think), it would have been taller than the Temple of Hera or any other building then standing in the sanctuary. It advances its left leg and draws back its right, so it is not really standing at all: it is walking, and its findspot, near the entrance of the sanctuary beside the Sacred Way, suggests that the statue (whatever the occasion for its original dedication) may have served as a marker guiding visitors moving into the precinct. Its arms are clenched and held at the sides. It is blocklike, conceived as the sum of four principal views (front, back, sides). The long, beaded hair (partly damaged) falls winglike behind the shoulders. The face is round, the eyes are wide and almond-shaped, and the thin mouth smiles a shallow smile. The blue-gray veining of the marble seems at first to have been ingeniously exploited to accentuate the lean, fluid anatomy of the statue – the concavity of the torso, for example, or the roundness of the buttocks, where concentric veins resemble topographical contour lines on a map.[6] But in fact the entire statue was probably painted brick red (the conventional skin color of men in Egyptian and other ancient art). Contrasting colors certainly enlivened the hair and eyes; rosette or star patterns were painted around the nipples; dark blue or brown paint filled in the pubic area (lightly raised in relief); and there may even have been a moustache painted above a line engraved over the upper lip.[7] On the front of the statue's left thigh (and not on its separate, rectangular base) there is a big, handsomely carved inscription that, like any Archaic text, was meant to be read aloud:

> Isches, the son of Rhesis, dedicated.

A word is missing and must have been supplied by the mind and voice of the spectator. To judge from similar dedicatory inscriptions, the word was probably "me," and so, as in the case of Phrasikleia's epitaph, the viewer/reader momentarily impersonates the statue, saying its words aloud: "Isches set me up."[8]

Of Achilles and Ajax

Not long after Aristion carved Phrasikleia, in the 530s, one of Archaic Athens' finest potters and vase painters made and decorated a wine amphora probably intended for use in a symposium, an upper-class "drinking-party" that was in essence a ritualized occasion for refreshment, conversation, entertainment, and, ultimately, sex.[9] Now in the Vatican (having found its way to an Etruscan tomb at Vulci), the vase bears a quintessentially Archaic image (see Figure 32). In a panel framed by rich, shiny black glaze, Achilles and Ajax, the two greatest Greek heroes at Troy, sit on stools and play dice in an almost perfectly symmetrical composition: with their shields leaning against the sides of the panel, the heroes stoop over the gaming table, drawing their right legs back, moving their pieces with their right hands, holding their spears with their left (the lines of the spears continue the downward thrust of the handles, binding the image to the architecture of the vase). The heads of the heroes are locked within the great V of the spears. Achilles wears his helmet, Ajax has set his on his shield, and their elaborately, meticulously incised armor and cloaks – the sheer *poikilia* ("lavishness," "ornamentality," "decorativeness") of it all exceeds even that of Phrasikleia's costume – differ in details.[10] Ajax uneasily raises his right heel; Achilles plants his right foot solidly on the ground. Otherwise, the heroes are nearly mirror images of each other: massive black silhouettes that seem pasted over the red-orange fabric of the vase, flat forms in an all but depthless space. Ajax's spears, it is true, cross in front of the table, whereas Achilles' disappear behind it; Ajax's left ankle overlaps his stool, Achilles' left ankle is overlapped by his; and so there is some indication of the third dimension, shallow though it may be. But essentially the scene adheres tightly to the plane, to the surface of the vase: the blackness of the figures within the panel and the blackness of the glaze outside it are visually equivalent. Both stick to the vase like a thin, lustrous skin.

The light ground of the image – the unpainted clay around the silhouettes of the heroes – is perceived not as air or space but as a neutral surface, something that can be written upon with words that, again, were meant to be read aloud by those symposiasts whose wine arrived in the jug, and who might have been expected to tell a tale about the heroes depicted upon it or elaborate upon the image they saw. Over Achilles' back the artist signed his handiwork: *Exekias epoiesen*, "Exekias made [me]" – the speaking reader necessarily supplying the "me" and thus giving voice to the vase or the image, as in the case of Phrasikleia's *kore* and Isches' colossos. Between Ajax and his armor a vertical inscription that has nothing to do with the heroes but everything to do with the Archaic vase-painter's sympotic audience and its homoerotic conventions praises a handsome local youth: *Onetorides kalos*, "Onetorides is beautiful" (the compliment, once spoken, might have initiated a tangential round of comments on the boy's good looks, making his beauty the topic of public discussion and so bestowing *kleos* upon him).[11] And then back to the myth: from the mouths of the heroes themselves stream words that give the score of the game. *Tria* (three), Ajax says, *tesara* (four), says Achilles, the greater hero and winner. And above them Exekias wrote the words *Akhileos* and *Aiantos*. Without these labels we could not be sure who the players are (and without hundreds of later variants of this scene we would not know that they are negligently playing a game when they should be driving Trojan intruders from their camp). But the labels are unusual in that they are written in the genitive case: that is, they mean not "Achilles" and "Ajax" but "*of* Achilles" and "*of* Ajax." A word is missing, once again to be understood and supplied by the viewer/reader. The word must have been something like *eidolon* or *eikon*, Greek words meaning "likeness" or "image." That is, around 540 or 530, Exekias acknowledged (and the reader of the vase was made to realize) that artists made semblances. The figures he painted were not Achilles or Ajax, but imitations of them.

But what did Aristion of Paros and the anonymous sculptor of the Isches colossos think they were making, and what did the viewers of these statues in cemetery and sanctuary think they were seeing? What did these statues mean, and how did they function in Archaic society? And what are the implications, if any, of Exekias' concession – of his artistic self-consciousness – for the course of the depiction of the human figure on vases?

Kore and Kouros

The kind of statue that served as Phrasikleia's memorial is (and was then) known as a *kore* (maiden). The kind of statue Isches dedicated is now known as a *kouros* (youth): what the type was called in antiquity we do not know. At all events, these are the two most familiar genres of Archaic Greek sculpture in the round, and they are often thought to epitomize Archaic aesthetic ideals and social ideologies. Now, Archaic sculpture itself is far older and more diverse than these types: it begins with small bronze figurines and ivory and wooden statuettes produced in the eighth century. The marble *kore* and *kouros* seem to have been invented only around the middle of the seventh century, under the impact of Greek exposure to Egypt and its monumental stone statuary. But they are hardly the only freestanding Archaic sculptural types from the seventh and sixth centuries: there are also clothed male figures, there are seated male and female ones, there are horsemen and offering-bearers and reclining figures and warriors and athletes. Moreover, although the *kore* and *kouros* are quintessentially Archaic, they were not universally so. The types appear variably in different parts of Greece. The *kore* and *kouros* are both common in east Greece and on Samos, on many Cycladic islands, and in Attica. In Boeotia the *kouros* is plentiful, but the *kore* is not. And both types are rare in the Peloponnesos. Even in those areas where they do appear they could be put to generally different uses: in Boeotia the *kouros* is typically a dedication in a sanctuary, whereas in Attica it is principally a funerary statue; the Attic *kore*, on the other hand, despite magnificent funerary examples such as Phrasikleia, is principally a dedication (Figure 33). Although not all Greeks were equally receptive to the types and although some Greeks preferred different uses for them, the *kore* and *kouros* nonetheless seem the principal expressions of Archaic attitudes – aesthetic and social – toward the human form.

A *kore*, again, represents an upright, clothed young woman standing either with both feet close together (like Phrasikleia, see Figure 30) or with one foot (usually the left) slightly advanced (see Figure 33).[12] Most often made of marble, occasionally of limestone, and sometimes (on a small scale) of bronze, terracotta, or wood, the *kore* may hold her hands in a variety of ways: she may keep them both down at her sides, or bring one arm across her chest, or pull at her dress with one hand while extending the other away from the body, or even extend both arms outwards. In her hands she may hold a variety of animals or objects: a bird, a hare, an apple, a flower, a pomegranate, a wreath, and so on. Early *korai* (and a few later ones) can be monumental – larger than life. But most are life-size or less. Whatever its size, the type is superficially – and the surface is what counts in Archaic art – a display of fashion, color, and ornament, an expression of the powerful Archaic impulse for *poikilia* that often leaves reality far behind. The *kore* can wear sandals or go barefoot; she can go bareheaded, or wear a hat or tiara or other headgear sometimes added in bronze. Her hair can be elaborately, even fantastically, coiffed in waves and long tresses. She can wear necklaces, earrings, and other jewelry. She can wear, by itself, a *peplos* (a heavy woolen tunic belted at the waist and pinned or sewn at the shoulders) or a *chiton* (a light, linen, sleeved tunic with buttons at the shoulders and an overfall over the belt).[13] At all events, *chiton*-wearing *korai* often obliquely drape a *himation* (a pleated mantle) over the right shoulder and below the left armpit, and it is even possible for a *peplos* to be worn over a *chiton*. There are other garments besides. Some areas of Greece prefer their *korai* dressed one way, some another, and different fashions are preferred at different times.

The question remains: what, exactly, does a *kore* depict besides a female figure in an elaborate costume? Does it have an identity? The question is first posed by what is probably the earliest *kore* of them all: an over life size (at 1.75 m or 5′9″ tall), planklike statue in Naxian marble dedicated by a woman named Nikandre to Artemis on the island of Delos around 660–50 (see Figure 34). Her monumentality and hard stone emulate Egyptian models; her so-called "Daidalic style" (characterized by a flat-topped, U-shaped face framed by triangular wedges of hair) was adopted from Near Eastern prototypes; her now eroded surface was once incised and brightly painted; and the three-line inscription on her left side hints at the circumstances of her creation and dedication:

> Nikandre dedicated me to the far-shooter, pourer of arrows,
> The excellent daughter of Deinodikes of Naxos, the sister of
> Deinomenes,
> And [now?] the wife of Phraxos.

The statue was apparently dedicated by Nikandre upon her marriage (and, possibly, her release from service as Artemis' priestess) and once again the statue speaks of itself ("me"). But whom does it represent? The choices are: the goddess Artemis (in which case the statue may have held a bronze bow and arrow in her drilled hands), Nikandre herself (in which case the statue may have held bronze flowers), or a Generic Woman – an excellent, beautifully adorned image that represented no woman in particular but the idea of woman, a fitting adornment and gift for the precinct of a goddess, an *agalma* ("delight," "pleasing gift," hence "statue").

That is essentially the choice any *kore* presents: goddess (or mythological heroine), real mortal woman, generic ideal woman. Some choices are easier to make than others: there is not much doubt that two *korai* who formed part of a six-figure dedication to Hera on Samos around 560 were supposed in some sense to be images of the dedicator's daughters Philippe and Ornithe – the names are inscribed upon them – just as the *kore* that stood atop Phrasikleia's grave was in some sense meant to be her substitute or double.[14] But in most cases the choice is hard to make, nowhere more so than on the Athenian Acropolis, where the finest collection of Archaic *korai* was assembled in the course of the sixth and early fifth centuries, especially in the years between 510 and 480, when, with the Persian destruction of the Acropolis, the history of the type seems to have come to an abrupt end.[15] Most Acropolis *korai* (see Figure 33) are under life size, though a few are monumental. A few wear the *peplos*, but most wear the *chiton* and *himation* (or a *chiton* alone). Many make offerings with outstretched hand or hands. But it is unclear who the Acropolis *korai* are supposed to be. We do not know the names of many dedicators of *korai* on the Acropolis, but those we do know – Epiteles, Nearchos, Naulochos and so on – are men: there is, then, no direct or necessary relationship between the sculptural type and the gender of the dedicant.[16] (So, too, we are told of a *kore* that stood elsewhere over the grave of a man named Midas,[17] and *korai* can be dedicated in the sanctuaries of male divinities.) The most popular theory has been that the Acropolis *korai* are simply generic images of young aristocratic womanhood: they are nonspecific *agalmata* meant as beautiful but anonymous adornments to the sanctuary of Athena, rich ornaments enhancing the *poikilia* of the Archaic precinct, marble maidens imaginatively placed in the service of the virgin goddess, eternal participants in (or at least witnesses of) the rituals and festivals that took place in their midst.[18] Increasingly, however, the generic interpretation has been found wanting. Some scholars have suggested that the *korai* represent minor Athenian divinities (such as nymphs) or heroines (such as the daughters of legendary kings).[19] Others have argued that most if not all Acropolis *korai* represent Athena herself – a few are certainly muscular enough to depict the goddess of war – whereas a few, such as the so-called "Peplos *kore*," might depict Artemis, who also had a sanctuary atop the citadel.[20] And there is now a theory that the Acropolis *korai*, individualized in appearance though similar in schema, were carved to represent real, living Athenian girls (for example, the *Arrhephoroi*, chosen each year to serve Athena on the Acropolis, or *kanephoroi*, high-born maidens who carried baskets in sacrificial processions, or even young women in the market for husbands) and so come close to being true portraits.[21]

Beyond the question of identity (and it is unlikely that one explanation fits all), there has been a recent tendency to see *korai* (and other draped female figures in Greek art) as objects of heterosexual desire, "sex objects" whose demure gestures indicated passive submission to the dominant male viewer, whose elaborate attire was intended to be seductive, and whose drapery folds even called to mind (in a common Greek metaphor) the furrows of the field and so invited imaginative phallic "plowing."[22] That metaphor, however, should probably be blocked: many *korai* stood on high bases and so literally over-looked those who looked upon them, never meeting their eyes, keeping a modest, decorous distance – they are maidens literally placed upon a pedestal.[23] And if some Acropolis *korai* were indeed images of the virgin goddess of the rock, then these at least were not properly available to the erotic male imagination: Athena cannot be plowed. In any case, the dedicatory *kore*, beautiful though it was, was a sacred gift for a divine recipient, to be possessed by the goddess and not by mortal men.

Whatever else they may be – and what they were depended upon their contexts, attributes, and identifying inscriptions – *korai* are displays of wealth and status commissioned and dedicated by aristocrats or well-to-do commoners who desired elite status: the largest Acropolis *kore* (some 7′ tall), and presumably the most expensive, was made by Antenor and was dedicated as a thank offering to Athena by Nearchos, probably the owner of a successful ceramics shop, who gratefully tithed his profits to pay for it.[24] The powerfully built Antenor *kore* (she has the shoulders, arms, and thighs of a tight end) probably represents Athena herself. But any *kore*, carved of expensive marble, bedecked in painted finery and jewelry, and often crowned in bronze, is a statement of economic prosperity, a beautiful commodity (just as real Greek women were "social valuables," possessions whose worth was exchanged from one family to another through marriage and dowries). In a sanctuary the *kore* pronounces the class or status of its dedicator (Figure 33). Over a grave such as Phrasikleia's (Figure 30), it not only displays the wealth of the girl's family but also, as the girl's double, embodies the economic loss that a potential husband has suffered with the death of the maiden, shown dressed for a wedding day that will never come.[25]

Like the *kore*, the *kouros* – the beardless, often smiling youth who stands foursquare with (usually) the left leg advanced and the right drawn back, arms down at the sides, fists clenched – was a type, a "blank," an endlessly repeatable schema that lent itself to a number of purposes and variations. Like the *kore*, it was either dedicatory or funerary in function. And like the *kore*, the *kouros*, through the addition of an attribute or an inscription or simply through its location and context, could acquire a specific identity. In most if not all cases it did: that is, it is unlikely that any *kouros* was meant to represent an anonymous or generic youth, or Youth in the abstract. Its form was conventional and it could, surely, embody abstract values such as *arete* (excellence, virtue) and the peculiarly aristocratic ideal of *kalokagathia* (the inextricable union of elite status with moral goodness and physical beauty, the idea that to look good was literally to be good). But Beautiful Youth was only the foundation of the type, its common denominator. Any *kouros* set over a tomb was surely meant to be a semblance or "copy" of the dead (however idealized it might be), and *kouroi* dedicated in sanctuaries (and, again, they could be dedicated in sanctuaries of goddesses as well as gods) could represent gods, heroes, mortals who acquired heroic status (such as Kleobis and Biton at Delphi), or even mortal dedicants, whose absence from the sanctuary was filled by the eternal presence of their stone doubles.[26] In short, *kouroi*, like *korai*, composed a genre, but no individual *kouros* was generic.

The type was invented in the Cyclades in the middle of the seventh century, after Greeks had been exposed to the colossal stone statues of Egypt (none of which were anonymous, incidentally) and to Egyptian techniques (a few early examples conform to a proportional canon then in use in Egypt).[27] The old idea that the earliest *kouroi* were images of Apollo, the god most associated with youth and beauty, who is in early poetry described (and in early art often represented) as a powerful long-haired youth who strides across heavens and earth, has lately been revived.[28] The *kouros* is certainly Apollonian – young, handsome, vigorous, and (most often) long-haired, like the god. And a number of *kouroi* may indeed actually represent him – a 10-m-tall colossus dedicated by the Naxians on Delos around 600 certainly did.[29] It is also telling that the largest single contingent of *kouroi* – some 120, a veritable battalion – have been found in the oracular hillside sanctuary of Apollo Ptoös in Boeotia.[30] But some seventh-century Cycladic vase-paintings show Apollo dressed and bearded, not nude and beardless,[31] and so at the time and place of the invention of the type there seems to have been no exact correspondence between painted conceptions of the god and the sculptured *kouros*. Elsewhere the type was adopted for different roles. Although most if not all of the *kouroi* at the Ptoön may be Apollos, *kouroi* are, again, found in the sanctuaries of other gods and even goddesses, and it is not easy to see why a statue of Apollo should have been considered an appropriate dedication to, say, Poseidon at Sounion or Hera at Samos. The Isches colossos (Figure 31) has, in fact, been interpreted as a

Samian or ancestral hero – its superhuman size, it is reasonably thought, removes it from the mortal realm.[32] And the few *kouroi* dedicated on the Acropolis in the sixth century may well have represented legendary Attic kings or heroes or, perhaps, mortal dedicants.[33] In any case, it is unlikely that any single, universalist interpretation fits all.

Nudity is the "costume" of the *kouros* and it is this (along with its lack of artificial supports and screens) that best distinguishes it from its Egyptian stone models (though it is not appreciated often enough that there are, in fact, Egyptian nude statues in wood).[34] In the Greek statue it is the nudity that counts, for it displays those physical characteristics that were considered most desirable in a male: broad shoulders, narrow waist, powerful buttocks and thighs, and small penis. The *kouros*, in short, embodied the ideal of male beauty and youth in a Youth and Beauty culture dominated by males – a dominance so complete and pervasive that even many *korai* have the proportions and physiques of men.[35] And in the Archaic period, when homoeroticism and pederasty were conventional, honorable, and virtually institutionalized, when it was acceptable and even desirable for an older man (an *erastes* or lover) to actively court and seduce a passive boy (an *eromenos* or beloved) so long as he was of the same social standing,[36] and when inscriptions on hundreds of vases such as the Vatican amphora (Figure 32) praise the beauty of a boy, it is easy to see how the type could be read as the object of erotic desire: the viewer becomes the *erastes* and the statue itself the *eromenos*.[37] But this formulation may be reductive. *Kouroi*, after all, look and smile blankly over and past the spectator; they resist engagement. At all events, the nudity of the *kouros* was not always total and its youth not always certain. Some examples wear belts (these are early), caps, boots, or jewelry.[38] Other *kouroi* had ornaments or other anatomical features added in paint now lost: the *kouros* buried with Phrasikleia, for example, had a painted necklace and pubic hair.[39] A few *kouroi* – probably even the Isches colossos (see Figure 31) – had mustaches. Many more might have had painted facial hair (sideburns or incipient beards?) or pubic hair that has simply faded away,[40] and so we may be interpreting the genre without crucial evidence. Facial hair effectively removes the *kouros* from the realm of *eromenoi* (at least it did for the Archaic poet we call Theognis, who says he will love his smooth-skinned boy only so long as his face remains hairless[41]), and so the range of ages represented by *kouroi* might be a lot wider than we have been used to thinking: some may not be youths after all.[42] Size and location or context may have removed some of them from the ranks of "beloveds," too. Although it is clear that the normal male visitor to the Heraion of Samos, for example, would have admired the beauty of the colossoi towering above him (Figure 31), it is difficult to believe he would have conceived the impulse to fondle or penetrate them, and pederastic longing seems an inappropriate response before *kouroi* that stood atop the graves of men.[43]

"Stop and mourn beside the tomb of Kroisos, dead..." reads the inscription on the base of the funerary *kouros* from Anavyssos (see Figure 35), and the rest of the inscription tells us that Kroisos died fighting in the battle's front ranks (*eni promachois*), a victim of raging Ares. Now, as A. Stewart has pointed out, to die as he did the real Kroisos had to have been a hoplite (or heavily armed footsoldier), and to have been a hoplite he had to have been of a certain age – older than 20, and so older than the usual *eromenos*.[44] That is, Kroisos was a mature man and so bearded. And yet his double, the *kouros* upon his grave, presents him as a youth: it presents him idealized, "youthened," at the height of his beauty, vigor, and power (though it also telescopes time by showing him wearing the kind of cap hoplites wore under their helmets). Thus, one role of the *kouros* was to idealize its mortal subject, to present him in his absence not as he was at death but at the height of his physical force and beauty – that is, in his youth – and so enhance his memory.[45] Ideals of beauty differed from place to place: Samians liked their *kouroi* rounded, Melians liked theirs slender, Athenians liked theirs thickly built with a highly defined musculature, and so on. But Archaic sculpture (like Classical sculpture later) was idealizing wherever you found it.

Ideals also change. In the century-long history of the Athenian *kouros*, for example, the type gradually seems to become more "naturalistic." Kroisos' *kouros* of ca. 530 is more anatomically correct than an Athenian *kouros* of 590, but it is itself less convincing as a representation of the human form than a *kouros* of 500 will be – say, the *kouros* that stood over the grave of Aristodikos in rural Attica, atop a base inscribed with a single word meaning "of Aristodikos" ("[marker, tomb] of Aristodikos" or, perhaps, "[image] of Aristodikos") (see Figure 36). Despite this internal stylistic evolution (which seems peculiar to Attic sculpture[46] and which in any case cannot be the result of Archaic sculptors actually trying to be naturalistic or Classical, because they did not know what "naturalism" and "the Classical" were), later *kouroi* stand essentially the way early *kouroi* do: left leg advanced, arms clenched at the sides, frontal and four-square. And this unchanging, endlessly reproducible stance must be at least part of the message of the type. Although nudity is, ironically, a social equalizer in real life – in a locker room it is hard to tell a naked commoner from a naked aristocrat – the nude *kouros*, whatever its specific identity, was the emblem of an elite that through the very dedication and expense of the statue promoted its own unchanging status and ideals such as *kalokagathia*. As a result, the formally conservative *kouros* became socially reactionary, its stance far more old-fashioned than the active, even daring poses adopted by sculptures that were beginning to fill temple pediments by the end of the sixth century, far more static even than the dynamic figures carved in relief on their own bases (Figure 37). Such discrepancies, as well as the contrast between its increasingly convincing anatomy and its own unconvincing pose, no longer made visual sense. And when the aristocracies or elites that had commissioned them by the hundreds (if not thousands) began to decline in late Archaic city-states like Athens, *kouroi* no longer made social sense, either.[47] The *kouros* gradually goes out of use around 500, and by around 480 the history of the type is over. Nude youths are still carved, but they are no longer *kouroi*. They do not smile, they do not walk, they shift their hips, they put all their weight on one leg and relax the other, they turn their heads, and so they look inward rather than outward (Figure 38). Revolutionary works such as the introverted Kritios and Blond Boys from the Acropolis, who stand the way they do because they seem to think the way they do, reject the schematic premises and ideologies of the extroverted, stiff, vacant *kouros* and announce the beginning of the Classical.

As Never Euphronios

Archaic art is prismatic and schematic. It analyzes the world, breaking it down into its component parts, putting it back together, and filling it with figures that are limited and conventional in the poses they strike and the gestures they make. It never intends to reproduce the world as we experience it or see it, a world that is momentary, changeable, and obscured. It is an art that establishes its own permanence and "truth." And so the first great Archaic vase-painting – a funeral scene painted on the front of a monumental amphora that was set over a grave in Athens' Dipylon cemetery around 760–50 – splits in two what was in fact a circular dance of mourners around the corpse lying on its couch and stretches both halves tight on either side of the bier (see Figure 39). As a result there is no overlapping of forms, and so there is no front and no back. The figures evenly adhere to the surface of the vase, a plane that is in essence equivalent to reality, a world without depth, without space, in which the bier has only two front legs and the nearly identical individual figures, consisting of profile heads, frontal shoulders and torsos, and profile legs, are uniformly presented and equally illuminated. The scene does not seek to duplicate the natural world with all its complexity, irregularity, flux, and depth. It seeks to make a world up – a world of absolute clarity and order, where nothing is hidden or implied. The Dipylon amphora presents an Archaic world at its starkest and most severe, but it is virtually the same world that Achilles and Ajax occupy on Exekias' amphora, painted over two centuries later (see Figure 32). The heroes there are not frontal-profile composites like the Dipylon figures: they are (with the exception of their frontal eyes) pure profiles. Still, their space is, as we have noted, almost as depthless as that of the Dipylon funeral, and their formal power resides solely in – it derives from – their adherence to the plane, to the surface of the vase. A lot had happened in Athenian vase-painting between the creations of the Dipylon and Vatican amphorae, but they are demonstrably products of the same continuous tradition, and the images they bear are Archaic in the same way.

Athenian vase painters, then, had painted dark brown or black figures over a light ground (the plain fabric of the clay) for hundreds of years before Exekias practiced the so-called Black Figure style, where lustrous black figures stand silhouetted against a red-orange fabric and interior details are sharply incised, with additional detail in pure white (for the skin of women, above all) or reddish-purple (for articles of clothing, male hair and beards, horses' manes, and so on). But just a few years after Exekias painted the Vatican amphora, around 525, another vase painter working, perhaps, just down the street in the Athenian potters' quarter turned Black Figure inside out simply by reversing its color scheme: now the figure was left in the reddish color of the clay and the areas around the figure were covered with rich black glaze. In this Red Figure technique a thin loaded brush is used to indicate details within the figure (anatomical features or details of clothing) with lines that vary in quality from a thick dark raised or "relief" line to a light dilute. The rendering of musculature or cloth could thus be more varied and subtle than the hard Black Figure incising tool (which created an even, unmodulated line) allowed, and with dilute there was even the possibility of shading, for indicating that light falls differently over the different contours of the human form. Red Figure is just as artificial a style as Black Figure, but the technique is inherently better suited to a more accurate rendering of human anatomy and for the depiction of figures that seem to twist and move and so break free from the picture plane, which had dictated the nature of representation for hundreds of years. By the end of the sixth century, in short, the world implied on Red

Figure vases is very different from the explicit world of Black Figure: it is a world of some depth and perspective, a world not of "truth" but of "seeming," a more complex world occupied by foreshortened figures who are figures of the moment and who exist in space as if spotlit on a darkened stage, not fixed and flat upon a seemingly backlit screen (Figure 40).[48]

What is not clear is whether the desire to represent such figures led to the invention of Red Figure, or whether the invention of Red Figure led to the representation of such figures. This much seems self-evident: whoever invented Red Figure was almost certainly trained as a Black Figure artist (if he was an Athenian vase painter he could not have been trained as anything else),[49] and so he must have been in some sense and for some reason dissatisfied with the style in which he had been schooled.[50] The dissatisfaction must have been either technological or aesthetic (or, perhaps, both). That is, either he was unhappy with the monotony of Black Figure and simply wished to add technical variety to his craft – to give himself more options, as it were – or he recognized the artistic limitations of Black Figure and consciously sought a new and different way to represent new kinds of figures. Whatever the case, other techniques (white ground, Six's technique) were developed at roughly the same time as Red Figure, and that suggests a strong desire to open up the possibilities of representation.[51]

The odds-on favorite candidate for the inventor of Red Figure is an anonymous painter who may have had some connection with Exekias but who certainly worked for a potter named Andokides, and so is called the Andokides Painter.[52] A number of his works are "bilinguals" – that is, vases that are decorated in both artistic "languages," with a Black Figure scene on one side and a virtually identical Red Figure scene on the other – and it is as if the artist were experimenting with or testing the different effects or characters of the two styles. On one bilingual cup, in fact, Red Figure warriors fight Black Figure ones: the two techniques are dueling each other from opposite sides of the vase, and the Red Figure warriors appear to be winning (see Figure 41).[53] Although the Black Figure sides of his bilingual vases are often (and probably rightly) assigned to a different artist (the Lysippides Painter, generally considered a pupil of Exekias), the Andokides Painter's scenes are formally or compositionally not much different: the figures are still flat, the action still planar. His Red Figure scenes are simply the "negative" of the Black – another silhouette style, a continuation or "pursuit of black-figure by other means."[54] That is, it is not that the Andokides Painter was merely incapable of fulfilling the potential of the new style: its potential simply never occurred to him. And so, if he was the inventor of the Red Figure, mimesis was not his motive or his goal. Instead, the Andokides Painter invented Red Figure not so that a new kind of figure could be depicted – a figure that was more anatomically accurate and generated its own space with twists and turns – or so that new illusionistic effects be explored, but simply to break Black Figure's monopoly, so that the Athenian vase painter would have another technique at his disposal and improve the overall commercial attractiveness of his product. His purpose was to add to the ornamental variety and decorative richness of the craft of vase painting itself – its *poikilia*. In this view, it was only the next generation of vase-painters – the so-called Pioneers (led by Euphronios, Euthymides (Figure 40), Phintias, and Smikros), working some ten to fifteen years after the Andokides Painter's invention – who realized what Red Figure was in fact capable of: the new technique came first, the new conception of the human figure came later.[55]

But Red Figure is itself less ornamental or *poikile* than Black Figure (which, with its added white and reddish-purple details, is by far the more decorative of the two styles), and it is the more demanding style, too.[56] That may be why Red Figure vases form only a small minority of vases produced in the last quarter of the sixth century: the new option, for all the *poikilia* it added to the craft, and for all its later success, was not immediately or readily seized upon by most vase painters. In any case, the Andokides Painter is not the only candidate for the inventor of Red Figure. Psiax (who also painted vases potted by Andokides) is another, and almost from the beginning he seems more inventive, more progressive, more interested in the foreshortening of figures than his contemporary the Andokides Painter (Figure 42): Psiax, in other words, is the true "father" of the Pioneers.[57] If it was Psiax who invented the new style, then it may after all have been to accommodate a more daring and experimental approach to the depiction of the human figure, to provide a new tool that allowed the artist to represent "better" figures as they appeared to the eye. In that case, the innovative aesthetic impulse preceded and called for the new technology.

Whatever the case, the late sixth-century Red Figure vase painter was not the only artist interested in the plausible depiction of the human form. Beginning around 525, relief sculptors, too, experimented with figures and objects shown in a variety of three-quarter, back, and frontal views, or in a kind of *trompe-l'oeil* even showed the same figures from two different points of view.[58] It is more likely that vase painters followed their lead in exploring visual effects rather than the reverse. Figures in relief were also normally set against a dark painted background (cf. Figure 37), and the change from Black Figure to Red may have been partly driven by the desire to emulate the light-on-dark effects of relief.[59] At all events, the representation of figures as they appeared to the eye – optically rather than conceptually – marks as fundamental a shift away from Archaic ways of making as the rejection of the foursquare *kouros* after 500. It may not be coincidence that the shift begins very soon after Exekias implied that he made mere images of Achilles and Ajax (see Figure 32) – that art was imitation, that he made figures not of "truth" but of "seeming." In any case, although the Archaic period conventionally ends only in 480, the beginning of the end of the Archaic style came much earlier. It came when partly carved, partly painted foreshortened chariots seemed to emerge from the background on the east frieze of the Siphnian Treasury and when on the north frieze Hermes charged obliquely toward the background to do battle with a giant;[60] when on a Red Figure cup by Psiax a kneeling archer, his right leg sharply foreshortened beneath him, showed the viewer his back and the sole of his right foot (Figure 42); when on the base of a missing *kouros* youths playing ball were shown in six different frontal, three-quarter, and back views and so presented a study guide to the human figure in action (see Figure 37);[61] and when variously foreshortened, drunken revelers on a vase by Euthymides (a Pioneer) made their tipsy way home, barely keeping their balance (see Figure 40), and Euthymides taunted his greatest rival with words, painted along the edge of the scene, that like other Archaic words were meant to be read aloud: "As never Euphronios." There is a double meaning in that: both "Euphronios [his name means Good Sense] never acted like this," but, more importantly, "Euphronios never painted anything like this."[62] Until then, no one else ever had, either.

Notes

1 Kaltsas 2002, 48–9 (Cat. 45). If Svenbro 1993, 12–13, is right that Phrasikleia's family was the prestigious and politically important clan known as the Alkmeonidai, and that the statues were buried to prevent their being vandalized by enemies of the family – specifically Peisistratos and his followers, who on the way to his third and final tyranny are said (by Isocrates, *Team of Horses*, 26) to have destroyed the houses and ransacked the graves of the Alkmeonidai– then Phrasikleia must date before 546 (not 540, the date Svenbro gives for Peisistratos's invasion of Attica). This scenario would explain the statue's excellent state of preservation. But the statue buried along with her seems a decade or so later (cf. Kaltsas 2002, 49 [Cat. 46], who dates the youth to the 530s), whereas Phrasikleia herself has also been dated more generally to the 540s or 530s (Stieber 2004, 142, improbably dates her around 520). A later exile of the Alkmeonidai(around 514) might best explain the

joint interment of the statues, whereas the threat of the Persian invasion of 490 or 480 remains a lesser possibility. On the struggles between Peisistratos and the Alkmeonidai, see also chapter 1, *The Peisistratids of Athens.*

2 Svenbro 1993, 14.

3 Similarly, the first line can be read as either "[This is] the marker . . . " or "[I am] the marker. . . . " Around the corner of the base, on its left side, the sculptor is identified in another inscription – "Aristion of Paros made me" – and the reader/spectator is called upon once again to give voice to the statue, assuming its identity ("me"). For more on orality and the role of words in early Greek images, see Hurwit 1990, Slater 1999, and Boardman 2003.

4 For more on Phrasikleia, see Day 1989, 26; Svenbro 1993, esp. 17–19; Stewart 1997, 66, 115; Steiner 2001, 13–14, 258–9; Karasaki 2004, esp. 121–6; Stieber 2004, 141–78.

5 Kyrieleis 1996.

6 Kyrieleis 1996, pl. 23.

7 Kyrieleis 1996, 23–6.

8 On the inscription, see Kyrieleis 1996, 45–6, 65–7.

9 Cf. Chapter 6 on poetry performed in the elite context of the symposium.

10 For *poikilia* as a fundamental principle of Archaic art, see Hurwit 1985, 23–5; also Neer 2002, 16, 33–4.

11 See Slater 1999. But see Boardman 2003, who disputes the notion that inscriptions on vases (and by extension texts on bases, such as Phrasikleia's, or on sculptures, such as the Isches colossos) were meant to be read aloud.

12 For *korai* in general, see Karakasi 2004.

13 The distinction is not always easy to make: some say Phrasikleia's dress is a *chiton* (cf. Kaltsas 2002, 48), some say a *peplos* (cf. Ridgway 1993, 139; Stieber 2004, 145). Karasaki 2004, calls it a *chiton* in her text (121) but a *peplos* in a table (169).]

14 For Philippe, Ornithe, and the so-called Geneleos Group, see Boardman 1978, Figures 91–3; Ridgway 1993, 135–6.

15 For the "bulge" in *korai* and other dedications on the Acropolis at this time, see Keesling 2003, 42–3, and *passim.* One *kore*, Acropolis 688, may date to just after 480.

16 For the list of the 15 or 16 known dedicators of *korai*, see Keesling 2003, 87.

17 *Greek Anthology* 7,153.

18 See, for example, Schneider 1975.

19 Harrison 1988, 54.

20 Ridgway 1993, 147–51; Keesling 2003, who stresses that her argument "applies only to a single votive context, the Athenian Acropolis, and does not presume that *korai* dedicated in other sanctuaries represented the same subjects as those dedicated on the Acropolis" (98).

21 Karasaki 2004, 136–9; Stieber 1994, 104–14, and 2004, who calls *korai* "mimetically realistic portrayals of the appearances of real Archaic women (140)." In the same vein, Stewart 1997 suggests that *korai* represent the daughters of "Athenian men who liked to honor Athena with [their] images" (137). But unlike Philippe, Ornithe, or Phrasikleia, no Acropolis *kore* is identified as an actual girl with a name inscribed on the statue itself or its base, and this seriously weakens Stieber's case; cf. Keesling 2003, 109.

22 Steiner 2001, 235; Stewart 1997, 128.

23 Steiner 2001, 237. Of course, their inaccessibility may only have added to their allure, and some *korai* (e.g., Acropolis 670, 671, 673, 674, and 682) set high atop bases or columns tilted their heads and lowered their eyes toward possible viewers on the ground, their eyes even physically distorted to take the steep angle of viewing into account; see Boardman 1978, Figures 111, 151, 152, 153, 158.

24 See Keesling 2003, 56–9.

25 Steiner 2001, 14–15.

26 For Kleobis and Biton (often now identified as the Dioskouroi), see Ridgway 1993, 74 and 107, n. 3.38.

27 Guralnick 1978, 1985.

28 *Iliad* 1.43–53; *Homeric Hymn to Apollo*, 133–5, 449–50; Deonna 1909; Ridgway 1993, 66–75. A nude, striding, long-haired god is found between nude women on a relief from a temple of Apollo at Prinias on Crete, datable to ca. 630, and one naturally thinks of Apollo, Artemis, and Leto; Boardman 1978, Figure 31.

29 Ridgway 1993, 61–2, 72.

30 See Chapter 9 for more discussion of the Ptoön sanctuary and the dedications made there.

31 Stewart 1997, 65; Boardman 1998, 111, Figure 250 (Parian amphora from Melos).

32 Kyrieleis 1996, 87–101.

33 Just as the Moschophoros (a statue of a bearded man carrying a sacrificial calf on his shoulders) dedicated by Rhonbos around 560 almost certainly represents Rhonbos himself; Boardman 1978, Figure 112.

34 Ridgway 1993, 71, 74. The life-size wooden statue of King Auibre Hor's *ka* from Dahshur (Thirteenth Dynasty) is often given as an example (see Smith 1981, 179), but in fact there are traces of a belt around the waist and there are holes drilled into the pelvis, undoubtedly for the attachment of a loincloth or kilt; see Tiradritti 1998, 135. On nudity as a costume, see Bonfante 1989.

35 Guralnick 1982.

36 See Chapter 4, *Initiation of Boys*, on the role of homoeroticism and pederasty in rites of passage.

37 Steiner 2001, 215; Stewart 1997, 67.

38 Ferrari 2002, 116–24, argues that the necklaces and earrings (as well as the hairstyles) that *kouroi* wear are marks of feminine beauty, and that the *kouros* "represents the moment of coming of age" when the youth sheds his "feminine skin." But Egyptian male statues wear jewelry, too, and such adornments on *kouroi* were probably not signs of femininity but of wealth and status (not to mention vanity), as they are for many men (even for macho professional athletes) today. Men who wore jewelry in antiquity did so to enhance their own *poikilia*. They were thus expressing not their "feminine" but their "Archaic" side.

39 Kaltsas 2002, 49.

40 See Ridgway 1993, 99, n. 3.17; Stewart 1997, 65; Ferrari 2002, 116.

41 Theognis 1327–8. The roughly 1400 verses attributed to Theognis are actually drawn from a variety of poems written as early as the seventh and as late as the early fifth centuries; there was a Theognis, but his corpus is a composite (cf. Chapter 6, on traditional role-playing personae in lyric poetry). About 150 lines of the *Theognidea* are concerned with the love of boys.

42 Cf. Ferrari 2002, who notes that some *kouroi* may have had facial hair (116) but who also claims that the paradigmatic *kouros* "never [grows] a man's beard" (124).

43 On the other hand, in Tyrtaios 10, lines 27–30, a man in the bloom of youth is said to be a wonder to men and an object of desire for women, beautiful even when he has fallen fighting in the front ranks (*promachoisi*). The diction seems echoed in the epitaph of the funerary Anavyssos *kouros*.

44 Stewart 1997, 66.

45 Such idealization was not universal in Archaic sculpture: Geneleos, for example, represented . . . arches (dedicator of that impressive group of statues on Samos c. 560–50) as a reclining fat man, and the Boxer Stele from the Athenian Kerameikos depicts its subject with a broken nose; see Boardman 1978, Figures 93 and 233.

46 Other local schools are far less interested in the investigation of anatomy; see Ridgway 1993, 71.

47 Stewart 1997, 68.

48 The illusionism of late sixth-century art is still very limited: scientific or linear perspective is unknown, and there is, with one or two possible exceptions, no diminution of objects or figures supposed to be in the distance; for one of the exceptions, see Hurwit 1991, 40.

49 Some have considered the possibility that the inventor of Red Figure was a sculptor of marble reliefs who changed specialties; but see Williams 1991a, 105; Robertson 1992, 9, 11–12.

50 Some hint of dissatisfaction with Black Figure is found even in the works of a quintessential Black Figure artist, the Amasis Painter, who instead of using white for the color of his female figures often outlined their flesh and left it in the color of the clay ("in reserve"). In other words, portions of some of his figures approximate Red Figure. It is not clear, however, whether this precedes and anticipates the invention of full Red Figure or is a response to its invention. See Boardman 1974, 55 and Figures 85, 87, 89.

51 Neer 2002, 32, 34–5.

52 Robertson 1992, 9–12; Boardman 2001, 81–2.

53 For more on bilinguals, see now Neer 2002, 32–43. Neer believes that Red Figure "makes its earliest appearance on 'bilingual' vases" (32), whereas Boardman 1975, 17, has suggested that most of the Andocides Painter's bilingual vases were painted relatively late in his career.

54 Neer 2002, 34; also Boardman 1975, 15; Robertson 1992, 10.

55 See Williams 1991b, 286; Neer 2002, 32, 37.

56 Robertson 1992, 7.

57 On Psiax, see Williams 1991a, 104, 106–7 ("teacher of Euphronius"); Williams 1991b, 287; Robertson 1992, 12–13. Like most scholars, Boardman 2001, 82, places Psiax a little later than the Andokides Painter, but the relative dating of vase painters in the last quarter of the sixth century is hardly an exact science, and it is impossible to say for sure that a given vase was painted around 520 rather than around 525.

58 Kaltsas 2002, 68–9 (Cat. No. 96).

59 It is not necessary to assume (as some have) that the first Red Figure vase painter was a relief sculptor who changed professions (see n. 49 above), only that he was impressed with the innovative reliefs he saw in the world around him. For other proposed influences (metalwork, textiles), see Williams 1991a, 106.

60 Boardman 1978, Figures 130, 212. The Andokides Painter's possible connection with the Siphnian Treasury frieze (executed around 530–25) has often been remarked upon; see, for example, Robertson 1992, 11–12; Neer 2002, 191–2.

61 Kaltsas 2002, 66–8 (Cat. No. 95).

62 For more on the taunt, see Neer 2002, 227, n. 74.

BIBLIOGRAPHY AND SUGGESTED READINGS

Boardman, J. 1974. *Athenian Black Figure Vases.*

______. 1975. *Athenian Red Figure Vases: The Archaic Period.*

______. 1978. *Greek Sculpture: The Archaic Period.*

______. 1998. *Early Greek Vase Painting.*

______. 2001. *The History of Greek Vases.*

______. 2003. "'Reading' Greek Vases?" *Oxford Journal of Archaeology* 22, 109–114.

Bonfante, L. 1989. "Nudity as a Costume in Classical Art." *American Journal of Archaeology* 93: 543–70.

Day, J. W. 1989. "Rituals in Stone: Early Greek Epigrams and Monuments." *Journal of Hellenic Studies* 109: 16–28.

Deonna, W. 1909. *Les Apollons archaïques.*

Ferrari, G. 2002. *Figures of Speech: Men and Maidens in Ancient Greece.*

Guralnick, E. 1978. "The Proportions of Kouroi." *American Journal of Archaeology* 82: 461–72.

______. 1982. "Profiles of Korai." *American Journal of Archaeology* 86: 172–82.

______. 1985. "Profiles of Kouroi." *American Journal of Archaeology* 89: 399–409.

Harrison, E. B. 1988. "Sculpture in Stone." In *The Human Figure in Early Greek Art.* Eds. J. Sweeney, L. Curry, and Y. Tzedakis. 5–54.

Hurwit, J. M. 1985. *The Art and Culture of Early Greece, 1100–480 BC.*

______. 1990. "The Words in the Image: Orality, Literacy, and Early Greek Art," *Word & Image* 6, 180–97.

______. 1991. "The Representation of Nature in Early Greek Art." In *New Perspectives in Early Greek Art.* Ed. D. Buitron-Oliver. 33–62.

Kaltsas, N. 2002. *Sculpture in the National Archaeological Museum, Athens.*

Karakasi, K. 2004. *Archaic Korai.*

Keesling, C. A. 2003. *The Votive Statues of the Athenian Acropolis.*

Kyrieleis, H. 1996. *Der Grosse Kuros von Samos.* (Samos X.)

Neer, R. T. 2002. *Style and Politics in Athenian Vase-Painting.*

Ridgway, B. S. 1993. *The Archaic Style in Greek Sculpture.* Second ed.

Robertson, M. 1992. *The Art of Vase-Painting in Classical Athens.*

Schneider, L. A. 1975. *Zur sozialen Bedeutung der archaischen Korenstatuen.*

Slater, N. 1999. "The Vase as Ventriloquist: *Kalos* Inscriptions and the Culture of Fame." In *Signs of Orality.* Ed. E. A. Mackay. 143–61.

Smith, W. S. 1981. *The Art and Architecture of Ancient Egypt.* Revised with additions by W. K. Simpson.

Steiner, D. T. 2001. *Images in Mind: Statues in Archaic Greek Literature and Thought.*

Stewart, A. F. 1986. "When Is a Kouros Not an Apollo? The Tenea 'Apollo' Revisited." In *Corinthiaca.* Eds. M. A. Del Chiaro and W. R. Biers. 54–70.

______. 1990. *Greek Sculpture: An Exploration.*

______. 1997. *Art, Desire, and the Body in Ancient Greece.*

Stieber, M. 1994. "Aeschylus' Theoroi and Realism in Greek Art." *Transactions of the American Philological Association* 124: 85–119.

______. 2004. *The Poetics of Appearance in the Attic Korai.*

Svenbro, J. 1993. *Phrasikleia: An Anthropology of Reading in Ancient Greece.*

Tiradritti, F. 1998. *Egyptian Treasures from the Egyptian Museum in Cairo.*

Williams, D. 1991a. "The Invention of the Red-Figure Technique and the Race between Vase-Painting and Free-Painting." In *Looking at Greek Vases*. Eds. T. Rasmussen and N. Spivey. 103–18.

______. 1991b. "The Drawing of the Human Figure on Early Red-Figure Vases." In *New Perspectives in Early Greek Art*. Ed. D. Buitron-Oliver. 285–301.

Zinserling, V. 1975. "Zum Bedeutungsgehalt des archaischen Kuros." *Eirene* 13: 13–33.

Index